Practical J2EE Application Architecture

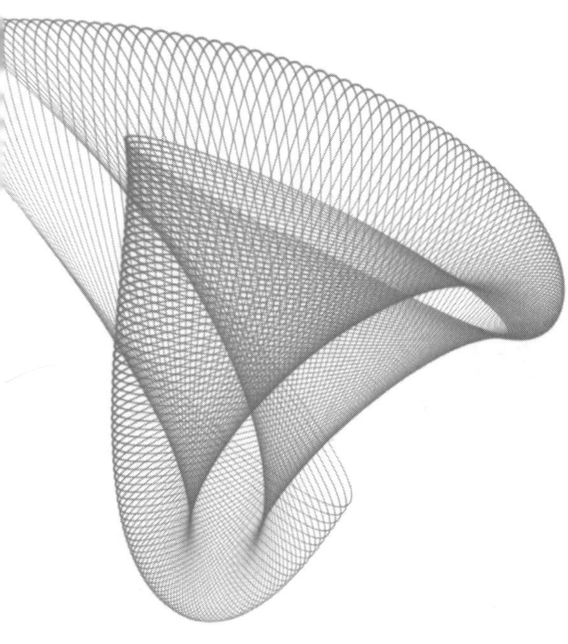

Practical J2EE Application Architecture

Nadir Gulzar

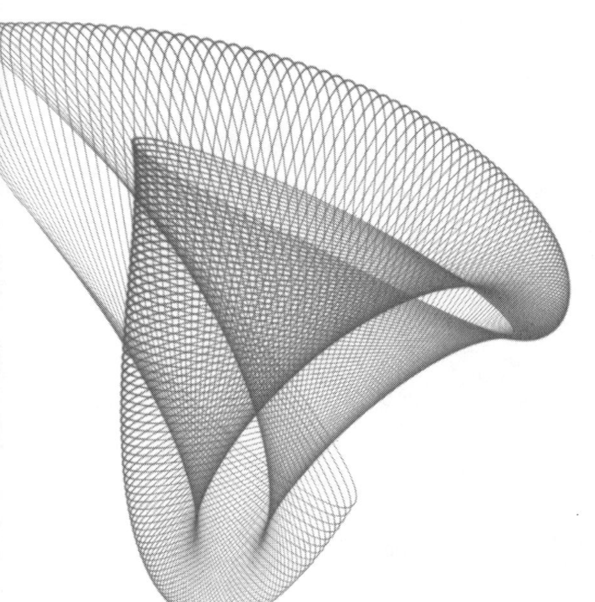

McGraw-Hill/Osborne

New York Chicago San Francisco
Lisbon London Madrid Mexico City Milan
New Delhi San Juan Seoul Singapore Sydney Toronto

The McGraw-Hill Companies

McGraw-Hill/Osborne
2100 Powell Street, 10th Floor
Emeryville, California 94608
U.S.A.

To arrange bulk purchase discounts for sales promotions, premiums, or fund-raisers, please contact **McGraw-Hill**/Osborne at the above address. For information on translations or book distributors outside the U.S.A., please see the International Contact Information page immediately following the index of this book.

Practical J2EE Application Architecture

1234567890 CUS CUS 019876543

ISBN 0-07-222711-7

Publisher	Brandon A. Nordin
Vice President & Associate Publisher	Scott Rogers
Editorial Director	Wendy Rinaldi
Project Editor	Julie M. Smith
Acquisitions Coordinator	Athena Honore
Technical Editor	Anne Horton
Copy Editor	Darren Meiss
Proofreader	Linda Medoff
Indexer	Valerie Perry
Computer Designers	Carie Abrew, Tabitha M. Cagan
Illustrators	Kathleen Edwards, Melinda Moore Lytle, Jackie Sieben, Lyssa Wald
Series Design	Roberta Steele
Cover Series Design	Greg Scott
Cover Illustration	Akira Inoue/Photonica

This book was composed with Corel VENTURA™ Publisher.

To Mother, Farrah, and Munira
The journey was hard but I had you

About the Author

Nadir Gulzar has over 16 years of IT industry experience. Over the last several years, he held the positions of senior architect, chief architect, and director of technology. Nadir is also a J2EE evangelist and mentor, and has created and delivered several training courses. He has worked on projects for global brand names like Sprint, Sears Roebuck, McKesson, and Visa International where he was responsible for architecting and designing medium to large-scale software systems. Nadir leads cross-functional teams comprising of business, creative, and technology personnel for delivering solutions based on object-oriented principles and concepts with particular emphasis on use case driven process.

About the Contributors

Govy Munamala is a Sr. Systems Architect at Inovant, a subsidiary of Visa International. Govy has been involved at Inovant with major re-architecture effort for creating next generation eCommerce applications using J2EE platform and XML-based technologies. Govy is involved in architecting high volume transaction validation system deployed globally by leveraging the latest advances in Java and XML-based technologies.

Kartik Ganeshan is a Java Architect with the Sun Software Services consulting organization focused on delivering application architecture services, Java technology expertise, best practices and methodologies for software development and design. Over the years, Kartik has had extensive involvement in leveraging J2SE and J2EE platforms including the Sun ONE architecture for building mission-critical enterprise applications and web services. His core interests include J2EE architecture, Web service technologies, XML, and security.

Mansour Kavianpour has extensive experience in systems integration, CORBA, J2EE and Web Services technologies. He is a well-known expert in the EAI community. Mansour was involved in the creation of several OMG specifications. He has developed many successful large-scale component-based systems.

Terry Markou has many years of experience in designing and developing various interactive Web applications, using J2EE and XML technologies. His clients encompass the transportation, real estate, medical, non-profit, and manufacturing industries, among others. He has unique understanding and proficiency in both the artistic as well as the technical aspects of Web application development.

Sarah Stritter Murgel is a usability and visual design specialist. She has worked on interactive projects for global brands such as BEA Systems, SBC, and Visa.

Enterpulse is fortunate to have professionals on its team who continue to pioneer the technology landscape—providing insight into the application frameworks we leverage to continually bring business value to our clients. Our team is committed to enhancing and evolving our capabilities through dedicated research into emerging technologies. This McGraw-Hill/Osborne Media publication, focusing specifically on application architecture using the J2EE platform, is a testament to that commitment.

Enterpulse (www.enterpulse.com) is the professional services firm that applies Internet technologies to improve human connections among customers, suppliers, and employees. The company's unique framework, ACE (Apply, Connect, ExtendSM), is a proven approach that creates business value by helping companies proactively understand customer expectations, better manage supplier relationships, and drive employee productivity while achieving the highest possible rates of return. We have deep competencies in advanced programming and system integration, business process analysis and vendor evaluation, and best-in-class partner platforms. Our content management, custom application, and portal solutions bring value to the entire enterprise.

Contents at a Glance

Contents

Part II Design and Construction

Part III Appendixes

Foreword

Consumers know what they want. Nowadays, the Internet is accessible to everybody. Our children start playing with it at a very early age, but there is no upper age limit for its use. We learn to be able to find any information we want quickly and easily. We have little patience for slow web sites, knowing that there's always somewhere else you can turn. Just think, what's your patience level for getting the information you want? Generally, people start becoming impatient after only four seconds! And now the same technology has become common in our workplace and we carry over those same levels of expectation onto our corporate web experience. We start complaining about the static content of our work systems and how we wish they were personalized and could learn from our use of them. Most of all we wish we didn't have to remember so many passwords and enter the same information repeatedly.

The technically high-level might say, "well that's all very simple—all you need is a Portal system with personalization capabilities, campaign management, a solid application server to support your business logic, single-sign-on security and probably some integration technology;" and in essence they are quite right. They are right in the same way that you only need a dam to control the Yangtze River in China—they're overlooking the implementation detail, which is often unexpectedly complex.

In the aerospace industry, this is very well known and we should all be thankful every time we step on a plane for the painstaking analysis and design phases that took place before the implementation and test phases began (of course, we're not thankful and hardly give a moments thought to the physics involved in getting a large metal tube to fly and all the interacting systems that have to work in order to keep it flying—perhaps it's better that we don't). Aerospace engineers have to get it right; lives are at stake. Even though we might think that commercial software does not require such stringent development, it shouldn't be that far removed. After all, there are plenty of implementations, especially in the financial sector where system downtime can cost millions of dollars per day. Even on a smaller scale, if your competitors have a system that is more flexible to change in customer demand than yours, your bottom line is likely to suffer.

So we have a paradox. User expectations on the systems we build are at an all-time high (and can only get greater) and the consequent system requirements are increasing rapidly. At the same time, the focus these days is on Return on Investment (ROI), value for money, speed to market and flexibility to change. So how do we resolve this paradox? Quite simply, *you need to design carefully.* As we have already observed, such sweeping statements are misleading and the design process can easily be a very involved undertaking. But at the end of the day, your system should be all the better for it. In all likelihood you will have avoided scope creep (adding new requirements part-way through development that derails the project planning) and, best of all, you may even have delivered what the customer wanted when they wanted it.

Understanding what your customer wants and rendering those requirements in a J2EE framework is what this book is all about. Enterprise application development can be a daunting task, so it is good to know there's now a contemporary source of relevant material to show you the way. This book pulls off the hardest trick of all—explaining complex topics simply, enabling you to see the relevance in your work. After all, chances are you are new to some or all of this technology and need to get up to speed in the fastest possible time.

So next time you check your account balance online or phone a support desk, gauge your expectations against the experience you receive. Do you think they designed their system well?

Simon Rowell
Director, Technical Management
Global Alliances, Western US
BEA Systems, Inc.

Acknowledgements

This book has been made possible by contributions from several individuals who provided text, insight, guidance, and support in shaping of the book's content.

I am indebted to Govy Munamala for his significant contributions in the shaping of Chapters 6 (Domain Model Design and Implementation) and Chapter 7 (Business Tier Design and Implementation), and in the design and development of business tier components and the creation of corresponding data model. Govy also provided the Ant build script explained in Chapter 9. My deepest appreciation to Kartik Ganeshan for contributing to the security-related content, and to Ali Siddiqui for helping shape the caching-related content that appears in Chapter 3. Special thanks go to Mansour Kavianpour for helping me shape Chapter 8 and for his significant contributions to this chapter. I am very grateful to Terry Markou for his assistance in the production of Web pages and to Sarah Murgel for creating the graphics for the site. Both Terry and Sarah provided assistance in validating the information architecture. I am very appreciative of the help provided by Enterpulse staff—most importantly the support provided by Geoff Faulkner, Jennifer Wilde, and Jacques Vigeant.

I am very grateful to the staff of McGraw-Hill/Osborne Media publication for their support throughout this project. The content of this book has the benefit of technical editing from Anne Horton and copy editing from Darren Meiss, and their efforts have greatly improved the presentation. Many thanks go to Athena Honore and Julie Smith for helping me focus on the delivery dates, and for providing the coordination, guidance, and encouragement during the project. Julie Smith worked tirelessly with the production team to get this book out on time. I am eternally grateful to Wendy Rinaldi for her encouragement and support, for without her belief in me this book would not have been written.

My very special thanks to Denyse Kehoe for introducing me to Osborne/McGraw-Hill publications.

I have benefited greatly from reading the works of other successful authors whose books have been mentioned in several chapters. My sincerest thanks to these authors for broadening my horizon in various disciplines of software development.

Last but most importantly, I would like to express my gratitude to my wonderful daughter Farrah and my lovely wife Munira for their infinite patience, support, and sacrifice during the course of this project.

Nadir Gulzar

Introduction

Developing large-scale enterprise applications involve several processes and technologies for creating a truly extensible, maintainable, and resilient object-oriented architecture. To be able to deliver an application that both completely meets the business goals set forth, and is able to evolve over the years without requiring significant redesign, warrants an open, flexible, and standards-friendly architecture. Careful articulation of the problem domain, and the requirements of its consumers, is just one aspect of ensuring that an architecture is created for supporting the current and future needs of the business. The problem domain definition must also become a means of driving the design, and development process. We should be able to trace the design and development artifacts to the original requirements to ensure consistency between the stated requirements and what is being delivered. This traceability between requirements and other project related artifacts ensure that the design view of the system is consistent with its use-case view.

Creating a use case view of the system is a meticulous process in which Information Architecture also plays a significant role. Translating the use case view into a corresponding design view for a multi-tiered architecture entails using the incremental and iterative process of domain modeling, business-tier process modeling, implementing presentation semantics—all within the context of a design that will allow maximum reuse within all tiers of the application. When you add to this compendium the need to understand the underlying component technologies, and the need to follow development methodologies and processes for managing project life-cycle, you can see that we are faced with a huge learning curve for creating a prototypical application that validates our approach for a large-scale solution. While the processes and technologies required to address all of the varied disciplines we just discussed are well-documented in several books, it is not practical for all J2EE enthusiasts to pour through each several-hundred page book before they're able to create a real world end-to-end solution. Serially learning each of the disciplines of software development is not efficient either, since it takes a lot more time, and is further compounded by our inability to retain unused information for long time. This book offers a "what you learn is what you use" approach that provides a blueprint for establishing a base-line architecture for most Web-based applications. This approach gives J2EE enthusiasts the opportunity for a fast ramp-up by allowing them to immediately apply the concepts they've learned to solve a real-world problem. It also provides both developers, and students aspiring to become architects, a one-stop source for the following:

- Use case driven modeling and development
- Role of Information Architecture in use case elaboration
- Formulating the security strategy of the application
- Understanding the need for presentation framework in the context of an MVC architecture
- Using the Struts framework
- Identifying implementation patterns for enabling Struts adoption in a consistent manner
- Capturing static aspects of the *Design View* of the system using class diagrams, and dynamic aspects using sequence diagrams
- Modeling interactions between the presentation tier components, interactions between the business tier components, and interactions between inter-tier components (between presentation and business tiers) using best practice design patterns
- Implementing the *Design View* using J2EE component technologies
- Implementing Web services using J2EE component technologies

Who Should Read This Book

Part I of this book is helpful for architects, developers, project managers, quality assurance teams, information architects, and anybody else who cares to understand the process of requirements analysis. The rest of the book is for budding architects, corporate developers, and students who are planning to build enterprise-class business applications for the J2EE platform. For Part II of this book, it is expected that the readers are familiar with object-oriented principles and concepts, and familiarity with UML is essential. This book assumes that the readers have familiarity with basic J2EE concepts, and the development and deployment of simple J2EE components.

Technology teams who will be creating a reference architecture or a prototypical programming model for upcoming projects will be able to harvest design templates from the accompanying material for their baseline architecture. Several best-practice J2EE design patterns, and their interactions and dependencies, have been captured in the accompanying sample application. The sample application provides a good place to start evolving the programming model based on your unique project requirements. Technology teams wanting to understand the architecture and adoption of presentation tier frameworks will benefit from the discussion on Struts.

The book's emphasis in on architecture and design and less on programming aspects, and as such, this book is not a complete coverage of the J2EE platform or Struts framework. Readers are provided with references to resources and books for completing their understanding of the material covered in this book. Also, this book is not exhaustive in its coverage of design patterns, as the subject of design patterns is vast and covered by large number of books, and there are several sites dedicated to discussing design patterns. The Web service implementation in this book is based on BEA WebLogic Workshop, which provides an abstraction over JAX-RPC API, as such programming with JAX-RPC API is not covered in this book.

How to Use This Book

Since this book employs a blueprint-like approach, it is best to read this book from beginning to end. This book develops the use cases for the sample philanthropic application *GreaterCause* in Chapter 1 and then discusses the impact of information architecture on evolving the use cases in Chapter 2. Chapter 3 is an optional read, however we encourage the readers to skim through the Application Architecture section as it sets the stage for the rest of the book. If you are already familiar with Struts and the related architecture then you can skip Chapter 4. Chapter 5 through 7 builds components for each of the application tiers and the associated use cases are realized incrementally in each of these chapters. Chapter 8 implements a Web service using the components developed in Chapters 6 and 7. Please note that the Web service implementation in Chapter 8 is based on BEA WebLogic Workshop. Chapter 9 provides information on installing and exercising the sample application. If your choice of application server is WebLogic, then Chapter 9 provides step-by-step instructions on installing the WebLogic Server 7.0, and deploying and exercising the sample application.

About Companion Website and Download

The sample application with accompanying binaries, source files, documentation, and errata links is available at http://www.osborne.com. Please follow the instructions provided by Osborne Media to locate the book specific links. References to source distribution in this book refers to the source made available in the download package. Complete information on the content of the download package is provided in Chapter 9.

Organization of this book

Part I, Requirements and Architecture Definition consists of Chapters 1 through 3.

Chapter 1, "*Requirements Analysis with Use Cases*" explains the process of defining the problem domain in the form of a use case view of the system. The sample application is decomposed into discrete functional units, with each such functional unit expressed as a separate use case. Each use case is explained using a standardized template, which explains the system behavior from the perspective of external entities interacting with the use case. A use case view is essential for creating a common understanding of the system behavior between the business domain experts, the application architect, and developers, without specifying how that behavior is implemented. The use case view developed for the sample application is prerequisite for understanding other chapters of this book.

Chapter 2, "*Information Architecture for Use Case Elaboration*" explains the impact of information architecture for comprehensively defining the use cases. In this chapter, we elaborate the use cases of our sample application by being more explicit in expressing the user interaction with the system, and the associated transactional semantics. Information architecture is crucial for devising schemes for organizing, labeling, navigating, indexing, and searching content. These aspects converge into a storyboard when creating a prototypical-view of the system's UI. The navigation semantics of the application are explained using a site flow that clearly articulates the page transitions associated with user actions—this information will be used when configuring the Struts framework.

Chapter 3, *"Application Architecture, Security, and Caching"* introduces important aspects of application architecture as it pertains to the J2EE platform (although the actual architecture of the sample application is gradually build throughout this book using a use case driven approach). This chapter discusses security, and provides a high-level architectural overview in the context of prominent technologies and specifications which should assist the readers in determining their unique security infrastructure needs, and the eventual selection of a best-of-breed solution. This chapter also covers *federated network identity* based on the *Project Liberty Architecture*. Finally, the chapter ends with a discussion on caching that explains common caching solutions and explores a basic caching architecture.

Part II, Design and Construction consists of Chapters 4 through 9.

Chapter 4, "*Struts-Based Application Architecture*" discusses the benefits and design considerations for a presentation-tier framework based on Model-View-Controller architecture. This chapter discusses key aspects of such a framework in the context of Struts. We explore Struts architecture, its implementation and configuration semantics, and basic usage for providing quick familiarity to our readers on varied aspects of Struts. The material provides under-the-hood information on Struts, giving readers the necessary background to evaluate its applicability in their problem domain. The information provided in this chapter will be adequate to follow the use case realizations in Chapter 5.

Chapter 5, *"Presentation Tier Design and Implementation"* is focused on use-case realization for the presentation tier functionality of the sample application. Emphasis in this chapter is on creating the static and dynamic models of the system while utilizing the best practice J2EE design patterns for realizing client-side semantics. This chapter also identifies Struts implementation patterns that provide repeatable solutions for solving complex user interactions. Templates can be derived from these patterns for assisting the development team in establishing a consistent design vocabulary and implementation across all use cases, thereby improving readability and maintainability of the code. These patterns will serve as a starting point from which to evolve.

Chapter 6, "*Domain Model Design and Implementation*" is focused on creating a domain model and the corresponding database schema for persisting the domain objects. In this chapter we identify domain entities and their relationships. We use J2EE container services to both access and persist the domain entities and their relationships. This chapter also discusses configuration aspects of container-managed fields and container-managed relationships for entity beans with container-managed persistence. The domain model implemented in this chapter forms the basis for implementing business tier components in Chapter 7.

Chapter 7, "*Business Tier Design and Implementation*" is focused on use-case realization for the business tier functionality of the sample application. This chapter discusses and implements several best-practice business tier design patterns. Emphasis in this chapter is on identification of appropriate design patterns in the context of our problem domain and the application of these patterns for solving common problems during the design and development of the business tier. This chapter also discusses the configuration aspects of stateful and stateless session beans and the transactional semantics associated with Enterprise JavaBeans.

Chapter 8, "*Web Services for Application Integration*" introduces the Web services technology and its associated standards. It brings to light key aspects of the WSDL and SOAP specification so that readers are able to discern the relationships between WSDL constructs and the corresponding SOAP message constructs. The concepts learned in this chapter are subsequently applied in the creation of a Web service in the context of our sample application using BEA WebLogic Workshop.

Chapter 9, "*Application Assembly and Deployment*" focuses on installing and configuring the WebLogic Platform 7.0, and deploying the sample *GreaterCause* application.

PART I

Requirements and Architecture Definition

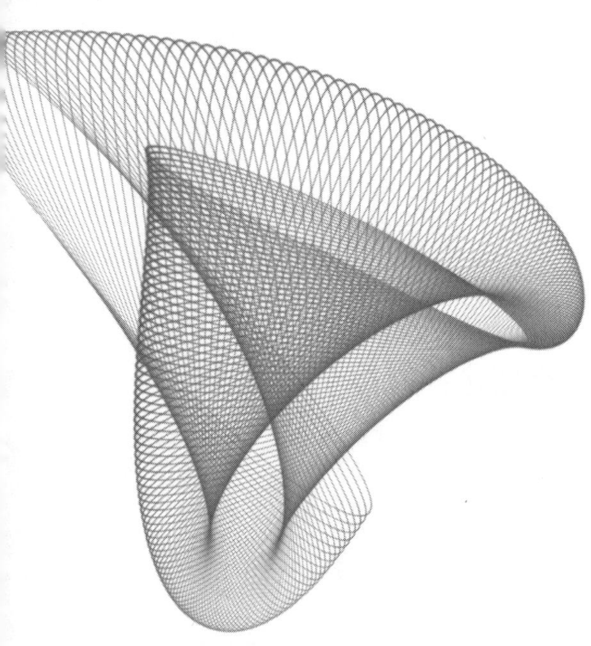

CHAPTER

1

Requirements Analysis with Use Cases

IN THIS CHAPTER:

Use Case Driven Modeling

Defining the Problem Domain

Identifying System Context

Identifying Risk Factors and Dependencies

Identifying Use Case Packages

Documenting Use Cases

GreaterCause Use Case Summary

Summary

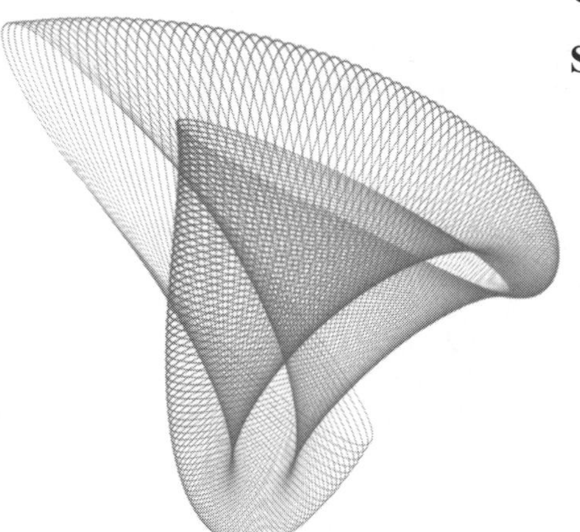

Developing large-scale software solutions reminds us of the many different perspectives that different stakeholders have about the end product. At the outset, there is nothing concrete to visually depict the semantics and mechanics of the end product. At this juncture of the project, we have an abstract view of the software to be developed. As such, it is imperative to find a common ground for all stakeholders to agree upon, without which we run the risk of creating a product that tends to lend itself to the vision of only a certain interest group. It is necessary to ensure creation of a product that is a representation of the organization's business needs and the needs of all its users and sponsors. Therefore, we must resort to providing a requirements vocabulary that is easily understood by all stakeholders. This chapter's focus is to assist the readers in creating such a vocabulary using use cases, activity diagrams, and flow of events.

However, before we begin, there has to be an expectation about the level of impact the artifacts in this chapter will have on defining a project's requirements. *Use cases* are at the center of this effort. Use cases can be created at different levels of abstraction. A use case diagram can be used to model the behavior of an entire system, subsystem, or a class. Getting too detailed in the first iteration could result in a lot of rework if the requirements are not well understood. Therefore, it is important to remain at a level of abstraction that clearly captures the requirements from the point of view of business domain experts, project sponsors, end users, customers, and executive management. We will call this group collectively *stakeholders*. For this group, we want to avoid too much, too fast, too early in the project. You will experience that just getting to agree on high-level requirements takes several iterations. This is not unusual since the process of requirements definition is evolutionary, and with every iteration we have opportunity to discover and improve. The requirements team is made up of stakeholders and one or more members of the technical staff; use cases are a contract between these two groups, and therefore appropriate representation from both sides is critical to the success of the project. Special needs of the project can be met by augmenting the requirements team with appropriately skilled members; for example, if the system is going to interface extensively with a CRM solution, it will be helpful to have assistance from a person experienced in the CRM space and CRM software.

Another viewpoint that we would like to suggest is that all through the process *think reuse* and *think decomposition*. This mode of thinking helps us factor common behavior into use cases, and finally package a set of related use cases into subsystems. The next chapter is a logical progression from this chapter and helps us map the requirements of this chapter in terms of *information architecture* that provides a prototype of the end product to the stakeholders and developers. Use cases will be elaborated during information architecture, therefore our endeavor for completely capturing functional requirements will conclude in Chapter 2. Use case realization is the focus of Chapters 5 through 8.

Use Case Driven Modeling

The Unified Modeling Language User Guide (UML) defines a use case as follows:

> A use case specifies the behavior of a system or a part of the system and is a description of a set of sequences of actions, including variants, that a system performs to yield an observable result of value to an actor.

A use case is an outside view of the system as seen by the entities interacting with the use case. It is used for capturing the requirements of a system. A use case is not atomic; a use case representing a complex system behavior can be further decomposed into more use cases. A use case is essential for creating a common understanding of the system behavior between the business domain experts, the application architect, and developers, without specifying how that behavior is implemented. During design, a use case is realized by a set of related objects working together to deliver the behavior prescribed by the use case. Models created during design must be able to map back to the requirements by their ability to satisfy each use case within the problem domain. The use cases therefore help validate the architecture. In an iterative design and development process, use cases enable catching of deviation from requirements early in the life cycle; all models and project artifacts are synchronized for accurately reflecting the purpose of the system all throughout the project life cycle. As such, risks are identified early in the process, therefore preventing major rework later.

Use cases document the system and form the bases of test cases for user acceptance, integration, regression, and system tests. This approach has built-in traceability because all design, development, and testing is performed based on use case scenarios. The use cases become a contract between the business units and the IT organization. By employing incremental and iterative approaches, this contract is enforced throughout the development life cycle by verifying intermediate artifacts against the behavior prescribed by the use cases. The use case model is central to all analysis and design artifacts, and for project planning.

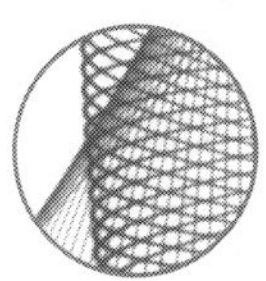

NOTE

This book consistently strives to live by the word "practical" in its name. Therefore, every concept presented in this book is explained using the fictitious GreaterCause application. The use cases discussed in this chapter will lay the foundation for understanding the problem domain. The use cases will be subsequently realized using architecture and design artifacts explained in the rest of the book.

Subsequent sections in this chapter explain what, why, when, and how to capture system requirements for the sample application. In this chapter, the following sections denote the artifacts created for the sample application:

- GreaterCause System Definition
- GreaterCause Context Diagrams and Actors
- GreaterCause Risk Factors
- GreaterCause Dependencies
- GreaterCause Use Case Packages
- GreaterCause Use Case Summary

Familiarity with the preceding structure will assist you in distinguishing the project artifacts from the commentary that surrounds the artifacts.

Defining the Problem Domain

To promote understanding of the problem domain, we ask ourselves several questions, some of which can be stated as follows:

- What business needs will the software try to solve?
- Who are the users of the system?
- What functionality will be supported by the system?
- What are the interactions between different subsystems?
- What components in the problem domain can be provided by a third party as off-the-shelf components?
- What components of the system can be isolated to form reusable, self-contained subsystems?

The answers to these and myriad other questions help us understand the solution space. We will be gradually answering these questions as we proceed through the book.

The first step in understanding the problem domain is to create a project description. A project description should explain the purpose of the project. It must be concise, and it should quickly demonstrate the business objective. You will be surprised how many different perspectives evolve at this time from different stakeholders. At this stage of the project, most stakeholders are concerned with return on investment. A project description is therefore the first consensus point between stakeholders because it clearly states the objectives of the new system.

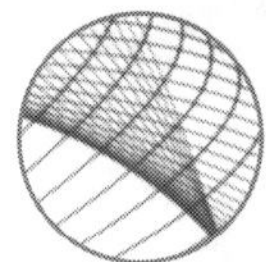

TIP

Before you begin to write the system description, you may find it helpful to define domain-specific terms for your audience; this will establish a common vocabulary for communication. You may optionally provide an operational model for added clarification, as shown in Figure 1-1.

GreaterCause System Definition

The following terminology is consistently used in defining the problem domain.

- GreaterCause is a philanthropic application that is hosted at a central location.
- GreaterCause.com is the domain name of the site where the GreaterCause application is accessible as a hosted service. For brevity, the term "site" will refer to the GreaterCause.com site.
- Portal is a personalized single point of access for business and consumer services.
- Portal-Domain is the domain that hosts a consumer portal or a corporate intranet.
- GreaterCause.com Portal-Alliance is formed as a result of portals providing a pass-through or gateway component, also called a *portlet*, on the portal page for redirecting portal users to the GreaterCause.com site.

- NPO is a non-profit organization that registers with GreaterCause.com site for soliciting charitable contributions from prospective donors.

The GreaterCause.com domain is responsible for hosting the GreaterCause charitable-giving application at a central location. The site is accessible to the donors via various consumer portals and corporate intranets.

Portal-providers create an alliance (i.e. a service contract) with GreaterCause to procure the GreaterCause services for their user base. An agreement between a portal-provider and GreaterCause to serve the portal's users is termed *Portal-Alliance*. Each portal-alliance has an associated administrator ID and password using which the portal-alliance Administrator (an employee of the portal provider, or its designate) can maintain the portal-related profile information. The portal-provider interposes itself as a gatekeeper to the GreaterCause application by using a portion of the portal's real estate to provide an intelligent gateway or pass-through to the GreaterCause site for their subscriber base. The GreaterCause pass-through is available as a portlet. This portlet is aggregated into the portal view of the partnering portal-domains.

Non-profit organizations (NPOs) register with GreaterCause to list themselves in the GreaterCause database for receiving charitable contributions (i.e. donations) from the visitors of the GreaterCause.com site. Each registered NPO is provided with an administrator ID and password using which the NPO administrator can maintain its related profile information.

Although, GreaterCause.com visitors can donate to any of the available charities (i.e. NPOs), a portal-provider can influence the decision of a donor in the selection of a preferred charity; this is done by campaigning for the preferred NPOs. Portal-alliance administrators

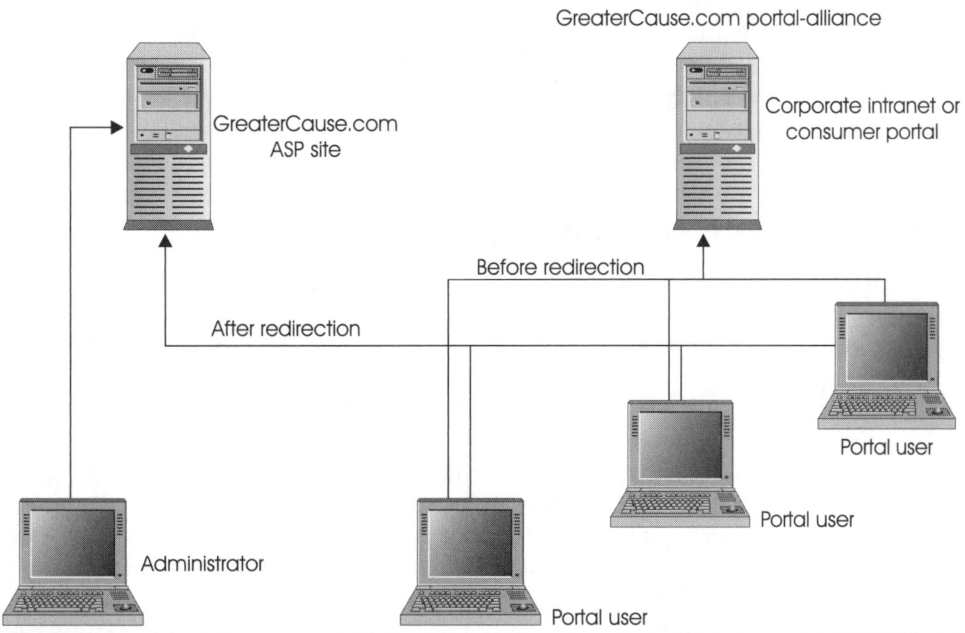

Figure 1-1 *GreaterCause operational model*

have the ability to log in to the GreaterCause.com site with their administrator ID and create campaigns for non-profit organizations at both the national and regional level. These portal-alliance–specific campaigns for preferred NPOs are stored at the GreaterCause.com site and subsequently featured by the portal-domains on their respective portal-page. The list of featured non-profit organizations (featured-NPOs), created by the portal-alliance administrator in the GreaterCause.com database, is provided via a web service to each portal-domain; this list is subsequently displayed by the portlet hosted within the portal-page. Prospective donors visiting the portals are provided with the option to donate to either the featured non-profit organizations, or pass through directly to the GreaterCause.com site for searching and donating to a non-profit organization of the donor's choice.

Once a portal-user is redirected to the GreaterCause.com site by the portal-provider, the GreaterCause service, as viewed by a portal-user, is customizable by portal-alliance administrators for preserving the branding and navigation structure of their respective portal-domains. The portal-domain, before redirecting the portal-user to GreaterCause.com, is responsible for authenticating the portal-user (a.ka. the donor). The portal-domain and the GreaterCause.com site mutually authenticate before redirecting the donors. Donor's registration information is provided by the portal-domain to GreaterCause.com during the redirection process.

All transaction history is logged using the donor's registration ID and portal-domain affiliation. Donors have the ability to view their history of donations for the current and previous year.

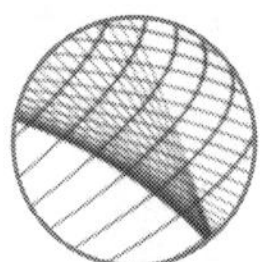

TIP

The description of the system provides a vocabulary that consists of real-world objects. Use case names are derived from this vocabulary and tend to express the behavior of the system in short, present-tense verb phrases in active voice; the use case being named must represent a reasonably atomic behavior of the system. In the use case context, a client is an external actor to the use case—which could be a human, another software system, or an asynchronous message. Therefore, a use case name is most effective when expressed from the perspective of the user.

Identifying System Context

The behavior and semantics of the system is best understood from the point of view provided by who needs the system, how they intend to use it, and who the system interacts with to satisfy the needs of its users. Each entity surrounding and interacting with the system constitutes the system's context, whether it be a consumer or a provider; this is illustrated in Figures 1-2 and 1-3 by the directed lines representing paths of communication.

Modeling the context of the system is useful in understanding how it interacts with other systems in an ecosystem of interconnected systems. An external entity communicating with the system is an instance of an *actor*; actors are not part of the system. An actor could be an individual, another software system, an asynchronous message, or a piece of external hardware. More specifically, an actor defines a particular role played by an entity within the context of the system; this implies that an entity may be represented by one or more actors because the entity takes different roles with regard to the system and, similarly, an actor represents one or more entities that represent the same role within the context of the system.

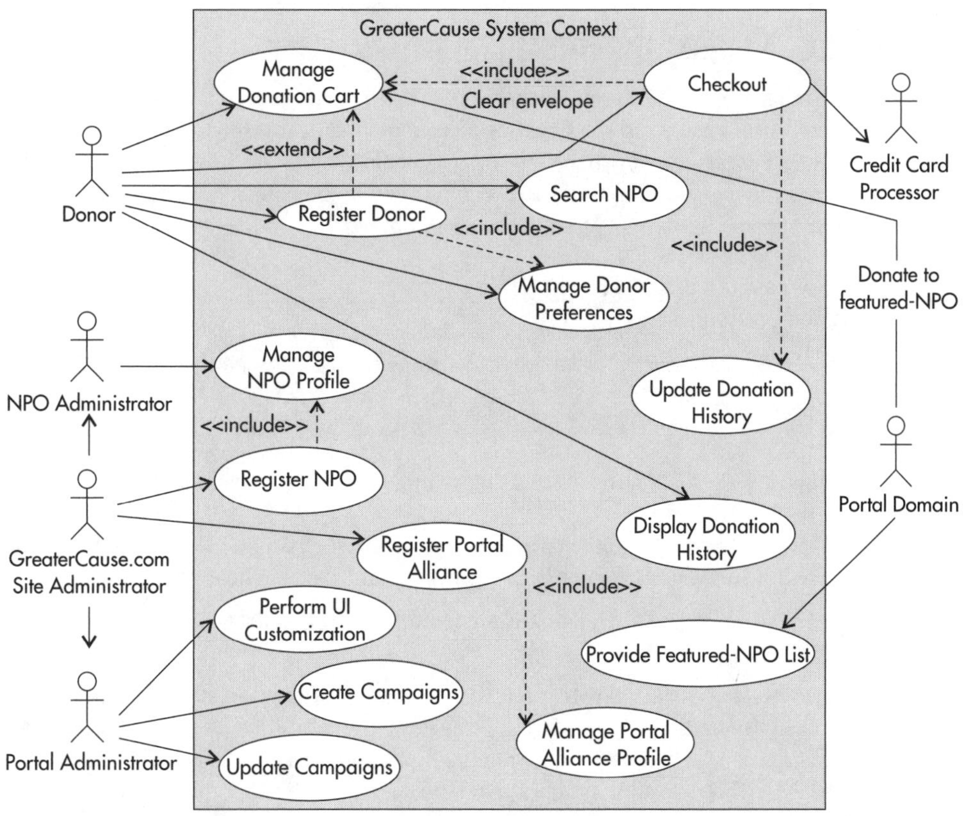

Figure 1-3 *GreaterCause System Context Diagram*

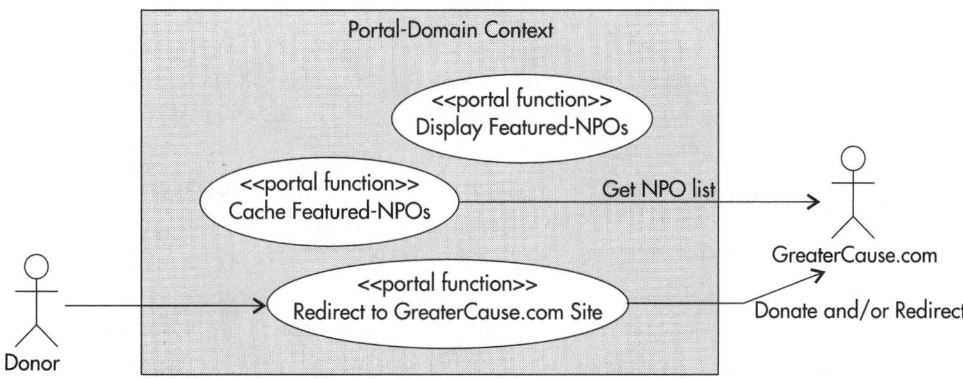

Figure 1-2 *Portal-domain context diagram*

GreaterCause Context Diagrams and Actors

It is apparent from the project description that we are dealing with two interacting systems, the core GreaterCause service and the GreaterCause components residing on the servers of the portal-domains. For brevity, we will not evolve the documentation for both systems separately but show separate models where appropriate. You will see in the context diagrams for the two systems that they appear as actors within the other's context.

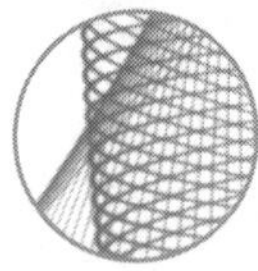

NOTE

Stereotyping is a UML extension mechanism, with which one can provide additional semantics to a model element in the context of a specific problem domain. We have extended the actors, packages, and use cases with two stereotypes, `<<GreaterCause.com>>` ***and*** `<<Portal Domain>>`, ***to identify entities or elements on the GreaterCause.com domain and on the portal-domain, respectively.***

The following is a list of all actors interacting with the GreaterCause application:

- **Donor** A donor is a user of the GreaterCause services. A donor has an affiliation with a portal, with which the donor can access the GreaterCause application.
- **Credit card processor** A credit card processor is an external system that processes the credit cards.
- **GreaterCause.com site administrator** The primary responsibility of a site administrator is to create configuration information for registering portal-alliances and NPOs. Only portals configured in the GreaterCause.com site can provide the GreaterCause services to its user base. The site administrator can *impersonate* an NPO administrator or a portal-alliance administrator; this allows a site administrator to function as a stand-in for an NPO administrator or portal-alliance administrator.
- **Portal-Alliance administrator** Portal-alliance administrators are responsible for creating global and regional campaigns for featuring non-profit organizations on their respective portals, and for maintaining the profile information for their portal-domain. Portal administrators are also responsible for providing the configuration information required to customize the UI experience of GreaterCause.com site users. Login credentials for portal-alliance administrators are created by the GreaterCause.com site administrator.
- **NPO administrator** The NPO administrator is responsible for maintaining the profile information for NPO. Login credentials for the NPO (non-profit organization) administrators are created by the GreaterCause.com site administrator.
- **Portal domain** Portal domains rely on the GreaterCause.com site to provide the list of featured-NPOs associated with active campaigns. The portal domains provide donors with an option to donate to one of the featured-NPOs before redirecting donors to the GreaterCause.com site.

The following is a list of all actors interacting with the portal-domain:

- **Donor** Explained in context with GreaterCause actors.
- **GreaterCause.com** GreaterCause.com provides charitable giving–related services to the users of the portal-domains. Additionally, it provides a list of featured-NPOs to the portal-domains.

Identifying Risk Factors and Dependencies

Once the project description is completed, the next step is to assess the risks and dependencies associated with the project. Knowing this information up front mitigates the risks early in the project life cycle. You must also document all assumptions. Once you obtain factual data, some of the assumptions become assertions and can be removed from the list. Some of the risk factors and dependencies for the GreaterCause application are listed in the following sections to illustrate some possibilities.

GreaterCause Risk Factors

Following are some of the GreaterCause risk factors:

- Portals may be restrictive in how they exchange information with GreaterCause.com site.
- Will a generic composite view template with limited UI customization meet the needs of the portal providers?
- Will the architecture support phase-2 functionality for funds disbursement?
- Will the portal provider agree to single sign-on semantics? It is expected that the portal-domain will authenticate the user before forwarding the request to the GreaterCause.com site.

GreaterCause Dependencies

Following are some of the GreaterCause dependencies:

- Project will use the Struts MVC framework. Engineers associated with this project will need to be trained on Struts.
- Site functionality can only be finalized after obtaining buy-in of pilot portal-alliances.
- Pilot portal-alliances must agree on using Web services for receiving the featured-NPO list.

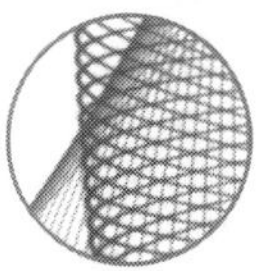

NOTE

Apart from documenting functional requirements of the system, one must also document the nonfunctional requirements that address the need for performance, load balancing, failover, platform dependencies, framework usage, adherence to standards, vendor preference, usability, etc. These are specific to organizations, applications, and platforms; as such, they will not be discussed in any detail in this book.

Identifying Use Case Packages

A use case diagram represents some behavioral aspect of a system, subsystem, or a class. It consists of a set of conceptually and semantically related use cases. The aggregate of all the use cases in all the use case diagrams represents the system functionality; this is also called the static use case view of a system. However, each individual use case with its associated set of sequences of actions constitutes the dynamic view of the system. The focus should be on creating use cases that factor common behavior, and then grouping use cases that are relevant to each other, both conceptually and semantically, in producing a desired system behavior. Such groupings form independent, self-contained functional units that could be packaged as subsystems during the analysis phase. Use cases in each package must have strong cohesion to each other and exhibit loose coupling with other packages.

Decomposing the system into packages has the advantage of modularizing the system, making it simpler to understand, manage, and document. The atomicity at the level of subsystems enables concurrent analysis, design, and development effort of different subsystems. The package hierarchy defined in the requirements phase can be used to model the structural view of the system during the analysis phase, and each package could potentially result in a subsystem. However, during the analysis phase you will also discover several supporting objects interacting with multiple packages. For example, the authentication module, the error reporting module, and the service locator module could be common to several packages; therefore, in the analysis phase, the package structure will need to be modified for housing such components. During the analysis phase, you may find the need to break down a package into subordinate packages; make sure the nesting is not more than a couple of levels, otherwise the packages get harder to manage.

Once the key abstractions are identified in the system context, we are able to distinguish functionally related use cases and move these into packages. Let's briefly define these groupings and then assess whether each grouping cohesively expresses an independent functional unit. Figure 1-4 depicts the system's use case packages with dependency relationships between several packages. This relationship is shown using a dashed line with an arrowhead pointing in the direction of the package that the other depends on. The dependency implies that a package is dependent on another package for some services or has structural knowledge about the elements in the other package.

GreaterCause Use Case Packages

GreaterCause use cases are distributed among packages shown in Figure 1-4. Refer to the use case diagrams corresponding to each package under the later section "GreaterCause Use Case Summary" for package description and for the use cases allocated to each package. The use case diagrams associated with each package in the section "GreaterCause Use Case Summary" depicts package interactions or dependencies using actors as stand-ins for related packages.

Once the decomposition has been accomplished, the use case diagrams can show package interactions or dependencies using actors as stand-ins for package-related functions. This notation supports the definition of a system context where every subsystem boundary scopes the behavior from the point of view of all the actors interacting with the subsystem.

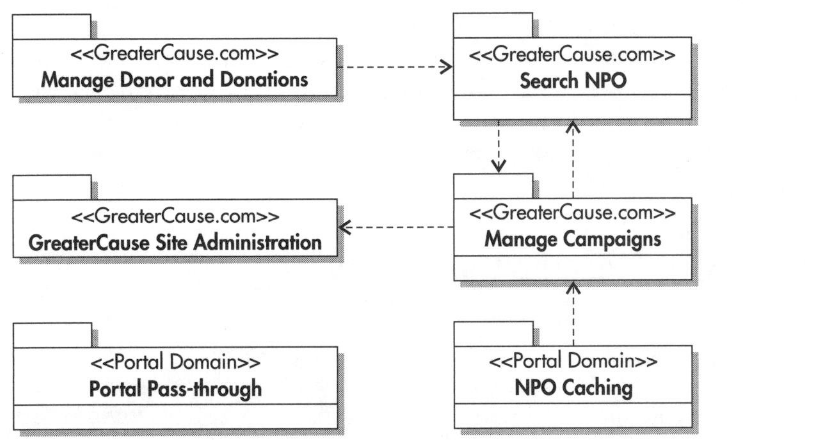

Figure 1-4 *Decomposing the system into packages*

Documenting Use Cases

Use cases can be documented quite extensively. One can include activity diagrams to model primary and alternate scenarios of the use cases, and sequence diagrams to model interaction between various actors and the system. Although one could model sequence diagrams for use cases, in most cases you will find that the activity diagrams are sufficient for documenting the various use case scenarios. Again, you do not have to have an activity diagram for every use case; use it to explain complex scenarios.

The use case documentation should be augmented by text that explains the *main flow of events* (primary scenarios) and *alternate flow of events* (secondary scenarios). These flows of events are documented in the language of the problem domain. Recall that a use case describes a set of sequences, therefore other than the main flow we need alternate flows to document those sequences that support exceptional behavior resulting from changes in system state, application exceptions, or an actor exercising different options. Each sequence or scenario is an instance of the use case the same way an object is an instance of a class. The flow of events must state the event or action that starts a use case, and it must clearly state how the use case ends. It must also include interactions with actors; this could include actions taken by the actor for requesting a system service or actions taken by the system for requesting service from the actors. The steps in a scenario are expressed as request-response interactions; for example, an actor requests a service and the system responds with an action. Scenarios are always written from an actor's viewpoint. This flow of events could be numbered for improved readability and may also contain preconditions and postconditions. We will see numbered flows of events, preconditions, and postconditions in Chapter 2, dealing with information architecture, where we will further elaborate a limited number of use cases using wire frames.

Use case documentation must clearly explain the purpose of the system without being too specific or too brief to cover essential system behavior. Focus should be on being complete rather than detailed in requirements analysis. Use cases have this duality of capturing requirements and expressing these requirements as behavior from an actor's viewpoint. Tailor the documentation to your audience and ask yourself, "Will the documentation effectively communicate the purpose of the system to the stakeholders, QA engineers, web production engineers, designers, and developers?" It may also help to engage a technical writer for documenting use cases. In this chapter, we are going to focus on a higher level of abstraction and then elaborate the use cases in Chapter 2.

Documenting Scenarios with Activity Diagrams

Activity diagrams model the dynamic aspects of a system. During use casing, an activity diagram helps a modeler to comprehensively depict a use case's dynamic behavior and its interaction with actors. Other than clearly articulating the flow of events for the stakeholders and developers, the knowledge derived from creating activity diagrams can be applied for adjusting the architecture such that conceptually and semantically related use cases with high degrees of cohesion are allocated in the same package. The cohesion between use cases is represented using the include or extend relationships, as explained in the next section, "Factoring Common Behavior and Variant Behavior." Should a readjustment in architecture lead to a use case being reallocated to another package, then any previously existing "include" relationships will become a "dependency" relationship.

Although the interaction diagram focuses on objects passing messages to each other, the activity diagrams focus on messages passed between objects. The messages make up the activity state in an activity diagram. The level of abstraction for depicting states in an activity diagram depends on whether you are using an *activity state* or an *action state*. An activity state is non-atomic and can be further decomposed in more activity states and/or action states. An action state represents an executable atomic computation that cannot be decomposed any further. A transition from a source state to target state is triggered by the completion of all activities in the source state.

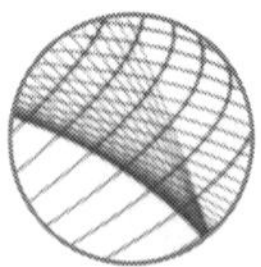

TIP

In an activity diagram, the transitions leaving a decision node (diamond-shaped node) can be labeled with guard conditions. These guard conditions represent if-else scenarios. Also, you can label a transition as an event.

Factoring Common Behavior and Variant Behavior

Use the "include" relationship to factor common behavior in use cases. Factoring common behavior into separate use cases makes the system modular and promotes reuse. Later, in section "Manage Donor and Donations" (Figure 1-5), you will observe that the *Register Donor* process always includes *Manage Donor Preferences*; this is because donor preferences are always set the first time the registration process is instantiated. Also, *Checkout* includes *Update Donation History* because a successful checkout results in the creation of transaction history.

The include relationship is used when a use case is always going to be included in another use case. Its execution is not conditional. For conditional includes, use the *extend* relationship. The extend relationship differs from the include relationship in that the use case in an extend

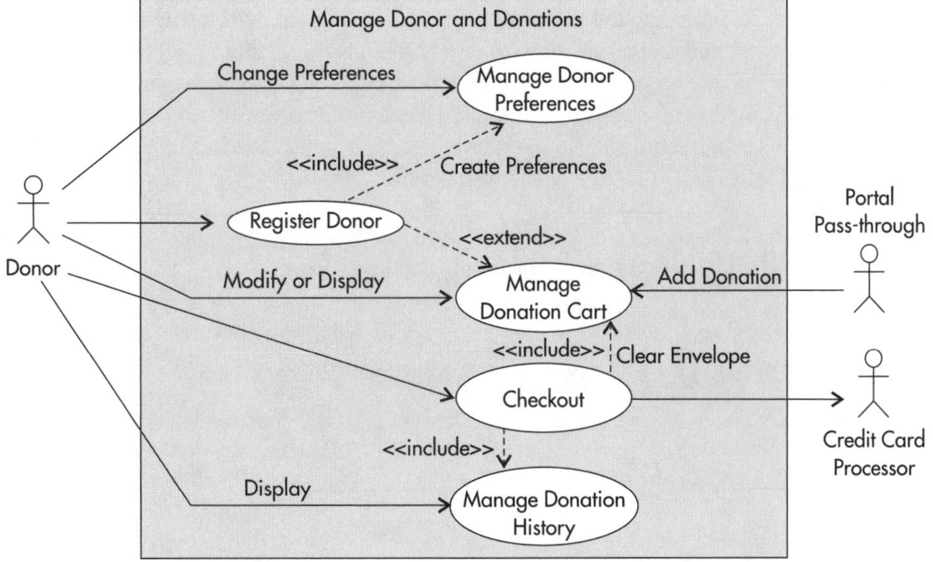

Figure 1-5 *Use case diagram—Manage Donor and Donations*

relationship conditionally injects itself into a base use case, at predetermined extension points. Factoring variants helps isolate exceptional behavior into separate use cases thereby simplifying the base use case.

An include relationship is represented by a directed link from the including use case to the included use case; an extend relationship is represented by a directed link from the extending use case to the use case that it extends. In the use case model, the include and extend relationships are rendered as stereotypes. In the flow of events, use the notation "include" (included use case) to include the behavior of another use case, as shown in the *Checkout* and *Register Donor* use cases in the package Manage Donor and Donations. Both include and extend must instantiate within the system boundary of its base use case; in other words, include or extend relationships cannot span between use case diagrams.

Creating a Use Case Summary

Consider a use case summary as an initial milestone in the requirements analysis effort. A use case summary is critical for several reasons:

- For quickly and accurately identifying the behavior of the system to stakeholders
- For requesting appropriate project funding and staff for subsequent phases of the project
- For project managers to prepare project plans
- For communicating requirements to the next phase of the project
- For fast ramp-up of individuals coming onboard the project team in the middle of the project

In this section, we will explain all the packages of the GreaterCause application, and their subordinate use cases and associated flow of events. Although explaining UML is beyond the scope of this book, wherever essential, we will explain how to appropriately use certain key notations accompanied with practical examples. The documentation style used in this book is suggestive and not prescriptive. You may have a variation of this based on your unique environment and team dynamics. For further information on applying use cases and associated techniques please refer to "Applying Use Cases" by Geri Schnieder et. al. [Use Cases], "Use Case Driven Modeling with UML" by Doug Rosenberg [Object Modeling], and "The Unified Modeling Language User Guide" by Grady Booch et. al. [UML].

GreaterCause Use Case Summary

This section documents each use case package independently. The packages are explained using use case diagrams and, where appropriate, activity diagrams are shown as well. The documentation also consists of a high-level summary of main and alternate flows of events for each use case.

Manage Donor and Donations

This package pertains to donor-related services. These services primarily include donor registration, making donations, managing the shopping cart, and providing donors with the ability to view their donation history (a.k.a. tax record) for the current and previous year.

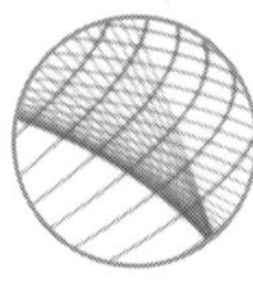

TIP

The activity diagram of Figure 1-6 is focused on communicating a single aspect of the system, and that is "Making a Donation." Use more activity diagrams to show other aspects of the system. Activity diagrams can be used to explain systems, subsystems, class, operations, and use cases. You want to create activity diagrams mostly for explaining complex processes.

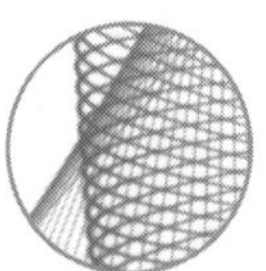

NOTE

The activity diagram of Figure 1-6 depicts the flow of events when a donor selects an NPO to donate to. The diagram clearly articulates the various processes involved in completing a donation process. The readers of the documentation will find it helpful to have a high-level view of certain complex sequences of events, especially the ones that illustrate a process flow.

Manage Donation Cart Use Case

This use case handles the process of displaying, adding, removing, and modifying donations in the donation cart.

Main Flow of Events The use case is instantiated when a donor selects an NPO on the search results page, or selects the donate function for a featured-NPO in a portal-page. The donor is presented the donation cart with the selected NPO added to the cart. The donor enters the donation amount for the new donation. At this time, the donor can also modify donation amounts for

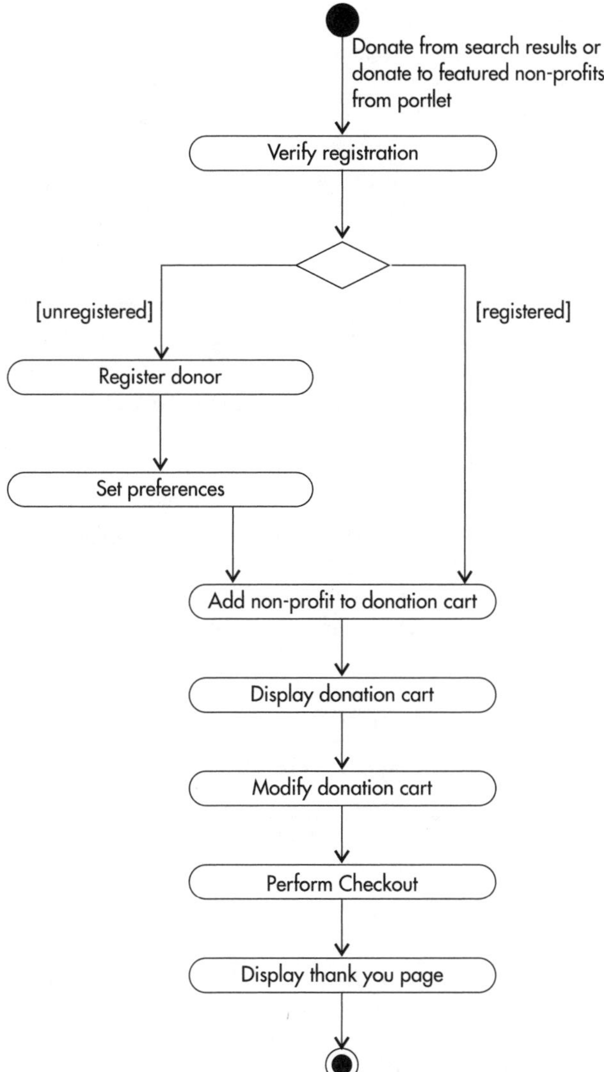

Figure 1-6 *Process Flow for "Making a Donation"*

existing donations and maybe decide to remove existing donations from the cart. The donor confirms the changes by selecting the checkout or update function, thus ending the use case.

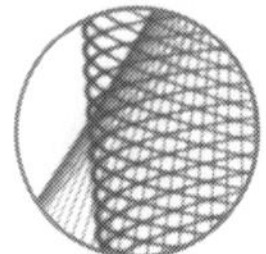

NOTE

In the preceding use case, notice that the emphasis is on behavior rather than the user interface. Wire frames depicting user interactions are developed as part of information architecture in Chapter 2. Wire frames, coupled with navigation semantics, will further augment the use cases.

Alternate Flow of Events If the donor is making a donation for the first time, the donor is presented with a registration form. The donor verifies the registration information, some of which could have been provided by the affiliated portal-domain, and submits the information to the system. The system validates this information and presents the new donor with a form that enables a donor to provide a set of preferences that personalizes a donor's donation experience. The donor provides this information to the system, which validates and stores the information in the database for future use. The donor is then presented with the donation cart.

Checkout Use Case

This use case interfaces with the credit card processor and creates transaction history. At the donor's discretion, this use case can also update credit card information.

Main Flow of Events The use case is instantiated when the donor selects the checkout function. The donor is presented with a checkout page. The donor has the option of changing the credit card information on this page and saving the new credit card information as part of the checkout process. When the donor confirms, the information is validated. If the validation is successful, the credit card processor is contacted. If the credit card transaction is successful, `include (Update Donation History)` for creating transaction history of all donations in the donation cart and `include (Manage Donation Cart)` for clearing the cart. A thank you page is presented to the donor, thus ending the use case.

Update Donation History Use Case

This use case records all transaction history.

Update History Main Flow of Events The use case is instantiated by the checkout function. Completed donations from the checkout function are added to the data store, and the use case ends.

Display Donation History Use Case

This use case also displays a cumulative history of a donor's donations for the current year and, optionally, the previous year. The current year's history is shown by default; the previous year's history is displayed only when selected.

Display History Main Flow of Events The use case is instantiated when a donor selects the reporting function. The system displays the transaction history for the current year, and the use case ends.

Display History Alternate Flow of Events The donor can select to display the previous year's history.

Register Donor Use Case

This use case creates a new donor in the GreaterCause data store.

Main Flow of Events The use case is instantiated for an unregistered donor. The donor is provided with a registration page. The registration page is initialized with a registration ID, and donor-related information provided by the portal-domain. The donor verifies or modifies the information. If the information entered by the donor is validated successfully, then use `include (Manage Donor Preferences)` and the use case ends.

Manage Donor Preferences Use Case

This use case enables a donor to input personal preferences for customizing his or her donation process.

Main Flow of Events The use case is instantiated either by the donor registration process or when the donor selects to modify his or her personal preferences. The donor makes the required changes and confirms. If the information entered by the donor is validated successfully by the system, the donor preferences are updated in the data store. The system acknowledges the changes and the use case ends.

Search NPO

This package provides the search functionality to donors, the site administrator, and portal-alliance administrators. NPO entries are analogous to items in a catalog. Searching a non-profit organization is analogous to searching an item from the catalog; in this context, the non-profit organization is itself an item in the supply-chain sense.

Search NPO Use Case

This use case provides search algorithms for searching the NPOs. A generic keyword-based search is available along with an advanced search capability for location-based searches.

Keyword Search Main Flow of Events This use case is instantiated when the donor uses the generic keyword search function. The system searches the database for matching NPOs and displays a results page to the user, and the use case ends.

Advanced Search Main Flow of Events This use case begins when the donor, the site administrator, or the portal-alliance administrator selects the advanced search function. The user is

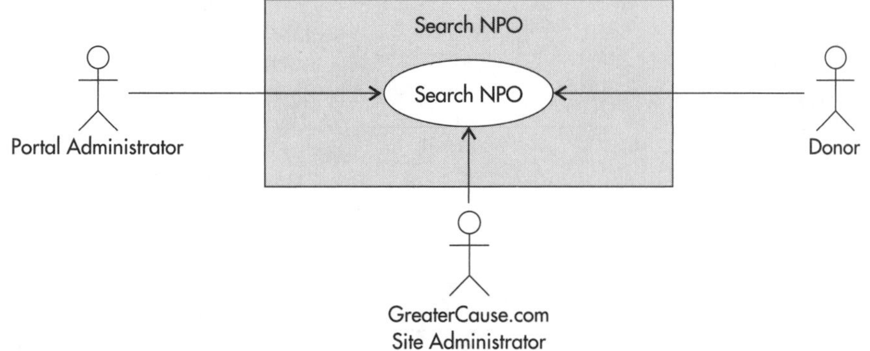

Figure 1-7 *Use case diagram—Search NPO*

presented with a query page. The user enters the search criteria. The system searches the database for matching NPOs and displays a results page to the user, thus ending the use case.

Perform GreaterCause.com Site Administration

This package enables the maintenance of the configuration information for proper operation of the site. Key facilities provided by this package are NPO registration, portal alliance registration, profile maintenance, and portal-specific UI customizations.

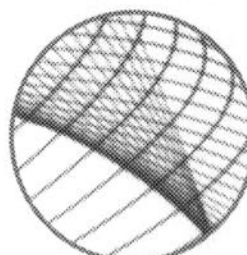

TIP

Actors can be organized using the generalization relationship. The inheritance semantics are the same as that in classes; the child inherits the behavior of the parent and can add to or override this behavior. For example, in Figure 1-8 the site administrator inherits from the NPO and portal-alliance administrators. Because Java does not support multiple inheritance, it is likely that during implementation the site administrator will extend a base class that has implemented the interfaces for NPO and portal-alliance administrators; this will allow the site administrator to be substituted wherever NPO and portal administrators can appear.

Register NPO Use Case

This use case is responsible for registering new NPOs for the site. Every NPO, prior to registration, is verified for validity. The NPO verification is an offline process.

Main Flow of Events The use case begins when the site administrator selects the NPO registration function. The site administrator enters all the necessary information pertaining

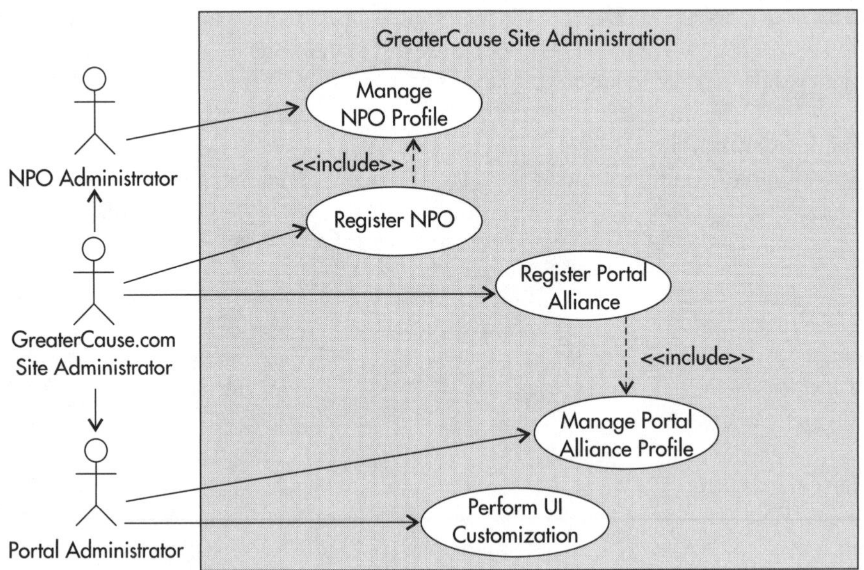

Figure 1-8 *Use case diagram—Perform GreaterCause.com Site Administration*

to a non-profit organization. The system validates the information. If the validation process is successful, the system stores the registration information in the data store. The system initializes an NPO profile record, acknowledges the actions, and the use case ends.

Manage NPO Profile Use Case

This use case enables the site administrator and NPO administrator to change the profile information associated with an NPO.

Main Flow of Events The use case starts when an NPO or site administrator selects the update profile function. The administrator is presented with a page with relevant profile information. The administrator updates the information and confirms changes. If the validation process is successful, the system commits those changes in the data store. The system acknowledges the changes, and the use case ends.

Register Portal-Alliance Use Case

This use case is responsible for registering new portal-alliances for the site. Only registered portal alliances can redirect their users to the GreaterCause.com site for making donations.

Main Flow of Events The use case begins when the site administrator selects the portal-alliance registration function. The site administrator enters the necessary information associated with the portal-domain. The system validates the information. If the validation process is successful, the system stores the registration information in the data store. The system acknowledges the actions, and the use case ends.

Manage Portal-Alliance Profile Use Case

This use case enables the site administrator and portal-alliance administrator to change the profile information associated with a portal-domain.

Main Flow of Events The use case starts when a portal-alliance administrator or site administrator selects the update profile function. The administrator is presented with a page with relevant profile information. The administrator updates the information and confirms changes. If the validation process is successful, the system commits those changes in the data store. The system acknowledges the changes, and the use case ends.

Perform UI Customization Use Case

This use case empowers the portal administrator and GreaterCause.com site administrator to provide portal-specific UI customizations. These customizations preserve the look and feel of the portal-domain when the users affiliated with a portal-domain are accessing the GreaterCause services.

Main Flow of Events The use case begins when the site administrator or portal administrator selects the UI customization feature. The administrator provides the location of a portal-specific custom navigation bar's HTML for portal branding. The system acknowledges the changes, and the use case ends.

Manage Campaigns

This package enables the portal administrators and site administrators to create portal-specific campaigns for featuring selected NPOs at both the global and regional levels. The campaign creation service is available only at the GreaterCause.com site. A list of featured- NPOs associated with active campaigns is made available as a Web service by GreaterCause for consumption by portal-domains. The portal-domains extract this information via the Web service and cache it locally. Subsequently, the portal-domains can exhibit the featured-NPOs in their portlets from a local cache rather than fetching that information from the GreaterCause.com site for every user signing on to the portal.

Create Campaign Use Case

This use case provides site and portal administrators with the ability to create campaigns for selected NPOs. NPOs could be promoted at the global or regional level, but no more than five NPOs can be displayed in the portlet (pass-through UI component) at any given time.

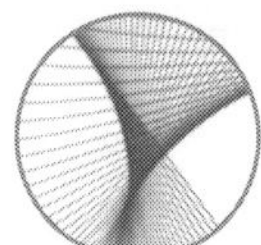

CAUTION

Be careful when using extend relationships. It is possible to end up with an extend relationship for simple logic. For example, in Figure 1-9, for use case Manage Campaigns we could have factored two variants, Manage National Campaigns and Manage Regional Campaigns, as two new use cases that extend the behavior of Manage Campaigns. For now, it is best not to express these variants as separate use cases because their behavior is only marginally different from each other.

Create Campaign Main Flow of Events The use case starts when the portal administrator or the site administrator selects the new campaign function. The search facility is invoked for finding the desired non-profit. The administrator selects a non-profit from the search result page. The system displays a campaign detail page with the selected NPO. The administrator enters the campaign dates and optionally a region code. The administrator then submits the information. The system validates the information and, on successful validation, saves the

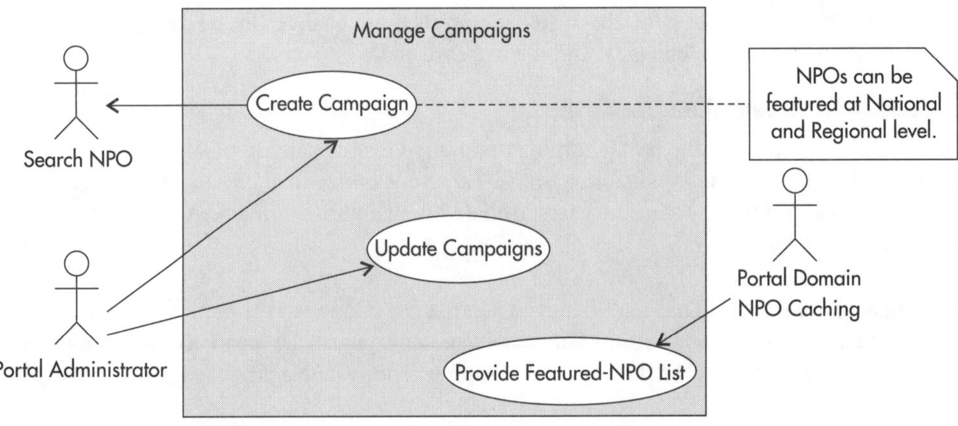

Figure 1-9 *Use case diagram—Manage Campaigns*

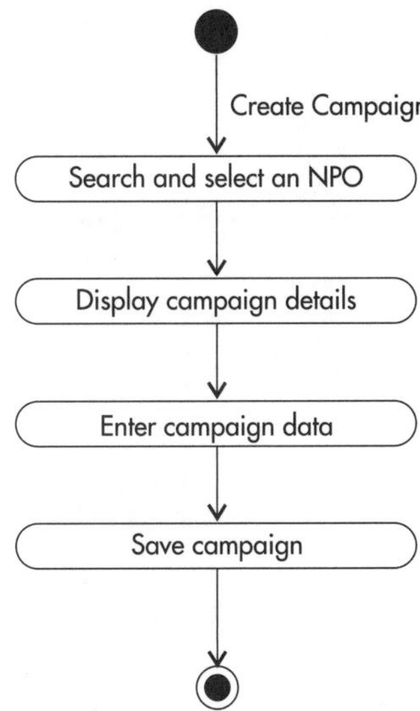

Figure 1-10 *Activity diagram for Create Campaign*

campaign in the data store. The system acknowledges the changes, and the use case ends. Figure 1-10 illustrates the Create Campaign main flow events.

Update Campaigns Use Case

This use case provides site and portal-alliance administrators the ability to modify existing campaigns.

Update Campaigns Main Flow of Events The use case starts when a portal or site administrator selects the function for modifying existing campaigns. The administrator either selects the global campaigns or supplies a region code for selecting regional campaigns for a specific region. The system displays the available active campaigns. The administrator modifies and submits the campaign information. The system updates the data store, thus ending the use case.

Provide Featured-NPO List Use Case

This use case enables the extraction of featured-NPOs for a given portal-domain. The featured-NPOs are made available to the portal-domain via a Web service.

Main Flow of Events This use case is instantiated as a result of Web service invocation. The GreaterCause.com domain provides the featured-NPO list to the portal-domain via the Web service, and the use case ends.

NPO Caching

This package enables the retrieval of a list of featured-NPOs from the GreaterCause.com domain; after the NPOs are retrieved, they are stored in a local cache.

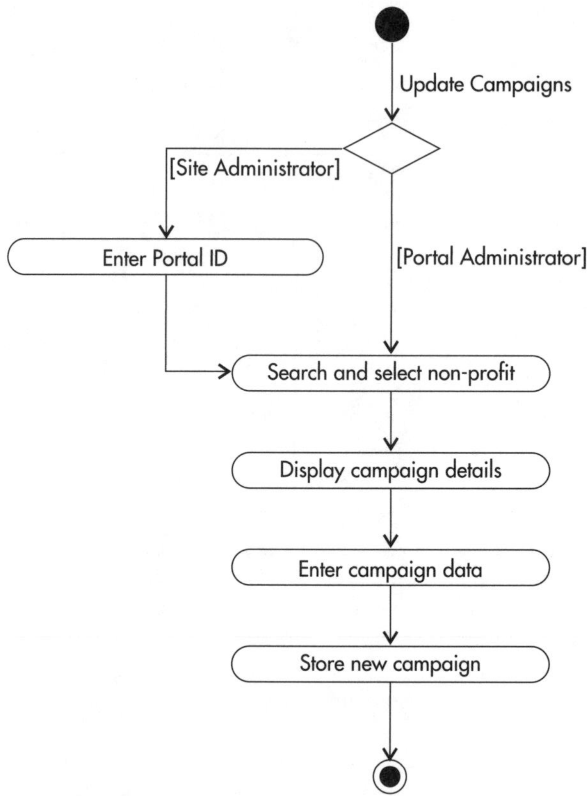

Figure 1-11 *Activity diagram for Update Campaigns*

Cache Featured-NPOs Use Case

This use case enables the caching of featured-NPOs. The portlet that represents a pass-through to the GreaterCause.com site uses this cache to display featured-NPOs, associated with active campaigns, to portal users.

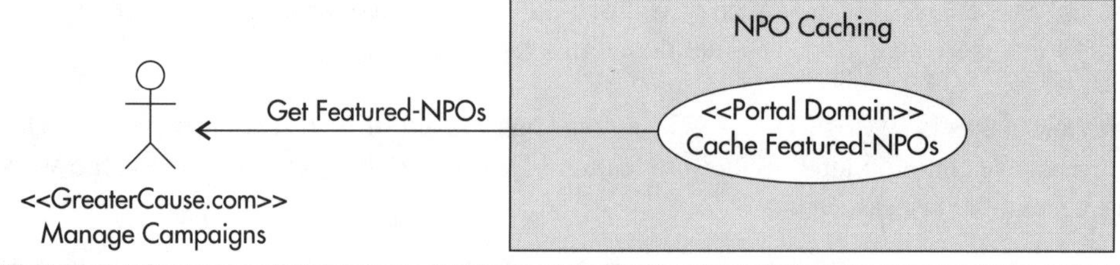

Figure 1-12 *Use case diagram—NPO Caching*

Main Flow of Events This use case is instantiated when the portal-domain invokes a Web service. The Web service provides a list of featured-NPOs that are retrieved and cached within the portal domain, thus ending the use case.

Portal Pass-through

This package enables the fetching and display of the cached featured-NPOs associated with active campaigns. The featured-NPOs are displayed in the GreaterCause-specific portlet provided within the portal page. The donor can choose to donate to one of the featured-NPOs. A donate action will signal the system to redirect the user to the GreaterCause.com site.

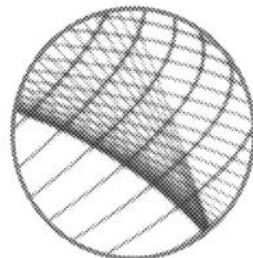

TIP

An ambiguity in the activity diagram is caused when two outbound transitions are specified for an activity or action state. For example, in Figure 1-13, we could put a self-recursion on Display National Campaign and Display Regional Campaign to display a maximum of five featured-NPOs, and then an outbound transition from these activity states to the next activity states; this will make the transitions ambiguous. Instead, you should implement an iteration logic with action states to set and increment the value of an iterator, and implement a decision node (branch node) to evaluate the completion of all iterations; only after the iterations are completed will you transition to another activity or action state.

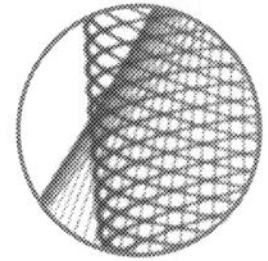

NOTE

The activity diagram of Figure 1-14 uses swimlanes to depict the activities across both the portal-domain and GreaterCause domain. The purpose of this diagram is to clearly show the activities and transitions within and across each domain. Swimlanes can be also be used for showing interactions between different subsystems and business objects.

Display Featured-NPOs Use Case

This use case displays global and regional featured-NPOs in the GreaterCause portlet within the portal.

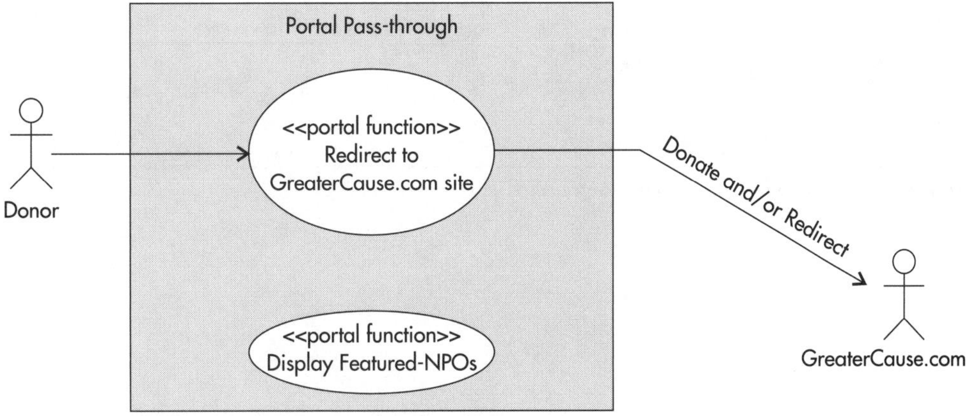

Figure 1-13 *Use case diagram—Portal Pass-through*

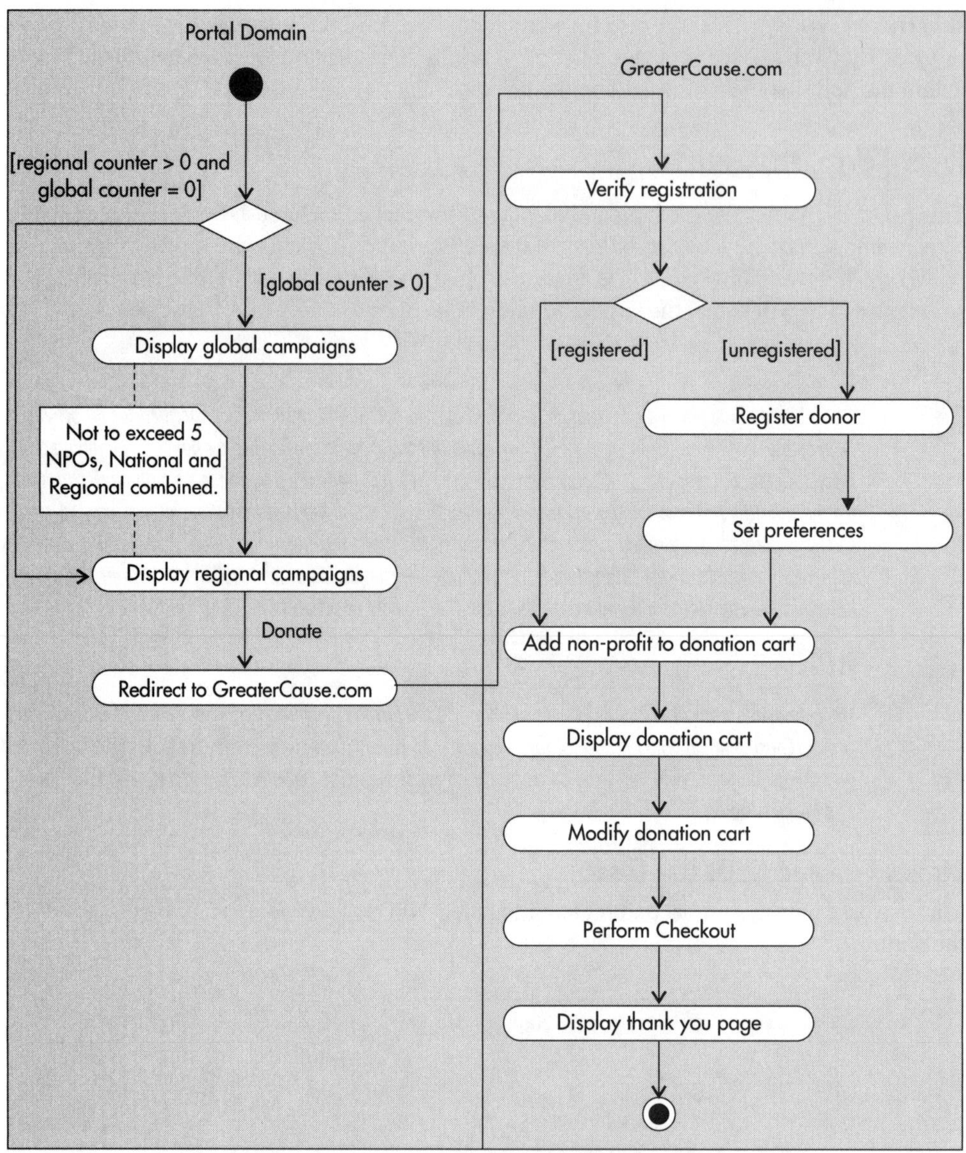

Figure 1-14 *Workflow for making a donation to a featured-NPO*

Main Flow of Events The use case begins when the portal-page is displayed to the portal user. The portlet's logic will display the featured-NPOs available in the local cache. A maximum of five NPOs are displayed, starting with NPOs associated with national campaigns. The successful rendering of the portlet within the portal's page terminates the use case.

Redirect to the GreaterCause.com Site Use Case

This use case is responsible for routing a portal user to the GreaterCause.com site.

Main Flow of Events The use case begins when the portal user selects the donate function for a featured-NPO. The portal-domain mutually authenticates with the GreaterCause.com domain. GreaterCause.com then generates an authentication token that will identify a valid redirection. The portal-domain assembles donor-specific information required for registration, and packages the token supplied by the GreaterCause.com domain. The system then redirects the donation request to the GreaterCause.com site with donor-specific information, along with the choice of NPO, thus ending the use case.

Alternate Flow of Events The portal user can select to pass-through to the GreaterCause.com site without selecting the donate function for a featured-NPO. In this case, the portal user is taken to the advanced search function of the GreaterCause application.

Summary

In a use case–driven approach, use cases are used as primary artifacts for understanding system requirements, for documenting the system, for validating the system's architecture, for driving the analysis and design models, for assessing project risks, for project planning, and for quality assurance. The next step in the process is to elaborate the use cases as part of information architecture. The use case scenarios are augmented once the site navigation semantics, wire frames, and field-level details are completed.

References

[UML] *The Unified Modeling Language User Guide* by Grady Booch et. al. (Addison Wesley, 1999)

[Object Modeling] *Use Case Driven Object Modeling with UML* by Doug Rosenberg (Addison Wesley, 1999)

[Use Cases] Applying Use Cases, A Practical Guide by Geri Schneider et. al. (Addison Wesley, 1998)

CHAPTER

2

Information Architecture for Use Case Elaboration

IN THIS CHAPTER:

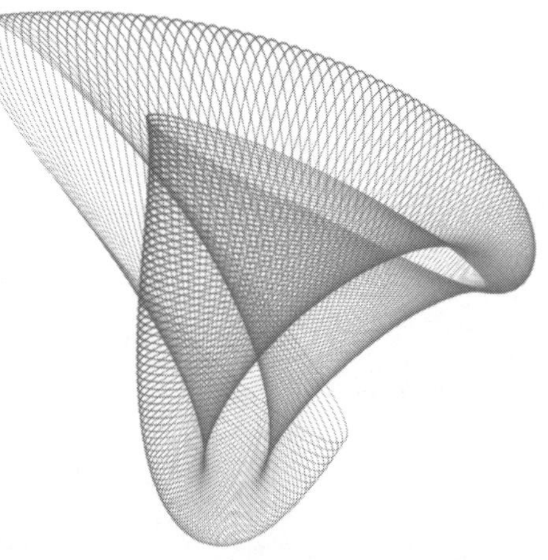

Success or failure of a project is dependent on several factors. At the outset, the single overwhelming factor is the ability to comprehensively define the behavior of the system as desired by its consumers. A large number of projects have seen their demise as a result of unstructured approach toward defining requirements. Traceability is the key word here. The use case model of Chapter 1 is a living document with built-in traceability. Any evolution of the system will be based on those use cases. At all times, the use cases will comprehensively reflect the behavior of the system. In this chapter, we will elaborate the use cases and be more explicit in expressing the user interaction and associated transactional semantics. We begin by answering the following questions:

- How do we articulate the user interaction semantics?
- How do we articulate the interactions between the use case and other parts of the system or external systems?
- How do we visualize these interactions?
- What information is exchanged during these interactions? How is this information affecting page transitions?
- How do we understand all possible flow of events?

To answer all of the preceding questions, we create an information architecture. Information architecture constitutes schemes for organizing, labeling, navigating, indexing, and searching content; these aspects converge into a storyboard that is the first mockup or prototypical view of the UI. The navigation semantics of UI is explained using a site flow that clearly articulates the page transitions associated with user actions. The information architecture is therefore very significant in defining system behavior from a UI perspective; this behavior is incorporated for comprehensively defining the detailed use cases of the system. The topic of information architecture is discussed in several books; we will keep our discussion limited to evolving the sample GreaterCause application and highlight a few important concepts of information architecture.

Beginning of Information Architecture

An information architect is a specialist who has the following focus:

- Creating a persona of the site's user base and tailoring the site to meet the needs of its audience.
- Devising schemes for organizing and labeling content. This effort results in the creation of a content taxonomy.
- Providing the access path to information from various touch points. This effort results in the creation of a navigation taxonomy.
- Spearheading the creation of a mockup UI; working with stakeholders and focus groups to refine the usability aspects of the site.

- Creating an information architecture style guide that controls the evolution of the site according to well-established guidelines.

For information architects to be successful in their efforts, they need the assistance of subject matter experts, business analysts, technology teams, graphics designers, and content editors.

- Subject matter experts and business analysts provide the business knowledge with related information to be made available in the site. They provide the context and significance of the information, and its impact to the business and to the information consumers.
- A representative from the technology team, usually the application architect, validates completeness of the information exchanged between the application and the user, assesses consistency in accessing information from multiple touch points, validates the transactional semantics, and generally comments on the technical complexity or risks associated with the recommended information architecture.
- Graphic designers provide the site with a consistent look and feel that represents the site's purpose and its identity. They prepare a style guide for ensuring consistent evolution of the site. With assistance from marketing, graphic designers also create the branding of the site.
- Content editors create guidelines for ensuring a consistent voice and tone in the creation of the site's content. Content editors may also perform copy editing and proofreading tasks, and be responsible for creating an editorial calendar.

In the entire information architecture process, two most significant aspects need to be constantly monitored by the project manager. These are expressed as follows:

- The site's functionality as expressed by the information architecture and its constituent mockup UI must be in line with the use case summary. The use case summary scopes the system, and any deviation from this could be considered as scope change. When scope changes occur, the use cases should be retrofitted and redistributed to stakeholders for consensus.
- The user interface is the most volatile component of the system; applications are always architectured with this awareness. However, once the development process begins, the information architecture cannot evolve radically to significantly change the transactional semantics, the business logic, or the functional requirements; the consequences of this are severe in terms of rework, cost escalation, and delivery schedule. Information architecture plays a significant role, although not the only role, in nailing down the behavior of the system; therefore, this process cannot be taken lightly.

Organizing Content

Site content must be organized from the perspective of its users; therefore, an information architect must think like a critical consumer. A user accessing a site is analogous to a shopper at a department store. A well-designed department store will clearly direct the shoppers to the appropriate aisle. The labeling used in identifying various sections of the store lets the shopper know what to expect when he or she gets there. For example, the Children's Apparel section will not be labeled as Children's Accessories because the word "accessories" is ambiguous in this context. A few visits to the store makes a shopper adapt to its organization, labeling, and navigation scheme, and he or she is able to find items more quickly.

There are several techniques for organizing a site's content. Some of these techniques are explained in the context of the sample application as follows:

- **Alphabetical** An example of alphabetical organization is a directory service that lists the entries by name. In the sample application, the non-profits resulting from a search query are ordered alphabetically.
- **Topical** An example of topical organization is an educational site that lists the content by subjects. Most sites use topical organization in conjunction with other organization schemes. In the sample application, the grouping of administrator services resembles a topical organization scheme, segregated from the grouping of donor services. In the following illustration, the services are arranged under Registration, Portal Configuration, and NPO Configuration.

- **Geographical** Examples of geographical organization are observed on sites dealing with weather forecasts, distribution centers, and store locators. Content on such sites is location specific. In the sample application, the featured non-profits are organized by the region code.
- **Hierarchical** An example of hierarchical organization is a corporate site that is structured according to divisions and departments. Hierarchical information is easily understood and therefore easier to navigate. This organization scheme is encountered very frequently in our day-to-day lives. Several simple hierarchies are present in the sample application.
- **Indexed** Indexed organization schemes are powerful for dynamic content. The content is usually indexed in a relational database, and the indexing mechanism drives

content selection. Templating mechanisms may use this organization scheme for serving dynamic content. In the sample application, the campaigns are indexed by portal-domain and the region code. Even though the campaigns are changing on a frequent basis, the indexing mechanism reorganizes the content and helps in the retrieval of only those campaigns that are relevant for a given portal-domain and region combination.

- **Role-oriented** For a given role, content can be organized statically according to a predetermined taxonomy or created dynamically on role detection. A role-oriented content organization scheme can be coupled with a goal- or task-oriented content organization scheme. In the sample application, each type of administrator is provided with an administrative page with a navigation bar based on the administrator's type; furthermore, the page sequence for a site administrator is different from the page sequence for a portal or an NPO administrator. The following illustration shows the navigation bar that is customized for different administrators.

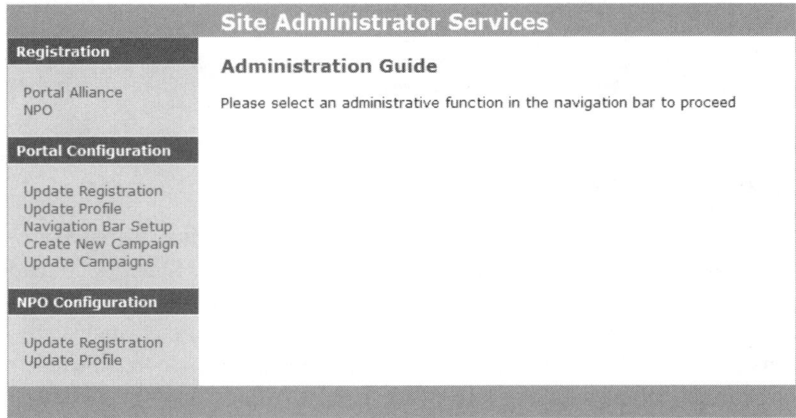

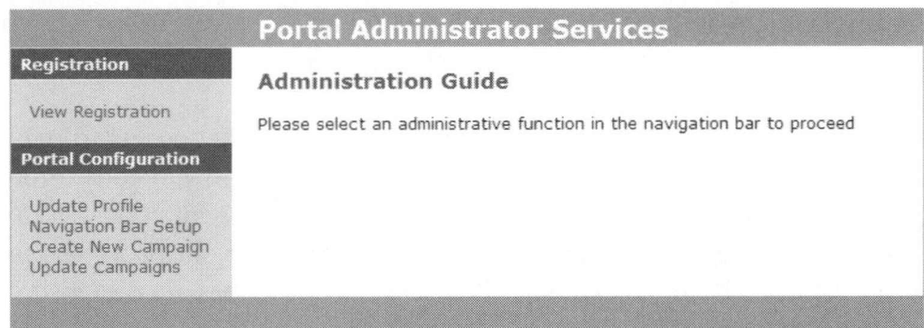

The following page only appears in the navigation scheme of a site administrator; this is because the site administrator has to identify the Portal ID for which he or she desires to act as a stand-in for the portal administrator.

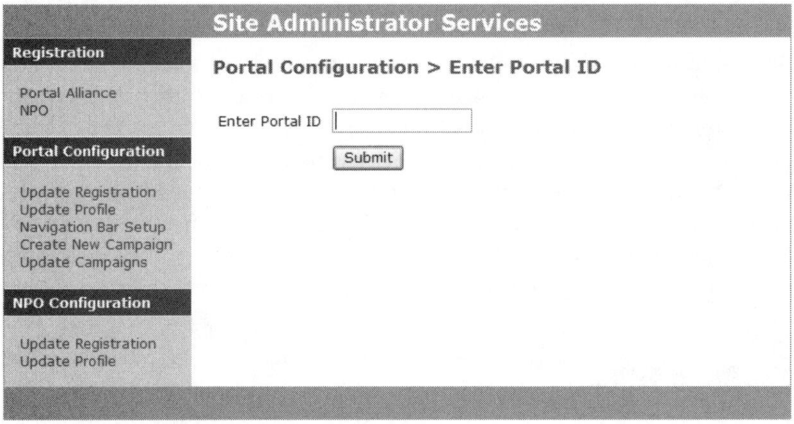

Site Administrator Services

Registration

Portal Alliance
NPO

Portal Configuration

Update Registration
Update Profile
Navigation Bar Setup
Create New Campaign
Update Campaigns

NPO Configuration

Update Registration
Update Profile

Portal Configuration > Enter Portal ID

Enter Portal ID

Submit

Navigating Content

The navigation aspect of a site must be intuitive for a first-time visitor; there are no second chances at making a good first impression. Navigation mechanisms that make it hard to find relevant information are discouraging, and users will lack the motivation to visit the site again. Although appropriately organized content is the first step toward creating a user-centric information access taxonomy, this taxonomy is ambiguous unless associated with a context. Navigation schemes complement the content taxonomies by providing the needed context, and they are augmented by an appropriate labeling scheme.

There are several approaches for creating an appropriate navigation scheme. Some of these approaches are explained in the context of the sample application as follows:

- **Global** The primary navigation bar of a site usually provides access to coarse-grained functionality with the capability to navigate both laterally and vertically through the site; this navigation bar is often referred to as the global navigation bar because the navigation elements are accessible consistently across the entire site or across conceptually and semantically related pages, also called subsites. Most sites are designed with global navigation at the top or bottom of the page.
- **Local** When the page hierarchy is traversed, we encounter several pages that are gateways to fine-grained content or functionality. A marketing page will have an information hierarchy that is different from the customer service page. To accommodate for functionally different subordinate information hierarchies, we use local navigation bars to support the navigation semantics that are specific to each of the subordinate information hierarchies. You can think of a local navigation bar as a form of nested navigation. In the sample application, each administrator page differs in the navigation

elements available to the type of administrator interacting with the system; as shown previously in the section "Organizing Content," the applicable local navigation bar for each type of administrator appears at center-left of the page. The selection of a navigation element in a local navigation scheme is often accentuated, for contextualization, by highlighting the selected element.

- **Bread crumbs** When shopping in Mall of America, we get our bearings by looking at "You are Here" signs. In a complex navigation scheme, it is always good to let the users know their locations within the overall site, and provide trails that they can take to get to certain pages; hence the bread crumbs analogy. Usually, an additional navigation bar is inserted at the top within the content portion of the page. This additional navigation bar is of the form Element1 > Element2 > Element3; selecting Element3 in the previous page results in the delivery of content for the current page.
- **Site map** A site map aggregates the navigational elements of a site. Representing a complex site structure using a site map could quickly clutter the map and make it unwieldy. Provide only the navigation elements essential to portraying the site's purpose while implementing a design that harmonizes form and function. The site map never provides an entry point in the middle of a workflow because this will jeopardize the transactional semantics of an application, which in turn could pose a serious security and data integrity risk.
- **TOC** A table of contents is often used for content that is hierarchical in nature. Sites offering user guides and documentation usually sport an ad hoc navigation scheme built around a table of contents. A TOC can be implemented inline with page transitions or as a separate window.
- **Embedded links** Often links are embedded within the content for creating an ad hoc navigation scheme.
- **Adaptive** A navigation scheme can adapt to reflect a user's preference and/or behavior. An example of this is apparent at online retail stores where a shopper could have additional navigation elements on a page added as a result of his or her shopping pattern.

Creating Wire Frames

In this section, we are going to apply the principles of information architecture in defining the user interface of an application. The user interface, or UI for short, is very critical for an eCommerce application. It synthesizes different aspects of information architecture into a common view. The organization and navigation taxonomies are clearly articulated through mockup user interfaces called wire frames. Creating a mockup or a prototypical UI early in the process, for systems with significant UI, will clarify the interaction semantics that could potentially change the behavior and scope of the system. Sharing a prototypical UI will assist the users in identifying serious problems with navigating the workflow and processes that they are so familiar with. Many times, new requirements are discovered at this stage, and its impact could be significant. At this state, there is always a possibility that the end users will ask for a lot more than scoped by the use case summary. A scope creep will jeopardize the time and cost commitments made through a preliminary project plan created in conjunction with the use case summary. The information architect and the application architect must assess and document such changes, and involve the stakeholders and/or decision makers for making the final call.

Appendix B illustrates a storyboard for the sample application. It consists of a set of wire frames that, in conjunction with the site flow, help the users understand the workflow associated with accomplishing various tasks. Storyboards are void of graphics; their main purpose is to illustrate the content and navigation taxonomies exposed to a user and to show the various site traversal scenarios. Appendix C illustrates a site flow. The site flow is an important artifact for articulating the navigation semantics and provides a bird's-eye view of the site. Site flow does not encompass each and every navigational aspect because doing so will make it less readable. To avoid the clutter, a common technique used for creating site flows is to draw it like a tree structure where most nodes have only one parent. The site flow will complete the storyboarding effect by showing the transitions between various uniquely numbered wire frames according to the navigation semantics established for the functional web site.

A wire frame can be further augmented with additional documentation as stated here:

- Relationships between navigation elements and corresponding pages or secondary navigation elements can be explained using a side bar.
- Content mapping details can be added for identifying the content, the content's source, and the contributors.
- Callouts can be used to provide additional context for page elements.

Detailing Use Cases

The following sections illustrate the results of applying information architecture to use cases. Among the available use cases, we have chosen to elaborate a cross-section of use cases for illustrating how information architecture can be used to refine the use cases. The scenarios depicted in the following detailed use cases contain more UI-specific information than found in the use case summary. We now have the ability to predict the sequencing of pages (or screens) and the associated navigation semantics, and specify this order in the use cases. In detailed use cases, the system's interactions with actors are more refined, and we are able to discern, to some degree, the flow of information between interacting subsystems. We have provided notes with the following use cases to annotate certain aspects for improved readability.

The format used in the upcoming section "GreaterCause Detailed Use Case Description" for detailing use cases is specified in Appendix A. This format is suggestive, and you may modify it according to the needs of your organization and project. Appendix B contains the wire frames essential for expressing the information architecture for the GreaterCause system. Appendix C contains the site flow and provides the navigation semantics for wire frames in Appendix B. Refer to Figure 2-1 for an abridged version of the site flow. The figure is distilled from Appendix C and is relevant for the discussion in the section.

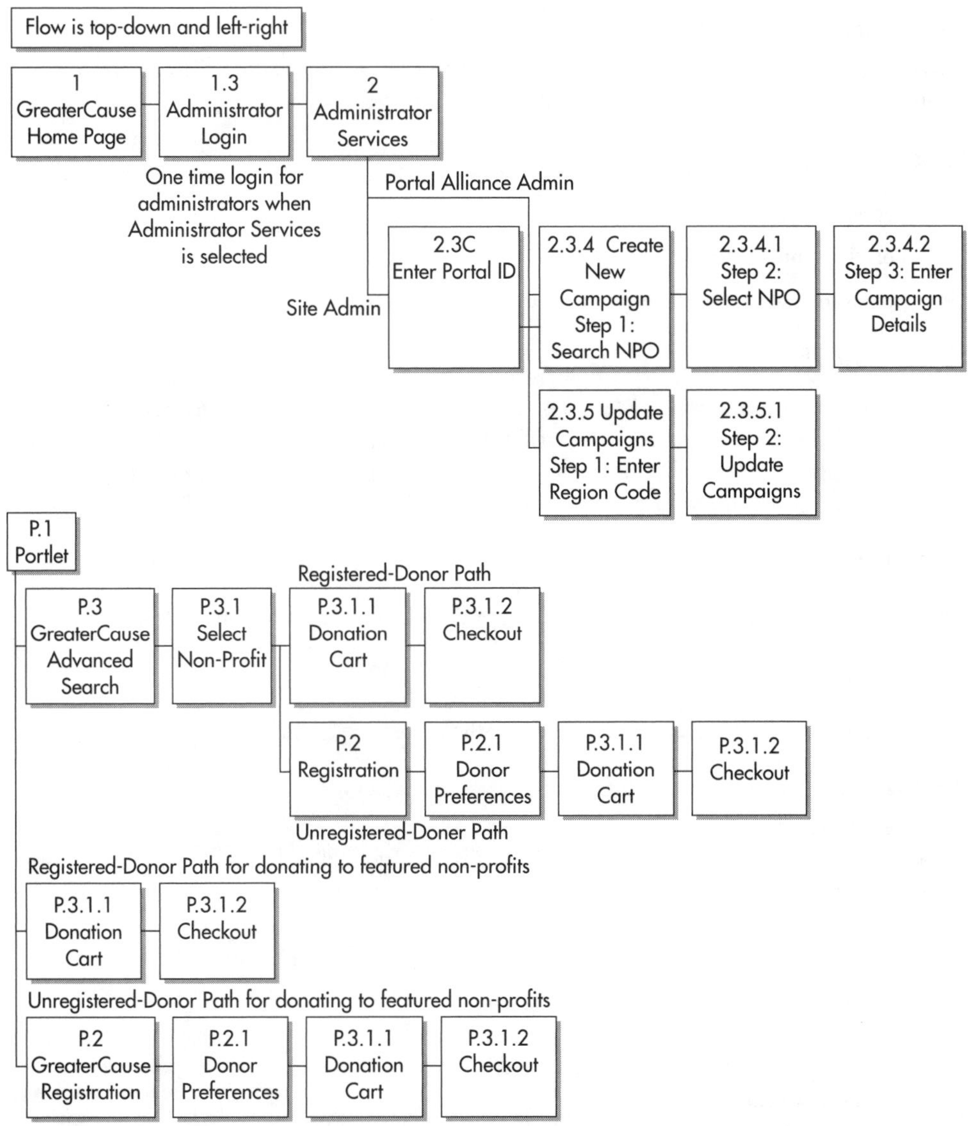

Figure 2-1 *GreaterCause abridged site flow*

GreaterCause Detailed Use Case Description

The following sections present the detailed use cases for the GreaterCause system. The use case description for each use case encompasses various aspects of information architecture, workflow transaction semantics, and system interactions. Where appropriate, an activity diagram is used for explaining a complex flow.

Create Campaign Use Case

This use case provides portal administrators and site administrators the ability to create campaigns for featuring selected non-profits on their respective portals.

Actors

- Search NPO
- Portal administrator
- Site administrator (as a stand-in for the portal administrator)

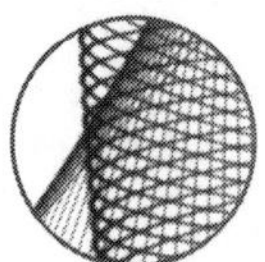

NOTE

Notice that in the preceding list of actors, the Search NPO package is an actor that represents an external subsystem. In most cases, the package classification usually translates into a separate subsystem or part of another subsystem implying that the functionality of the Create Campaigns use case will always be in a different subsystem than that of the Search NPO.

Precondition(s)

- An administrator is logged in as a portal administrator or a site administrator.

Postcondition(s)

- A new campaign is created and saved by the system.

User Interface The following illustrates the user interface for Create Campaign use case.

2.3	Home > Site Administrator Services > Portal Configuration > Enter Portal ID

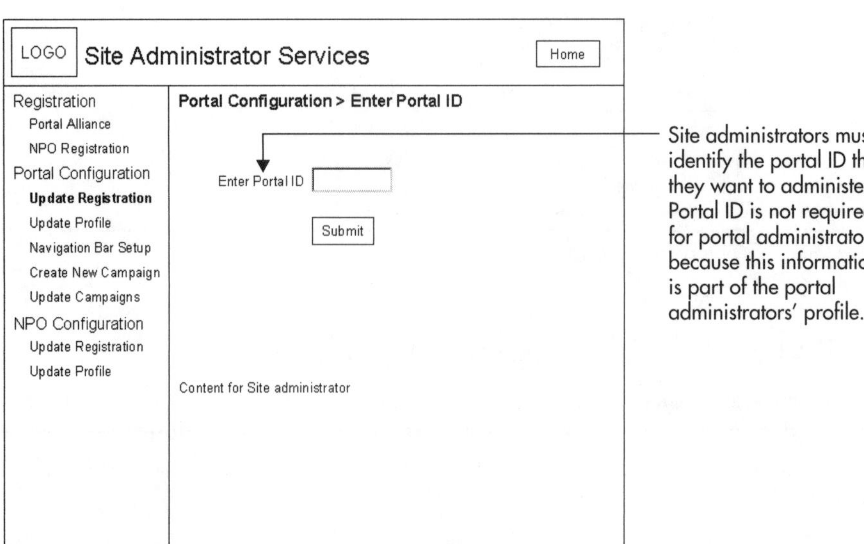

2.3.4.2	Home > Site Administrator Services > Portal Configuration > Create New Campaign

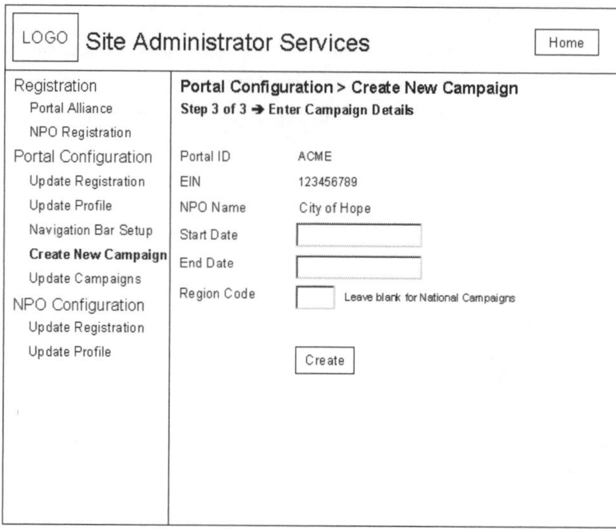

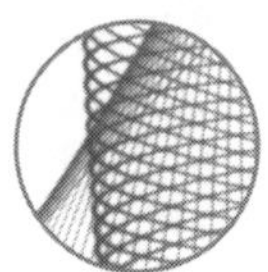

NOTE

The granularity chosen for this use case is pretty coarse. This has resulted in a situation where several UI interactions are being addressed by a single use case. The advantage of a coarse-grained use case in this instance is that we are able to explain the flow of events as a related set of actions.

Create Campaign Main Flow of Events

1. The use case is instantiated when an administrator or site administrator selects Create New Campaign on the Administrator Services page.
2. If the administrator is a site administrator,
    a. The system displays the Enter Portal ID page.
    b. The site administrator provides the portal ID for which he or she wants to perform administration functions.
    c. The system validates the portal ID; if the validation is successful, the system allows further processing, else the site administrator is requested to re-enter the portal ID.
3. The Create Campaign use case invokes the services of the Search NPO use case for searching and selecting an NPO. The Search NPO function delivers the selected NPO to the Enter Campaign Details page.
4. The administrator furnishes the start date, the end date, and the region code.
5. The administrator requests the creation of a new campaign.
6. The system validates the campaign attributes supplied by the administrator and on successful validation stores the campaign in the system.
7. The system acknowledges the creation of a new campaign, and the use case ends.

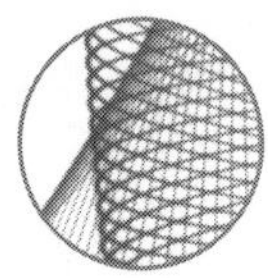

NOTE

Comparing the preceding flow of events with the flow of events in the use case summary, it is apparent that the information architecture and the resulting wire frames have enabled us to visualize, to a much greater degree, the interactions between the user and the system. The details added to the use case description as a result of the information architecture will make it possible to use it as a contract between the stakeholders and implementation team. This level of detail also serves as a starting point for generating test cases. We can freeze requirements at this juncture and start design and development.

Activity Diagram The following illustrates the activity diagram for the Create Campaign use case.

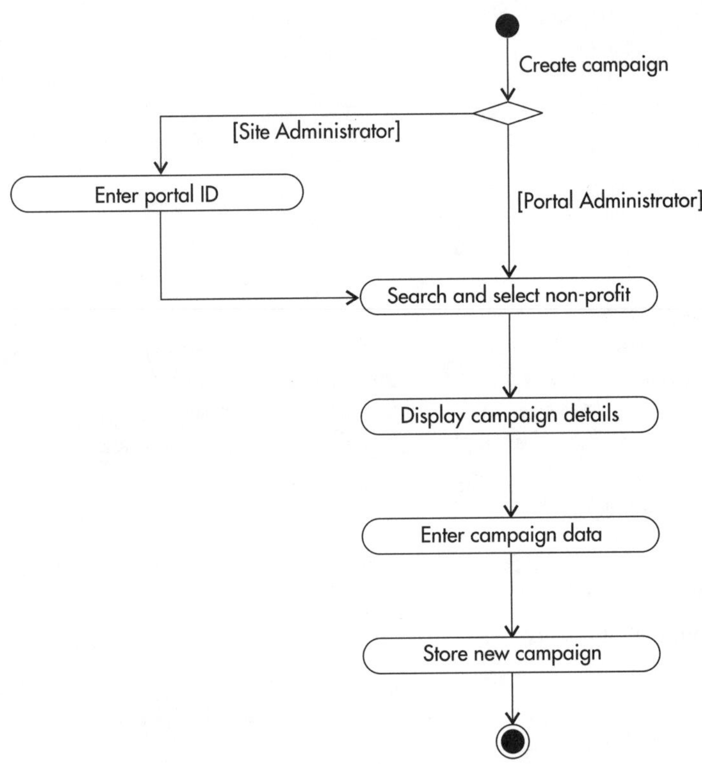

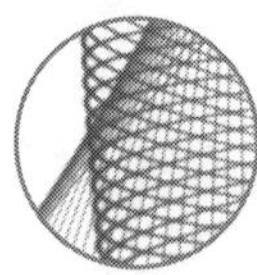

NOTE

Activity diagrams, although at a coarser grain than the textual flow of events, provide a comprehensive view into the use case by depicting all possible main and alternate flows.

Update Campaigns Use Case

This use case provides portal administrators and site administrators the ability to update existing campaigns for a given portal-domain.

Actors

- Portal administrator
- Site administrator (as a stand-in for the portal administrator)

Precondition(s)

- An administrator is logged in as a portal administrator or a site administrator.

Postcondition(s)

- Changes to campaigns are saved by the system.

User Interface The following illustrates the user interface for the Update Campaigns use case.

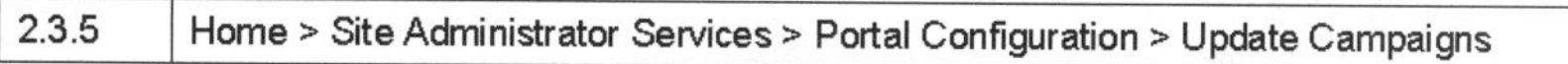

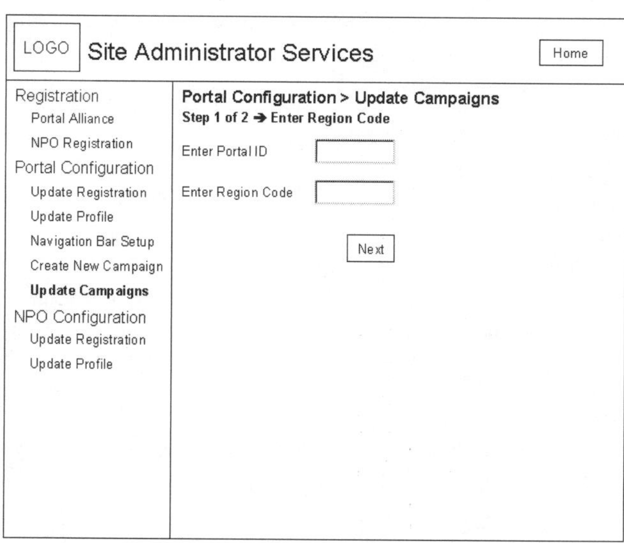

2.3.5.1	Home > Site Administrator Services > Portal Configuration > Update Campaigns

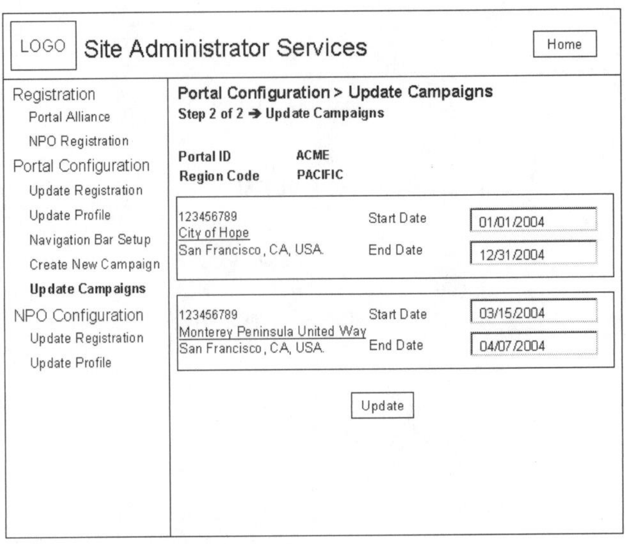

Update Campaigns Main Flow of Events

1. The use case is instantiated when a portal administrator selects Update Campaigns on the Administrator Services page.
2. If the administrator is a site administrator,
   a. The system displays the Enter Region Code page, which requires the administrator to provide a portal ID and the region code.
   b. The site administrator provides the portal ID for which he or she wants to perform administration functions. The administrator submits the region code for which campaigns are to be updated or leaves the field blank for updating global campaigns.
   c. The system validates the portal ID; if the validation is successful, the system allows further processing, else the site administrator is requested to reenter the portal ID.
3. If the administrator is a portal administrator,
   a. The system requests a region code.
   b. The administrator submits the region code for which campaigns are to be updated or leaves the field blank for updating global campaigns.
4. The system displays active campaigns in the Update Campaigns page. Active campaigns are those whose end dates have not expired.

5. The administrator modifies the campaigns and submits the changes to the system.
6. The system validates the campaign attributes supplied by the administrator, and on successful validation stores the changes in the system.
7. The system acknowledges the changes, and the use case ends.

Activity Diagram The following illustrates the activity diagram for the Update Campaigns use case.

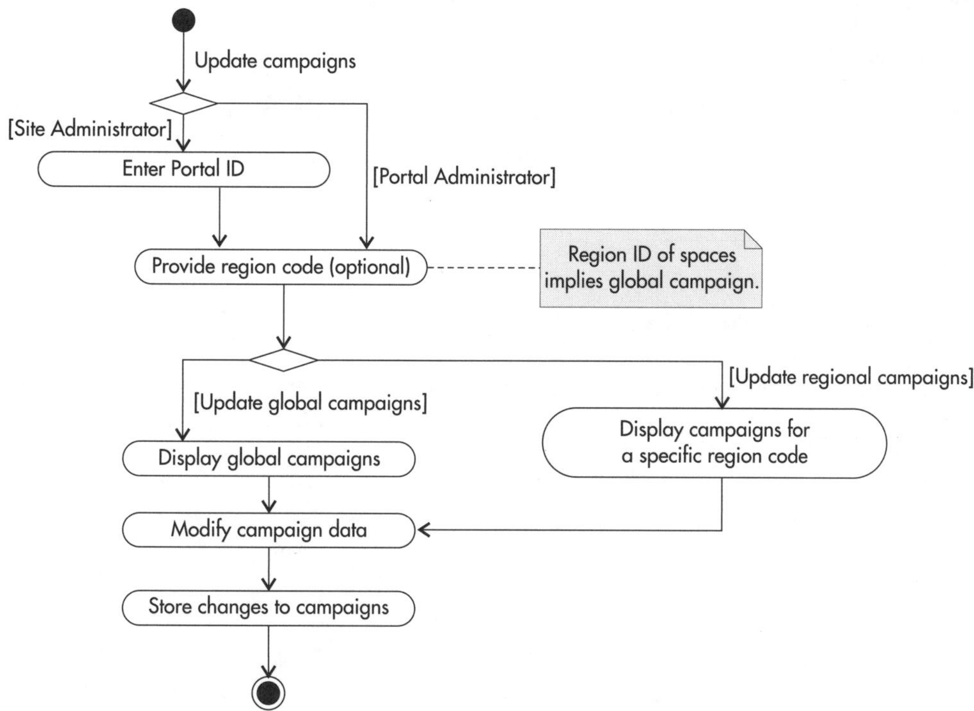

Manage Donation Cart Use Case

This use case handles the process of displaying, adding, removing, and modifying donations in the donation envelope.

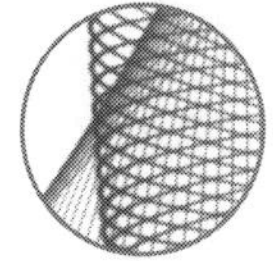

NOTE

This use case was selected for elaboration to depict the usage of nested "includes." The Manage Donation Cart use case is extended by the Register Donor use case, which in turn includes the Manage Donor Preferences use case. The Manage Donation Cart use case interacts with an external subsystem Portal Pass-through.

Actors

- Donor
- Portal Pass-through

Precondition(s)

- Portal-domain of the donor is registered with GreaterCause.

Postcondition(s)

- Donation Cart is updated according to the action taken by the actor.
- Unregistered donors are registered by the system.

Include/Extend Use Cases

- Register Donor
- Manage Donor Preferences

User Interface The following illustrates the user interface for the Manage Donation Cart use case.

P.3.1.1	Donation Cart

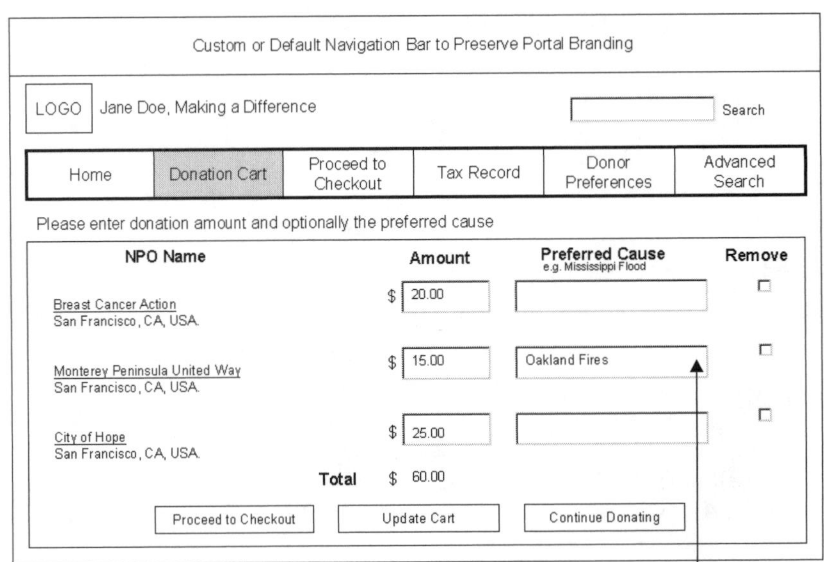

UnitedWay will be accepting donations for several causes.

Manage Donation Cart Main Flow of Events

1. The use case is instantiated when a donor either selects to donate to a non-profit from the search results page, or donates to a featured-NPO from the portal-domain's portlet. The system adds the selected NPO to the Donation Cart.
2. (set unregistered).
3. The system displays the Donation Cart.

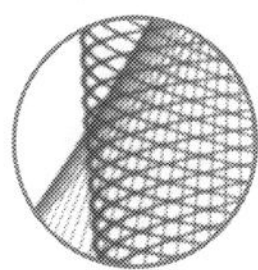

NOTE

(set unregistered) is a label used for the extension point where the use case Register Donor will conditionally inject itself in the Manage Donation Cart use case if the donor is not a registered donor. The label "unregistered" may appear in the flow of the Manage Donation Cart, which is the base use case.

4. The donor provides the donation amount and the preferred cause.
5. The donor requests Proceed To Checkout.
6. The use case ends.

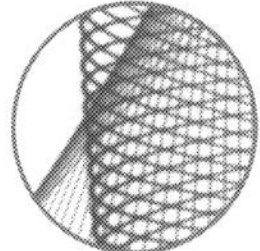

NOTE

Exceptional flow of events infer most of the action-sequence from the main flow, therefore terseness is acceptable.

Exceptional Flow of Events

- **Donor selects Update Cart** After editing the Donation Cart, the donor could select Update Cart instead of Proceed To Checkout.
- **Donor selects Continue Donating** After editing the Donation Cart, the donor could select Continue Donating instead of Proceed To Checkout.
- **Donor removes NPOs from Donation Cart** While editing the cart, the donor could select certain non-profits for removal.

Register Donor Use Case

This use case creates a new donor identity in the system. The identity is provided by the portal-domain with which the donor has affiliation. This is a one-time process for donors. The donor need only log in once to the portal, and access to GreaterCause does not require another login.

Actors

- Donor

Precondition(s)

- Prospective donor wants to make his or her first donation.

Postcondition(s)

- Donor is registered, and donor preferences are created in the system.
- Donor is taken to the Donation Cart page.

Include Use Cases

- Manage Donor Preferences

User Interface

The following illustrates the user interface for Register Donor use case.

Main Flow of Events

1. The use case is instantiated by the Manage Donation Cart use case, when an unregistered user attempts to make a donation.
2. The system verifies the authentication token presented by the donor.
3. The donor is presented with a Registration page. The registration page is pre-populated with attributes that were provided by the portal-domain.
4. The donor provides the missing information and submits the registration information.

5. The system will validate and store the registration information. The system will also create a Donor Preferences record and initialize it with a registration ID.
6. Include (Manage Donor Preferences).
7. The use case ends.

Manage Donor Preferences Use Case

This use case enables donors to create personal preferences for customizing their donation process.

Actors

- Donor

Precondition(s)

- Donor is already registered into the system.

Postcondition(s)

- Modified preferences are stored in the system.

User Interface The following illustrates the user interface for the Manage Donor Preferences use case.

P.2.1	Donor Preferences

Custom or Default Navigation Bar to Preserve Portal Branding

LOGO Jane Doe, Making a Difference

Search

Home	Donation Cart	Proceed to Checkout	Tax Record	Donor Preferences	Advanced Search

For best experience, customize following settings. All information is optional.

Default Donation Amount

Limit Search to non-profits

Primary Email*

Disclose Name and Address to Non-Profits Yes No

Submit Preferences

* Primary email will supersede registration email

Your Credit Card Information

Name on Card

Card Type

Card Number

Expiry Day Expiry Year

Following is your registration information. To change click here.

Jane Doe
555 Bay Drive
Fremont, CA 94555
USA
Email: jdoe@americaunited.com

Main Flow of Events

1. This use case is instantiated either by the donor registration process or when the donors select to modify their personal preferences.
2. The donor is presented with the Donor Preferences page.
3. The donor makes the required changes to the attributes and submits the information.
4. On successful validation, the system stores the donor preferences.
5. The system acknowledges the changes, and the use case ends.

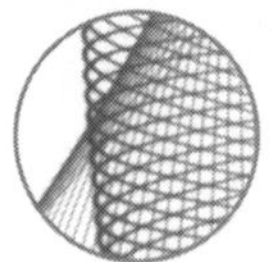

NOTE

Now that we have elaborated selected use cases, compare it with summary-level use cases of Chapter 1. It is apparent that with the help of the detailed use cases, we are able to discern the invocation order of each use case for realizing a specific process flow, and the associated transaction semantics, from the point of view of the system user.

Summary

During information architecture, we create schemes for organizing, labeling, and navigating the content of a site. Storyboard and site flow are reflective of the taxonomies produced during this process. For systems with significant UI, information architecture provides a much needed reality check for users, stakeholders, and implementers of the system at the very outset. It is used for flushing out the detailed requirements of workflows and processes, the implications of which are immediately reflected in the detailed use case description of the system. The consensus on detailed use case descriptions among stakeholders, users, information architects, and the technical team ensures that the vision set forth by the extended team addresses both the business needs and technical feasibility of the system within the specified time and budget.

CHAPTER

3

Application Architecture, Security, and Caching

IN THIS CHAPTER:

Application Architecture

Planning Application Security

Digital Signatures

Single Sign-On

Java Authentication and Authorization Service

Federated Network Identity

Caching Overview

Cache Architecture

Summary

References

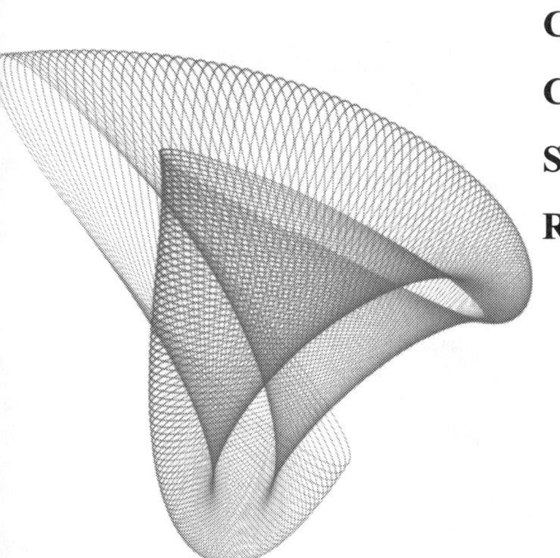

This book progressively builds the application using a use case driven approach. Chapters 4 through 8 explicitly discuss the design, J2EE component development, and configuration aspects of the sample GreaterCause application. However, before we start developing the application, we need to look at several other aspects of the design to ensure a reliable, scalable, extensible, and robust operational environment for the application. In addition to discussing the architecture elements, this chapter assists in putting a perspective around the application security. The discussion on security will assist the readers in envisioning ahead of time the specific needs of their application and plan toward a solution that adequately secures the system from malicious use. Since vendor-specific security implementations and the application requirements differ significantly from one application to another, the focus in this chapter is to provide a high-level overview based on prominent technologies and specifications. This should assist the readers in determining their unique design needs and arriving at a solution that takes advantage of best of breed solutions. Please note that the declarative security provided by the J2EE platform, and the J2EE platform security API used for programmatic security, are discussed in Chapter 5. The final section in this chapter focuses on the design aspects in the creation of an application-level cache. Since this chapter is not a prerequisite for the rest of the book, you may decide to come back to it later.

We assume that J2EE is a platform of your choice, and hence we do not get into the details of why it is a good choice. Several books do a good job at explaining this. We highly recommend *Designing Enterprise Applications with the J2EE Platform* [J2EE] for getting a solid roundup of all pertinent J2EE technologies. We also recommend *Core J2EE Patterns* [Core], which covers several of the patterns implemented in this book. For the purpose of reading this book, we expect that the readers have only a basic knowledge of JSP, servlet, and EJB technologies. Some excellent tutorials are available at java.sun.com to quickly bring you up to speed with these technologies.

Application Architecture

The subject of architecture is exhaustive as it refers to several design aspects and relevant artifacts used for the construction of an application. Several of the design artifacts developed during the course of this book contribute to the overall architecture but represent architecture at different levels of granularity. For example, the MVC architecture discussed in Chapter 4 addresses tier-level responsibilities, whereas the design patterns used for implementing EJBs (discussed in Chapter 7) address component-level responsibilities. A security architecture that complements the application architecture will also be at different levels of granularity, as explained in the section "Planning Application Security." Some discernable artifacts and processes of an architecture can therefore be summarized as follows:

- *Functionality* of the system as expressed by use cases and augmented by wire frames.
- Application *layers*, their interactions, responsibilities, and the elements they contain for satisfying the use cases.
- *Components* identified for each layer and their interactions, dependencies, and their roles. This will include both infrastructure and application components.

- Composition of these components; expressing their interaction using appropriate design patterns to form *fundamental structural elements* that provide repeatable, reusable, and extensible solutions.
- Composition of fundamental structural elements into larger units called *modules*, or *subsystems*.
- Composition of the software modules and corresponding configuration files into *deployable units*.

The 4+1 View Model of Architecture

The overall architecture of a system can be modeled with the following interlocking view as proposed by Philippe Kruchten in a paper "The 4+1 View Model of Architecture" [Kruchten].

- The Use Case View of a system constitutes the use cases that describe the behavior of the system from the perspective of external entities interacting with the use case. The use case view is a static view of the system. It captures requirements that are used in the creation of the system's architecture. This view ties all other views together.
- The Logical View (also called the *Design View)* of a system consists of classes, interfaces, and their collaborations.
- The Implementation View describes the physical organization of the software and includes the components, files, libraries, and so, on required to assemble the system.
- The Deployment View focuses on hardware topology consisting of physical nodes and computing hardware on which the executables are deployed.
- The Process View is concerned with the concurrency and synchronization aspects of the software—for example, the processes, tasks, and threads.

This book focuses explicitly on the Use Case View and the Logical View of the system. The Use Case View of the sample application was created in Chapters 1 and 2. The static aspects of the Logical View are captured using class diagrams of Chapter 5 where we model interactions between the presentation tier components, and in Chapter 6 where we model interactions between the domain entities, and in Chapter 7 where we model the interactions between various EJBs and helper classes for realizing the business tier functionality. The dynamic aspects of the Logical View are represented using sequence, collaboration, state-chart, and activity diagrams. Sequence diagrams are used extensively in Chapters 5, 6, and 7 to show the interactions between application objects. The Logical View helps create the vocabulary of the problem and its solution. This vocabulary is complemented by the vocabulary of the design patterns employed to solve recurring problems within the system. Design patterns help us articulate commonly occurring interactions between objects in the problem domain and are discussed in several chapters.

Creating a J2EE Architecture Blueprint

Architecture is the software's blueprint, which is derived from the use cases created in Chapters 1 and 2. However, we cannot expect to take the use cases and arrive at the final architecture without going through a refinement process. The architecture of a system evolves as decisions are made in terms of feasibility, technical challenges, trade-offs, cohesion between stated requirements, fluctuating needs of the stakeholders, and so on. This is very much an iterative process where use cases will provide a starting point but there will be a need to modify or extend the use cases as the architect creates the Design View of the system.

The J2EE architectural style does not strictly recommend adherence to a layer-like architecture in which layers have a hierarchical structure and each layer can only communicate with the layer above or below. Instead, it encourages a tiered approach in which different tiers can communicate based on the way the requirements are implemented. Several scenarios depict this approach, as shown in Figure 3-1.

- Clients can interact directly with a Web tier; the Web tier accesses the database tier (database tier is shown as EIS tier).
- Clients can interact directly with the EJB tier; the EJB tier accesses the database tier.
- Clients can interact directly with the Web tier; the Web tier interacts with the EJB tier, and the EJB tier accesses the database tier.

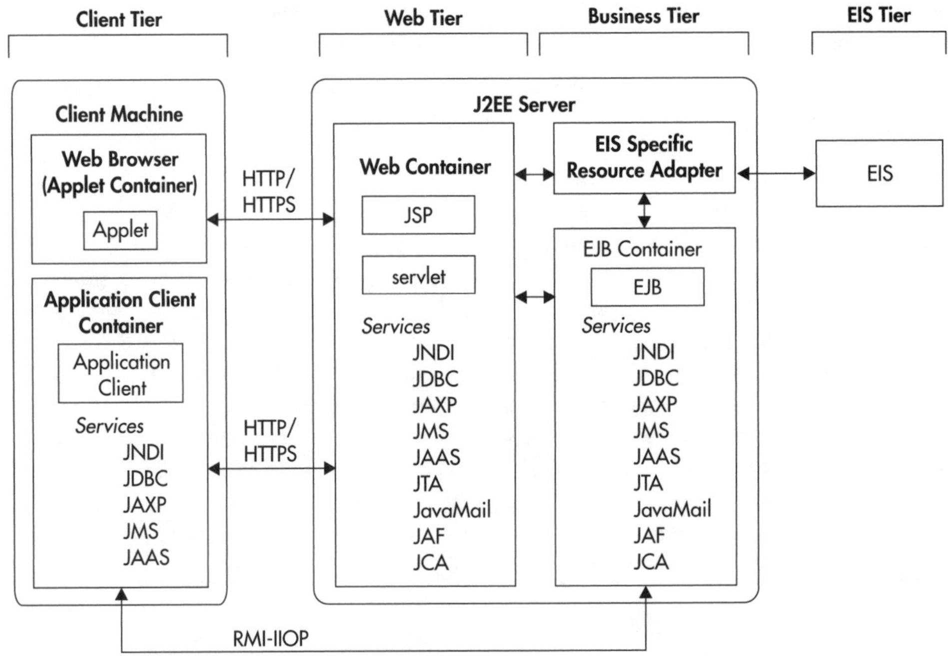

Figure 3-1 *J2EE architecture*

From Figure 3-1, it is apparent that the role of the container is central to the J2EE architecture. The container interposes itself between the application components and the J2EE platform services. This gives the container the ability to transparently inject the platform services based on the configuration information declaratively specified in the deployment descriptors. An *EJB container*, running on the J2EE server, manages the execution of all EJBs for one J2EE application. It handles the life cycle of EJBs and provides all the system-level services for the EJB. It provides transaction management, security, resource management, and naming services for the EJBs. A *web container*, running on the J2EE server, manages the execution of JSPs and Servlets for one J2EE application. The *application client container*, running on the client machine, manages the execution of application client components for one J2EE application.

The purpose of this book is to sufficiently demonstrate the architecture of a J2EE-based solution for large-scale development. As such, we have used the multi-tiered approach identified by the third item in the preceding list. We have employed container-managed persistence for data access and manipulation, which is covered in Chapters 6 and 7. For accessing a large volume of read-only data, we have favored using a session bean with Data Access Object Pattern [Core] for accessing data directly from the data store when implementing the Value List Handler Pattern [Core]. Please refer to Chapter 7 for design and implementation details.

Employing Frameworks

The architecture employed in this book is greatly simplified as a result of using the open source Struts framework. Struts employs MVC (Model-View-Controller)–style semantics for breaking up the application responsibilities between three distinct layers as suggested by the name. Struts framework is discussed in detail in Chapter 4, with corresponding implementation for the sample application in Chapter 5. Employing frameworks such as Struts provides an architect with the ability to focus on creating elements that plug into the framework and/or framework-related extensions. We therefore architect based on the extension points and the framework's ability to interact with other elements of the application for realizing the use cases. The usage of framework therefore provides a standard way of implementing a specific system functionality, which in this case is the mapping of user actions in the presentation tier to the services offered by the business tier.

A presentation-layer framework will typically solve a recurring problem, namely, mapping of user actions to an application service. This problem space is solved using best-practice patterns such as Front Controller [Core], View Helper [Core], or a combination pattern such as Service to Worker [Core] or Dispatcher View [Core]. Creating a custom application-specific framework (a one-off solution) is not a trivial undertaking, as is obvious in the discussion of Struts framework in Chapter 4. The class diagrams of Chapter 5 clearly show how simplistic the approach is when designing with a framework like Struts. We simply focus on implementing abstract methods or subclass Struts-provided request handler class. By employing a few design patterns, such as Command [Gof], Business Delegate [Core], Service Locator [Core], and Session Façade [Core], we are able to create a design vocabulary that is consistently replicated across most use cases. This greatly promotes understanding between developers who create implementations for realizing different use cases but with the semantics that adhere to the common design vocabulary of the system.

Designing for a responsibility-driven tiered architecture enables construction of software in a manner that addresses the objective of isolating infrastructure-specific functionality from application-specific functionality (that is, custom functionality) for each tier. With the Struts framework, the Model-View-Controller semantics provide for three different layers of responsibilities.

Generally speaking, use of a framework could impose an architectural template for building applications within a specific domain. However, frameworks provide reusable infrastructure service that are used by many use cases in the system. Bypassing the framework approach will entail that each use case with a common set of functionality will have to address its needs by creating a one-off solution. Obviously such approaches are self-defeating in the long run since they create inflexible and hard to maintain code.

J2EE Components in an Architecture

When developing business applications, a large amount of time could be spent building core system services like transaction management, resource management, security, remote connectivity, and object relational mapping services. These services are essential to all enterprise applications and can be abstracted into a reusable and declaratively configurable framework that could provide these essential services to all applications at runtime. Such a framework enables architects and engineers to focus on solving the business problem, thus simplifying the designing and coding effort and offering consistent implementation semantics for all applications using the framework. The J2EE architecture offers a standard set of system services to application components as part of the runtime environment referred to as *containers*.

J2EE provides component-based approach for the design, development, assembly, and deployment of enterprise applications. There is clear separation of responsibility between the different tiers, as shown in Figure 3-1. The tiered approach decomposes a problem domain into fundamental units of application functionality that are appropriate for each tier. This makes it possible to offer a highly reusable component-based architecture in which a Model-View-Controller (MVC) architecture is a natural fit.

The services offered by the containers are configurable declaratively and interpreted at deployment time, thus insulating code from any modification should there be a need to modify the behavior of these system-level services. For example, transactional semantics are specified declaratively for a set of interrelated components composing a service. The components from one domain can be mixed with components from another domain to offer a new set of services whose transactional semantics could be specified differently (and declaratively) using XML-based deployment descriptors. Similar discussion is true for configuring security roles for describing access privileges for a set of users in the newly composed application. The deployment descriptors are explained in Chapters 5, 6, and 7 for components of the sample GreaterCause application. The J2EE specification ensures that code written in accordance with the specification will be portable across various vendors.

Planning Application Security

The Internet is an established vehicle for personal, communal, and commercial interactions. All forms of information from personal e-mails to high-value financial transactions are dispatched over the Internet. It is a known fact that information constitutes what is arguably the most valuable asset of an individual or an organization. Protecting these assets is almost as important as the tasks or business they are intended for.

System security is an extremely sought after "ingredient" in any mission-critical enterprise application, almost at par with the coveted application feature-list. Security is also very unique in that it is one of the most pervasive components in an application. This implies that security isn't necessarily limited to a particular part of a system, such as its presentation, business logic, database, servers, or networks, but in fact applies to *all* aspects of the system. It is therefore crucial that any design or analysis of a system take a *holistic* approach to addressing security rather than that of a *modular* one. Though security may be realized differently in various parts of the system, all security operations must seamlessly tie together in order to achieve a manageable and secure system. Securing an enterprise application, a complex task in many regards follows three basic tenets (outlined in this section and the next).

> *Tenet I: "It is a doctrine of war not to assume the enemy will not come, but rather to rely on one's readiness to meet him; not to presume that he will not attack, but rather to make one's self invincible." (Sun Tzu, "The Art of War")*

Security in electronic commerce is vital for every business application. It is foolhardy to assume that information sent and received over the Internet will not be listened to, intercepted, or manipulated in any way, shape, or form. Instead it is always considered prudent when security requirements and security limitations of the data and operations of an enterprise application are thoroughly understood and communicated to the appropriate stakeholders.

Identifying Security Requirements

It is very important that all enterprise applications, internal or external, client-facing or back-office enabling, must go through constant "security preparedness" analysis during their entire project life cycle. These reviews and analyses allow stakeholders to become aware of the capabilities and vulnerabilities of the system. These reviews are not necessarily meant to build a "perfect" defense but rather to increase one's preparedness by determining the following:

- **Risk estimation** A deterministic estimation of the system's overall security scope (intranet, extranet, Internet, protected back-end, and so on) and specific measures taken to ensure against relevant attack scenarios provide an accurate picture of the system's risk exposure. An untainted declaration of known security limitations and vulnerabilities provides stakeholders with information necessary for making an informed decision on the acceptability of the system given the sensitivity of data and operations involved.
- **Damage estimations** Damage estimations provide the "silent" scenarios wherein damage (financial, political, opportunity, and so on) caused by a breach in the system is summarized and estimated. This information is critical to allow organizations to be prepared for eventual fallouts (financial, legal, public, and so on) if and when their systems are compromised.
- **Security breach identification and recovery procedures** Recovery procedures provide organizations with guidelines on how to identify and recover from a security

breach quickly and effectively. These procedures must also provide a recovery process detailing the manner in which to recover from the identified breach in the shortest possible period of time. This may include creating a patch, and subsequently testing and deploying it in the production environment. Severe, unexpected compromises in system security may require that the system (or part of it) be taken offline.

- **Evolutionary requirements** From a security perspective, it is important to understand the evolution of the enterprise application or system being built. Major security concerns that may need to be addressed for an evolving application include the following:
  - Communication scope (intranet, extranet, Internet) and encryption requirements
  - Establishing partnerships, trust relationships, and identities
  - Authorization requirements
  - Resource protection and access control

It is essential that an application's security design is adequately flexible and extensible in order to incorporate demands made during "foreseeable" future evolutions of the application. This will increase the trust level placed in the system, ensuring that it can effectively meet the security demands made by an ever-changing environment of trusted relationships.

> *Tenet II: "There are no invincible countries, no foolproof defenses and no impregnable fortifications. Those who passively wait to be attacked are vulnerable." (Sun Tzu, "The Art of War")*

The term "secure" is a relative concept and hence the notion of "perfect security" is non-existent. Instead it is more practical to investigate what constitutes a "secure-enough" environment for the enterprise system being built. The following aspects (among others) must be taken into account when providing such an environment:

- **Resources** Building a secure-enough system has a lot to do with resources and often comes with a price. In order to be secure enough, it is necessary to stay one step ahead of the resources committed toward malicious acts. It requires a talented and seasoned skill set, top-notch hardware (often required to overcome security-related performance bottlenecks), and people knowledgable about existing security processes within an organization. Such resources are either expensive and/or difficult to find.
- **Risk exposure** The scope or exposure (intranet, extranet, Internet, and so on) of the system being built is an important factor in building a secure-enough environment. Standard technologies (such as SSL, digital signatures, shared-key encryption, public key infrastructure, and so on) can be selected once basic scope requirements have been identified.
- **Trust** A notable limitation, but yet an ever-present component of anything related to securing a system is trust. No matter what the nature of defense, or the amount of resources committed to designing and installing secure technologies, there are certain entities that must be trusted.

Since trusted entities are critical links in determining the overall strength of a defense, it is crucial that usage of such *trusted* technologies or relationships, their capabilities, and the processes that manage them are clearly documented and communicated to the parties concerned. For example, SSL, a technology that is often used for mission-critical Internet applications forms the basis of *trust* for all secure communications.

> *Tenet III: "If you know your enemy and know yourself, you will not be defeated in a hundred battles." (Sun Tzu, "The Art of War")*

An important aspect of designing secure-enough systems involves a good understanding of possible attack scenarios and how those malicious acts, if committed, may exploit the system. This critical and strategic observation consists of two fundamental aspects :

- **Internal and external system boundaries** There are many interaction points in an application. Some interactions points in the system are externally facing (that is, interact with computing services or users outside the organization that owns the system) and some are internal. Each such interaction point must clearly be documented from a security standpoint, including its relevance to the system, its sensitivity, and most importantly the processes put in place that manage them.
- **Assailants and attacks** A thorough profile of possible malicious acts that target internal and external interaction points as well as the assailants that orchestrate them is needed. Such profiles detail, among other things, an assailant's capabilities, resources, and their ability to inflict damage using information appropriated through unauthorized means. As stated previously in Tenet II, securing "everything" from "everyone" is an impossible task. Thus, such profiles, examined in the context of the sensitivity of operations involved, help determine whether the measures taken to protect the system are sufficient.

Functional Classification of Application Security

Security-related issues cover a wide range of subject matter from network hacking and denial-of-service attacks to managing a user's network identity. Covering all such aspects in detail would require its own book and is not the goal of this chapter. This section provides a perspective on how application security can be functionally classified under distinct areas of responsibilities. Security at the application layer can be logically partitioned into three primary *areas* of responsibility, or *zones*, each handling a specific set of tasks that contribute to the overall security of the system. These three zones (shown in Figure 3-2) are as follows:

- Channel security
- Network identity management
- Authentication and authorization

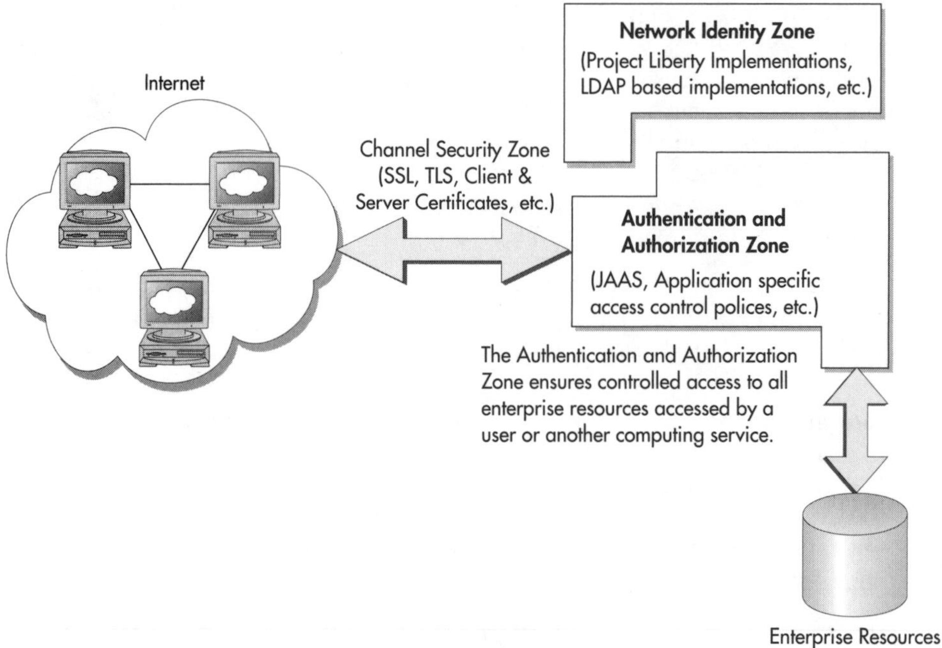

Figure 3-2 *Application security zones*

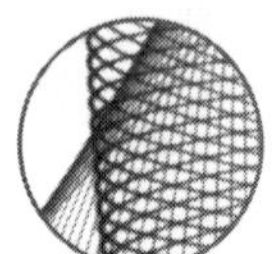

NOTE

These zones are logical partitions based on areas of responsibility and are not related to the physical infrastructure in which they are deployed.

The rest of this section provides a high-level overview of each zone, following which we discuss technologies applicable to these zones.

Channel Security

Channel security addresses how the communication between various entities on the Internet takes place. The most commonly used technology is Secure Sockets Layer (or SSL), which preserves confidentiality and integrity of data between communicating endpoints. Certificates are also used as part of SSL communication to establish the identity of the communicating endpoints on either end of a secure channel. Message security addresses the mechanisms that may be applied to discrete pieces of information or documents that are passed between communicating endpoints. In order to preserve data *integrity*, *authenticity*, and *non-repudiation* of the information exchanged, digital signatures (discussed further in the section "Digital Signatures") are used.

The following table provides a summary of the various technologies employed in this zone and their use.

Mechanism	Channel Security	Channel Message Security
Confidentiality	SSL, TLS	
Data integrity		Message transformation algorithms and message-digests
Authentication	Client- and server-side certificates for transport-level encryption	
Data origin authentication		Certificates used for digital signature verification
Non-repudiation		Digital signatures

Network Identity Management

As more and more people, communities, and businesses use the Internet as their primary means of interaction, the notion of an *identity* (just as in real life) becomes a crucial part of online communication. Simply put, an identity consists of a set of attributes that uniquely defines who you are as a system user and how you are represented in various system interactions. Albeit, the concept of a user identity may sound simple, however, defining and establishing identities for sophisticated multiuser enterprise applications is a task much easier said than done. Couple that with the possibility that identities may need to be "portable" in order to be shared among various networked services and you have a complex problem at hand. Today, a person's Internet identity is strewn across various entities connected to the Internet including portals, business services, organizations, and so on. This fragmentation of information results in "closed," inextensible and isolated relationships.

Federated network identity is the key to addressing the issue of identity fragmentation, and in doing so, it enables businesses to realize new opportunities and explore revenue potential in relatively new economies of scale. In this world of identity federation, a user's online identity, personal profile, interests, preferences, purchase history, and so on, can be administered securely by the user and privately shared with trusted organizations of the user's choosing. The natural means to realizing this goal will first involve the establishment of a standardized method to create, disseminate, and manage simple federated identities across multiple identity management systems (a.k.a. identity providers) based on commonly deployed technologies. Project Liberty (http://www.projectlibery.org), an alliance consisting of a broad spectrum of industries, envisions such a world in which businesses and their users can engage in virtually any type of interaction without compromising the privacy and security of their identity. An overview of the Liberty 1.1 architecture, and the vendors implementing this specification, is provided in section "Liberty Architecture."

The network identity management zone is the basis for conducting most system transactions. It is this zone that determines *who* you are and defines *what* you can do. The identity of a user must therefore be established in this zone before any application services can be accessed, and thus it is crucial that mechanisms used in this zone are protected, isolated, and managed by clearly defined processes. The network identity zone is often a cornerstone for sophisticated identity-related operations. For example, during user logon

- The user submits his/her credentials via a secure channel for authentication.

- User authentication is performed by retrieving the user credentials stored within the identity zone and validating it against the one submitted by the user.

It is therefore obvious that a breach in the network identity zone may prove fatal in that the system will be unable to distinguish a valid user from a malicious one.

Authentication and Authorization

The authentication and authorization zone have two main functions in the system—the first being that of establishing the authenticity of user credentials (authentication) and the second, "translating" a user's identity into permissible actions (authorization). The authentication and authorization zone is more a "gatekeeper" to system resources and data rather than an "administrator" to the information used to access its protected assets. This zone consists of polices, rules, and processes that protect resources and ensure that system operations are executed securely in a manageable and consistent manner. Authentication and authorization functionality are complex and nontrivial but are unarguably a crucial component in almost all enterprise applications. They often are combined with network identity solutions and offered as a centralized, integratable service to allow for improved manageability. It is thus recommended that functions of this zone be designed and built based on established standards to increase extensibility and preserve vendor neutrality. One such technology is Java Authentication and Authorization Service (JAAS), which is discussed in the section "Java Authentication and Authorization Service."

Authentication is a relatively simple process since the tasks involved are few and bounded. After all, only a finite set of credentials (for example, username and password) are validated to establish user identity. Thus the authentication module need only be designed to handle those specific types of credentials.

Authorization, in contrast, requires a completely different approach. This is because authorization in general is involved in a significantly larger number of transactions whose design is closely tied to business processes and regulations. This, however, does not imply that the *entire* authorization process must be designed and built from scratch for each application. The authorization process, though different in each application, does have a common set of fundamental concepts such as roles, actions, permissions, rules, access control lists, and so on. In fact, well-designed authorization frameworks contain both infrastructure- and application-specific components. The main goal of such frameworks is to *minimize* tight coupling between the authorization process and the application. For example, in order to grant access to a protected resource to users of role "myRole," one should ideally require simple modification to policy files rather than a change to the application.

Introduction to Single Sign-On A popular and widely implemented extension to the authentication process is single sign-on (SSO). A technical overview of the single sign-on process, its motivations, and issues is provided in the "Single Sign-On" section. Single sign-on defines a series of interactions that occur between trusted systems in order to sign on an authenticated user without his/her direct involvement to one or more systems. The following steps detail the SSO process:

1. Two systems, A and B, establish *trust* that allows them to *share* user identity information. This implies (among other things) that any user identity information originating from A or B and destined for B or A, respectively, is considered to be trustworthy, valid, and secure.
2. User identity is first established at one trusted source (say A) using a standard sign-on process involving a direct user challenge.
3. User then attempts to access a service hosted in system B from A.
4. System A forwards the user's identity to system B on behalf of the user.
5. Since system B trusts system A (step 1), system B accepts user identity information sent by system A.
6. System B validates and establishes the user's identity in its system without explicitly challenging the user and provides access to the requested service.
7. User has thus *single signed-on* to system B as the user was challenged only *once* to provide his/her credentials (at system A in step 2).

The crux of the interactions that occur within this zone are defined by the *metadata* and *schemas* (discussed in the "Single Sign-On" section) conveyed as part of these interactions. Metadata and schemas generically refer to the identity information, and the formats in which they are exchanged between the various systems participating in single sign-on operations. The main classes of information exchanged include account/identity, authentication context, and participant metadata, which are explained here:

- **Account/identity** This is simply the user's account/identity information accessed through a *handle* (refer to the section "Single Sign-On and Identity Federation"). The comprehensive list of attributes in a user's account/identity is application specific.
- **Authentication context** Many mechanisms and techniques are available to authenticate users into a system. Different parties may choose different technologies and follow different processes, and may be bound by myriad legal obligations regarding how they authenticate their users. The choices made in this area will largely be driven by the requirements of each party, the nature of the service, the sensitivity of information exchanged, financial constraints, and risk tolerance. Additionally, if a service is to trust the user authentication data it receives from an external source, the service *may* wish to know the technologies, protocols, and processes that were employed by that source to obtain the data. The authentication context provides a means for the exchange of such information.
- **Provider metadata** In order for identity sources and target services to communicate, they must have obtained metadata about each other. Such metadata primarily aid in establishing trust and operational agreements between the two communicating parties.

Digital Signatures

Security technologies deployed today in run-of-the-mill Internet environments are inadequate for securing mission-critical business transactions. For example, the Secure Sockets Layer

(SSL) does guarantee the secure exchange of confidential data, but once the data has been received, it is decrypted and often retained in its original form for processing. Thus, SSL only protects the data while it is in "secure" transport, *neither* before *nor* after. This shortcoming is further exacerbated when messages are routed through multiple nodes and unencrypted for processing at each node. This may leave the data vulnerable to unauthorized alteration on relatively insecure servers. In addition to protecting the sensitivity of the data transacted, ensuring the data's long-term integrity, authenticity, and origin is crucial. This allows for non-repudiation—the ability to unequivocally assure both the sender and recipient of the data that its origin is authentic, its contents unchanged and as the sender intended.

Digital signatures address the need of transacting and storing highly sensitive commercial data both during and after the life of the transaction thus ensuring long-term non-repudiation. As XML becomes the de facto standard for conducting electronic business transactions, a trusted and secure XML-message exchange mechanism is essential. XML digital signature is a key technology enabling both long-tem integrity and origin authenticity of the document. The XML Signature specification is a promising standard that provides a means for signing XML documents. Capturing resulting signatures using the very same XML syntax allows for seamless integration into XML-based business applications.

Public Key Cryptography in Digital Signatures

Digital signatures use a prominent and well-known technology called public key cryptography. Public key cryptography provides the transactions the confidence that data involved in the transaction will not be modified or appropriated by anyone other than the intended recipient. This is accomplished by generating a public and a private key combination known as asymmetric keys. The asymmetric key set has the following unique characteristics:

- The relationship between the private and public key is such that any cryptographic operation that is performed using one key can only be reversed by the other. Thus a message encrypted using the public key component of the asymmetric key-pair can only be decrypted by the private key of the very same key-pair.
- Unlike symmetric key cryptography, this technique does not require that the sender or receiver exchange any secret information as part of the transaction.

The characteristics of public key cryptography just described make it an absolute "must-have" to construct reliable digital signatures. The functionality offered by public key cryptography include

- **Integrity** Ensuring that any changes to the original message can be unambiguously identified (explained in the upcoming section "Ensuring Data Integrity").
- **Authenticity** Ensuring that the origin of the message can be unambiguously identified.

This functionality, and through it, the realization of non-repudiation, give electronic transactions qualities similar to that of signatures on standard paper transactions known and used by all.

Certificate Authorities

A digital signature is created by providing a confidential private key as an input to a PKCS (Public Key Cryptography Standard) transform (for example, multi-prime RSA algorithm) that is applied to the data to be signed. Since only the public key of the asymmetric key-pair can reverse that transform, the recipient of the "signed" data on successfully reversing the applied transform with the public key, can be confident that the data is in fact from the sender.

It is also important to note that the validity of the digital signature stems from the confidence that the public key does, in fact, belong to the sender. It is for these reasons that Certification Authorities (for example Verisign Inc.) issue certificates that assert the validity of the relationship between the public key and that of the certificate's owner/subject.

Ensuring Data Integrity

Due to the computationally intensive nature of PKCS algorithms, only a small document/message identifier is actually signed with the private key. This identifier is commonly known as a *hash* or *message-digest*. The hash or digest for a given input data-stream is unique in that it is highly unlikely that there exists a single computed hash value for two dissimilar data-streams. Hence an alteration to the data content will fail to produce the same hash value indicating that the content was changed in transit. The computed hash value is then transformed, in other words *signed*, with the sender's private key thus allowing the recipient to verify, using the sender's public key, that the content/document is in fact from the sender. Thus, the *signed* hash/digest preserves both the integrity and the authenticity of the transacted data.

The received data is verified by first obtaining its hash value by applying a reverse PCKS transform on the signature using the sender's public key. The hash value is then recomputed on the received data and compared with the data's original *hash* value. If they are the same, the recipient can then be confident that the data indeed came from the sender, unaltered.

XML Signatures

The same challenges associated with encryption, integrity, and non-repudiation also exist for XML data. Two new XML specifications addressing the subject of securing, encrypting, and non-repudiating XML data are XML Signature and XML Encryption.

A unique feature in XML Signature is the ability to allow only specific parts of an XML document to be signed. This becomes extremely useful if an XML document is to be handled by multiple parties, each with certain delegated responsibilities that are to be unequivocally captured in the document. This ensures the integrity of all *signed* portions of the document. An example in context is business process workflows. A business process workflow may involve an XML document exchange between multiple participants where each participant may wish to sign only specific parts of the document maintaining a certain level of commitment for which they are liable. Prior digital signature standards did not provide the capability to address signatures at such a high level of granularity, nor did they provide a means to specify signed portions of a document by multiple parties. Figure 3-3 provides an overview of the various components in an XML Signature.

XML-based interchange formats allow data to be easily understood between two or more communicating parties. XML schema rules allow for flexible data representation. The very

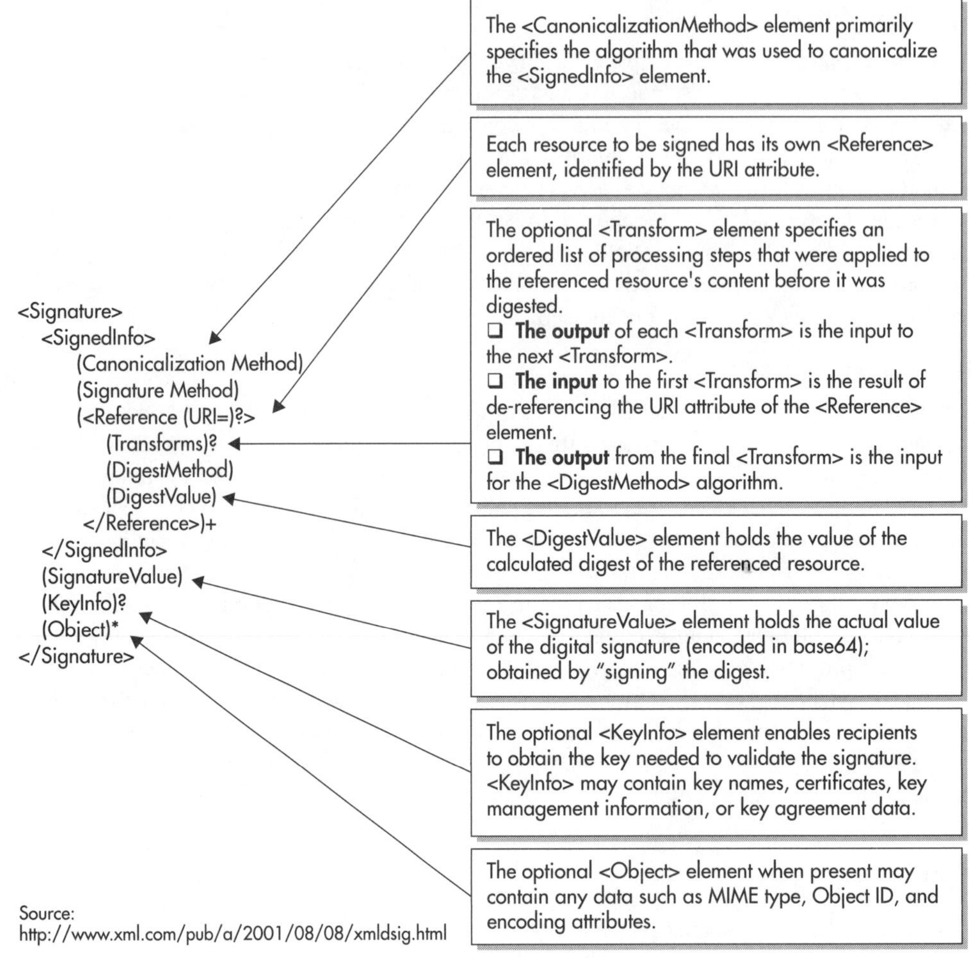

Figure 3-3 *Components of an XML Signature*

same piece of data may be represented in different XML structures (or documents). Consider the following XML document fragments:

```
<?xml version="1.0"?>
<books>
    <book type="fiction" cost="15" binding="soft"/>
    <book type="history" cost="29  binding="hard"/>
</books>

<?xml version="1.0"?>
<books>
```

```
    <book type="fiction" binding="soft" cost="15"/>
    <book type="history" binding="hard" cost="29"/>
</books>
```

These XML document fragments though logically equivalent do not contain the same sequence or ordering of characters. In this particular scenario, the fragments differ by the order of attributes that appear in the "book" element.

In order to determine that two XML documents or fragments are logically equivalent, it is necessary to arrive at a unified (or canonical) format. In order to address this issue there exists canonicalization algorithms that transform XML documents into canonical forms that can be compared octet by octet. XML canonicalization is essential to the process of signing and verifying XML documents. Prior to signing an XML document, the document is first canonicalized using accepted algorithms based on W3C rules for XML canonicalization. It is the canonicalized form of the document that is digitally signed, not the document's original form.During verification, it is the digital signature of the canonicalized form of the XML document that is verified. Thus the verification of the digital signatures of all logically equivalent versions of the signed XML document should be successful.

An important aspect to consider is the performance characteristics of canonicalization. As can be inferred from the description of the canonicalization operations in prior sections, canonicalization operations may involve multiple traverses of the XML document. Furthermore, conversion of an XML document to a uniform canonicalized format (such as octet sequences) may be resource intensive. The performance characateristics are further exacerbated as the XML document size increases.

Single Sign-On

As the number of enterprise applications increases in large organizations, coordinating authentication and authorization operations for these applications becomes a complex task. In addition to dealing with the security aspects of each application, a centralized and robust policy management infrastructure is essential. This ensures that the organization's information and services are accessed in a consistent manner.

Usability considerations in a diverse environment consisting of multiple security domains requires integration of user sign-on functions with that of identity management. This need is addressed by a service or a set of services that coordinate user authentication and credential forwarding between security domains. This is commonly known as single sign-on (SSO), termed after the end user's perception of this functionality. SSO provides operational and cost benefits through the following:

- Increased simplicity of user sign-on function
- Improved user experience
- Reduced management overhead as administrators may easily add, remove, or limit a user's access to enterprise resources in a consistent manner as dictated by access policies

The single sign-on process can be envisioned as a method of authenticating to multiple resources or services, each in its own security domain, by only being challenged once to submit authentication credentials. A high-level overview of the single sign-on process is shown in Figure 3-4. Important elements of SSO include the following:

- **Primary domain** The domain that initially challenges the user for his/her credentials. This domain is responsible for mapping sign-on credentials (example, userid and password) to accounts in other security domains.
- **Secondary domains** All other security domains that authenticate the user based on credentials provided by the primary domain.

Trust is a crucial factor in any secure operation and is no different in SSO. In SSO, the secondary domains trust the primary domain to do the following:

- Accurately assert the authentication credentials submitted by the end user
- Prevent user credentials from unauthorized use

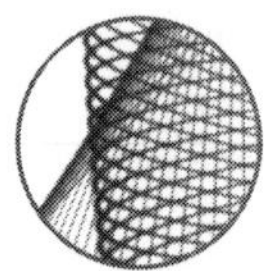

NOTE

The primary and secondary domains do not necessarily represent entities within the bounds of an enterprise system or an organization. These domains may be systems belonging to external organizations and those that share user identity information though well-established trust and operational agreements.

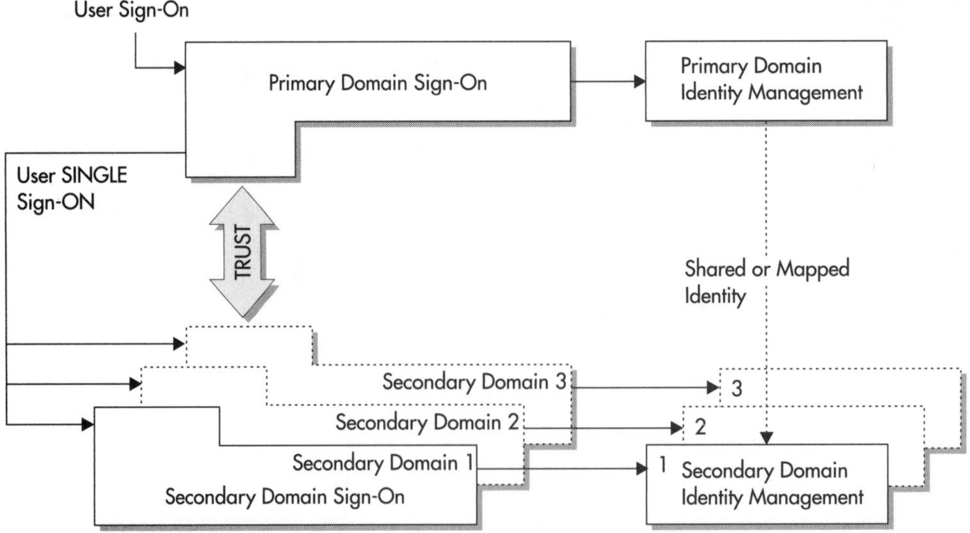

Figure 3-4 *Single sign-on architecture*

Credential Mapping in SSO

Usually, user-supplied credentials submitted to a primary domain are first forwarded to a centralized identity management infrastructure where these credentials are used to obtain the user's identity profile. Through this profile a user is mapped to another set of independent credentials, in the context of the secondary domain, which are then used for user sign-on to the secondary domain. Credential mapping, though complex from a design standpoint, yields many advantages with regard to security, manageability, and user experience.

For example, a user may wish to access divisional sales reports through a corporate portal. The user is challenged only once when entering the corporate portal. Signing on to the reporting service is automatically handled via the single sign-on process using the credential mapping process as explained earlier.

One way to optimally map users between domains is through roles. Since the secondary domain trusts the primary domain and its authenticated users, the secondary domain can control access to its resources and services through roles. Role mapping is advantageous in that as users are added and removed from the system, the application remains unaffected. Role mapping may also be combined with other credentials to customize access control mechanisms as each application's authorization needs (which may be implemented using JAAS, please refer to section "Java Authentication and Authorization Service" for details) are unique.

Elements of Single Sign-On

Single sign-on, as described earlier, is a means by which a primary domain conveys to a secondary domain that the user is in fact authenticated. However, as simple as this operation may sound, there are various elements related to designing, deploying, and managing this operation in a mission-critical environment. The following sections discuss various elements of the single sign-on process.

Profiles

As part of the single sign-on operation, user identity is exchanged securely between primary and secondary domains using profiles. Profiles map messages exchanged between primary and secondary domains to a specific protocol such as HTTP, SOAP, and so on. These profiles are required to clearly define the sequence of interactions, format, message content, and *trust* attributes established between participating domains. Profiles may be designed using a proprietary approach or based on standardized profiles (for example, Project Liberty—see http://www.projectliberty.org).

Credentials

Identity in a system is established by validating a set of credentials that corroborate a set of one or more *identity* assertions. For example, in a *role-based* system, with a password-based authentication model, a username and password would be considered as credentials that prove a user's assertion that he/she belongs to a specific *role*. Credentials are used in various

Preventing Replay Attacks

Often, system-generated URLs have some user identification information for authenticated users. Such URLs maintain time-bound information and are required to have the property of a *nonce.* A nonce is a random, non-repeating value incorporated as part of the data exchanged by a protocol to protect against *replay* attacks. A replay attack occurs when a message that has a definite *validity period* is replayed (that is, sent again) after its validity has expired. Using a nonce ensures that a time-bound entity such as a URL that is valid at a given point in time cannot be *replayed* or *reused* after it expires. Since the contents of a replayed (expired) message may look authentic (formatting, credentials, signatures, and so on), unsuspecting server processes may end up reprocessing the message constituting a serious security breach. Thus time-based assurance of the *freshness* of the message must be employed to protect against such an occurrence.

ways in a single sign-on operation and are often the basis for establishing trust with the credential bearer. Examples of credentials include the following:

- Sensitive information such as private cryptographic keys, pin numbers, passwords, and so on, that are required to be protected from unauthorized access. Such information may also be protected from tampering or fabrication.
- Shared information such as public key certificates, pseudonyms, and so on.

Multi-Layered Authentication

It may be possible that credentials and the mechanisms used for authentication or authorization are not of sufficient quality to complete an attempted operation. For example, after initial sign-on, a user attempts to conduct a high-valued operation (such as an account withdrawal) that requires a more secure form of authentication. In such a scenario, a user may be required to provide a stronger assertion of identity, such as a digital signature or personal pin number. This action is known as *re-authentication*, and the overall process as *multi-layered authentication.* Employing multi-layered authentication can be a policy decision, a contractual agreement, or at the discretion of the service. Such polices and agreements may include details about the following:

- User identification methods when enrolling (registering) credentials
- Credential renewal policies
- Credential storage, protection, and distribution (for example, encryption, access controls, and so on)

Authentication assertions should provide an indication of the quality of credentials and the mechanism in which they are exchanged between security domains. For example, authentication assertion established between security domains may be deemed of type *strong* if the following are true:

- Digital certificates and SSL are used to authenticate the user.
- Biometric identity verification in addition to digitally signed documentation are used during user registration/enrollment.

Thus, if a security domain provides authentication assertions of type *strong* to a secondary domain as part of single sign-on, the secondary domain may trust the assertions to a certain degree. However, this degree of trust is unlikely to be placed on assertions that originate from other security domains that do not use assertions of type *strong*. Thus, it is crucial that single sign-on participants clearly define their authentication type and multi-layered authentication process.

Mutual Authentication

Another extension to the standard authentication mechanism is *mutual* authentication. Mutual authentication implies that both the user and the service authenticate themselves with each other in a reciprocal manner. For example, when establishing an SSL connection, the client and server may mutually authenticate themselves using client-side and server-side certificates, respectively. Though this feature may provide greater assurance, it does introduce a certain degree of vulnerability in that a user/client may not be adequately prepared to discern or evaluate bogus server certificates.

Validating Liveness

Liveness simply refers to whether a user attempting to perform an operation at time t_1 is the same user who was authenticated into the system at time t_0. For example, after logging in, the user may conduct several operations and then attempt to conduct an operation that the service deems high-value. The service may thus decide to initiate re-authentication to ensure that the user attempting to conduct the high-valued operation is in fact the same authenticated user. Though this approach does not protect against rogue users, it does augment the service's audit trail.

Java Authentication and Authorization Service

Java and J2EE technology today is being used in large-scale, multi-user environments. This requires the ability to deal with multiple users concurrently, as well as handle their credentials, privileges, and identities in a consistent, manageable fashion. The Java Authentication and Authorization Services (JAAS) provides a framework and a standard API for user authentication, privilege management, and credential verification for the Java 2 and J2EE platforms. This section provides an overview of JAAS and its importance in securing enterprise applications.

In the Java platform, security policies can place fine-grained access control upon protected resources by verifying the identity of code source and who signed it. However, this model lacks enforcing control based on the user who runs the code. The code-centric model is important for executing code that is downloaded from other sources, as is common in browser-based applications. However, most applications are used in a multi-user environment and serve the needs of a wide audience with different levels of access privileges. JAAS complements the code-centric model by providing user-based authentication and authorization on top of the existing Java security model.

Subjects, Principals, and Credentials

In JAAS, a user or a computing service that desires to access protected resources or other protected computing services is represented as a subject. A subject interacts with a computing service using an identifier and will typically have a unique identifier with each service it interacts with. The JAAS specification calls this identifier a *name.* The term *principal* represents a name associated with a subject. A subject therefore comprises a set of principals as shown here:

```
public interface Principal {
    public String getName();
}
public final class Subject {
    public Set getPrincipals() { }
}
```

During the authentication process, a user or a computing service (subject) presents some form of evidence to another computing service (another subject) to prove its identity. The credentials provided during authentication may be userid/password and/or digital certificates, signed data, and so on. The JAAS security model takes into account that most services rely on named principals to access protected resources. Principals are associated with a subject once it successfully authenticates to a service.

Services that implement a conventional access control mechanism define a set of protected resources that may be accessed by a named principal. Principals in large-scale enterprise applications may use verifiable public key as identifier to ensure a unique, indisputable identity. In addition to principals, services may also require the subject to present added security-related attributes that may include password, PIN, public key certificates, and so on, as part of the request to access the service. These attributes are known as credentials in the JAAS framework and are typically used for SSO operations. JAAS credentials can be any type of object. Therefore, existing and third-party implementation may be plugged into the framework. Credential implementation may reference data that may physically reside on a separate server or even in hardware devices like smart cards. A credential implementation may also delegate to third parties using its own delegation protocol.

JAAS credentials are of two types: public and private. Public credentials include a subject's public identity attributes like PKCS certificates that are accessible without requiring any permission. Private credentials include a subject's private security-related attributes such as PCKS private keys, password, and so on, that have access controls. Please refer to the JAAS API for further details on the *Subject* class.

Authentication

Each service may have an authentication mechanism that is specific to it. Therefore the security-related attributes required by each service may be different. The JAAS framework supports a flexible architecture that allows the plugging in of different authentication services (called LoginModules) to meet the security requirements of an application. This architecture creates a loose coupling between the applications and the authentication services, thus enabling modification or replacement of authentication services without affecting the existing applications.

JAAS authentication framework is based on pluggable authentication module (PAM) framework and therefore supports the notion of stacked LoginModules. The JAAS *LoginContext* class represents a Java implementation of the PAM framework as shown here:

```
public final class LoginContext {
    public LoginContext(String name) { }
    public void login() { }
    public void logout() { }
    public Subject getSubject() { }
}
public interface LoginModule {
    boolean login();
    boolean commit();
    boolean abort();
    boolean logout();
}
```

The *LoginContext* consults a configuration file to determine the list of configured *LoginModules*. A sample configuration file that identifies the *LoginModule*(s) is shown here:

```
GreaterCauseModules {com.gc.security.donor.DonorLoginModule required;}
```

Note the use of the *required* flag in the configuration file. Other possible values are *Requisite*, *Sufficient*, and *Optional*. These flags control the overall behavior of the authentication process. More information about these flags is available at http://java.sun.com/j2se/1.4.1/docs/api/javax/security/auth/login/Configuration.html.

The *LoginContext* is instantiated as follows:

```
LoginContext lc = new LoginContext ("GreaterCauseModules",
    new myCallbackHandler());
```

Objects implementing the *CallbackHandler* interface are used for performing the user interaction for obtaining the credentials required for successful authentication. This is because there are various ways of communicating with a user, and we need to keep the *LoginModule*(s) independent of the different types of user interactions.

JAAS performs the authentication steps in two phases:

- In the first phase, the *LoginContext*'s login method invokes the *login* method of each *LoginModule* specified in the configuration file. The *login* method of each *LoginModule* performs the authentication (for example, prompting/challenging the user for username and password). The *LoginModule*'s *login* method will return true or false (indicating success or failure, respectively), or it may throw a *LoginException*. In case of a failure, if an application decides to retry the authentication, then phase 1 is repeated.
- In the second phase, if the *LoginContext*'s overall authentication succeeded, then the *commit* method on each configured *LoginModule* is invoked. The *commit* method of the *LoginModule* will check its internal state to ensure if its own authentication succeeded.

Once it is verified that both the overall *LoginContext*'s authentication and the *LoginModule*'s authentication has succeeded, then the relevant principals (authenticated identities) and credentials are associated with the subject.

Authorization

JAAS authorization is accomplished by enforcing the appropriate access controls on the principals associated to the subject during the authentication process. Services based on the JAAS access control model define a set of protected resources and the means through which principals may access them. The JAAS policy is built on top of the Java 2 codesource-based security policy, forming a complete authorization scheme for the Java 2 runtime system. The following code snippet is a sample principal-based policy entry supported by JAAS:

```
grant Codebase "http://www.gc.com", Signedby "gcadmin",
   Principal com.gc.Principal "pHolmes"  {
      Permission com.gc.siteAdmin.AccessPermission "administrator"
           }
```

This example grants code loaded from the remote resource "http://www.gc.com", that has been digitally signed by "gcadmin", and executed by "pHolmes" permissions to administer the site. To be executed by "pHolmes", the subject associated with the current access control context (explained later in this section), must contain a principal of class com.gc.Principal, whose *getName* function returns "pHolmes".

Roles are treated as "named" principals by JAAS. Access controls can thus be applied to roles just like to any other principal, as shown in the following code snippet:

```
grant Codebase "http://www.gc.com", Signedby "gcadmin",
   Principal com.gc.Role "administrator"  {
      Permission com.gc.siteAdmin.AccessPermission "administrator"
           }
```

The JAAS authorization framework also allows for the *Principal* class in a particular policy entry to programmatically determine if the principal is "implied" by a given subject. In this scenario, the *Principal* class (specified in the policy entry) "implements" the *PrincipalComparator*, whose *implies* method is invoked when permissions are determined for a subject.

```
Public interface PrincipalComparator {
   boolean implies (Subject subject);
}
```

Role hierarchies may be realized in this manner where a specific role (such as com.gc.Role) implements the *PrincipalComparator* interface and returns "true" if a specified subject contains an "administrator" role principal.

Associating a Subject with an AccessControlContext The *java.lang.SecurityManager* is consulted any time an untrusted code attempts to access protected resources. To determine whether the subject has sufficient authority to access a protected resource, the *SecurityManager* delegates to *java.security.AccessController*, which ensures that the *AccessControlContext* contains sufficient permission to allow access to the resource. JAAS dynamically associates an authenticated subject to *AccessControlContext* by providing a *Subject.doAs* method.

After a service performs user authentication, and before protected resources can be accessed, the service can associate the subject with the current access control context. This is done by preparing the operation to be performed as a *java.security.PrivilegedAction* and then calling the static *Subject.doAs* method and passing it an authenticated subject and a *java.security.PrivilegedAction* object. The *doAs* method associates the subject with the current access control context and then invokes the *run* method from the *PrivilegedAction* object. The action thus executes as the specified subject. When security checks occur during this execution, the *SecurityManager* queries the JAAS policy and updates the current *AccessControlContext* with the permissions granted to the subject and the executing codesource, and then performs its regular permission checks. When the *PrivilegedAction* run method finally completes, the *doAs* method removes the subject from the current *AccessControlContext*, and returns the result back to the caller.

Federated Network Identity

Users accessing Internet-based services often use such services in ways that cater to their personal tastes and preferences. Each user *account* associates the user with his/her information that may include anything from personal preferences on web pages to more sensitive data such as credit card and bank account numbers. The network identity of the user is the complete set of all such information constituting the user's different accounts. However, in today's world, user accounts are scattered all over the Internet and the concept of a *portable* and *flexible* network identity is rare.

Project Liberty (http://www.projectliberty.org), a broad alliance of a wide spectrum of industries, attempts to address this issue through a series of technical specifications that can be used to realize a wide range of network-identity operations. Project Liberty implementations may ultimately provide a convenient and secure framework in which organizations may leverage new or existing relationships with customers and partners allowing for new business opportunities and increased customer satisfaction. Project Liberty provides a standards-based approach to network identity management. Several products supporting Liberty Alliance 1.1 specifications are now available—a complete list can be obtained at http://www.projectliberty.org. The solution providers include RSA Security, Entrust, Sun Microsystems, Oblix, Novell, and many others. This section primarily discusses key concepts of Project Liberty's *Federated Network Identity* architecture.

In a federated identity system, it is crucial that the following key objectives are realized:

- The privacy and security of personal information.
- Participating entities must be able to manage trusted relationships using a standards-based approach rather than a one-off solution.

- The realization of single sign-on standards that allow decentralized authentication and authorization of users, that is, each service provider must be able to authenticate and authorize users without having to forward user credentials to other non-essential third parties.

These objectives are realized by establishing circles of trust, an agreement common to all participants. It is based on such circles of trust that operational agreements and trust relationships are formed between service providers and users. Users can choose to federate (share) their local identities, and include them into circles of trust. A circle of trust thus becomes a federation of trusted participants that provide a seamless environment in which to conduct secure transactions. Figure 3-5 illustrates circles of trust within a federated network identity framework.

Liberty Architecture

This section provides a high-level overview of the Liberty architecture, its components, and its processes.

Definitions

The provider definitions are as follows:

- **Service provider** Organizations providing Internet-based services. These may include virtually anything with a web presence, including businesses, portals, banks, media portals, government, and so on.
- **Identity provider** A type of service provider that offers identity-related services that are the basis for forming trust circles between affiliated service providers. An example of an identity provider may be a trusted system that manages employee identities across an organization and its subsidiaries.

The Liberty-enabled implementations must support the following functional requirements:

- **Identity federation** Protocols and stipulations that ensure users, service providers, and identity providers within a circle of trust are notified when identities are federated and de-federated (that is, added and removed from circles of trust). These protocols also mandate that all service and identity providers provide each of its users a list of the user's federated identities at that provider.
- **Authentication** The authentication processes in a networked identity federation requires that the following minimal scenarios be supported:
  - Navigating between identity and service providers (to exchange user-related information.
  - Preserving confidentiality, authenticity, and integrity of any information exchanged between user agents and identity providers, or between identity and service providers.
  - Presentating verifiable form(s) of identity by the Identity provider to the user before the user provides credentials or personal information to that provider.

- Enabling service providers to request the identity provider to re-authenticate a user using the same or a different authentication class.

- **Support for pseudonyms** The ability to support pseudonyms (that is, aliases, assumed names, and so on) that are unique to each identity federation, across all identity and service providers.
- **Global logout** Support for "logout" notifications (on user logout) to related identity and service providers with whom the user has established a federated identity.

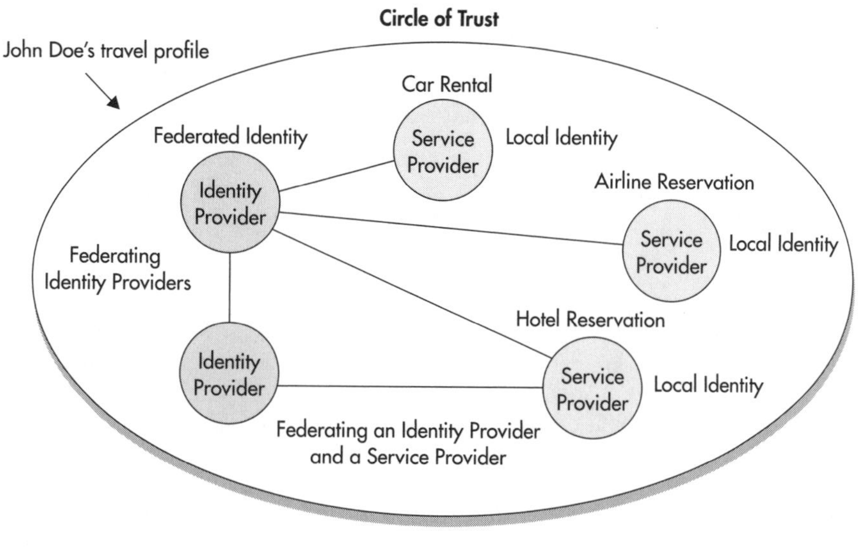

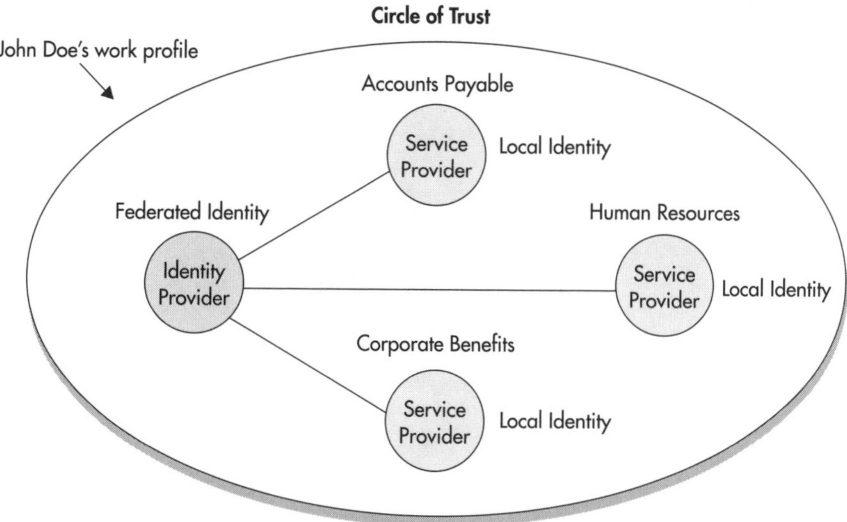

Figure 3-5 *Circles of trust*

Figure 3-6 illustrates the overall Liberty architecture. The Liberty architecture is based on three orthogonal components:

- **Web redirection** Enables Liberty entities such as service provider, identity providers, and user agents to interact over today's installed http-based environments. On attempting to access a service hosted at a service provider, the user is first redirected to the identity provider for sign-on, subsequent to which the user is redirected back to the service provider.
- **Web services** Liberty protocols detail various interactions that occur between two or more Liberty-enabled providers. Each set of interactions is based on RPC-like call semantics conveyed via Simple Object Access Protocol (refer to Chapter 8 for details on RPC-oriented SOAP messages). SOAP is a well-recognized specification for conducting RPC-like interactions using XML over HTTP and is thus useful for realizing Liberty-specific protocols and orchestrations.
- **Schemas and metadata** A set of data formats employed by Liberty entities to exchange provider-specific information and other identity artifacts among each other. Please refer to section 5.3 of the Liberty Architecture Overview [Version 1.1] document for further information.

Single Sign-On and Identity Federation

The first time that users use an identity provider to log in to a service provider, they must be provided with an option to federate their existing local identity on that service provider with the identity provider. This allows the identity provider to use the user's federated identity in a

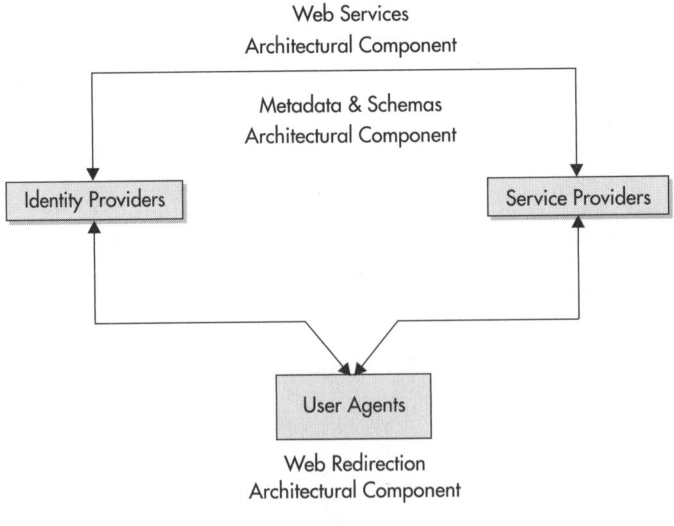

Figure 3-6 *Liberty architecture*

confidential manner for single sign-on purposes with service providers within the same circle of trust. This is explained further in this section in conjunction with Figure 3-7.

In a federated identity system it is essential that users must be uniquely identified and asserted across all service and identity providers. A quick solution that comes to mind is the use of a Global ID (global identifier). However, implementing global identifiers that are not provider specific and are "portable" across services is a significant challenge. Furthermore global identities pose risks—if they are compromised, malicious users can gain access into virtually every provider in the federation.

As an alternative to global identifiers, Liberty employs explicit *trust relationships* that are created when a user decides to federate his/her identity between an identity and service provider. When federating a user's identity, opaque *handles* (also know as name identifiers) instead of actual account identifiers are used to uniquely resolve users. An explicit trust relationship is created when the user chooses to federate his/her identity the first time a user logs in to a service provider using an identity provider. Figure 3-7 illustrates the creation of handles.

As shown in Figure 3-7, upon identity federation, the user directories of the identity provider and the service provider make use of opaque handles to reference the user account on either provider. In this way, the *real* identity of the user is concealed and the usage of a specific alias is restricted only to this link as other links may use different aliases. This mechanism securely establishes a federated user identity without the use of a single global identifier.

Federation Scenarios

Based on the federated identity mechanism discussed in the preceding, it is possible to realize three useful scenarios.

Federating Single Identity Provider, Multiple Service Providers A user may use a single identity provider to access multiple service providers. To allow the service providers to exchange information about the user, the user must explicitly federate the two service provider identities. The following hold true in this scenario:

- Service providers cannot directly exchange information about a user identity federated through an identity provider. The service providers may only communicate with the identity provider individually.

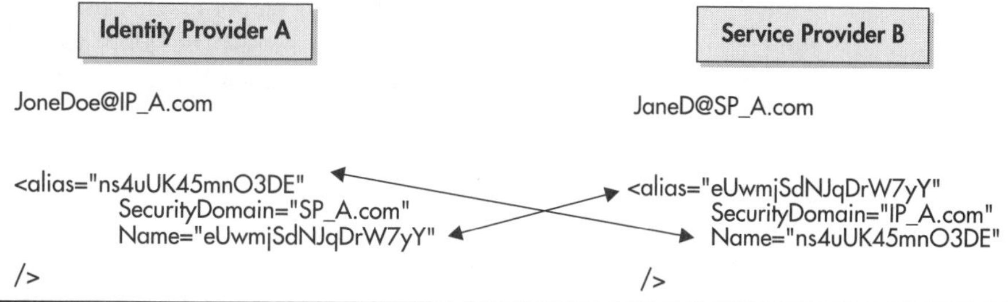

Figure 3-7 *Identity federation between an identity provider and a service provider*

- The identity provider holds individual/isolated relationships with each service provider (through separate user handles), thus ensuring privacy and confidentiality of user information.
- User can sign on to multiple service providers using a single identity provider.

Federating Multiple Identity Providers, Single Service Provider A user may use multiple identity providers to access a single service provider. A federated identity between multiple identity providers and a service provider can be very useful if a user requires access to a designated service from multiple locations. For example, when a user *switches* from a corporate intranet to the Internet, or to a mobile device, the user may typically use different identity providers, each within a different circle of trust in order to access the service.

Federating Multiple Identity Providers In order for the user to avoid having to "remember" to federate a new service with multiple identity providers a user may federate identity providers together allowing them to access each other's information. Thus when a new service is made accessible to a primary identity provider, all other identity providers privy to that information may be used to access the service. When a user's identity is federated across many identity providers, an explicit link exists between each identity on different identity providers, forming a *trust chain*. Providers cannot *skip* identities in a trust chain to access services or request information because user identity must be checked at each step.

The following are issues and risks are associated with federating identity providers:

- Liberty protocols do not dictate the underlying semantics of federated relationships. Reasons for not doing so could be due to the variable factors that often drive the design and implementation of such semantics. Such factors may include organizational agreements between providers, capabilities of the Liberty implementations deployed, political influences, and legal liabilities.
- How trust relationships between identity providers are established, and how those relationships are represented to service providers, are unspecified. Organizations that host identity providers must define policies that govern such trust relationships and the means for representing them.
- Agreements and policies that govern circles of trust must also address how federation failures are communicated to users.
- Creating several local identities with many service providers and/or identity providers and then federating them constitutes a security risk when identity providers possess reusable user credentials such as a username and password. Such reusable credentials can be used to impersonate the user at every service provider federated with that account.

The Liberty approach is *more* secure than a global identifier in the following ways:

- If an identity provider in a circle of trust is compromised, the rest of the members in the trust circle need to just record the incident and "sever" links to that provider to re-establish secure access. Since the identities compromised at that provider are only useful to access other providers at adjacent links, only the adjacent providers need to be *cleansed* of any reference to compromised identities. In contrast, if a global unique identifier is compromised, *every* provider in the circle of trust is affected, and hence recovery becomes a more arduous task.

- In the Liberty network identity architecture, information about a user may be "spread-out" over multiple identity providers in a trust circle. Hence if a provider is compromised, only the user information at that provider is exposed. In contrast, if a global unique identifier is compromised potentially all personal information of a user may be exposed, which constitutes a serious privacy violation.

Defederation

Users have the ability to terminate federations, or defederate identities. Defederation is the process of terminating the validity of a federated identity at a service or identity provider. The defederation process may be initiated at the identity or service provider. When defederation is initiated at an identity provider, the identity provider is stating to the service provider that it will no longer provide user identity information to the service provider, and it will no longer respond to any requests by the service provider made on behalf of the user. When defederation is initiated at a service provider, the service provider is stating to the identity provider that that user has requested that the identity provider no longer provide the user identity information to the service provider and that the service provider will no longer ask the identity provider to do anything on behalf of the user.

Caching Overview

A typical enterprise application spans multiple tiers and may be distributed over several machines. Data may be accessed from any of these tiers based on the application design. For example, in a multi-tiered J2EE application, data from the persistent store will usually be accessed in the EJB tier. An application with high transaction volume and with a need to provide short response time to the clients may have multiple machines in the EJB tier accessing a single data store. In such applications, access to the data store can become very expensive because generally the backend data stores run on high-performance expensive hardware and software. Even when expensive hardware and software is used, the system may not easily scale when more users and information are added to the data store since the amount of information to be retrieved could grow exponentially. In order to provide a scalable solution, a cache should be incorporated in the enterprise applications. A cache provides the following benefits:

- Reduces the number of network calls by minimizing calls to the data store
- Reduces application latency
- Improves response time of the application

Common solutions offered today include the following:

- A web-tier cache is generally used to cache HTML pages or JSP fragments and sits in the web tier in front of the web server. More and more applications are moving toward JSP fragment caching. Some vendors provide custom tags for caching JSP fragments, which enables caching content produced within the body of the tag. The contents cached can be the final view of the content, or simply the values calculated for variables. The latter is useful when the presentation is independent of the computed data. The JSP Tag Library for Edge Side Includes, or JESI (JSR 128 at www.jcp.org), is a specification for a custom tag library that developers can use to automatically generate ESI code (ESI is a markup language that enables partial page caching for HTML fragments) using JSP syntax. For more on the ESI standard, refer to http://www.esi.org.
- An application-level cache is generally useful in applications that access data store directly in servlets, JSPs, session beans, or entity beans with bean-managed persistence. The cache then sits between the application and the data store. In this case, a JCACHE specification (JSR 107 at www.jcp.org)–compliant cache can be used to provide caching of Java objects once the objects are retrieved from the data store and transformed to its appropriate Java type. JCACHE standardizes caching of Java objects and provides for cache expiration, spooling, and cache consistency. For entity beans with container-managed persistence, the containers employ appropriate caching strategies. Vendors may provide some control over the caching strategy by using vendor-specific deployment descriptors.
- Some container vendors offer EJBs classified as read-only entity beans. This allows caching of entity beans that were marked as read-only. The configuration of caching attributes are provided via the vendor-specific deployment descriptor. Vendors also provide proprietary API for invalidating cached data. This solution is vendor specific and therefore not portable. It is expected that read-only entity beans with container-managed persistence will become part of the post-EJB 2.1 standard.
- Data stores also implement sophisticated caches. For example, an RDBMS will have a database cache to speed up database access and minimize the expensive disk block access and look ups. In this section, we discuss only application-level caches.

Application Data Caching

J2EE technology provides infrastructure support to enable developers to build multi-tiered, distributed applications using EJBs. In most multi-tiered applications, the most expensive resource from a price and access perspective is a data source such as an RDBMS. In such applications, it is beneficial to architect and design an application-level data cache.

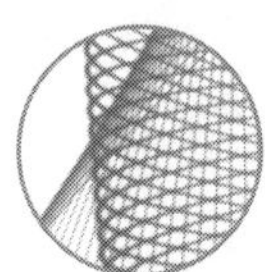

NOTE

It is most beneficial if an architect adheres to Java standards such as JCACHE when designing and implementing a cache.

Most application being built today have two types of data access needs:

- **Transactional data** In this case, the application reads and writes data to the data store.
- **Read only data** In this case, the application only reads data from the data store.

Transactional data does not lend itself well to caching. Generally, the frequency of changes to data causes too many cache invalidations. The frequency of updates also does not allow for a stable cache. This results in too many cache misses and defeats the purpose of caching. Thus, it is not a good practice to have a cache of transactional data. This is also true for any data where the frequency of updates can be measured in seconds and minutes rather than hours and days. In this scenario, the services offered by a J2EE container and the contracts specified for a container-managed persistence bean will be adequate. In cases where data is read-only, or it is updated less frequently, caching application data can provide good benefits. Resources permitting, read-only data is a prime candidate for caching in memory.

Cache Architecture

It is very important that the cache architecture clearly defines the objectives of a cache up front. There are several important issues to consider:

- **Distributed caching** Is a distributed cache needed? Is a hierarchical/tiered cache required?
- **Capacity planning** What is the size of the cache?
  - **Caching algorithm** Which algorithm to use in order to purge a cached object: algorithm based on LRU (least recently used), frequency of usage, or LRU and frequency combined?
  - **Cache population** Define process for loading the cache. Is there a cache priming process like populating the cache in a servlet's *init()* method?
  - **Cached data invalidation** Define process for invalidating a cache when data changes in a data store and define process for propagating this change to other JVMs in a distributed caching scheme.

Cached Data Invalidation in a Distributed Cache

When an object is in memory, its corresponding image can be changed on disk, or it can be changed by another thread in memory. In this scenario, the object needs to be purged from the cache. The object can either be read back immediately into the memory or read into memory the next time it is requested. In a distributed cache, invalidation is more complicated. An object may be in several distributed JVMs, in which case, if an object in the cache is made dirty then all the caches in a distributed caching topology need to be notified. Similarly, if the object is changed on the disk then all the caches need to be notified. JMS can be used to provide this notification and synchronization between distributed caches. J2EE offers a mature network communications infrastructure and is designed from the ground up to support distributed computing, therefore it is well suited for a distributed cache. Vendors such as spiritsoft offer caching frameworks based on JCache, which allows users to implement multi-tiered caching solutions using JMS for intercache communication. SpiritCache from spiritsoft offers such services as clustering, fault-tolerance, and XA transactions.

Desirable features for a cache will include the following:

- Distributed cache across JVMs
- JMS-based invalidation and refresh
- A CacheFactory to handle cache creation via specialized data-aware cache-creator classes, such as *Named cache*
- Cache priming or bulk loading at a predefined time
- Built-in statistics via ValueObject (see Figure 3-8) objects to help in invalidation and cache sizing based on the following:
  - Frequency of use (accessed how many times?)
  - Last accessed (when was it last accessed?)
  - Time bound expiration (how long in the memory?)

Figure 3-8 depicts important elements of a cache.

The possible interactions between different cache objects are as follows:

- The *CacheFactory* is used to create a named cache such as an instance of *TokenCache*. The factory object creates a *CacheManager* object and associates it with the *TokenCache*.
- The *TokenCache* implementation may use a *HashMap* object in which case we can use a key/value pair (that is, a concrete implementation of *ValueObjectKey*/*ValueObject*) for storing and retrieving objects. *TokenCache* is implemented as a Singleton object. Appropriate synchronization semantics should be associated with the cache.
- The *ValueObject* implementation maintains a reference to the cache that contains it. This reference can be used to inform the cache when a *ValueObject* is invalidated or updated. The *ValueObject* is an abstract class providing the base implementation for certain methods. The *TokenCache* is populated with the *ValueObject* subclass (*TokenObject*), as shown in Figure 3-8.
- The factory associates a *CacheEventListener* object (a concrete implementation of this interface could be a JMS-based listener subscribing to a JMS topic associated with the cache) with the *CacheManager*. This event listener responds to events such as INVALIDATE and RELOAD.
- The factory associates a *CacheItemCreator* object (implemented by a concrete class *TokenCacheItemCreator*) with the *CacheManager*.
- When the *get* method of *TokenCache* is called, and if there is a *miss*, the *CacheManager* calls the *create* method of *TokenCacheItemCreator* object. This will load the data from the data store.

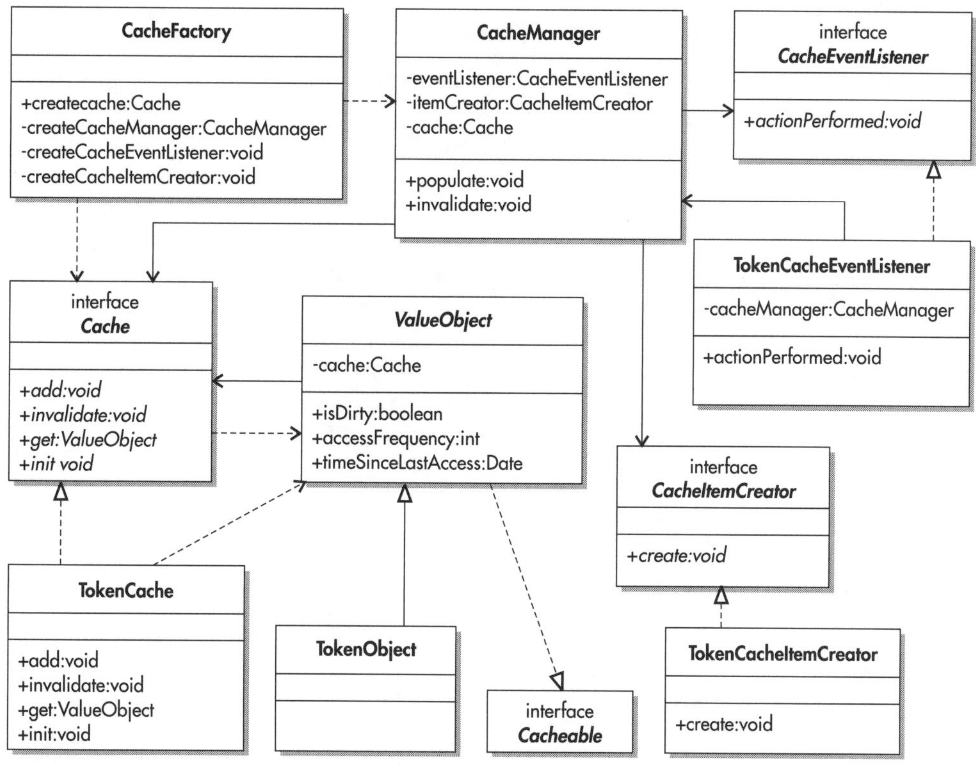

Figure 3-8 *Elements of a cache*

- When a *TokenCache* object is updated by a client, or when an object is invalidated, the *CacheManager* sends an invalidate notification to all the caches in a distributed caching topology. This is done by posting an INVALIDATE event for that object to the JMS topic.
- An INVALIDATE event will invoke the event listener's *actionPerformed* method, which will instruct the *CacheManager* of the invalidation. The *CacheManager* will in turn call the invalidate method of the *TokenCache*. An invalidation results in the removal of the corresponding item from all the caches.

Cache Optimization

When designing an application-level cache, one needs to optimize cache hits. A cache *hit* means that the data was found in the cache and hence the request can be serviced from the cache. If there is cache *miss*, the client needs to be serviced from the data store. The bigger the cache size, the better the chance of a cache hit. An architect needs to optimize the application cache size such that the cache hit is at a ratio above the acceptable threshold. Since applications have only finite resources available, the cache size is limited by the amount of memory available to the application. It is advisable to build a prototype cache and simulate the cache hits. With Java, it is best to fix a cache size and not let it grow above a certain threshold. This works well with the Java memory model and garbage collection since memory is not given back to the operating system even after the garbage collector frees it. Fixing the cache size, instead of constant readjustment, will therefore prevent the operating system process from growing out of bounds.

To put a limit on the cache size implies creating a purging algorithm for keeping the cache optimally configured. The most common purging algorithms are LRU (least recently used) and access-frequency-based (popularity-based). In the LRU case, an object is purged because it was accessed the longest time ago. In the access-frequency case, an object is purged based on the number of times the object was accessed. For example an object with three accesses is purged before an object with five accesses. A more generalized algorithm is to use a combination of LRU and access-frequency. The combination can give each parameter a different weight. The weight is determined by the data access pattern of the particular application:

```
Weight = accessFrequency * exponent ((-decayConstant) * timeSinceLastAccess);
```

- **accessFrequency** Number of times the object was accessed since it has been in the cache.
- **timeSinceLastAccess** Time elapsed since the object has was last accessed.
- **decayConstant** This is normalized to be between 0 and 1. If *accessFrequency* is to be given more weight, set *decayConstant* close to 0. If *timeSinceLastAccess* is to be given more weight, set *decayConstant* close to 1. Adjust *decayConstant* for getting the right value based on cache optimization needs.

Summary

Although this chapter introduced the significant aspects of architecture as it pertains to the J2EE platform, the actual architecture of the sample application is gradually built throughout this book using a use case–driven approach. In the chapters to come, we will incrementally build out each use case in the presentation and business tier employing an MVC-based architecture. Central to our discussion are the various design patterns that can be leveraged to provide consistent implementation across all use cases.

Application security is another important aspect of the overall application design for controlling access to protected resources. Security is pervasive in an application, at the same time the security must be incorporated in a manner that offers a high degree of loose coupling between the security components and the components that implement the business logic. A change in the access control mechanism should have little or no effect on the business logic. Classifying the security requirements in terms of channel security, network identity management, and authentication and authorization offers us the opportunity to clearly discern the interaction points between the application and the security infrastructure. This further assists in the creation of guidelines that are helpful in the evaluation of third-party products that may provide either part of the solution or the complete solution.

References

[RUP] *The Rational Unified Process, An Introduction, Second Edition* by Philippe Kruchten (Addison-Wesley, 2000)
[Core] *Core J2EE Patterns* by Deepak Alur et al. (Prentice-Hall, 2001)
[Gof] *Design Patterns* by Erich Gamma et al. (Addison-Wesley, 1995)
[Kruchten] *The 4+1 View Model of Architecture* by Phillippe Kruchten (IEEE Software 12 (6), November 1995)

PART II

Design and Construction

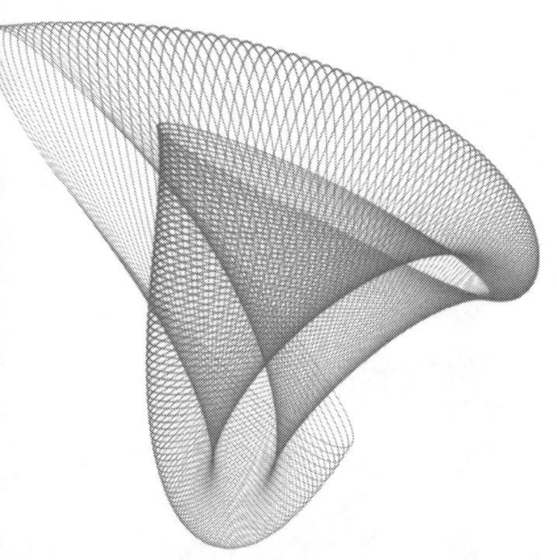

CHAPTER

4

Struts-Based Application Architecture

IN THIS CHAPTER:

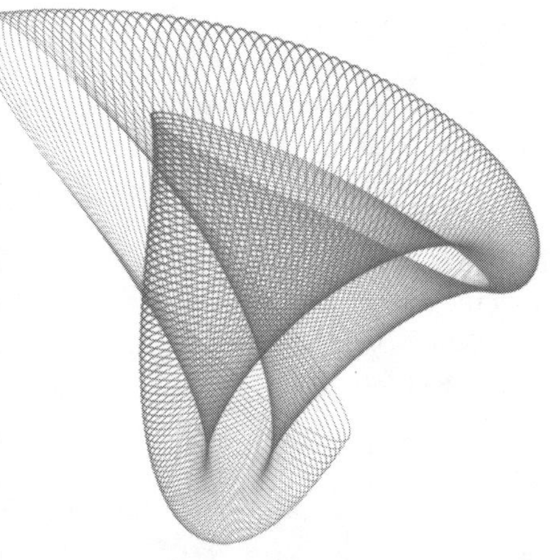

For enterprise software development, we constantly strive to use standards-based platforms and software. Standards-based software offers the flexibility of developing solutions that are interoperable, use industry best practices, and provide the option of selecting the infrastructure from any vendor without the risk of breaking the architecture. JSP, Servlet, and EJB specifications, among others, have enabled the programmers to declaratively obtain system-level services from the implementations of these standards; the result is that the developers have been able to experience large productivity gains by focusing on business problems rather than trying to deal with system-level services such as transaction, security, and resource management.

Standards-based development factors common system functionality into core platform services that use proven design patterns and best practices; this creates a foundation framework on which custom functionality can be built. However, one area where a standard was not prescribed, for an infrastructure-level service, was the mapping of client-side actions (or events) to server-side method invocation on business components using the HTTP protocol, the corresponding navigation semantics, and HTML forms processing. The challenge of assimilating a request/response-based HTTP protocol in an event-based MVC (Model-View-Controller) pattern has resulted in another industry of solution providers. During the early years of J2EE, an enterprise application architect who was dealing with large projects involving a large number of Web pages was expected to roll his or her own version of a presentation framework that implemented an MVC-like architectural style; as you will appreciate, this was no small feat to accomplish. The more recent JavaServer Faces standard addresses issues such as representing UI components and their state management, defining navigational semantics, event handling, forms validation, internalization support, and so on. However, the Jarkarta open source project 'Struts' has already achieved the mind share and acceptance from enterprise architects as a viable MVC-based presentation framework that supports much of the functionality offered by JavaServer Faces. At the time of this writing, the expectation is that Struts-based implementations will use JavaServer Faces components for component-level functionality within a page, but continue to use the their own application model for dealing with higher level functionality, such as forms and actions. For more information on JavaServer Faces, refer to http://java.sun.com/j2ee/javaserverfaces. The future direction of Struts is to transition over to JavaServer Pages Standard Tag Library (JSTL) and JavaServer Faces tags.

Another framework that is worth mentioning is the XMLC-based Barracuda Presentation Framework. XMLC is an XML compiler that converts document templates, including HTML, cHTML, WML, XHTML, and XML, into Java objects that implement the DOM interface. Java programs can manipulate the DOM representations of these documents on the server side by merging the state information from the application's model into the DOM representations. Once the DOM is modified, it can be serialized into the source document type or other XML-compliant format that represents the response; this enables a high degree of separation between the presentation and the business logic. A web production engineer (a.k.a. form designer), therefore, works completely independent of the application engineer, who depends only on finding and replacing tags with certain ID and class attributes set by the production engineer; XMLC generates access methods for these special tags, and these access methods serve as a formal interface between production engineer and the application engineer. You can get more information on Barracuda by visiting http://www.enhydra.org.

In this chapter, we define the requirements of a robust presentation framework and simultaneously discuss how these requirements are implemented in the Struts framework. We also explore the design patterns implemented by Struts and the semantics of the controller and associated helper components, and we examine various Struts-related configuration resources; this knowledge will be useful when designing components that will interact with the framework, and when there is a need for extending the framework for accommodating special needs of a project. Struts-based application architecture with practical examples will be covered in Chapter 5 where we have identified several Struts-related patterns that can be used as implementation templates in implementing complex behaviors. This chapter cites several examples, where appropriate, from Chapter 5. We cover "under the hood" semantics of Struts to gain a better understanding of how Struts is architectured, and what possibilities exist should you decide to extend the framework; as such, only limited coverage of examples have been provided in this chapter, with the rest of the discussion deferred to Chapter 5.

Struts as a Presentation Framework

This section discusses some of the most common requirements that are essential for a viable presentation framework. Along with identifying the requirements, we map these to the features offered by Struts and corresponding usage scenarios.

MVC Implementation

The MVC (Model-View-Controller) architecture is a way of decomposing an application into three parts: the model, the view, and the controller. It was originally applied in the graphical user interaction model of input, processing, and output.

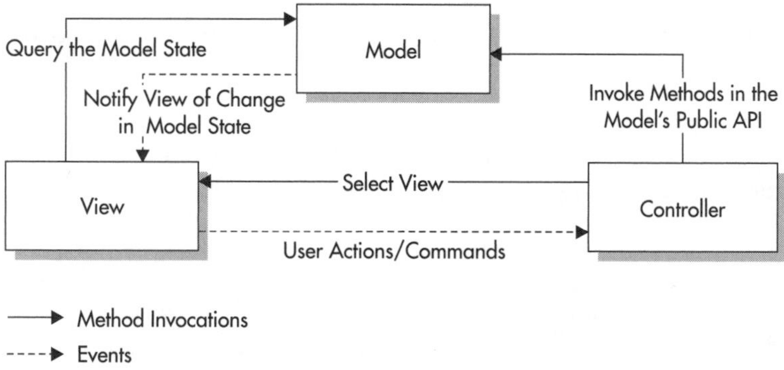

Model A model represents an application's data and contains the logic for accessing and manipulating that data. Any data that is part of the persistent state of the application should reside in the model objects. The services that a model exposes must be generic enough to support a variety of clients. By glancing at the model's public method list, it should be easy to understand how to control the model's behavior. A model groups related data and operations for providing a specific service; these groups of operations wrap and abstract the functionality of the business process being modeled. A model's interface exposes methods for accessing and updating the state of the model and for executing complex processes encapsulated inside the model. Model services are accessed by the controller for either querying or effecting a change in the model state. The model notifies the view when a state change occurs in the model.

View The view is responsible for rendering the state of the model. The presentation semantics are encapsulated within the view, therefore model data can be adapted for several different kinds of clients. The view modifies itself when a change in the model is communicated to the view. A view forwards user input to the controller.

Controller The controller is responsible for intercepting and translating user actions into command objects [Gof] that invoke methods on the model's public API. The controller is responsible for selecting the next view based on user actions and the outcome of model operations.

In a J2EE-based application, MVC architecture is used for separating business layer functionality represented by JavaBeans or EJBs (the model) from the presentation layer functionality represented by JSPs (the view) using an intermediate servlet-based controller. However, a controller design must accommodate input from various types of clients, including HTTP requests from web clients, WML from wireless clients, and XML-based documents from suppliers and business partners. For the HTTP Request/Response paradigm, incoming HTTP requests are routed to a central controller, which in turn interprets and delegates the request to the appropriate request handlers. This is also referred to as MVC Type-II (Model 2) Architecture. Request handlers are hooks into the framework provided to the developers for implementing request-specific logic that interacts with the model. Depending on the outcome of this interaction, the controller can determine the next view for generating the correct response.

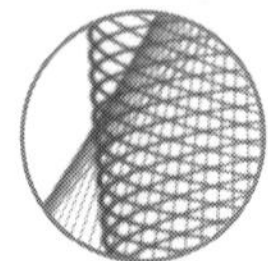

NOTE

In this book, the term Request Handler is used interchangeably with Action class and its subclasses.

The following is an illustration of the MVC implementation in Struts. Struts implements the MVC pattern using the *Service to Worker* pattern [Core]; we discuss this further in the section "Struts MVC Semantics."

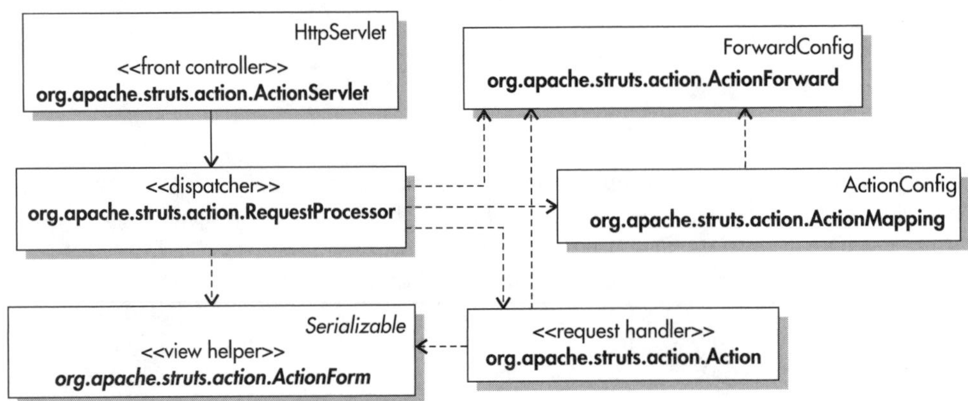

The following discusses the interactions depicted in the preceding illustration.

Controller

In Struts, the Controller is implemented by the *ActionServlet* class. The *ActionServlet* is declared in web.xml (the deployment descriptor) as follows:

```
<servlet>
    <servlet-name>action</servlet-name>
    <servlet-class>org.apache.struts.action.ActionServlet</servlet-class>
</servlet>
```

All request URIs with the pattern **.do* are mapped to this servlet in the deployment descriptor as follows:

```
<servlet-mapping>
    <servlet-name>action</servlet-name>
    <url-pattern>*.do</url-pattern>
</servlet-mapping>
```

A request URI that matches this pattern will have the following form:

http://www.my_site_name.com/mycontext/action_Name.do.

The preceding mapping is called *extension mapping*, however, you can also specify path mapping where a pattern ends with /*, as shown here:

```
<servlet-mapping>
    <servlet-name>action</servlet-name>
    <url-pattern>/do/*</url-pattern>
</servlet-mapping>
```

A request URI that matches this pattern will have the following form: http://www.my_site_name.com/mycontext/do/action_Name.

In Struts 1.1, the Struts required configurations are loaded in the *ActionServlet.init()* method. The configurations control the behavior of the framework; this includes mapping of URIs to request handlers (discussed in section "Model Interaction with Request Handlers"), configuring message resources, providing access to external resources via plug-ins, and so on. In fact, processing of incoming requests actually occur in the *RequestProcessor* to which *ActionServlet* delegates all the input requests.

Dispatcher

All incoming requests are delegated by the controller to the dispatcher, which is the *org.apache.struts.action.RequestProcessor* object.

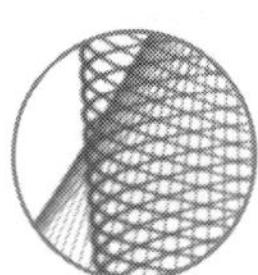

NOTE

The behavior of the dispatcher, and the behavior of the request handlers that the dispatcher interacts with, is controlled via a configuration file struts–config.xml. Various aspects of this configuration file are explained throughout this chapter.

The *RequestProcessor* examines the request URI for an action identifier, creates a request handler instance using the information in the *ActionMapping* configuration object (explained in the next section), and calls the *requesthandler.*execute method. The *execute* method of the request handler is responsible for interacting with the application model. Depending on the outcome, the request handler will return an *ActionForward* configuration object (*ActionForward* is the runtime representation of the `<forward>` element and is explained in the section "Navigation Using ActionForward") to the *RequestProcessor.* The *RequestProcessor* will use the *ActionForward* object for invoking the next view by calling either *RequestDispatcher.forward* or *response .sendRedirect*, depending on the configuration.

Command Pattern Using ActionMapping

Struts provides a declarative way to specify the mapping between the servlet path in the request URI and an appropriate request handler using XML syntax. This implementation is very similar to the command pattern [Gof]. The following snippet is from the struts-config.xml file; these declarations are used for creating an *ActionMapping* configuration object, which is the runtime representation of the `<action>` element.

```
<action-mappings>
    <action path="/PortalAllianceRegistration"
            type="com.gc.prez.admin.PortalAllianceRegistrationAction"
            name="PortalAllianceRegistrationForm"
            scope="session"
            validate="false">
        <forward name="ShowPage" path="/2_1_PortalAllianceRegistration.jsp"/>
        <forward name="EnterPortalID" path="/2_3A_EnterPortalID.jsp"/>
        <forward name="success" path="/2_SiteAdministratorServicesMainPage.jsp"/>
    </action>
</action-mappings>
```

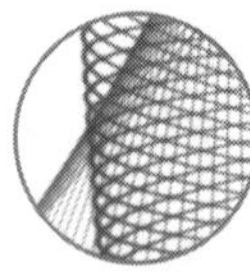

NOTE

All examples used in this chapter are from Chapter 5. Should you need to explore the examples in parallel (not necessary), please refer to the accompanying source distribution for fully functional code.

The following briefly explains the attributes used in the preceding declaration:

path The context relative path in the HTTP request that is used for identifying this action mapping.

type Class name that will be used for creating an instance of the request handler for handling this request.

name The logical name of a JavaBean, also called a form-bean, that will be used to hold form data. The form-bean will be saved in the specified scope using this name.

scope Request or session scope for saving the form-bean.

Dynamic URL Generation

Dynamic URL generation for the *action* attribute using the custom *org.apache.struts .taglib.html.FormTag* (explained further in Chapter 5) will protect the HTML documents from being adversely impacted as a result of change of context path or `<url-pattern>`. For a **.do* URL pattern, the custom FormTag `<html:form action="/editCustomerProfile?customerType=preferred">` will dynamically generate an HTML `<form>` tag with the *action* attribute containing the following server-relative URL:

```
<form action="/contextPath/editCustomerProfile.do?customerType=preferred"/>
```

The path attribute shown in the preceding snippet maps to the `action` attribute of the HTML `<form>` element. The declarative specifications prevent hard coding of mappings in the code base and enable convenient visualization of how servlet path specifications in HTML forms are mapped to instances of request handlers; in addition, application behavior and navigation semantics can be changed by simply altering the action mappings. A request handler is a subclass of the Struts-provided Action class.

Using the *name* attribute, an action mapping can declaratively specify a JavaBean whose properties will hold the parameters from the HTTP request; this JavaBean is subclassed from the *ActionForm* class. The *name* in the action mapping declaration is a unique identifier using which the instances of *ActionForm* classes are stored in the specified scope. The *ActionForm* subclass is declared in the struts-config.xml file using the `<form-beans>` tag as follows.

```
<form-bean  name="PortalAllianceRegistrationForm "
       type="packageName.PortalAllianceRegistrationForm "/>
```

Model Interaction with Request Handlers

A subclass of *Action* is used as an adaptor between incoming requests and the model. The *Action* subclass, also called the request handler, is created specific to every request. The base *Action* class provides common functions for accessing framework-related resources and methods for saving errors detected by the *execute(...)* method of its subclass. The errors are subsequently extracted and displayed in the HTML form using the custom *org.apache.struts.taglib.html.ErrorsTag* as explained in the section "Displaying Errors with ErrorsTag." *The execute(...)* method of a request handler should contain control flow for dealing with request parameters and the associated *ActionForm*, it should encapsulate model interaction semantics, and it should provide the next view based on the outcome of model operations. Request handlers are cached by the *RequestProcessor* when first created, and subsequently made available to other incoming requests; as such, request handlers must not contain user-specific state information; also, request handlers must synchronize access to resources that require serialized access. More discussion on request handlers is available in the section "Request Handler Semantics."

The following is a simple request handler *PortalAllianceRegistrationAction*. Refer to the GreaterCause directory in the accompanying source distribution for complete code listing.

```
public class PortalAllianceRegistrationAction extends Action {
    public ActionForward execute( ActionMapping mapping, ActionForm form,
    HttpServletRequest req, HttpServletResponse res ) throws Exception {
        PortalAllianceRegistrationForm regForm =
                             ( PortalAllianceRegistrationForm )form;
        String action = regForm.getAction();
        if ( action.equals( "Create" ) )
        { return ( createRegistration( mapping, form, req, res ) ); }
        else if ( action.equals( "Update" ) ) {
            return ( updateRegistration( mapping, form, req, res ) );
        }
        else if ( action.equals( "View" ) )
        { return ( viewRegistration( mapping, form, req, res ) ); }
        else { return null; }
    }
    public ActionForward createRegistration( ActionMapping mapping,
    ActionForm form, HttpServletRequest req,
    HttpServletResponse res ) throws Exception {
    ..
    ..
    //return an ActionForward object for displaying the next view
    }
    public ActionForward updateRegistration( ActionMapping mapping,
    ActionForm form,
    HttpServletRequest req, HttpServletResponse res ) throws Exception {
    ..
    ..
    //return an ActionForward object for displaying the next view
    }
    public ActionForward viewRegistration( ActionMapping mapping,
    ActionForm form,
    HttpServletRequest req, HttpServletResponse res ) throws Exception {
    ..
    ..
    //return an ActionForward object for displaying the next view
    }
}
```

Navigation Using ActionForward

ActionForward objects are configuration objects. These configuration objects have a unique identifier to enable their lookup based on meaningful names like "success," "failure," and so on. *ActionForward* objects encapsulate the forwarding URL path and are used by request handlers for identifying the target view. *ActionForward* objects are created from the `<forward>` elements in struts-config.xml. The following is an example of a `<forward>` element in Struts that is in the local scope of an `<action>` element:

```
<action-mappings>
    <action path="/PortalAllianceRegistration"
            type="com.gc.prez.admin.PortalAllianceRegistrationAction"
            name="PortalAllianceRegistrationForm"
            scope="session"
            validate="false">
        <forward name="ShowPage" path="/2_1_PortalAllianceRegistration.jsp"/>
        <forward name="EnterPortalID" path="/2_3A_EnterPortalID.jsp"/>
        <forward name="success"
                path="/2_SiteAdministratorServicesMainPage.jsp"/>
    </action>
</action-mappings>
```

Global <forward> elements are typically specified for common destinations within the application as illustrated by the following example:

```
<global-forwards>
    <forward   name="success"  path="/1_HomePage.jsp"/>
    <forward name="failure"
          path="/1_3_AdministratorLoginFailure.jsp"/>
</global-forwards>
```

Based on the outcome of processing in the request handler's *execute* method, the next view can be selected by a developer in the *execute* method by using the convenience *org.apache.struts.action.ActionMapping.findForward* method while passing a value that matches the value specified in the *name* attribute of the <forward> element. This is illustrated by the following snippet.

```
return mapping.findForward( "ShowPage" );
```

The *ActionMapping.findForward* method will provide an *ActionForward* object either from its local scope, or from the global scope, and the *ActionForward* object is returned to the *RequestProcessor* for invoking the next view using the *RequestDispatcher.forward(...)* method or *response.sendRedirect*.The *RequestDispatcher.forward* method is called when the <forward> element has an attribute of *redirect="false"* or the *redirect* attribute is absent; *redirect="true"* will invoke the *sendRedirect* method. The following snippet illustrates the *redirect* attribute usage:

```
<forward name="success"  path="/1_HomePage.jsp"  redirect="true"/>
```

The <controller> element in the struts-config.xml file provides yet another feature for controlling how the <forward> element's *name* attribute is interpreted; the <controller> element is used in conjunction with the *input* attribute on the <action> element, as shown here:

```
<action-mappings>
    <action path="/PortalAllianceRegistration"
            type="com.gc.prez.admin.PortalAllianceRegistrationAction"
            name="PortalAllianceRegistrationForm"
```

```
            scope="session"
            input="ShowPage"
            validate="false">
        <forward name="ShowPage" path="/2_1_PortalAllianceRegistration.jsp"/>
        <forward name="EnterPortalID" path="/2_3A_EnterPortalID.jsp"/>
        <forward name="success"
                path="/2_SiteAdministratorServicesMainPage.jsp"/>
    </action>
</action-mappings>

<controller>
    <set-property property="inputForward" value="true"/>
</controller>
```

The preceding <action> element has an *input* attribute with a forward name; this forward name is identical to the one used in the <forward> element. With the preceding <controller> configuration, when the *ActionForm.validate* returns a non-empty or non-null *ActionErrors* object, the *RequestProcessor* will select the <forward> element whose *name* attribute has the same value as the *input* attribute of the <action> element; unless overridden by a subclass of *RequestProcessor*, this behavior is standard when validation errors are encountered. With the following <controller> element declaration, when the *ActionForm.validate* returns a non-empty or non-null *ActionErrors* object, the *input* attribute provides a forwarding URL instead of an *ActionForward* name to which the forward occurs. In the absence of the *inputForward* property, this is the default behavior.

```
<controller>
    <set-property property="inputForward" value="false"/>
</controller>
```

The forward is done to the specified path, with a / (slash) prepended if not already included in the *path* specification. For forward or redirect, URLs in Struts are created internally by the *RequestProcessor* with the following structure:

- If *redirect=true*, the URL is created as /contextPath/path because for *HttpServletResponse.sendRedirect* the container interprets a URL with a leading / (slash) as relative to the servlet container root.
- If *redirect=false*, the URI is created as /path because *ServletContext.getRequestDisptacher* uses context-relative URL.

Internationalization and Localization Support

Internationalization, or I18N, is the process of engineering an application such that it can be adapted to various languages and regions without requiring any change to the application logic. For internationalization support, an application must consider the following:

- Textual content, error messages, exception messages, and labels on GUI components must be externalized into resource files. These resource files will contain locale-specific information as discussed shortly.
- Date, time, currency, numbers, measurements, and phone numbers must be formatted based on local preferences and culture.

In today's global marketplace, it is important to design the applications with internationalization; doing this upfront takes relatively less time and effort than incorporating I18N after the application has been developed. The JDK provides the *Locale* class that is used by internationalized classes to behave in a locale-sensitive way. A *Locale* object represents a specific geographical, political, or cultural region. The following is a discussion on how Struts implements I18N and localization.

The Locale Object

Struts classes providing I18N support retrieve the locale-specific information from the *HttpSession* using *getAttribute(Action.LOCALE_KEY)*. The *Locale* object is saved in the session in several different ways, as explained next.

Using HtmlTag The custom tag *org.apache.struts.taglib.html.HtmlTag* is inserted in a JSP as `<html:html locale="true">`. This is a declarative way of populating *Locale* in the session. When *locale=true* is specified, the tag logic will retrieve the *Locale* object using the *HttpServletRequest.getLocale()* method. The *getLocale()* method returns the preferred *Locale* that a client browser will accept content based on the Accept-Language header. A default locale for the server is returned when the client does not provide an Accept-Language header. A session object is created if it does not exist, and the *Locale* object is then stored in the session object using *Action.LOCALE_KEY*. The HTML tag is subsequently written to the output stream with the *lang* attribute set to the language specified in the locale. The *Locale* object is stored only once in this manner; subsequent *locale=true* specification will not be able to replace the *Locale* object in the session. This method of setting locale works best when the users have their browsers set with the preferred locale list.

Using the Action Object For programmatically changing the *Locale* object, the *Action* class provides the *setLocale(...)* method for saving the *Locale* object in the session using *Action.LOCALE_KEY*. This method of setting locale works best when a user has the option of choosing locale in the HTML form by clicking a UI component. However, using this method can sometimes cause problems if locale-specific resources are preloaded and a user is allowed to switch locale in the middle of a process flow. It is best to allow this functionality in a controlled manner and reset all locale-specific resources when a locale change is requested.

Using <controller> Element Under this scheme, the `<controller>` tag from the struts-config.xml file is used to flag the *RequestProcessor* to get the locale from the *HttpServletRequest* object and put it in the session using *Action.LOCALE_KEY*. This is illustrated here:

```
<controller>
    <set-property property="locale" value="true"/>
</controller>
```

If *value=true*, then the *Locale* object obtained from request *getLocale()* is saved in the session if not previously saved.

Internationalized Messaging and Labeling

For I18N support, all error messages, instructional messages, informational messages, titles, labels for GUI components, and labels for input fields must be stored externally and accessed in a locale-specific way. The Struts framework provides the *MessageResources* class that mimics the *ResourceBundle* class provided by the JDK. Locale-specific resource bundles provide a way of isolating locale-specific information. Resource bundles belong to families whose members share a common base name, but whose names also have additional components that identify their locales. The default resource bundle has the same name as the base name of a family of resource bundles and is the bundle of last resort when locale-specific bundles are not found. Locale-specific bundles extend the base bundle name with locale-specific identifiers like the language, country, and variant of a locale. Consider the following example.

If base *ResourceBundle* name is *MyApplicationResources*, resource bundles belonging to this family may be identified as follows:

- *MyApplicationResources_en* identifies the bundle for the English language.
- *MyApplicationResources_fr* identifies the bundle for the French language.
- *MyApplicationResources_fr_FR* identifies the bundle for the French language for France.
- *MyApplicationResources_fr_CA* identifies the bundle for the French language for Canada.

If the desired locale is *fr_FR* and the default locale is en_US, the search order for accessing resource bundles can be summarized as follows. The search goes from being more specific to less specific:

- *MyApplicationResources_fr_FR* The desired resource bundle
- *MyApplicationResources_fr* Less specific bundle if the desired bundle is not found
- *MyApplicationResources_en_US* The default bundle if no matching bundles are found thus far
- *MyApplicationResources_en* Less specific bundle if the default bundle is not found
- *MyApplicationResources* The base bundle

Struts provides a facility for accomplishing the preceding mechanism using *MessageResources* objects. *MessageResources* objects are initialized from the key/value pairs specified in underlying properties files. You have to specify only the base name for a *MessageResources* properties file in the struts-config.xml file to access all the locale-specific properties files using search order that is similar to the one specified for the *ResourceBundle*(s). The following depicts how message resources are declared in the struts-config.xml file:

```
<message-resources parameter="packageName.MyApplicationResources" key="MyResources"/>
```

The value of the *parameter* attribute declares the base non-locale-specific properties file. This base resource file will have the name *MyApplicationResources.properties*, while locale-specific files will have the name *MyApplicationResoures*_localeSpecificExtension*.properties*. For each application, we can specify one or more base bundle names. *MessageResources* objects are created by the controller, that is *ActionServlet*, and saved in the *ServletContext* using either a generic key *Globals.MESSAGES_KEY* (same as *Action.MESSAGES_KEY*) or using the *key* attribute provided in the `<message-resources>` element (in case of multiple *MessageResources*).

For accessing message resources objects in request handlers, the *Action* class provides a convenience method—*Action.getResources*—for retrieving a message resource from the *ServletContext* using the key (i.e., unique identifier) associated with the *MessageResources* object. Each *MessageResources* object will be responsible for getting locale-specific messages by accessing the underlying set of locale-specific properties files; the properties files are identified by the base *MessageResources* name specified by the *parameter* attribute in the `<message-resources>` tag.

To retrieve a locale-specific message, use *MessageResources.getMessage* while passing locale and message key as arguments as follows:

```
protected static MessageResources messages =
   MessageResources.getMessageResources("packageName.MyApplicationResources ");
```

The locale can be retrieved from the session using *Action.LOCALE_KEY*. When an *Object[]* is provided as an argument for *MessageResources.getMessage*, the message retrieved is treated as a message format pattern and is converted to a *MessageFormat* object. The *MessageFormat* object is subsequently used for calling the *MessageFormat.format* method while passing the *object[]* to be appropriately formatted and inserted into the pattern at appropriate places. The *MessageFormat* class is not locale specific, therefore the corresponding message format pattern and the *Object[]* must take localization into account. *MessageResources* API provides several convenience methods for retrieving messages; the corresponding Javadoc is available at http://jakarta.apache.org/struts/api/index.html. On most occasions, the logic for retrieving messages from a resource bundle is transparent to the Struts user; this is explained in the next section. Refer to the section "Message Resources Semantics" in this chapter for additional information on this topic.

Error Handling

Most form interactions require that the user be informed of the possible outcome of the form submission. Displaying error and informational messages in a consistent manner is a desirable feature of a framework. In the preceding section, we discussed locale-specific messaging using the *MessageResources* objects. The set of properties files associated with each *MessageResources* object has key/value pairs. A Struts-based application will accumulate, for message lookup, the keys associated with validation and informational messages in an

ActionErrors object as a precursor to accessing resource bundles. The following static model illustrates the classes involved in the error handling mechanism provided by Struts.

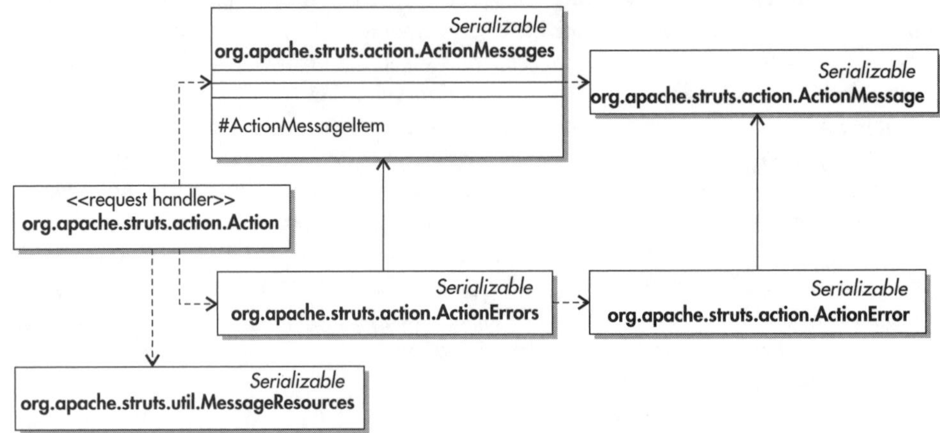

We will briefly discuss the interactions depicted in the preceding illustration. This discussion will provide us with insight on how message keys are captured in Struts to get locale-specific messages, and how the messages are rendered in a consistent manner in the view. For this discussion the view component is a JSP.

Identifying Errors with ActionError

Implementations of *Action.execute* or *ActionForm.validate* form. validation (discussed in the section "Storing Form Data Using ActionForm") should capture validation and application-specific errors in *ActionErrors* objects, which aggregates *ActionError* objects. An *ActionError* object consists of a message key and optionally an *object[]* to be used for parametric replacement in the retrieved message. Refer to earlier section "Internationalized Messaging and Labeling" for relevant information. *ActionError* objects must be created without worrying about the locale or the associated resource bundles. We will deal with I18N when the *ActionError* objects are used for retrieving messages. Refer to the *ActionError* API for a complete list of available convenience methods for creating *ActionError* objects. Once an *ActionError* object is created, it should be added to the *ActionErrors* object using the *ActionErrors.add* method while passing as arguments the *ActionError* and the property name for which a validation error was detected. The following snippet from the *ManagePortalAllianceAction* class illustrates this. Chapter 5 discusses the implementation of the sample application in detail.

```
public ActionForward execute( ActionMapping mapping, ActionForm form,
HttpServletRequest req, HttpServletResponse res ) throws Exception {
    ManagePortalAllianceForm portalForm =
                ( ManagePortalAllianceForm )form;
    ActionErrors errors = portalForm.validate( mapping, req );
    String action = portalForm.getAction();
    if ( !errors.empty() && portalForm.getPage() == 1 ) {
      saveErrors( req, errors );
      return mapping.findForward( "EnterPortalID" );
```

```
    }
    if ( ( !errors.empty() ) && ( portalForm.getPage() == 2 ) &&
    ( action.equals( "updateProfile" ) ) ) {
      saveErrors( req, errors );
      return mapping.findForward( "ShowPortalProfile" );
    }
    if ( ( !errors.empty() ) && ( portalForm.getPage() == 2 ) &&
    ( action.equals( "navigationBarSetup" ) ) ) {
      saveErrors( req, errors );
      return mapping.findForward( "ShowNavigationBarSetup" );
    }
// rest of the code
}
```

Within the associated *ManagePortalAllianceForm*, the *validate()* method will add error messages to the *errors* object as follows:

```
public ActionErrors validate( ActionMapping mapping,
       HttpServletRequest req ) {
       ActionErrors errors = new ActionErrors();
      if ( ( page == 1 ) && ( ( portalID == null ) ||
         ( portalID.trim().length() < 1 ) ) ) {
          errors.add( "portalID", new ActionError( "error.portalID.required" ) );
      }
      else if ( ( page == 2 ) && ( action.equals( "updateProfile" ) ) ) {
          errors = super.validate( mapping, req );
          if ( searchLimit.intValue() < 10 ) {
            errors.add( "searchLimit",
                new ActionError( "error.PortalAllianceProfile.SearchLimit" ) );
          }
      }
```

For saving error messages not related with a property, a convenience instance member *ActionErrors.GLOBAL_ERROR* is available for use in place of a property argument in *ActionErrors.add(...)*. Usage of property name in creating an *ActionErrors* object is clarified in the upcoming section "Compiling Errors ActionErrors."

Compiling Errors with ActionErrors

ActionErrors objects hold all *ActionError* objects in a *HashMap* whose key is the name of the property for which messages have been accumulated, and the value is an *ActionMessageItem* object. *ActionMessageItem* is declared as an inner class of *ActionMessages*. Each *ActionMessageItem* object consists of a unique sequence number and an *ArrayList* object representing all possible validation errors for a given property. The sequence number is used for sorting the *ActionMessageItem* collection such that validation errors are reported according to the property that was first flagged as invalid. *ActionErrors.get* returns an *Iterator* on an *ArrayList* containing *ActionError* objects. This *Iterator* object is referenced by the custom tag *ErrorsTag* and will be discussed in the next section, "Displaying Errors with ErrorsTag."

In request handlers, i.e., in the *Action.execute* method, *ActionErrors* should be saved in the *HttpServletRequest* using the attribute name *Action.ERROR_KEY*; this is done by calling a convenience *saveErrors* method on the base *Action* class while passing as arguments the request object and the *ActionErrors* object The *ActionErrors* generated as a result of *ActionForm.validate* are saved by *RequestProcessor (the dispatcher)* in the request object using *Action.ERROR_KEY*. The next view can use the *ErrorsTag* for retrieving the *ActionErrors* object; the *ErrorsTag* can be used in a JSP as follows:

```
<%@ taglib uri="/WEB-INF/struts-html.tld" prefix="html" %>
<html:errors/>
```

The *ActionErrors* class extends the *ActionMessages* class. *ActionErrors* provides the static member *GLOBAL_ERROR* and *ActionMessages* provides the static member *GLOBAL_MESSAGE*; these static members can be used as keys when the messages are not property specific. For saving the *ActionMessages* object in a request handler, the convenience *Action.saveMessages* method can be used while passing the request object and the *ActionMessages* object; the *ActionMessages* object is saved in the request using the *Action.MESSAGE_KEY*.

For simply capturing message keys, without the property name and the substitution parameters, a convenience method *org.apache.struts.util.RequestUtils.getActionErrors* is available for converting a *String* object, a *String* array, or an *ErrorMessages* object (a Vector of message keys) into an *ActionErrors* object. For these implementations, the *getActionErrors* method will use the *ActionErrors.GLOBAL_ERROR* in place of a property argument.

Displaying Errors with ErrorsTag

This custom tag renders the messages in an HTML document. It retrieves the *ActionErrors* from the *HttpServletRequest* using *Action.ERROR_KEY* and then using the *ActionErrors.get()* method retrieves an *Iterator* on an *ArrayList* containing *ActionError* objects. For each *ActionError* object in the *ArrayList*, a locale-specific message is retrieved and sent to the response stream. By default, the *locale* object in the session is used; but an alternate *locale* attribute can be specified for the tag. By default, the resource bundle saved in the ServletContext with the key *Action.MESSAGES_KEY* will be used unless overridden by the *bundle* attribute on the tag. You will need to override the resource bundle if more than one base resource file is being used for manageability. As of Struts 1.1 beta 2, an *ErrorsTag* can only use one resource bundle family (i.e., the bundles have the same base name), therefore all errors in the *ActionErrors* object must be available in this resource bundle family. Because all *ActionError* objects within the *ActionErrors* object are logged by a property name, the messages displayed can be restricted to a single property by specifying a *property* attribute specification on the *ErrorsTag*.

The sample application 'GreaterCause' uses a default resource bundle 'ApplicationResources.properties'. Following is a snippet from this properties file.

```
error.portalID.required=<li>Portal ID must be provided</li>
error.invalidToken=<li>Either this form has been submitted once already, or,
this form is not in proper submission sequence</l1>
error.ein.required=<li>EIN must be provided</li>
```

The *ErrorsTag* uses message keys 'errors.header' and 'errors.footer' for providing caption and formatting around error messages, as shown here:

```
errors.header=<h3><font color="red">Please review following message(s) before
proceeding:</font></h3><ul>
errors.footer=</ul>
```

Exception Handling

In addition to an error handling mechanism, a presentation framework must provide a mechanism for showing locale-specific exceptions of meaning and relevance to the user. A recommended way to do this is to capture the actual exception and its context in a log file and then send a meaningful informational message for assisting the user in determining a suitable course of action. Uncaught exceptions in JSPs are handled by the *errorPage* mechanism as specified in JSP 1.2 specification. Similarly, uncaught exceptions in servlets are handled using the `<error-page>` specification in the web.xml deployment descriptor. Struts provides a simple mechanism that is somewhat similar to the error page mechanism provided by JSP and servlet containers. The following configuration can be specified in the struts-config.xml file:

```
<action  path="/editCustomerProfile"
         type="packageName.EditCustomerProfileAction"
         name="customerProfileForm"
         scope="request"
         input="profile">
    <forward name="profile"  path="/CustomerProfile.jsp"/>
    <forward name="success"  path="/MainMenu.jsp"/>
    <exception
         key="profile.inaccessible"
         type=" packageName.ProfileAccessException"
         path="/login.jsp"/>
</action>
```

The exception handling mechanism builds on top of the error handling mechanism and therefore uses the *MessageResources* for providing locale-specific messages. The following static model illustrates the classes involved in the exception handling mechanism provided by Struts. The discussion that follows explains the Exception mechanism provided with Struts.

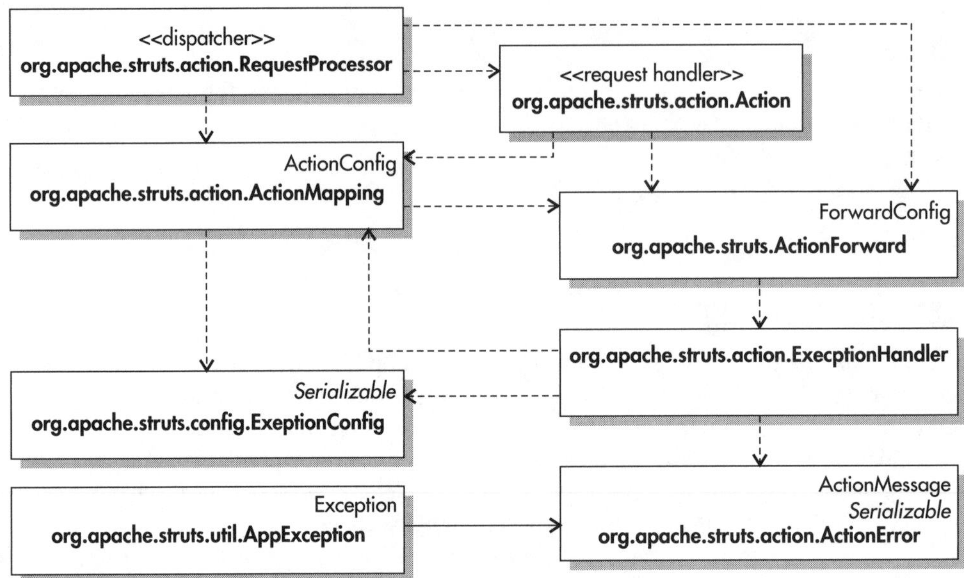

Role of the Dispatcher

As discussed in the section "Dispatcher," the dispatcher (a.k.a. the request processor) calls the *execute* method of the request handler. Any exception thrown by the request handler is caught by the *RequestProcessor* and interrogated for a possible match with the `<exception>` elements in the struts-config.xml file. The *RequestProcessor* will call the *ActionMapping.findException* method to find an *ExceptionConfig* configuration object (*ExceptionConfig* objects are runtime representations of `<exception>` elements) whose *type* attribute matches the type of the exception. If an attempt to find an `<exception>` configuration for the original exception fails, the *findException* method will look up the exception superclass chain for a suitable match until it reaches the top of the chain. *ActionMapping.findException* will search for the `<exception>` element both in the local scope of the *ActionMapping* object, and in the global scope.

Global `<exception>` elements are typically specified for common exceptions within the application as illustrated by the following example:

```
<global-exceptions>
    <exception
         key="profile.inaccessible"
         type=" packageName.ProfileAccessException"
         path="/logon.jsp"/>
</global-exceptions>
```

If an *ExceptionConfig* object is found for a given exception type, the *RequestProcessor* will create an exception handler and call its *execute* method; this is explained further in the section "Converting an Exception into ActionErrors." The *RequestProcessor* will forward to the URL specified in the *ActionForward* object returned by the exception handler.

Exception Handling with AppException

This is a convenience base class for creating exceptions within the request handlers. It encapsulates both, the attribute causing an exception (optional) and associated *ActionError* object. A subclass of *AppException* will be responsible for providing the appropriate constructors for correctly instantiating this object by using a message key, and optionally the attribute name and an *object[]* for parametric substitution. The message key can be extracted from the *ExceptionConfig* object that corresponds to this exception. Refer to the section "Struts Configuration Semantics" for information on navigating the configuration objects. Refer to the *AppException* API for an available list of constructors that can be called from the constructor of its subclass. The *AppException* is passed as an argument in the *ExceptionHandler.execute(...)* method.

Converting an Exception into ActionErrors

The *RequestProcessor* checks the *ExceptionConfig* for an exception handler specification. The *RequestProcessor* creates the specified *ExceptionHandler* and calls its *execute(...)* method while passing the *AppException* as one of the arguments. A default exception handler specification of *org.apache.struts.action.ExceptionHandler* is preconfigured in the *ExceptionConfig* object. The *ExceptionHandler* retrieves the *ActionError* from the *AppException* object and creates an *ActionErrors* object for consumption by *ErrorsTag*. If the exception is not of type *AppException* or one of its derived classes, then the *ExceptionHandler* will create the *ActionErrors* object using the key specified in the `<exception>` element; this alleviates the request handler developer from writing extra code for exception handling; however this limits the ability of the framework to call only a single constructor of *ActionError* that only accepts a key value. Use the *handler* attribute on the `<exception>` element to override the default exception handler if desired. The *ExceptionHandler* or a subclass of *ExceptionHandler* will create an *ActionForward* object using the *path* property of the *ExceptionConfig*; if this path is not specified, it will use the path specified in the *input* attribute of the *ActionMapping* configuration object. The *ExceptionHandler* will also save the original exception in the request object using *Action.EXCEPTION_KEY*. A view is free to access this information in any way desired. The *Action.EXCEPTION_KEY* can be also be used to retrieve and rethrow the original exception for using the error-page mechanism provided by the servlet container.

Once-Only Form Submission

A problem always encountered in developing browser-based clients is the possibility of a form getting submitted more than once. It is apparent that such submissions are undesirable in any eCommerce application. Struts provides a mechanism to protect the model layer from the adverse effect of multiple form submissions by using a token generated by the base

Action class *generateToken* method. To control transactional integrity and atomicity, simply call the *saveToken* method in a request handler before selecting the next view with an *ActionForward.* The *saveToken* method calls the *generateToken* method to create a unique identifier and then saves it in the session with the key *Action.TRANSACTION_ TOKEN_KEY.* The *FormTag* retrieves the token from the session and saves it as a hidden field with the name *Constants.TOKEN_KEY.*

On a subsequent request, the request handler can check for token validity by calling the convenience *isTokenValid* method on the base *Action* class. Should this method return *false*, the request handler must implement suitable logic to account for the problem. An example of this is illustrated here:

```
ActionErrors errors = new ActionErrors();
if ( !isTokenValid( req ) ) {
    errors.add( ActionErrors.GLOBAL_ERROR, new ActionError( "error.invalidToken" ) );
    saveErrors( req, errors );
    return mapping.findForward( "ShowPage" );
}
resetToken( req );
```

The *isTokenValid(...)* method synchronizes the session object to prevent multiple requests from accessing the token. In the request handlers, the method *isTokenValid(...)* must be followed by a *resetToken(...)* to remove the token from the session; this will ensure that any subsequent request will result in *isTokenValid(...)* returning *false*, thus preventing a form from multiple submissions. The *saveToken(...)* should be called in the request handler to recreate a new transaction token for the next request. A call to the *resetToken* is not required when the *isTokenValid* method parameter list includes the *reset* flag.

Capturing Form Data

The JSP specification provides a standard way for extracting and storing form data at request time in JavaBeans using `<jsp:useBean>` and `<jsp:setProperty>`. However, this solution creates a strong coupling between the presentation layer and the JavaBeans; furthermore, the HTML document creator has to be aware of such components and their correct usage in the context of a page. Because the JavaBeans can be created and placed in a specified scope by the `<jsp:useBean>` tag or by another server component, there could be problems with bean life cycle management between different components sharing the JavaBean. Struts provides a mechanism for extracting, storing, and validating form data; at the same time, it overcomes the shortcomings of the `<jsp:useBean>` and `<jsp:setProperty>`.

The following is a recap of the `<action>` and `<form-bean>` elements:

```
<form-bean  name="PortalAllianceRegistrationForm"
       type="packageName.PortalAllianceRegistrationForm"/>
```

```
<action-mappings>
    <action path="/PortalAllianceRegistration"
            type="com.gc.prez.admin.PortalAllianceRegistrationAction"
            name="PortalAllianceRegistrationForm"
            scope="session"
            input="ShowPage"
            validate="false">
        <forward name="ShowPage"
                 path="/2_1_PortalAllianceRegistration.jsp"/>
        <forward name="EnterPortalID"
                 path="/2_3A_EnterPortalID.jsp"/>
        <forward name="success"
                 path="/2_SiteAdministratorServicesMainPage.jsp"/>
    </action>
</action-mappings>
```

The preceding snippet maps a JavaBean of type=*packageName*.PortalAllianceRegistrationForm with *name*= "PortalAllianceRegistrationForm" (unique identifier) to an <action> element with *name*= "PortalAllianceRegistrationForm;" the request handler is uniquely identified by the path / PortalAllianceRegistration in the incoming request. The semantics of the form creation and usage are illustrated with the following static model.

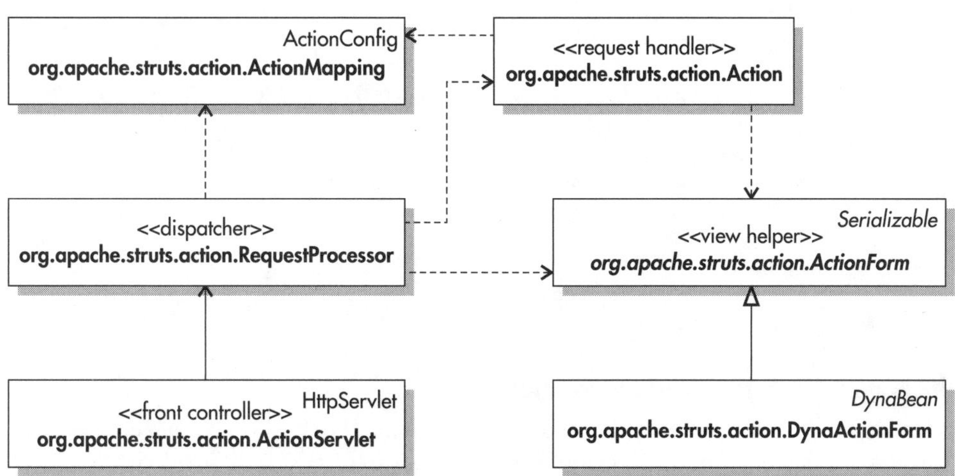

First, we will explore the semantics of forms processing while employing simple JavaBeans objects. These objects are subclassed from as *ActionForm* and are also referred to as form-beans. We will then discuss forms processing using the *DynaActionForm* object that can support dynamic sets of properties at request time.

The following is an abbreviated version of the *PortalAllianceRegistrationForm* from the sample application. Please note that the *ValidatorForm* extends the *ActionForm*. *ValidatorForm* is discussed in detail in Chapter 5.

```
public class PortalAllianceRegistrationForm extends ValidatorForm implements
Serializable {
    public PortalAllianceRegistrationForm() {
    }
    public String getPortalID() {
        return portalID;
    }
    public void setPortalID( String portalID ) {
        this.portalID = portalID;
    }
    public String getPortalName() {
        return portalName;
    }
    public void setPortalName( String portalName ) {
        this.portalName = portalName;
    }
    private String portalID;
    private String portalName;
    // rest of the code goes here
    public void reset( ActionMapping mapping, HttpServletRequest req ) {
        portalName = null;
        // rest of the code goes here
    }
    public ActionErrors validate( ActionMapping mapping, HttpServletRequest req ) {
        ActionErrors errors = super.validate( mapping, req ); //Struts Validator
        if ( errors == null ) {
            errors = new ActionErrors();
            // Additional validations to be placed here
        }
        return errors;
    }
}
```

Initializing ActionForm Objects in FormTag

As mentioned earlier in this section, the action URL in the HTML form is mapped to an `<action>` configuration, which in turn is mapped to a `<form-bean>` configuration. The URL specified in the *action* property of the *FormTag* is translated by the *FormTag* into a URL whose path structure conforms to the `<url-pattern>` specified in the deployment descriptor. For extension mapping, this implies that the resource extension is the same as that specified for the `<url-pattern>`. Therefore, a URL of the form */editCustomerProfile?customerType=preferred*, is translated into /contextName/ *editCustomerProfile.do?customerType=preferred*.

The *FormTag* calls the *org.apache.struts.util.RequestUtils.createActionForm* method, which will search for an *ActionFormBean* configuration object (*ActionFormBean* is the runtime representation of the `<form-bean>` element) with a name that matches the *name* specified on the corresponding `<action>` element. A new instance of the *ActionForm* is created using the *type* attribute of the `<form-bean>` element; a new instance is created when the ActionForm instance is not found in the specified scope, otherwise the *FormTag* calls the *ActionForm.reset* method on the existing form-bean to clear it in preparation for the form data from the next request. The scope is specified by the *scope* attribute in the `<action>` element; the new *ActionForm* instance or the existing reinitialized instance is saved in the specified scope using the *name* attribute.

Storing Form Data Using ActionForm

The *ActionForm*-derived objects are used for storing the parameters from a request object, and therefore they are tightly coupled to a user. An *ActionForm* subclass is a JavaBean with accessor methods for properties corresponding to parameters in the *HttpServletRequest* object. If an *ActionForm* object is created by the *FormTag* (discussed in the preceding section), then in the request subsequent to form rendering by the *FormTag*, the *RequestProcessor* (that is, the dispatcher) will access the form from the specified scope; the form to be retrieved is identified by the related action mapping. The *RequestProcessor* will then reset the form properties, populate the form with request time parameters, and then call the *validate* method on the form object to perform server-side validation of user input. The *validate* method is called only when the *validate* property in the *ActionMapping* object is set to true; this is the default behavior. The result of validation could be an *ActionErrors* object, explained in the section "Error Handling," which is used by *org.apache.struts.taglib.html.ErrorsTag* to display the validation errors to the user. The *ActionForm* can also be used for storing intermediate model state, which is subsequently referenced by a view (a JSP) for presenting to the user.

An *ActionForm* class can also be created by the *RequestProcessor*. This happens when a forward is done to a URL that maps to the controller servlet rather than a JSP and the corresponding action mapping specifies the *form* property. In this case, an attempt by the *RequestProcessor* to look up the form-bean may result in the creation of a new *ActionForm* object if not found in the specified scope. The *ActionForm* objects are found in the specified scope using the *name* attribute specified in the `<action>` element; when a form-bean is found by the *RequestProcessor*, it is passed to the request handler's *execute* method. You may also decide to instantiate an action form in a request handler; you may find this need when initializing instance variables based on application state. This is illustrated by the following example.

```
public class CreateCampaignAction extends Action {

public ActionForward execute( ActionMapping mapping, ActionForm form,
HttpServletRequest req, HttpServletResponse res ) throws Exception {
        ManageCampaignsForm campaignForm = ( ManageCampaignsForm )form;
        // other code appears here
        return ( searchAndSelectNPO( mapping, form, req, res ) );
```

```
    }
public ActionForward searchAndSelectNPO( ActionMapping mapping, ActionForm form,
HttpServletRequest req,
    HttpServletResponse res ) {
        ManageCampaignsForm campaignForm = ( ManageCampaignsForm )form;
        SearchAndListNPOForm searchForm =
        ( SearchAndListNPOForm )req.getSession().getAttribute
                ( "SearchAndListNPOForm" );
        if ( searchForm == null ) {
            searchForm = new SearchAndListNPOForm();
            req.getSession().setAttribute( "SearchAndListNPOForm", searchForm );
        }
        /* Initialize state information with the objective of Search */
        searchForm.setAction( "createNewCampaign" );
        campaignForm.setAction( "createNewCampaign" );
        return mapping.findForward( "ShowSearch" );
    }
}
```

Form objects created for the purpose of providing intermediate model state to the JSP should use request scope; this will ensure that the objects do not hang around after their usefulness expires. By default, all forms are saved in the session scope. The existence of form objects in the session beyond their usefulness could result in wasted memory, as such, the request handlers must track the life cycle of form objects stored in the session. A good practice for capturing form data is to use a single form-bean for related forms that span several user interactions. form-beans can also be used to store intermediate model state, which can be adapted by custom tags for use in a view at response time. Tag usage prevents incorporation of Java code (scriptlets) in the view, thus achieving a good division of responsibility between a web production team that primarily deals with markup, and an application development team that primarily deals with writing Java code. The tags factor out logic for accessing intermediate model state; this logic could be quite complex when accessing nested objects or when iterating through a collection.

Creating ActionForm with Dynamic Properties

A *DynaActionForm* object is an object with a dynamic set of properties. *DynaActionForm* extends the *ActionForm*; its usage permits creation of a form object through declarations made in the struts-config.xml as follows:

```
<form-bean  name="logonForm"
type="org.apache.struts.action.DynaActionForm">
    <form-property name="username" type="java.lang.String"/>
    <form-property name="password" type="java.lang.String"/>
</form-bean>
```

The *RequestProcessor* creates, populates, and validates the *DynaActionForm* in the same way it does *ActionForm*, i.e., the parameters in the request object are populated in the *DynaActionForm* for the dynamic set of properties specified in the `<form-bean>` element; other parameters are simply skipped.

Request Parameter Type-Conversion

This discussion focuses on how *String[]* type retrieved by Struts framework using *request .getParameterValues(*parameterName*)* is converted to the target property type of the form-bean object. The following is a list of supported target types:

```
java.lang.BigDecimal
java.lang.BigInteger
boolean and java.lang.Boolean
byte and java.lang.Byte
char and java.lang.Character
double and java.lang.Double
float and java.lang.Float
int and java.lang.Integer
long and java.lang.Long
short and java.lang.Short
java.lang.String
java.sql.Date
java.sql.Time
java.sql.Timestamp
```

The target types, i.e., the type associated with form-bean object properties, are found using an introspection mechanism; a Struts-specific custom introspection mechanism is used for *DynaActionForm* objects. Struts also supports indexed parameter names of the form *parameterName[n]*; where the index *n* is zero based. The form-bean methods corresponding to this naming convention are created according to the indexed property design patterns prescribed by the JavaBeans specification, as shown next.

The following methods are used to access all array elements of an indexed property:

```
public <PropertyType>[] get<PropertyName>();
public void set<PropertyName>(<PropertyType>[] value);
```

The following methods are used to access individual array elements:

```
public <PropertyType> get<PropertyName>(int index)
public void set<PropertyName>(int index, <PropertyType> value)
```

The following describes the usage scenarios for indexed properties and simple properties:

1. When the bean property is an array, and the parameter name in the request does not use the indexing notation *parameterName[n]*, the *String[]* returned by *request.getParameterValues(*parameterName*)* is converted to an array of target component type. The *ActionForm* subclass should be defined with the following method signatures:

   ```
   public void set<PropertyName>(<PropertyType>[] value)
   public <PropertyType>[] get<PropertyName>();
   ```

2. When the bean property is of type array, and the parameter name in the request uses the indexing notation *parameterName[n]*, the *String[]* returned by *request .getParameterValues(*parameterName*)* is assumed to be containing only a single value; as such, only *String[0]* is converted to the component type of the array. The *ActionForm* subclass should be defined with the following method signatures that accept an index argument:

```
public void set<PropertyName>(int index, <PropertyType> value)
public <PropertyType> get<PropertyName>(int index)
```

   These method signatures follow the design patterns of indexed properties as stated in the JavaBeans specification. In the absence of these methods, indexed access using the indexing notation is also possible by implementing the following method:

```
public <PropertyType>[] get<PropertyName>();
```

   In this scenario, the required array element to *set* is accessed by the Struts framework by first getting the underlying array object, accessing the element for the given index, and finally setting the accessed object. This pattern can also support a *List*-based implementation for request parameters that use the indexing notation *parameterName[n]*. We discuss a *List*-based implementation next in the section "A Simple Example of Nested Properties."

3. For simple property types, the *String[]* returned by *request .getParameterValues(*parameterName*)* is assumed to be containing only a single value; as such only *String[0]* is converted to the target type. For simple properties, the *ActionForm* subclass should be defined with the following method signatures.

```
public void set<PropertyName>(<PropertyType> value)
public <PropertyType> get<PropertyName>();
```

A Simple Example of Nested Properties

An example of *List*-based implementation with *List* update capability is illustrated in this section. Following is a stripped-down version of the JSP code from *2_3_5_1_UpdateCampaigns.jsp* that can be found in the GreaterCause directory. In the following snippet, *Collection* "campaigns" is extracted from the *ActionForm* "ManageCampaignsForm" using *getCampaigns()* and saved in the session using the identifier "campaignDTO"; this identifier is subsequently used to retrieve the elements of the collection in the <iterate> tag.

```
<logic:iterate id="campaignDTO" name="ManageCampaignsForm" property="campaigns">
    <table>
        <tr>

<%-- Each element of the Collection campaigns (identified in the session by
the identifier campaignDTO) is iterated and the corresponding nested property written
```

```
to the output stream. The property indexed="true" will create an index for
each form field where this property is specified; the index is zero based and
increments for each iteration --%>
            <html:hidden name="campaignDTO" property="ein" indexed="true"/>
                <td><bean:write name="campaignDTO" property="ein"/></td>
                <td><bean:message key="prompt.StartDate"/></td>
                <td><html:text name="campaignDTO" property="startDate" size="10"
                    maxlength="10" indexed="true"/></td>
        </tr>
        <tr>
            <td class="txt">
            <!-- other HTML appears here -->
            </td>
            <td><bean:message key="prompt.EndDate"/></td>
            <td><html:text name="campaignDTO" property="endDate" size="10"
                maxlength="10" indexed="true"/></td>
        </tr>
    </table>
    <br>
</logic:iterate>
```

The preceding <iterate> tag will result in the following HTML that shows two iterations of the <iterate> logic, and results in indexes [0] and [1]. The field name *campaignDTO[0].ein* can be decomposed as follows: *campaignDTO* references the *Collection* "campaigns" in the *ActionForm* "ManageCampaignsForm"; the index [0] references the first element of the *Collection* "campaigns", which is made available using the method *getCampaignDTO(int index)* in the ActionForm; the simple property *ein* is an instance variable of the first element of the *Collection* "campaigns"; each element of the *Collection* is an object of the type *CampaignDTO*. When the form is submitted, the Struts framework applies the updates to the corresponding simple properties in the CampaignDTO by first calling the method *getCampaignDTO(int index)*; it then applies the form input to the corresponding instance variable in the DTO. It is important to reiterate here that when the framework retrieves the campaign DTO object, the framework takes the responsibility of updating the individual instance variables of campaign DTO objects.

```
<table>
    <tr>
        <input type="hidden" name="campaignDTO[0].ein"value="EIN0">
        <td>EIN0</td>
        <td>Start Date</td>
        <td><input type="text" name="campaignDTO[0].startDate" maxlength="10"
            size="10" value="2003-12-12"></td>
    </tr>
    <tr>
        <td>
        <!-- other HTML appears here -->
        </td>
        <td>End Date</td>
```

```
        <td><input type="text" name="campaignDTO[0].endDate" maxlength="10"
            size="10" value="2004-12-12"></td>
    </tr>
</table>
<br>

<table>
    <tr>
        <input type="hidden" name="campaignDTO[1].ein"value="EIN1">
        <td>EIN1</td>
        <td>Start Date</td>
        <td><input type="text" name="campaignDTO[1].startDate" maxlength="10"
            size="10" value="2003-01-01"></td>
    </tr>
    <tr>
        <td>
        <!-- other HTML appears here -->
        </td>
        <td>End Date</td>
        <td><input type="text" name="campaignDTO[1].endDate" maxlength="10"
            size="10" value="2003-12-31"></td>
    </tr>
</table>
<br>
```

For the preceding logic to work correctly, we need the following *ActionForm* definition.

```
public class ManageCampaignsForm extends ValidatorForm implements
    Serializable {
    public ManageCampaignsForm() {
    }
    public String getEin() {
        return ein;
    }
    public void setEin( String ein ) {
        this.ein = ein;
    }
    public String getStartDate() {
        return startDate;
    }
    public void setStartDate( String startDate ) {
        this.startDate = startDate;
    }
    public String getEndDate() {
        return endDate;
    }
    public void setEndDate( String endDate ) {
        this.endDate = endDate;
    }
```

```
    /** Coarse grained DTO is provided by the service layer */
    public void setCampaigns( List campaigns ) {
        this.campaigns = campaigns;
    }
    /** Coarse grained DTO is provided to the service layer */
    public List getCampaigns() {
        return campaigns;
    }
    private String ein;
    private String startDate;
    private String endDate;
    private List campaigns;
    /* The identifier CampaignDTO specified in the <iterate> tag is used to get
    the appropriate element from the underlying Collection campaigns */
    public CampaignDTO getCampaignDTO( int index ) {
        return ( CampaignDTO )campaigns.get( index );
    }
}
```

The nested property can nest to any number of levels, using both indexed and non-indexed properties. Chapter 5 implements the use case Update Campaigns that employs simple and indexed properties in a nested combination.

Custom Extensions with Plug-Ins

A framework must provide a facility for creating custom extensions by allowing a mechanism for plugging external services seamlessly into the framework. This implies that the framework must provide extension points, using which the life cycle management (i.e., *init()* and *destroy()*) of the pluggable component is possible. By providing such extension points, a developer can write a service that conforms to the interface supported by the extension mechanism, in this case the *PlugIn* interface, for controlling the creation, usage, and cleanup of the service and its corresponding resources within the context of the framework.

The Struts Validator is an example of a plug-in that enables declarative form validation. The corresponding entry in struts-config.xml is depicted here:

```
<plug-in className="org.apache.struts.validator.ValidatorPlugIn">
    <set-property property="pathnames"
                  value="/WEB-INF/validator-rules.xml,/WEB-INF/validation.xml"/>
</plug-in>
```

The *ValidatorPlugIn* class, and all other plug-in classes, are instantiated by the controller during its initialization. Each plug-in object is instantiated using the *className* attribute in the `<plug-in>` element. This plug-in object adheres to the design patterns of JavaBeans specification by providing the property accessor methods for each property specified in the `<plug-in>` element. Once a plug-in is instantiated, its *init* method is called to enable the developer to perform plug-in–specific initialization. For example, the *ValidatorPlugIn.init* method will initialize its resources and save the resources in the ServletContext using *ValidatorPlugIn.VALIDATOR_KEY*; these resources are subsequently used for creating an instance of the class *org.apache.commons.validator.Validator* in the context of the framework. The plug-in(s) instantiated by the controller are saved in the ServletContext as an array of *org.apache.struts.action.PlugIn* objects using the key *Action.PLUG_INS_KEY*. This array is subsequently used by the controller's *destroy()* method to call the *destroy* method on each plug-in for releasing acquired resources. Plug-in usage provides an elegant solution for initializing and saving objects that provide a specific set of services and whose usage can augment the functionality of the framework.

Struts Configuration Semantics

This section discusses the configuration objects that the controller creates, caches, and uses for controlling the behavior of the framework. All configuration objects are available to a developer in request handlers via the *ModuleConfig* object; this object can be accessed using the *Action.getModuleConfig()* method; the configuration objects can be extended for implementing custom functionality.

Parsing the Configuration File

The configuration file, struts-config.xml, is parsed in the controller's *init()* method using an instance of *org.apache.commons.digester.Digester*; the Digester extends *org.xml.sax.helpers.DefaultHandler*. Internally, the Digester uses a SAX parser to parse the configuration file. From the configuration file, the Digester constructs an object hierarchy of configuration objects, rooted in the *ModuleConfig* object, using the rules specified in *org.apache.struts.config.ConfigRuleSet*; these rules govern object creation and population. More information about Digester is available at http://jakarta.apache.org/commons/digester.html. The rule set provided by *ConfigRuleSet* can be augmented by specifying the *rulesets* initialization parameter that provides a comma-delimited list of class names containing additional rules. The configuration file location is provided in web.xml by the *config* initialization parameter as follows:

```
<servlet>
    <servlet-name>action</servlet-name>
    <servlet-class>org.apache.struts.action.ActionServlet</servlet-class>
    <init-param>
      <param-name>config</param-name>
      <param-value>/WEB-INF/struts-config.xml</param-value>
    </init-param>
</servlet>
```

The configuration object hierarchy is created in the *init()* method of the controller and saved in the ServletContext using org.apache.struts.Globals.MODULE. At the root of the configuration hierarchy is the *ModuleConfig* object. The *ModuleConfig* object contains references to collections of all other configuration objects, with convenience methods for saving and retrieving these objects. The semantics of creating a configuration object tree is explained in the section "Creating Configuration Objects." The following sections briefly explain the purpose for each configuration object.

ActionMapping This object is created from the `<action>` element. It provides the mapping between an incoming request and the corresponding request handler. It also embeds *ExceptionConfig* and *ActionForward* objects; these subordinate objects are in the local scope of the *ActionMapping* object.

ActionForward This object is created from the `<forward>` element. It provides the URI of the next web component. *ActionForward*(s) are specified both in the local and global scope. Global scope is used when a required *ActionForward* is not found in the scope of the current *ActionMapping* object.

ActionFormBean This object is created from the `<form-bean>` element. It provides the mapping between a form name in the *ActionMapping* to an *ActionForm* subclass.

FormPropertyConfig This object is created from the `<form-property>` element. It provides the dynamic attribute names and types for creating a *DynaActionForm* object.

DataSourceConfig This object is created from the `<data-source>` element. It provides information for configuring a data source in the framework.

MessageResourcesConfig This object is created from the `<message-resources>` element. It provides the base name of a family of resource bundles.

ExceptionConfig This object is created from the `<exception>` element. It provides a message key and a URI of the next web component when an exception of a given type is thrown by the request handlers. *ExceptionConfig*(s) are specified both in the local and global scope. Global scope is used when a required *ExceptionConfig* is not found in the scope of the current *ActionMapping* object.

PlugInConfig This object is created from the `<plug-in>` element. It provides the class name of an external resource that needs to be instantiated within the framework, and whose *init* and *destroy* methods are to be called by the framework.

ControllerConfig This object is created from the `<controller>` element. It provides information for configuring the framework.

For a complete list of all the attributes that can be specified for each configuration object, refer to the API at http://jakarta.apache.org/struts/api/index.html.

ModuleConfig The *ModuleConfig* object caches configuration information as follows:

1. *ActionMapping* objects are cached using a *HashMap*, keyed by the *path* attribute of the `<action>` element. The default *ActionMapping* class *org.apache.struts.action.ActionMapping* specified in the *ModuleConfig* class can be overridden using the *mapping* initialization parameter in the `<servlet>` declaration.

   Each *ActionMapping* object caches subordinate configuration information as follows:

   - *ActionForward* objects are cached using a *HashMap*, keyed by the *name* attribute in the `<forward>` element nested within the `<action>` tag.
   - *ExceptionConfig* objects are cached using a *HashMap*, keyed by the *type* attribute in the `<exception>` element nested in the `<action>` tag.
2. *ActionForward* objects are cached using a *HashMap*, keyed by the *name* attribute of the `<forward>` element nested within the `<global-forwards>` tag.
3. *ActionFormBean* objects are cached using a *HashMap*, keyed by the *name* attribute of the `<form-bean>` element.

   Each *ActionFormBean* caches subordinate configuration information as follows:

   - *FormPropertyConfig* objects are cached using a *HashMap*, keyed by *name* attribute of the `<form-property>` element nested within the `<form-bean>` tag.
4. *DataSourceConfig* objects are cached using a *HashMap*, keyed by a default *Globals.DATA_SOURCE_KEY* or the *key* attribute on the `<data-source>` element.
5. *ExceptionConfig* objects are cached using a *HashMap*, keyed by the *type* attribute of the `<exception>` element nested in the `<global-exceptions>` tag.
6. *MessageResourcesConfig* objects are cached using a *HashMap*, keyed by a default *Globals.MESSAGES_KEY* or *key* attribute of the `<message-resources>` element.
7. *PlugInConfig* objects are cached using an *ArrayList*.
8. A single *ControllerConfig* is placed in the *ModuleConfig*.

Creating Configuration Objects

Each rule in the *ConfigRuleSet* is associated with an element nesting pattern; an example pattern appears as the first argument in the *addObjectCreate (...)* signature shown next. The patterns and associated rules are first registered with the Digester using several *add*RuleName*(...)* methods encapsulated in *ConfigRuleSet* class. During struts-config.xml parsing, the rules are fired when an element nesting pattern in the struts-config.xml file matches with a pattern for which a rule is registered. For a given pattern, there could be more than one registered rule; in this case all matching rules are evaluated in the order they were first registered. Refer to the API documentation at http://jakarta.apache.org/commons/digester/api/index.html for additional information.

In this section, the *ConfigRuleSet* is annotated for clarifying the relationship between different configuration objects and their creation sequence. The following convention is used for adding rules to the digester's rules cache.

```
digester.addObjectCreate("struts-config/data-sources/data-source",
         "org.apache.struts.config.DataSourceConfig",
         "className");
```

The preceding snippet is equivalent to the following code:

```
digester.addRule("struts-config/data-sources/data-source",
     new ObjectCreateRule("org.apache.struts.config.DataSourceConfig", "className"));
```

Annotated ConfigRuleSet

It is not necessary to read this subsection if your intent is only to use the Struts framework; however, if you wanted to extend the framework to suite the needs of your project, this "under the hood" discussion can provide you with useful information on how you can declaratively add additional properties to the various configuration objects used by Struts, and even add new configuration objects.

Digester uses a stack to create the configuration object hierarchy. It pushes the most recently created object on top of the stack, therefore, the object to which all rules apply is the object that was most recently created and pushed on the stack by the Digester using the *ObjectCreateRule*. The object on the top of the stack goes out of scope, and is subsequently popped, when the corresponding tag in struts-config.xml goes out of scope. It is convenient to equate the *ModuleConfig* object to document root, which is `<struts-config>`. The runtime representation of rules are concrete objects that extend the *Rule* class. The order of rules firing, as depicted next, is important for creating an appropriate object hierarchy.

The *ObjectCreateRule* instantiated as a result of the element nesting pattern *struts-config/data-sources/data-source* shown here will create a *DataSourceConfig* object. If the `<data-source>` element specifies a *className* attribute, the class specified by this attribute will be used, instead of *DataSourceConfig*, for creating the configuration object. The default *DataSource* object created by *DataSourceConfig* is of the type *org.apache.struts.util .GenericDataSource*.

```
digester.addObjectCreate("struts-config/data-sources/data-source",
         "org.apache.struts.config.DataSourceConfig",
         "className");
```

The *SetPropertiesRule* shown next will set the properties of this object with attributes specified in the `<data-source>` element of the configuration file.

```
digester.addSetProperties("struts-config/data-sources/data-source");
```

The *SetNextRule* shown next will call the *addDataSourceConfig* method of the root object in the configuration hierarchy to add a reference to the *DataSourceConfig* object in the root object; the configuration root object is *ModuleConfig*.

```
digester.addSetNext("struts-config/data-sources/data-source",
         "addDataSourceConfig",
         "org.apache.struts.config.DataSourceConfig");
```

The *AddDataSourcePropertyRule* instantiated as a result of the element nesting pattern *struts-config/data-sources/data-source/set-property* shown next will add dynamic properties and their values to the *DataSourceConfig* object as specified in the `<set-property>` element of the configuration file.

```
digester.addRule("struts-config/data-sources/data-source/set-property",
        new AddDataSourcePropertyRule(digester));
```

The struts-config.xml file will have following declarations for the preceding rule:

```
<struts-config>
  <data-sources>
    <data-source>
      <set-property property="autoCommit"  value="false"/>
      <set-property property="password"    value="mypassword"/>
    </data-source>
  </data-sources>
</struts-config>
```

The *SetActionMappingClassRule* instantiated as a result of the element nesting pattern *struts-config/action-mappings*, as shown next, will set the class name of the action mapping class for instantiating *ActionMapping* objects. The action mapping class name is set in the *ModuleConfig* object using the *type* attribute in the `<action-mappings>` element. A default action mapping class *org.apache.struts.action.ActionMapping* is preconfigured in *ModuleConfig*.

```
digester.addRule("struts-config/action-mappings",
        new SetActionMappingClassRule(digester));
//As of Struts 1.1 beta 2, SetActionMappingClassRule class is in
ConfigRuleSet.java file
```

The *FactoryCreateRule* is instantiated as a result of the element nesting pattern *struts-config/action-mappings/action*, as shown next. This rule will instantiate an *ActionMapping* object via the *ActionMappingFactory.createObject(...)* method which uses the class specified by the *className* attribute in the `<action>` element; if this element is not specified, it will use the action mapping class specified in the *ModuleConfig* object.

```
digester.addFactoryCreate("struts-config/action-mappings/action",
        new ActionMappingFactory());
//As of Struts 1.1, ActionMappingFactory class is in
ConfigRuleSet.java file
```

The *SetPropertiesRule* shown next will set the properties of the *ActionMapping* object with attributes specified on the `<action>` element of the configuration file; the *SetNextRule* shown next will call the *addActionConfig* method to add a reference to this *ActionMapping* object in the parent object, which is *ModuleConfig*. As discussed in the earlier section "Parsing the Configuration File," all *ActionMapping* objects are cached inside the *ModuleConfig* in a

HashMap. Similar discussion holds good for all other configuration objects with the exception of *PlugInConfig*, which is cached in an *ArrayList*.

```
digester.addSetProperties("struts-config/action-mappings/action");
digester.addSetNext("struts-config/action-mappings/action",
          "addActionConfig",
          "org.apache.struts.config.ActionConfig");
```

The *SetPropertyRule* shown next is instantiated as a result of the element nesting pattern *struts-config/action-mappings/action/set-property*. This rule allows declaration of two attributes; the first attribute will contain the name of the property, and the second attribute will contain the property value. Incidentally, in the following example, the first attribute that will contain the name of the property has a value "property", and the second attribute that will contain the property value is named "value". The *ActionMapping* object accessor is called for setting the value of the specified property for each `<set-property>` element. This is just another way of setting properties of the configuration objects.

```
digester.addSetProperty("struts-config/action-mappings/action/set-property",
"property", "value");
```

The struts-config.xml file will have the following declarations for the preceding rule:

```
<struts-config>
  <action-mappings>
    <action  path="/editCustomerProfile"
             type="packageName.EditCustomerAction"
             name="customerProfileForm"
             scope="request">
      <set-property property="scope"  value="request"/>
    </action>
  </action-mappings>
</struts-config>
```

The following snippet creates the *ExceptionConfig* object, sets it properties as specified in the `<exception>` element of the configuration file, and sets a reference in its parent object, which is currently the *ActionMapping* object. The parent object is apparent from the element nesting pattern */action/exception*:

```
digester.addObjectCreate("struts-config/action-mappings/action/exception",
         "org.apache.struts.config.ExceptionConfig",
         "className");
digester.addSetProperties("struts-config/action-mappings/action/exception");
digester.addSetNext("struts-config/action-mappings/action/exception",
         "addExceptionConfig",
         "org.apache.struts.config.ExceptionConfig");
digester.addSetProperty("struts-config/action-mappings/action/exception/set-
property",
         "property", "value");
```

The following snippet creates the *ActionForward* object, sets it properties as specified in the <forward> element of the configuration file, and sets a reference in its parent object, which is currently the *ActionMapping* object. The parent object is apparent from element nesting pattern */action/forward*:

```
digester.addObjectCreate("struts-config/action-mappings/action/forward",
        "org.apache.struts.action.ActionForward",
        "className");
digester.addSetProperties("struts-config/action-mappings/action/forward");
digester.addSetNext("struts-config/action-mappings/action/forward",
        "addForwardConfig",
        "org.apache.struts.config.ForwardConfig");
digester.addSetProperty("struts-config/action-mappings/action/forward/set-prop
erty",
        "property", "value");
```

For the next rule, notice that the parent object is again the *ModuleConfig* object that is associated with the document root <struts-config>. The following snippet creates the *ControllerConfig* object, sets it properties as specified in the <controller> element of the configuration file, and sets a reference in its parent object, which is currently the *ModuleConfig* object:

```
digester.addObjectCreate("struts-config/controller",
        "org.apache.struts.config.ControllerConfig",
        "className");
digester.addSetProperties("struts-config/controller");
digester.addSetNext("struts-config/controller",
        "setControllerConfig",
        "org.apache.struts.config.ControllerConfig");
digester.addSetProperty("struts-config/controller/set-property",
        "property", "value");
```

The following creates the ActionFormBean object, sets it properties as specified in the <form-bean> element of the configuration file, and sets a reference in its parent object, which is currently the *ModuleConfig* object:

```
digester.addObjectCreate("struts-config/form-beans/form-bean",
        "org.apache.struts.action.ActionFormBean",
        "className");
digester.addSetProperties("struts-config/form-beans/form-bean");
digester.addSetNext("struts-config/form-beans/form-bean",
        "addFormBeanConfig",
        "org.apache.struts.config.FormBeanConfig");
digester.addSetProperty("struts-config/form-beans/form-bean/set-property",
        "property", "value");
```

The following snippet creates the *FormPropertyConfig* object, sets it properties as specified in the <form-property> element of the configuration file, and sets a reference in its parent object, which is currently the *ActionFormBean* object:

```
digester.addObjectCreate("struts-config/form-beans/form-bean/form-property",
        "org.apache.struts.config.FormPropertyConfig",
        "className");
digester.addSetProperties("struts-config/form-beans/form-bean/form-property");
digester.addSetNext("struts-config/form-beans/form-bean/form-property",
        "addFormPropertyConfig",
        "org.apache.struts.config.FormPropertyConfig");
digester.addSetProperty(
        "struts-config/form-beans/form-bean/form-property/set-property",
        "property", "value");
```

The following snippet creates the global *ExceptionConfig* object, sets it properties as specified in the `<exception>` element of the configuration file, and sets a reference in its parent object, which is currently the *ModuleConfig* object:

```
digester.addObjectCreate("struts-config/global-exceptions/exception",
        "org.apache.struts.config.ExceptionConfig",
        "className");
digester.addSetProperties("struts-config/global-exceptions/exception");
digester.addSetNext("struts-config/global-exceptions/exception",
        "addExceptionConfig",
        "org.apache.struts.config.ExceptionConfig");
digester.addSetProperty("struts-config/global-exceptions/exception/set-property",
        "property", "value");
```

The following snippet creates the global *ActionForward* object, sets it properties as specified in the `<forward>` element of the configuration file, and sets a reference in its parent object, which is currently the *ModuleConfig* object:

```
digester.addObjectCreate("struts-config/global-forwards/forward",
        "org.apache.struts.action.ActionForward",
        "className");
digester.addSetProperties("struts-config/global-forwards/forward");
digester.addSetNext("struts-config/global-forwards/forward",
        "addForwardConfig",
        "org.apache.struts.config.ForwardConfig");
digester.addSetProperty("struts-config/global-forwards/forward/set-property",
        "property", "value");
```

The following snippet creates the *MessageResourcesConfig* object, sets it properties as specified in the `<message-resources>` element of the configuration file, and sets a reference in its parent object, which is currently the *ModuleConfig* object:

```
digester.addObjectCreate("struts-config/message-resources",
        "org.apache.struts.config.MessageResourcesConfig",
        "className");
digester.addSetProperties("struts-config/message-resources");
digester.addSetNext("struts-config/message-resources",
        "addMessageResourcesConfig",
        "org.apache.struts.config.MessageResourcesConfig");
```

```
digester.addSetProperty("struts-config/message-resources/set-property",
        "property", "value");
```

The following snippet creates the *PlugInConfig* object, sets it properties as specified in the `<plug-in>` element of the configuration file, and sets a reference in its parent object, which is currently the *ModuleConfig* object:

```
digester.addObjectCreate("struts-config/plug-in",
        "org.apache.struts.config.PlugInConfig");
digester.addSetProperties("struts-config/plug-in");
digester.addSetNext("struts-config/plug-in",
        "addPlugInConfig",
        "org.apache.struts.config.PlugInConfig");
digester.addRule("struts-config/plug-in/set-property",
        new PlugInSetPropertyRule(digester));
//As of Struts 1.1, PlugInSetProperty class is in ConfigRuleSet.java file
```

Struts MVC Semantics

Building upon the knowledge of how Struts offers various infrastructure services, this section will discuss the design patterns and implementation details of the key components of the framework. The semantics of key Struts components will assist in recapping this chapter, and at the same time offer an "under the hood" view that will be helpful in extending the framework, should such a need arise. The Struts framework uses the Service to Worker design pattern [Core].

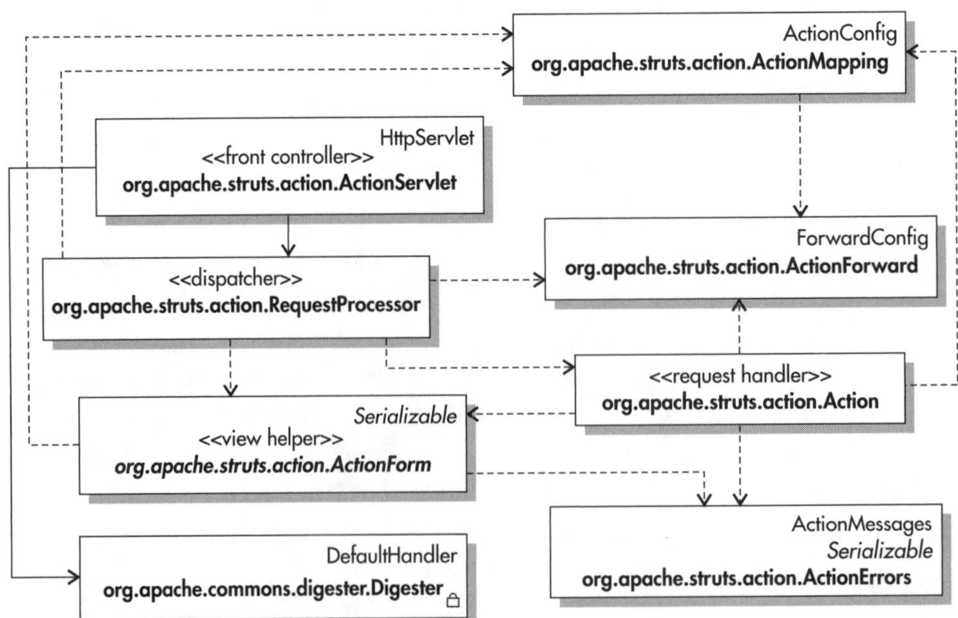

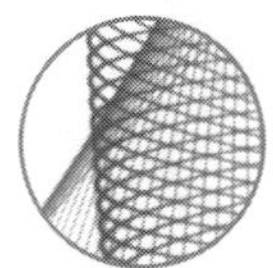

NOTE

Struts is constantly evolving, as such, it is very likely that the semantics captured here may change to some degree as the 1.1 beta undergoes bug fixes and optimizations.

The Controller Object

The controller semantics are realized by the *ActionServlet* class. It provides a central place for handling all client requests. This promotes a cleaner division of labor for the controller layer that typically deals with view and navigation management, leaving the model access and manipulation to request handlers (Command objects [Gof]) that are typically request specific. All incoming requests are mapped to the central controller in the deployment descriptor as follows:

```
<servlet>
    <servlet-name>action</servlet-name>
    <servlet-class>org.apache.struts.action.ActionServlet</servlet-class>
</servlet>
<servlet-mapping>
    <servlet-name>action</servlet-name>
    <url-pattern>*.do</url-pattern>
</servlet-mapping>
```

The logical mapping of resources depicted in the preceding permits modification of resource mappings within the configuration file without the need to change any application code; this mapping scheme is also referred to as *Multiplexed Resource Mapping*. The controller provides a centralized access point for all presentation-tier requests. The controller delegates each incoming request to the *RequestProcessor*, which in turn dispatches the request to the associated form bean for form validation, and to a request handler for accessing the model. The combination of controller and *RequestProcessor* forms the core controller process. The abstraction provided by the controller alleviates a developer from creating common application services such as managing views, sessions, and form data; a developer leverages standardized mechanisms such as error and exception handling, navigation, internalization, data validation, data conversion, and so on.

Controller Object Semantics

The controller servlet (*ActionServlet*) essentially initializes the resources required for controlling the behavior of the framework; all request processing function is delegated by the controller to the *RequestProcessor*. The following is a listing of the *init()* method–related key controller operations in the order of execution sequence:

1. Get the initialization parameters declared in the deployment descriptor (refer to the *ActionServlet* API for a complete list of available initialization parameters and their usage).
2. Parse the web.xml deployment descriptor to retrieve the `<url-pattern>` element's body; this will assist the *RequestProcessor* in understanding how to extract the path information from the request URI and strip the .do extension. The URL mapping is saved in the ServletContext using *Action.SERVLET_KEY*.
3. Parse the struts-config.xml using the Digester instance and the *ConfigRuleSet* (discussed earlier in this section), and create the configuration object hierarchy rooted in the *ModuleConfig* object. The *ModuleConfig* is saved in the context using *Globals.MODULE_KEY*.
4. Create a *MessageResources* object for each *MessageResourcesConfig* object and save it in the ServletContext using the key supplied for each message resource, or the default key *Action.MESSAGES_KEY* (a.k.a. *Globals.MESSAGES_KEY*).
5. Create a *DataSource* object for each *DataSourceConfig* object and save it in the ServletContext using the key supplied for each data source, or the default key *Action.DATA_SOURCE_KEY* (a.k.a. *Globals.DATA_SOURCE_KEY*).
6. Create a *PlugIn[]* object for all *PlugInConfig* objects and save the array in the ServletContext using the key *Action.PLUG_INS_KEY.* Initialize each *PlugIn* object with the properties available in the corresponding *PlugInConfig* object. For each *PlugIn* object created, call its *init(...)* method.
7. Freeze the configuration from further modification. This logic prevents changes to the configuration objects once the servlet begins accepting client requests.

In the *process(...)* method, the *ActionServlet* will create a *RequestProcessor* if it has not been created already, and delegate the request processing to the *RequestProcessor* by calling the *process(...)* method of the *RequestProcessor*. In the following section, we will continue the discussion on the *RequestProcessor.process(...)* method.

The Dispatcher Object

The *RequestProcessor* functions as a dispatcher and handles client requests by instantiating (or reusing) a request handler, and a corresponding form bean. The errors created, or exceptions thrown by the form beans and the request handlers, (and processed by the *RequestProcessor*) which influences the view management function of the *RequestProcessor*. Form beans assist *RequestProcessor* in storing the form data and/or staging intermediate model data required by the view. The *RequestProcessor* uses the `<action>` declarations, as shown next, for instantiating request specific request handlers.

```
<form-bean  name="PortalAllianceRegistrationForm"
       type="packageName.PortalAllianceRegistrationForm"/>
```

```
<action-mappings>
    <action path="/PortalAllianceRegistration"
            type="com.gc.prez.admin.PortalAllianceRegistrationAction"
            name="PortalAllianceRegistrationForm"
            scope="session"
            input="ShowPage"
            validate="false">
        <forward name="ShowPage" path="/2_1_PortalAllianceRegistration.jsp"/>
        <forward name="EnterPortalID" path="/2_3A_EnterPortalID.jsp"/>
        <forward name="success" path="/2_SiteAdministratorServicesMainPage.jsp"/>
    </action>
</action-mappings>
```

The path specified in the request URI is used for locating the corresponding `<action>` element (which is the corresponding ActionMapping object) whose type property specifies the class for instantiating request handler objects.

Dispatcher Object Semantics

The following is a listing of *process* method–related key dispatcher operations in the order of execution sequence:

1. From the servlet path, get the path information (after stripping the .do extension). This path information will be used to find the matching *ActionMapping* object. (A client request encapsulates the desired action in the request URI as servlet path.)
2. If *ControllerConfig* specifies *locale="true"*, get the locale from the request and store it in the user's session using *Action.LOCALE_KEY*. If the locale is already existing, no action is taken.
3. If *ControllerConfig* provides a content type, set the content type for responses.
4. If *ControllerConfig* specifies *nocache="true"", set no-cache HTTP headers on each response.*
5. Call the *processPreprocess* method. This method is provided for doing any custom processing prior to form processing. A return value of true indicates success, otherwise the *process* method is terminated with a *return*.
6. Get the *ActionMapping* object from *ModuleConfig* for the given path; if a match is not found, an *ActionMapping* object associated with the property *unknown="true"* is used. The resulting *ActionMapping* is saved in the request scope using *Action.MAPPING_KEY*. If no mapping is found, the *response.sendError* method is called for sending an error message to the client, and the *process* method is terminated with a *return*.
7. Perform Java Authentication and Authorization Service (JAAS)–based authentication using the *request.isUserInRole* method for verifying privilege to perform the current action; the roles are specified as a comma-delimited string in the *roles* property of the *ActionMapping*. If no roles are provided in the action mapping object, or the user is in the appropriate role, then the processing will continue, otherwise the *response.sendError* is called for sending an error message to the client, and the *process* method is terminated with a *return*.

8. Try finding the *ActionForm* associated with *ActionMapping* in the specified scope. If found, use this *ActionForm*, else, create a new *ActionForm* object or *DynaActionForm* object using the *type* property of the corresponding *ActionFormBean*; save the form in the specified scope using the *name* property from the *ActionFormBean*. Call the *reset(...)* method of the *ActionForm* object or *DynaActionForm* object to initialize the form; populate the form object with the parameters in the request object.
9. The form object's *validation* method is called if the *validate* property of the *ActionMapping* object is set to true. If the validation is successful, then we proceed to the next step. If the validation returns a non-null or non-empty *ActionErrors* object, an *ActionForward* object with the *name* property that is the same as the *input* property of *ActionMapping* object is chosen as the candidate *ActionForward* object. The *ActionForward* object provides the URL (*path* property of *ActionForward*) of the next view. This is usually the same view whose processing generated the *ActionErrors*. The *ActionErrors* object is saved in the request object using the key *Action.ERROR_KEY.*
10. Check for presence of the *forward* property in the *ActionMapping* object. This property is mutually exclusive with the *type* and *include* property. If found, the URI specified by the *forward* property is used for forwarding the current request instead of using a request handler object to handle this request. After the forward is done, the *process(...)* method is terminated with a *return*.
11. Check for presence of the *include* property in the *ActionMapping* object. This property is mutually exclusive with the *type* and *forward* properties. If found, the URI specified by the *include* property is used in *RequestDispatcher.include()* for processing the current request instead of using a request handler object to process this request. After the include is done, the *process* method is terminated with a *return*. If an *include* property was not specified then we precede to the next step.
12. Find an instance of the request handler from the request handler cache using its fully qualified class name specified by the type property of the *ActionMapping* object. If an instance is found, use this instance for the next step, else create a new instance of the class specified by the type property and save it in the cache.
13. Call the *execute* method of the request handler. The request handler will return an *ActionForward* object depending on the outcome of its processing.
14. The *path* property in the *ActionForward* object is used for forwarding the current request to the next view.

The Request Handler

A subclass of an *Action* class is used as an adaptor between incoming requests and the model. A request is intercepted initially by the *RequestProcessor*, which in turn instantiates a corresponding request handler. This *Action* class–derived object, also called the request handler, is created specific to every request as explained in the preceding section. The request handler implements the *Command* pattern [Gof]. A client request encapsulates the desired action in the request URI as servlet path, the path information is subsequently extracted by the dispatcher (*RequestProcessor*) for creating an instance of the corresponding request handler. The command pattern decouples the UI from request handlers.

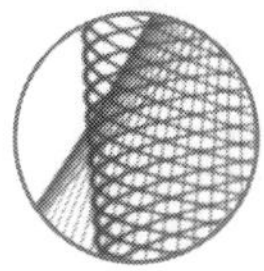

NOTE

User-specific state information must not be stored in request handlers because they are used for servicing requests from all users.

Request Handler Semantics

For distributed applications, an action class houses the control logic required for interacting with business logic in EJB components and will typically use a *Business Delegate* [Core] object for this purpose. Business delegate shields the request handlers from having to deal with the complexity of accessing distributed components. The business delegate design pattern promotes loose coupling between the request handlers and the server-side components since the logic for accessing server-side components is embedded in the business delegate. A request handler is written by a developer working in the presentation tier; a business delegate is usually written by a developer responsible for creating the business tier services. For smaller nondistributed applications, the action class may contain business logic. When distributed processing is not required, and business logic is embedded in request handlers, a *Data Access Object* [Core] can be used to abstract the underlying data access implementation; this provides a loose coupling between the request handlers and the data access layer, thus protecting the presentation tier from implementation changes in the integration tier. The base *Action* class of request handlers provides several convenience methods; please refer to the API documentation at http://jakarta.apache.org/struts/api/index.html.

Message Resources Semantics

This section will briefly discuss the semantics of *MessageResources* and *PropertyMessageResources* classes. Each message resource bundle has a base name, which corresponds to the name of a properties file, as discussed in the section "Internationalized Messaging and Labeling." This base name is identified by the *property* attribute in the `<message-resources>` element of the configuration file. The controller creates a *MessageResourcesConfig* object for every `<message-resources>` element in the configuration file. The controller then creates a *MessageResources* object for each *MessageResourcesConfig* object and saves it in the context using the key supplied for each message resource, or the default key *Action.MESSAGES_KEY* (a.k.a. *Globals.MESSAGES_KEY*).

The *MessageResources* objects are created using a *MessageResourcesFactory*. A factory class can be specified using the factory attribute in the `<message-resources>` element. However, for the accessing messages housed in a properties file, a default factory *org.apache.struts.util.PropertyMessageResourcesFactory* is preconfigured in the *MessageResourcesConfig* object; the *ActionServlet* uses this factory object for instantiating the *PropertyMessageResources* object. The following illustration depicts the static model providing internationalized messaging and labeling facility.

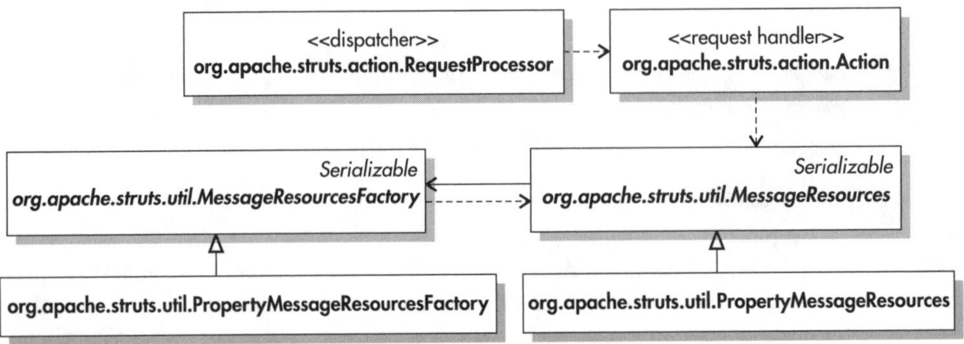

A message from a specific resource bundle is retrieved by the framework by first retrieving the *PropertyMessageResources* object from the context using the appropriate key and then calling its *getMessage(...)* method while passing a locale and a message key. *PropertyMessageResources.getMessage(...)* is used when the retrieved message does not require parametric substitution; otherwise, for parametric substitution *the MessageResources.getMessage(...)* method is used, which accepts a locale, a message key, and an *Object[]* as arguments. When an *Object[]* is specified, the *MessageResources.getMessage(...)* method retrieves the message format pattern by calling the *PropertyMessageResources.getMessage(...)* method and uses this format pattern in the *MessageFormat.format(...)* method to perform parametric substitution of *Object[]*.

A cache of locale (converted to its String value) is maintained in the *PropertyMessageResource* object to identify if messages for a particular locale have already been loaded in the message cache. If a locale is not found in the locale cache, the entire properties file associated with that locale is loaded into the message cache. Refer to the section "Internationalized Messaging and Labeling" for naming conventions used for the properties files. The message cache is keyed by '*locale.toString() + "." +* key' and the value is the value in the properties file for the corresponding key. When retrieving messages, it is possible that after loading the properties file for a particular locale, the desired key may not exist. In such situations, an attempt is made to find a key that is less restrictive for the specified locale; this is accomplished by stripping the locale variant from the key, if present, and doing another search with the less restrictive key; if this search is unsuccessful, then the locale's country code is stripped from the key and another search is performed. If the key is found using the less restrictive version of the locale, then the corresponding message is added to the message cache using the complete original key without country code or variant stripping; this increases the number of messages in the cache but provides faster response time for finding messages. If the key is not found even after locale stripping, the default locale is loaded in the message cache, if it already hasn't been loaded, and the key search is performed with the key modified for the default locale; if this search is unsuccessful, the base resource bundle without any locale specification is searched. If the key is found using the default locale or the base bundle, the corresponding message is added to the message cache using the complete original key.

Summary

Before embarking on a major project, it is always beneficial to evaluate off-the-shelf or out-of-box solutions that address a significant part of the requirements. Implementing MVC semantics for a request/response-based HTTP protocol demands significant investment of time and effort. Selecting a suitable framework for solving this problem provides a head start for a project while allowing the architects and developers to focus on realizing the business use cases rather than integration semantics. This chapter has provided insight into Struts framework, its MVC semantics, its configuration semantics, and the core services it offers out-of-box. The knowledge gained from this chapter is instrumental in designing and implementing the presentation tier components of Chapter 5. Chapter 5 will also cover the Struts Validator for declarative form validation. More information on Struts and the related configuration and installation instructions can be found at http://jakarta.apache.org/struts/userGuide/index.html. Because Struts development is an ongoing endeavor, it is likely that by the time you read this chapter, some of the implementation may change, therefore it is best to complement the information provided in this chapter with release notes and updates posted at http:// jakarta.apache.org/struts.

References

[Core] *Core J2EE Patterns* by Deepak Alur et al. (Prentice-Hall, 2001)

[Gof] *Design Patterns* by Erich Gamma et al. (Addison-Wesley, 1995)

CHAPTER

5

Presentation Tier Design and Implementation

IN THIS CHAPTER:

Implementing Struts Request Handlers and Form-Beans

Implementing Presentation Tier Design Patterns

Designing with Struts Tags and Validator

Implementing Application Security

Realization of the Sample Application Use Cases

Abstracting Patterns from the Sample Application

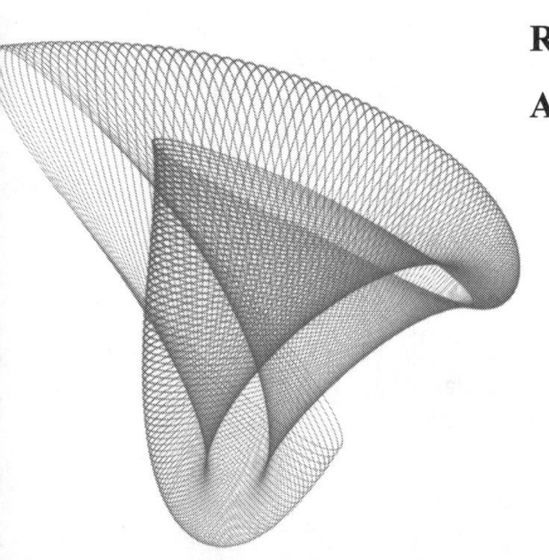

Chapter 1 started out with a high-level use case view. Chapter 2 employed information architecture to move toward a detailed use case view. Chapter 2 provided us a sense of process flow, transactional semantics, and subsystem interactions. Chapter 4 was a look at using Struts as a framework of choice for implementing the presentation tier. If you have not reviewed Chapter 4, please do so before proceeding with this chapter. The use case view developed in Chapters 1 and 2 is employed for creating a project plan; this use case view can provide us with essential information for planning work allocation to development teams, while identifying architecturally significant use cases for building our first thread of end-to-end functionality. The development process in this chapter follows the use case-driven approach; this will provide us with the traceability required for adhering to the functionality prescribed by the use cases in Chapters 1 and 2.

While the focus of Chapter 4 was to explain the architecture employed in creating a presentation framework, and to provide the essential base for working with Struts, this chapter focuses mainly on implementing the use cases using the Struts framework. Emphasis in this chapter is on creating the static and dynamic models of the system, and identifying patterns that provide repeatable solutions for solving complex user interactions. Templates can be derived from these patterns for assisting the development team in establishing consistent design vocabulary and implementation across all use cases. In this chapter, we will develop presentation-side tier functionality for all the use cases identified by the packages GreaterCause Site Administration, Manage Campaigns, and Search NPO. We have endeavored to implement these use cases using different design implementation patterns to provide readers with insight into leveraging the Struts framework in different ways; these patterns will serve as a starting point from which to evolve and create more repeatable solutions by leveraging several other features of Struts not covered by this book. Since the focus of this book is architecture, a large portion of this chapter is dedicated to discussing design implementation patterns that can be used repeatedly in creating consistent solutions across the system.

To follow along with this chapter, you may want to install the GreaterCause application, as explained in Chapter 9. The complete administration functionality of the GreaterCause application is rooted in the Administrator Services button on the GreaterCause.com home page. Appendix C provides a complete site flow for Administrator Services.

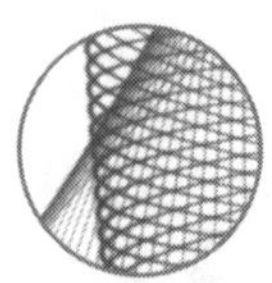

NOTE

Readers of this book should have a basic knowledge of servlet and JSP technologies. In order to provide an optimum reading time, we have deliberately tried to avoid explaining these technologies. Should you desire to learn about servlets and JSPs, excellent tutorials are available at java.sun.com and at the sites of J2EE container vendors.

The class diagrams depicted in this chapter will cover the presentation tier components and related vocabulary; the business tier (service layer) model and associated design patterns are explained and developed in Chapter 6 and Chapter 7. So long as the business interfaces are clearly defined for the business tier, construction of components in the presentation tier can be done in parallel with the construction of components in the business tier. In large projects, we tend to use the specialized skill of a web production team, presentation tier engineers, and business tier engineers. Therefore, for each use case being developed, the artifacts created by this cross-functional team must be available at the right time for integration testing to proceed. Parallel development of different tiers has to be managed effectively in order to provide a cohesive set of deliverables that can be tested end-to-end; the key learning from the integration testing can be leveraged by the subsequent iterations in creating quality deliverables.

Implementing Presentation Tier Classes

Because the presentation tier leverages the Struts framework for providing the controller component, the number of classes participating in realizing each GreaterCause use case are minimal; the heavy duty work is performed by the Struts itself. Whether you have a preference for Struts or not, one important aspect of this discussion is to understand how simple the development process is when an MVC-based implementation is provided as a bundled solution. Our focus is on creating request handlers, and supporting helper classes such as business Delegates, ActionForm subclasses (form-beans), and DTOs (data transfer objects). We endeavor to identify the relationships between request handlers and the rest of the helper classes, and use sequence diagrams to model the interactions between these classes. For each use case, we shall create a single class diagram, and subsequently identify design patterns that will abstract key interactions between the Views (JSPs), the Struts Framework, and the classes participating in the realization of each use case.

The detailed use case view provides us with a clear understanding of the work flow involved in accomplishing various application tasks. These application tasks, or actions, can be represented as methods in the request handlers, and subsequently mapped to the business interfaces provided by the service layer via the business delegates. At this juncture, we may find the need to evolve the coarse-grained tasks defined in the use case into its constituent parts, and identify suitable operations for these tasks on the class diagrams.

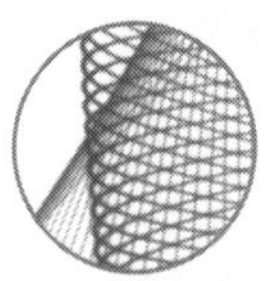

DEFINITION

A DTO (Data Transfer Object) *represents a coarse-grained object that aggregates server side data before it is serialized and marshalled across the wire from the business tier to the presentation tier or vice versa. The purpose of using DTO is to reduce network traffic since calls made to EJBs are expensive. The DTO pattern is explained in Chapter 7, in the section "Data Transfer Object Pattern."*

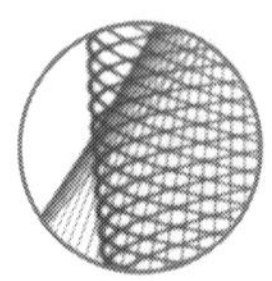

DEFINITION

A Business Delegate *is used to reduce the coupling between the presentation tier and the business tier; it hides the implementation details of the business interfaces. Details are available in the section "Implementing the Business Delegate Pattern."*

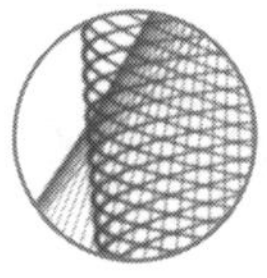

NOTE

The sequence diagrams depicted in this chapter have been distilled to make them easy to read while maintaining focus on the key aspects of object interactions. As such, please refer to the code illustrations or the accompanying source distribution for complete details.

Implementing ActionForm Subclasses

The properties defined in an ActionForm subclass follow the JavaBean patterns described in Chapter 4. The Struts framework uses these patterns, that is the *get* and *set* accessor methods, to manage the ActionForm (a.k.a. the form-bean, which is discussed in Chapter 4) state. Struts uses the org.apache.commons.beanutils package to perform operations on JavaBeans; this includes automatic type conversion (from request parameters to the form-bean, and vice versa), handling simple and nested bean properties, and automatic field initialization based on field type. The *beanutils* package provides increased productivity and convenience of working with JavaBean-compliant classes.

Capturing Form Data

The primary function of an ActionForm subclass is to capture form data submitted by an HTML document. The key/value pairs submitted as part of the HTTP request are used to populate the properties specified in the ActionForm subclass. As such, you can implement an ActionForm subclass for staging the data provided by the HTML form. The form-beans used by the GreaterCause application are not limited to capturing information from a single form. In our sample application, the site administrator has to typically go through two screens, one for identifying the entity that it is going to impersonate (either the portal-alliance or a non-profit), and the other for working with data pertaining to the entity. Multi-page interactions are explained in the section "Multi-Page Pattern." Another case of multi-page interaction is involved with search semantics, where up to four screen interactions are possible; this is explained in the section "Shared Request Handler Pattern." As explained in Chapter 4, the data types used in form-beans are transformed automatically from the String type of HTTP protocol to the target type used by the bean properties. The initial value for blank fields is also set automatically by the framework using helper classes from the *beanutils* package. Care should be taken to ensure that all form fields are represented in the form-bean, otherwise the Struts framework simply ignores extra parameters in the request. Also, you must try to prevent naming conflicts between the field names used in the HTML form with the field names used within the form-bean for the purpose of managing application state. In several cases, you can design a form that can handle input from multiple pages; this technique reduces the number of forms used by the application, which in turn reduces form clutter, increases manageability, and promotes modularity.

Validating Data

The ActionForm bean can optionally contain a validate method that is called either by the framework or through the request handler classes. If the validate method is not to be invoked by the framework, then you must set the *validate* attribute in the `<action>` element of the struts-config.xml to "false"; otherwise the framework will automatically call the *validate* method immediately after populating the form-bean. The semantics of the framework are explained in Chapter 4. An alternate technique allowing declarative validation is provided by the framework by extending the form-bean with the *ValidatorForm* class; this is discussed in the section "Factoring Validator into the Design Process."

For our sample application, we have deliberately set the *validate* attribute to "false". One reason for doing this is the way the *ValidatorForm* behaves when used with the *page* property. The validation.xml file (explained later) contains declarative validation, which could be tied to a numeric page identifier. The *page* attribute in validation.xml controls which validations must be evaluated based on the value of the *page* property in the form-bean. If the page number associated with the *page* property of the form is *n*, then all validations with *page* value *n* and less are evaluated. For the GreaterCause application, this behavior is not desired since the sequence of pages shown to the user is based on the administrator type, and therefore the set of validations associated with a site administrator will fail for other types of administrators for whom a corresponding form was not processed and the data was not collected; the sample application therefore explicitly calls the *validate* method from the request handlers. Another reason for not letting the framework automatically call the validation is to have control over which pages get shown when the validation fails. The automatic *validate* method by the framework is inflexible when dealing with several `<forward>` possibilities. Should a validation fail, the framework will automatically invoke the URL associated with the `<forward>` element that has the same *name* attribute as the *input* attribute on the `<action>` element. Using automatic validation implies that only one response view is possible no matter which form gets submitted. The GreaterCause application has several `<forward>` elements associated with an `<action>` element, therefore the *validate* method is explicitly called by the request handlers, and the use of the *input* attribute on `<action>` elements is not entertained.

Managing Application State

The GreaterCause application uses form-beans to manage the application state. One reason for doing this is because the state of the application is very much influenced by the form-bean's *page* and *action* properties; the second reason is that state information cannot be stored in the request handlers since request handlers are not thread safe. The *action* property is used in identifying an action associated with a link or a button that the system remembers and adapts its behavior based on the value; one such case is when a single form is used to create, update, and view the registration information associated with a Portal-Alliance or a non-profit (NPO). The *page* property is useful in identifying the pages in a multi-page interaction; the *ValidatorForm* (that extends ActionForm) contains the *page* property that can be used to number the forms participating in a multi-form interaction. The *page* property is useful in creation of wizard-like behavior. The *action* property combined with the *page* property makes the request handlers highly modular in that a single request handler can be used to handle a variety of forms and user actions. The multi-page pattern, multi-action pattern, and Shared Request Handler pattern (all patterns are explained later in the chapter) rely on this mechanism in creating highly flexible request handlers. Using state information, we are able to package related functionality within a single request handler class rather than spreading out related functionality across multiple action classes; this increases manageability and promotes modularity.

Transferring ActionForm Properties to DTO

Although form-beans can function as data transfer objects (DTOs), it is not advisable to do so because form-beans are "presentation layer centric." The UI is the most volatile part of the system, therefore we want to shield the business tier from changes in the form-beans of the presentation tier. For service layer calls, especially when using EJBs, it is desirable to make fewer calls to increase throughput. The Value Object pattern recommended by Core J2EE Patterns [Core] is used for transferring data between application tiers using objects (a.k.a. DTOs) whose level of granularity is coarse; this is further explained in Chapter 7. The process of transferring form data staged in the form-bean to data transfer objects, and vice versa, is greatly simplified if data transfer object and form-beans use the same naming convention for property accessors. The *beanutils* package provides helper classes for transferring the state from one bean to another; the GreaterCause application uses the method *PropertyUtils.copyProperties(toBean, fromBean)* from the *beanutils* package to accomplish this transfer in a single method call. The DTOs are typically designed by the service layer developer and contain flags for identifying whether a particular property was modified; these flags are used in optimizing method calls in the domain layer (see Chapter 6 for details) when modifying entity bean properties. The DTOs are packaged with both the web module (.war) and the EJB module (.jar) because these objects are common to both the web tier (presentation tier) and the EJB tier (business tier for GreaterCause).

Managing the Form-Bean Life Cycle

The *scope* attribute on the `<action>` element in the struts-config.xml file instructs the Struts framework about placement of the form-bean, upon its creation, in either the *request* object or the *session* object. When request scope is chosen, the form is placed in the *request* object and made available to the next resource invoked by the framework using the *RequestDisptacher.forward* method. The *request* objects are valid only within the scope of a servlet's service method, therefore the form-bean is not valid in the next invocation of the service method. The GreaterCause application uses the session scope to store all forms because all form-beans are designed to support multiple forms; employing this technique puts the responsibility of removing the form-beans on the developer when such beans are no longer useful. Keeping the form-beans in the session provides an added benefit of reuse when existing form-beans need to be frequently recycled during a user session; for such forms the reset method is implemented to prevent the annoyance of stale data being displayed to the users. Recall from Chapter 4 that the reset method is automatically called by the Struts framework just prior to form-bean population, so care must be taken in creating a reset method for cases where form data is captured from multiple forms. For such cases, it is best to check the *page* property and then conditionally initialize form-bean properties.

Implementing Request Handlers

Request handlers implement the Command pattern [Gof]. The controller servlet maps a request to the *execute* method of a request handler. The request handler is a subclass of the *Action* class, or any of the classes specified in the org.apache.struts.actions package; all classes in this package extend the *Action* class. In our sample application, we use the *Action* class as well as a variant of this class, the *DispatchAction* class from the *actions* package. The request handlers are cached by the controller and used for servicing subsequent requests from any user, as such, the request handlers are not thread safe; any state information pertaining to a user must not be stored in request handlers. Consider request handlers as an extension of the controller servlet; as discussed in Chapter 4, it is the controller servlet that instantiates the dispatcher, which in turn instantiates a request handler. One can write directly to the response stream from request handlers or pass control to another resource using the *RequestDispatcher .forward* method; the common practice is that a request handler will service a request, and when exiting its *execute* method, it will return an *ActionForward* object to the dispatcher instructing the dispatcher which view should be displayed next. When the request handler uses the *RequestDispatcher.forward* method, it can return a null as *ActionForward* to indicate to the controller that a response has already been sent and that the controller should take no further action. A typical request handler will have the following logic. This snippet has been taken from the class *PortalAllianceRegistrationAction* (Register Portal-Alliance use case); the code has been modified and made generic. Please refer to the accompanying source distribution for the exact code.

```
public ActionForward execute( ActionMapping mapping, ActionForm form,
HttpServletRequest req,HttpServletResponse res ) throws Exception {
    PortalAllianceRegistrationForm regForm =
                     ( PortalAllianceRegistrationForm )form;
    ActionErrors errors = new ActionErrors();
    /* Check transaction token to ensure that the page is not stale.
     * This check will also invalidate the token. isTokenValid()
     * method is synchronized on the session object */
    if ( !isTokenValid( req, true ) ) {
        errors.add( ActionErrors.GLOBAL_ERROR,
        new ActionError( "error.invalidToken" ) );
        saveErrors( req, errors );
        /* Redisplay the input form; this stale page does not
         * need transaction token */
        return mapping.findForward( "ShowPage" );
    }
    /* Validate the form fields */
    errors = form.validate( mapping, req );
    if ( !errors.empty() ) {
        saveErrors( req, errors );
        saveToken( req );
       /* Redisplay the input form */
       return mapping.findForward( "ShowPage" );
    }
    PortalAllianceRegistrationDTO dto = new PortalAllianceRegistrationDTO();
    /* Transfer form properties to DTO */
    try { PropertyUtils.copyProperties( dto, regForm ); }
    catch ( InvocationTargetException e ) {
        Throwable rootCause = e.getTargetException();
        if ( rootCause == null ) { rootCause = e; }
        throw new ServletException( rootCause );
    }
    catch ( Throwable e ) { throw new ServletException( e ); }
    /* Access service layer using the delegate */
    PortalAllianceRegistrationDelegate delegate =
            PortalAllianceRegistrationDelegate.getInstance();
```

```
    try { delegate.createPortalAllianceRegistration( req, dto ); }
    /* Catch service layer Exception */
    catch ( GCNestingException e ) {
        errors.add( ActionErrors.GLOBAL_ERROR,
        new ActionError( e.getMessageToken() ) );
        saveErrors( req, errors );
        /* Create a new token before redisplaying the page */
        saveToken( req );
        return mapping.findForward( "ShowPage" );
    }
    /* Clean up the form-bean */
    req.getSession().removeAttribute( "PortalAllianceRegistrationForm" );
    /* Specify the next View */
    return mapping.findForward( "success" );
}
```

The request handler can check the transaction token, perform form validations, and interact with the model using the business delegate. Token usage is discussed in Chapter 4. The sample application sets the transaction token for every transactional page; it then checks this token for validity when the request handler gets the control, and rejects any request with a stale token.

Managing User-Specific State

An *ActionMapping* object, created from the `<action>` element of the struts-config.xml file, is associated with a single request handler and a single form-bean. Other than the simplest scenarios, one can seldom expect that a single request handler will process a single page with a single operation. An example of such operations (which we subsequently refer to as "action") in the context of the sample application are the create/update/view actions on the registration page. It is highly unlikely that one will create three different request handlers for accommodating three different actions, because it will create manageability issues and defeat modularity. Among the available solutions, we will discuss the multi-page pattern and the multi-action pattern (using both the *Action* subclass strategy and *DispatchAction* subclass strategy) that uses the form-bean to manage application state; this state is queried by the request handler for deciding the process flow.

Although in most cases the Struts framework will instantiate and initialize the form-bean associated with a request handler (as specified by the *type* attribute in the `<form-bean>` element of struts-config.xml file), sometimes it becomes necessary for the request handlers to instantiate the form-beans required by a subsequent view. The sample application uses this technique when it invokes the search facility. The search facility is a common service available to any request handler wanting to couple itself with the search facility. The search facility's request handler has to remember the calling request handler such that it can seamlessly transfer control back to the calling request handler after the search request is satisfied. To enable this, the calling request handler has to instantiate the form-bean associated with the search facility and set the *action* property that will instruct the search facility which *ActionForward* it should use when exiting; this is explained in the section "Shared Request Handler Pattern."

Implementing the Business Delegate Pattern

A business delegate [Core] provides an extra level of indirection in accessing business tier services. A delegate essentially decouples the presentation tier from the business tier by brokering all calls from the presentation tier to the business tier. This design protects the presentation tier from changes in the business tier interfaces so long as the delegate is able to adapt the new business tier interface to existing method calls from the presentation tier. The business delegate also encapsulates the JNDI lookups, which reduces the complexity of the request handlers. Following is an example of a business delegate that is implemented to access the registration services of the EJB com.gc.services.admin.SiteAdminBean. The complete code is available in the accompanying source distribution. If you want to learn more about the package structure and naming conventions used by the sample application, please refer to the section "Identifying Package Dependencies."

```
package com.gc.prez.admin;
public class ManageNPODelegate {
    private ManageNPODelegate() {
        super();
    }
    /* Implement the Singleton pattern */
    public static ManageNPODelegate delegate =
        new ManageNPODelegate();
    public static ManageNPODelegate getInstance() {
        return delegate;
    }
    /* Get the remote reference of the EJB */
    public NPOAdmin getBusinessInterface( HttpServletRequest req )
    throws Exception {
            /* Use the generic Service Locator */
        ServiceLocator service = ServiceLocator.getInstance();
        NPOAdmin businessInterface =
        ( NPOAdmin )service.getRemoteForStateless( NPOAdminHome.class );
        return businessInterface;
    }
    /* Access the business tier service */
    public NPOProfileDTO getNPOProfileDTO( HttpServletRequest req,
    String ein, String adminID ) throws Exception {
        NPOAdmin businessInterface =
        getBusinessInterface( req );
        try {
            return ( NPOProfileDTO )businessInterface.getNPOProfile(
            ein, adminID );
```

```
        }
        catch ( RemoteException e ) {
            throw new ServletException
            ( Constants.Communication_Error, e );
        }
    }
    ... rest of the code ...
}
```

The sequence diagram of Figure 5-1 illustrates the business delegate interactions. The request handler method *ManageNPOAction.showNPOProfile()* will access the delegate. The delegate in

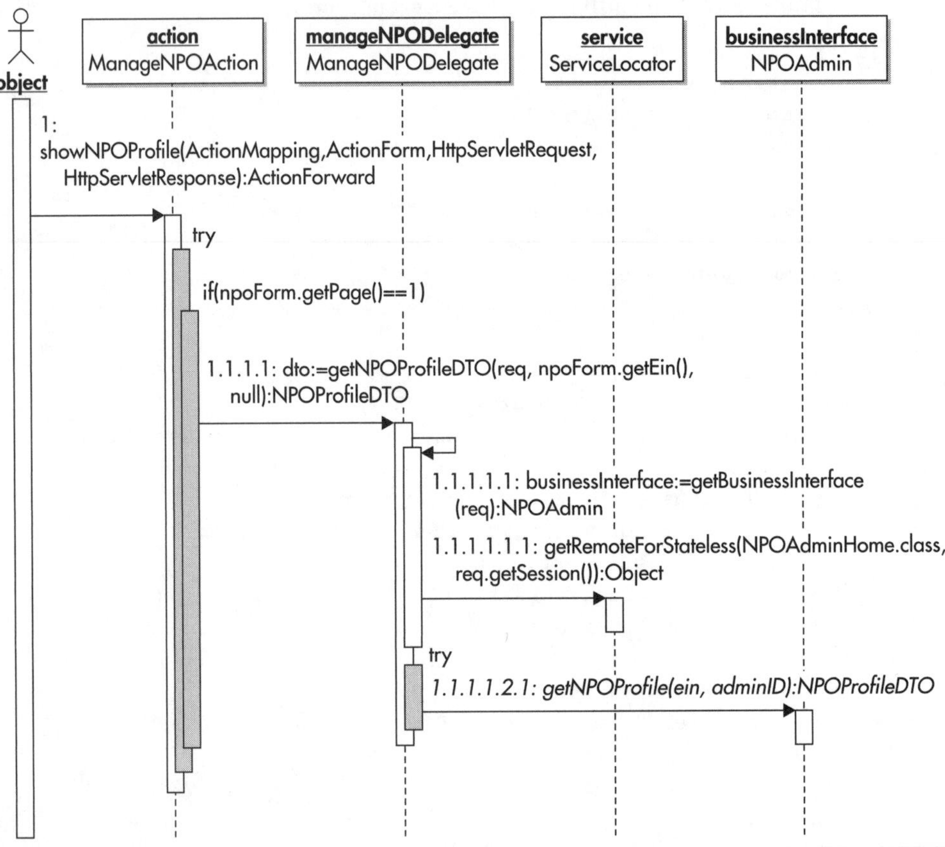

Figure 5-1 *Business delegate sequence diagram*

turn will get the remote reference to the business layer EJB using the *getBusinessInterface* method, and subsequently access the business tier service *getNPOProfile()*.

Implementing the Service Locator Pattern

The Service Locator encapsulates the logic for creating the initial context, JNDI lookup, and EJB remote reference creation. The service locator also optimizes access to EJBs by caching home references and EJB objects. It reduces code complexity for the business delegates whose only concern is to obtain the remote reference from the service locator and use it for making calls to the business tier. The sample application provides a more generic approach to implementing service locators using the reflection API; this has resulted in a single service locator for the entire GreaterCause application. You may want to evolve this implementation to suit your unique project requirements. The service locator implemented with the GreaterCause application provides the following generic service locator methods.

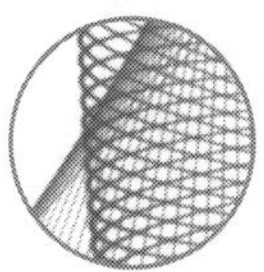

NOTE

For the GreaterCause application, the JNDI names follow the naming convention ejb/homeInterfaceName. *This convention is used while implementing the methods of the service locator.*

- *getRemoteForStateless(Class homeClass,)* This method will accept a stateless EJB home interface name and return a remote reference for the EJB. Home reference caching is used for optimization.
- *getRemoteForStateless(Class homeClass, Object[] args,)* This method will accept a stateless EJB home interface name and return a remote reference for the EJB. This method is called when the *create* method of the home interface accepts arguments; the arguments are passed to the *create* method using *Object[]*. Home reference caching is used for optimization.
- *getRemoteForStateful*(Class homeClass, HttpSession session) This method will accept a stateful EJB home interface name and return a remote reference for the EJB. This method caches an EJB handle in the HttpSession for subsequently getting the remote reference. Because the bean is stateful in nature, the corresponding EJB handle is saved in HttpSession as against a globally available cache that was used for caching home references in getRemoteForStateless method implementations. An EJB handle object is saved in the HttpSession instead of the remote reference because remote references are not guaranteed to be serializable when the HttpSession is passivated by the servlet engine.

The following demonstrates a simple service locator implementation that employs the reflection API. Please note that this version is abridged for improved readability; only one method from those listed is shown. The complete code is available in the accompanying source distribution.

```
package com.gc.prez.common;
public class ServiceLocator {
    /* Implement Singleton Pattern */
    private static ServiceLocator service = new ServiceLocator();
    private Class[] parmsGlobal          = new Class[0];
    private Object[] argsGlobal                  = new Object[0];
    private HashMap ejbHomeCache
    private ServiceLocator() {
        super();
    }
    public static ServiceLocator getInstance() {
        return service;
    }
    /* Get InitialContext for JNDI lookup() */
    private InitialContext getInitialContext() throws ServletException {
        Properties env = new Properties();
        env.put( Context.INITIAL_CONTEXT_FACTORY,
               "weblogic.jndi.WLInitialContextFactory" );
        /* Provide the appropriate URL based on your server configuration */
        env.put( Context.PROVIDER_URL, "t3://localhost:7001" );
        try {
            return new InitialContext( env );
        }
        catch ( NamingException e ) {
        ... rest of the code ...
        }
    }
    public Object getRemoteForStateless( Class homeClass,
    session ) throws ServletException {
        /* Get the cached home reference (EJBHome reference) */
        Object ejbHomeInterface = ejbHomeCache.get( homeClass.getName() );
        try {
            if ( ejbHomeInterface == null ) {
                InitialContext ic = this.getInitialContext();
                Object home = ic.lookup( "ejb/" +
                homeClass.getName() );
                /* Create home reference (EJBHome reference) */
                ejbHomeInterface =
                PortableRemoteObject.narrow( home, homeClass );
```

```
            ejbHomeCache.put( homeClass.getName(),
            ejbHomeInterface );
        }
        Method method = homeClass.getMethod( "create", parmsGlobal );
        /* Create remote reference (EJBObject reference) */
        Object ejbRemoteInterface =
               method.invoke( ejbHomeInterface, argsGlobal );
        return ejbRemoteInterface;
    }
    catch ( NamingException e ) {
    ... rest of the code ...
}
```

Factoring Tags into Design Process

Custom tags bundled with Struts are organized into several tag libraries; the sample application uses Struts-provided *bean*, *html*, and *logic* tag libraries along with an application-specific GreaterCause tag library. Only some of the custom tags provided with Struts depend on the Struts framework; most tags can be used without the Struts framework. The following brief discussion has been included to demonstrate the impact of tags on the design process. Tags are like any other Java classes and should be factored into your overall design process. For additional details and a full list of custom tags and their functionality, please refer to http://jakarta.apache.org/struts/userGuide/index.html, and http://jakarta.apache.org/struts/resources/index.html; the resources section at this URL lists several good books for learning about Struts in greater detail.

The main purpose of using custom tags is to avoid coding scriptlets in JSPs. Scriptlet usage is highly discouraged because it embeds Java code within the JSP, which makes the JSP less modular and maintainable. Factoring all logic from JSP into tags reduces the complexity of the JSP, and provides flexibility for web production engineers who have to only work with a defined set of tags without concern for coding any logic. Code reuse is yet another reason why Java code must not be embedded in JSPs. The sample application uses the custom *bean* tags to retrieve bean properties for dynamic HTML generation; it uses the custom *logic* tags to test the values of form-bean properties for conditional processing; and it uses the custom *html* tags for dynamically generating HTML page elements.

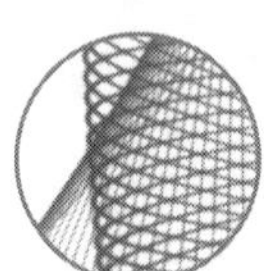

NOTE

Several tags designed to work with JavaBeans have three essential attributes. The* name *attribute provides an identifier using which a JavaBean is saved and retrieved from the context specified by the* scope *attribute, and the* property *attribute specifies the property of the named JavaBean.

The following is a sampling of custom tags used in the JSP page 2_1_PortalAllianceRegistration .jsp. The process of portal-alliance registration is explained in the use case "Register Portal Alliance" in Chapter 1. Let's examine how some of these custom tags factor into the design decisions:

- **<html:errors/>** The request handlers and form-beans accumulate validation errors in the *ActionErrors* object. The sample application uses the `<html:errors/>` tag for subsequently displaying the accumulated errors. Chapter 4 discusses this tag in detail. Struts 1.1 offers the `<html:messages>` tag, which has more capabilities than the `<html:errors/>` tag.
- **<html:form method="POST" action="/PortalAllianceRegistration.do">** This tag makes use of the Struts framework in identifying the *ActionMapping* configuration object associated with the *path="/PortalAllianceRegistration"*. The mapping specification assists the tag in identifying and creating (if not already existing in the specified scope) the form-bean associated with the *ActionMapping* object, and pre-populating the HTML form with the values specified in the form-bean. The *action* attribute of the HTML form tag is dynamically generated using the context-relative path name. This is important when changing the context path name because no corresponding change is required in the JSP since it is not hard coded in the JSP.
- **<html:hidden property="page" value="2"/>** This tag is used to create an HTML `<input>` element with an input type of hidden. The sample application uses hidden fields for saving process flow–related state of the application in the form-beans. The request handlers of the sample application use hidden properties in the HTML form for tracking multi-page form interaction using the page property of the form beans, and for tracking the actions embedded within the forms using the action property of the form-beans.
- **<bean:message key="PortalAdminServices.registration"/>** The sample application is an internationalized application. This tag plays a vital role in internationalizing the application. It accepts a key and a set of optional arguments to generate a localized label, prompt, error message, or a heading from the resource bundle specified by the `<message-resources>` tag in the struts-xml.config file. Please refer to Chapter 4 for information on internalization and localization.
- **<bean:write name="PortalAllianceRegistrationForm" property= "activationDate"/>** This tag is used to extract the specified property from the bean PortalAllianceRegistrationForm that is stored in one of the contexts, and write it to the output stream. The sample application uses the `<bean:write>` tag for fields that are read-only, as is the case when viewing the registration data, or displaying the Portal ID, or the EIN.
- **<logic:equal name="PortalAllianceRegistrationForm" property="action" scope="session" value="Create">** This tag is used in the sample application for enabling a single JSP to create different views based on the *action* property of the

form- bean PortalAllianceRegistrationForm. The *action* property associated with the form-bean PortalAllianceRegistrationForm stores the processing state of the application, which could take the value Create, Update, or View. Conditionally executing logic based on the value of the *action* property renders the same page differently for each *action* property variation.

Several other tags are used in the sample application. You can learn more about these tags at the URL suggested earlier in this section. The procedure for installing and using tag libraries is explained in Chapter 9. It is apparent from the preceding discussion that a good part of application functionality that pertains to rendering views can be factored into tags; as such, the architect must be cognizant of its impact to the overall development process, and define appropriated usage scenarios or patterns for the development team.

Factoring Validator into the Design Process

Use of the Jakarta Commons Validator influences the design direction by providing yet another option for the creation of form-beans. The *validate* method of the *ActionForm* subclass, or the validations embedded within the request handlers are only one way of doing server-side validations. By extending the form-bean with the *ValidatorForm* class, the framework provides the ability to perform both client-side and server-side validations using declarative style of validations. This declarative style of specifying validations for form elements greatly reduces the need to code common validations that are used with almost every form submission. Common validations such as required fields, field formats (date, phone, zip, e-mail address, and so on), numeric or not, field length checking, and so on, are repeatedly coded by developers, therefore increasing the code volume and redundancy. Abstracting these common validations into another layer promotes reuse.

The Validator services are injected into the Struts framework using the following declaration in the struts-config.xml file:

```
<plug-in className="org.apache.struts.validator.ValidatorPlugIn">
    <set-property property="pathnames"
        value="/WEB-INF/validator-rules.xml,/WEB-INF/validation.xml"/>
</plug-in>
```

The Validator requires the following two configuration files:

- **Validator-rules.xml** This file contains the basic validators that are packaged with the framework.
- **Validation.xml** In this configuration file, we specify the validations associated with the form-bean properties. A condensed version of this file from the sample application is shown next; it demonstrates several different kinds of validations.

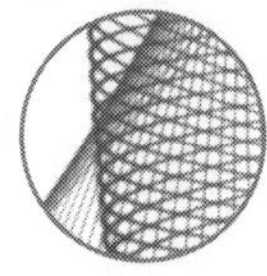

NOTE

A detailed discussion of Validator is available at http://home.earthlink.net/~dwinterfeldt/overview.html. For installation instructions, please refer to Chapter 9.

```
<form-validation>
    <formset>
        <form name="PortalAllianceRegistrationForm">
            <field property="portalID" page="1"
                    depends="required,minlength,maxlength">
                <arg0   key="prompt.PortalID"/>
                <arg1   key="${var:minlength}" name="minlength"
                   resource="false"/>
                <arg2   key="${var:maxlength}" name="maxlength"
                   resource="false"/>
                <var>
                    <var-name>maxlength</var-name>
                    <var-value>16</var-value>
                </var>
                <var>
                    <var-name>minlength</var-name>
                    <var-value>3</var-value>
                </var>
            </field>
            ... rest of the declarations ...
            <field property="email" page="2" depends="required,email">
                <arg0   key="prompt.email"/>
            </field>
            <field property="activationDate" page="2"
                    depends="required,date">
                <arg0   key="prompt.ActivationDate"/>
                <var>
                    <var-name>datePatternStrict</var-name>
                    <var-value>yyyy-MM-dd</var-value>
                </var>
            </field>
            ... rest of the declarations ...
        </form>
        <form name="ManagePortalAllianceForm">
            <field property="firstName" depends="required">
                    <arg0   key="prompt.FirstName"/>
                </field>
            <field property="lastName" depends="required">
                    <arg0   key="prompt.LastName"/>
            </field>
```

```
            <field property="email" depends="required,email">
                    <arg0   key="prompt.email"/>
            </field>
            <field property="phone" depends="required">
                    <arg0   key="prompt.Phone"/>
            </field>
            <field property="searchLimit" depends="required,Integer">
                    <arg0   key="prompt.SearchLimitLabel"/>
            </field>
        </form>
        ... rest of the declarations ...
    </formset>
</form-validation>
```

The Validator framework provides support for internationalization by using the same resource bundle as the Struts framework. For the sample application, this resource file is identified in the struts-config.xml file using the `<message-resources>` element. In the validation.xml file, the *page* attribute has been used on several `<field>` elements. The purpose of this attribute is to selectively fire away the validations depending on the value of the *page* property in the form-bean. The *page* property is provided by the base class *ValidatorForm*, and is populated from a hidden field specified within an HTML form. For a given page with value *n*, all validations that pertain to the page numbered *n* and less will be evaluated. When the page property is not specified in a JSP, it is initialized to 0 by the form-bean (unless initialized previously to some other value).

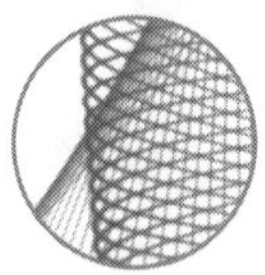

NOTE

Since this book is focused on architecture and design, we have deliberately kept the examples light on programming aspects such as writing comprehensive validations. Effort has been made to bring to light those components of the application that are significant in understanding the architecture and design aspects during the development life cycle.

When the basic validations provided by the Validator are inadequate, you may need to override the *validate* method of the *ValidationForm* subclass. When additional validations are desired in a form-bean, create a *validate* method in the *ValidatorForm* subclass that calls *super.validate* method to perform Validator-based validations, and then perform additional validations in the subclass's *validate* method. The following sample application uses this technique for the *ManagePortalAllianceForm.validate* method; refer to the section "Manage Portal-Alliance Profile Use Case" for additional details. By employing the *page* attribute property in the *ManagePortalAllianceForm.validate* method, we are able to process different sets of validations for different process flows.

```
public ActionErrors validate( ActionMapping mapping,
HttpServletRequest req ) {
    ActionErrors errors = new ActionErrors();
    /* page 1 is for identifying a Portal ID */
    if ( ( page == 1 ) && ( ( portalID == null ) ||
```

```
                        ( portalID.trim().length() < 1 ) ) ) {
            errors.add( "portalID", new ActionError( "error.portalID.required" ) );
        }
        /* page 2 is for updating the profile of a portal-alliance */
        else if ( ( page == 2 ) && ( action.equals( "updateProfile" ) ) ) {
            errors = super.validate( mapping, req );
            if ( searchLimit.intValue() < 10 ) {
                errors.add( "searchLimit",
                    new ActionError( "error.PortalAllianceProfile.SearchLimit" ) );
            }
        }
        return errors;
    }
```

Identifying Package Dependencies

Let's revisit the package diagram depicted in Chapter 1 (Figure 1-4); the package dependencies depicted in this diagram were an approximation based on our requirements. After creating the class diagrams for the use case packages GreaterCause Site Administration, Manage Campaigns, and Search NPO, we are able to discern the true dependencies between these packages. Although it is likely that the design time packages may deviate from the analysis model, the simple nature of our system follows the same packaging convention, both at analysis and design time. For the sake of manageability, the package naming conventions used by the sample application in the presentation tier and the business tier follow the following convention.

Presentation Tier	Business Tier
com.gc.prez.admin	com.gc.services.admin
com.gc.prez.managecampaigns	com.gc.services.managecampaigns
com.gc.prez.searchnpo	com.gc.services.searchnpo

This naming convention makes the process of identifying related components fairly intuitive. The package dependencies are illustrated in Figure 5-2.

Packaging is convenient for collocating related classes into self-contained units. When a large number of classes are responsible for realizing use cases, then it is best to use an extra level of package nesting; nesting more than a couple of levels will make the packaging structure unwieldy. Packaging is very helpful in promoting parallel development since each package and its constituent use cases expose an interface that provides the required services to the dependent packages. It is not uncommon to call each package a subsystem. A subsystem is a grouping of components whose behavior constitutes the behavior offered by the contained elements. The dependencies between packages shows the impact the dependent classes can have when package elements are modified. In Chapter 1, while modeling the system context of a use case, package dependencies were articulated by showing use cases in other packages as actors.

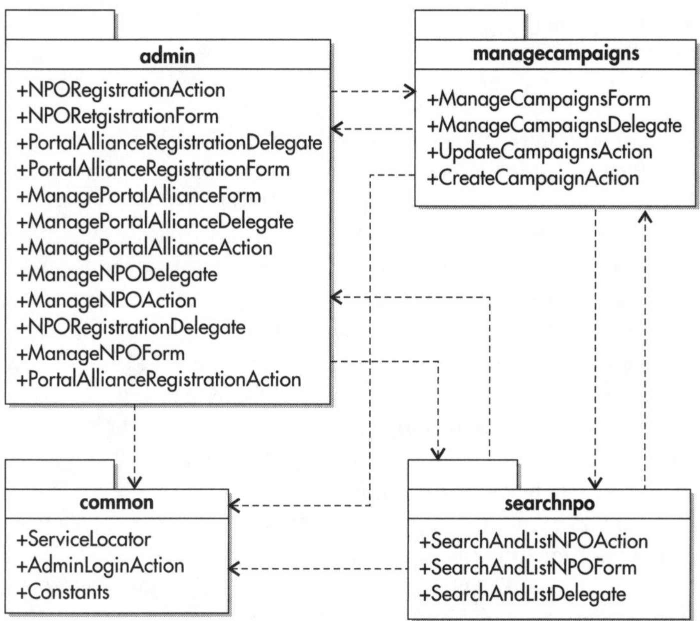

Figure 5-2 *Administration Services package diagram*

Implementing Application Security

The sample application uses a container-provided authentication and authorization mechanism. The servlet specification prescribes declarative security, which is the means of expressing an application's security structure including roles, access control, and authentication requirements in a form external to the application. For the sample application, the security configuration is specified declaratively in the deployment descriptor (web.xml) using the <security-constraint> element for protecting web resources as follows:

```
<security-constraint>
    <display-name>Administration Gateway</display-name>
    <web-resource-collection>
        <web-resource-name/>
        <description>Administration Menu</description>
        <url-pattern>/AdministratorServices.do</url-pattern>
        <http-method>POST</http-method>
        <http-method>GET</http-method>
    </web-resource-collection>
    <auth-constraint>
        <description>Administrator Access</description>
        <role-name>NPOAdministrator</role-name>
        <role-name>PortalAdministrator</role-name>
```

```
        <role-name>SiteAdministrator</role-name>
    </auth-constraint>
</security-constraint>
```

In this deployment descriptor specification, the resource identified by the *<url-pattern>* element (*/AdministatorServices.do*) is protected by the container from unauthorized access. The security constraints apply to the specified HTTP methods. Only users in the role specified by the `<role-name>` (within `<auth-constraint>`) specification will be able to access this resource. The security constraints are effective only when the client tries to directly access the protected resources; resources are not protected when a servlet invokes another resource using the *RequestDispatcher.forward()* or *RequestDisptacher.include()*.

It is advisable to control resource access using container provided authentication and authorization because the process of requesting user credentials, validating and maintaining login credentials, and subsequently tracking access to requested resources is provided by the container based on standards established for providing these services. This significantly reduces custom code and leverages the security solutions provided by vendors. J2EE application servers use the JAAS (Java Authentication and Authorization Service) framework for providing user authentication, and for enforcing access control. The JAAS authentication framework is based on Pluggable Authentication Module (PAM), and therefore supports an architecture that allows system administrators to plug in the appropriate authentication services to meet their security requirements. With the availability of new or updated authentication services, system administrators can easily plug them in without having to change existing applications. To write your own LoginModule for the JAAS framework, please refer to http://java.sun.com/j2se/1.4/docs/guide/security/jaas/JAASLMDevGuide.html, and http://java.sun.com/security/jaas/doc/api.html. Container vendors also provide useful templates as a starting point for writing JAAS extensions. JAAS was also discussed in Chapter 3.

The sample application uses the default security realm provided by the container; this security realm has limitations, but one could write custom JAAS LoginModules or procure a vendor-provided extension that seamlessly plugs into the JAAS framework. This style of managing security employs container-managed authentication and authorization, which makes the code portable across different vendor implementations. Also, third-party vendors provide support for JAAS framework, thus enabling wider choice of security solutions.

The sample application also employs programmatic security. Programmatic security is provided using the following methods of the HttpServletRequest interface:

- *getRemoteUser*
- *isUserInRole*
- *getUserPrincipal*

The *getRemoteUser* method returns the username that was used in the login page. The login page is shown to an unauthenticated remote user when the user tries to access a protected resource. Form-based authentication is used when a developer wants to control the look and feel of the login screen. The login form must contain fields with the name j_username for entering a username, and j_password for entering the password; the *action* of the login form must always be j_security_check. The login form used by the sample application is shown here. Refer to AdministratorLogin.jsp for complete code.

```
<form method="POST" action="j_security_check" name="adminLogin">
  <table border="0" cellspacing="0" cellpadding="5">
    <tr>
      <td class="txt"><bean:message key="Login.AdministratorID"/></td>
      <td><input type="text" name="j_username" size="16", maxlength="16"></td>
    </tr>
    <tr>
      <td class="txt"><bean:message key="Login.Password"/></td>
      <td><input type="password" name="j_password" size="16" maxlength="16"></td>
    </tr>
    <tr>
      <td> </td>
      <td><html:submit><bean:message key="prompt.submit"/><html:submit></td>
    </tr>
  </table>
</form>
```

When the user tries to access a protected resource, the container will send the login form to the user. Once the user posts the username and password to the server, the container will attempt to authenticate the user. Upon successful authentication the container will redirect the user, along with the original request parameters, to the resource originally requested; the redirection to the requested resource will occur only if the user is in the role authorized for accessing the resource. Form-based authentication is usually used with a secure transport mechanism like SSL (using HTTPS protocol). In order to use HTTPS, specify `<user-data-constraint>` in the deployment descriptor as follows.

```
<security-constraint>
    <display-name>Administration Gateway</display-name>
    <web-resource-collection>
    ... rest of the declarations ...
    </web-resource-collection>
    <auth-constraint>
    ... rest of the declarations ...
    </auth-constraint>
    <user-data-constraint>
        <transport-guarantee>CONFIDENTIAL</transport-guarantee>
    <user-date-constraint>
</security-constraint>
```

If the original request was over HTTP, and *CONFIDENTIAL* is specified, the container will redirect the client to the HTTPS port. For further information on switching between the HTTP and HTTPS protocols using the Struts framework, please refer to http://sslext.sourceforge.net.

The Ffollowing declarations are used in the web.xml file to specify a login page that uses form-based authentication:

```
<login-config>
    <auth-method>FORM</auth-method>
    <realm-name>myrealm</realm-name>
    <form-login-config>
        <form-login-page>/1_3_AdministratorLogin.jsp</form-login-page>
        <form-error-page>/1_3_AdministratorLoginFailure.jsp</form-error-page>
    </form-login-config>
</login-config>
```

Other forms of authentication include basic, digest, and client authentication. Please refer to the URL http://java.sun.com/j2ee/tutorial/1_3-fcs/doc/Security.html for further information.

The use of *isUserInRole* determines if a remote user is in a specified security role. A group is a collection of users; users within a group inherit the access privileges assigned to the group. Roles are assigned either at the group level or user level. The container enforces access to resources based on roles. We saw previously how this is accomplished using the `<auth-constraint>` declarations in the deployment descriptor.

The System Administrator creates groups and users (called *principals*) in the security realm. Please refer to Chapter 9 for complete details on setting up groups and users in the security realm. The principal-to-role mapping is declared in the WebLogic-specific deployment descriptor *weblogic.xml* as follows:

```
<security-role-assignment>
    <role-name>NPOAdministrator</role-name>
    <principal-name>NPOAdmin</principal-name>
</security-role-assignment>
<security-role-assignment>
    <role-name>PortalAdministrator</role-name>
    <principal-name>PortalAdmin</principal-name>
</security-role-assignment>
<security-role-assignment>
    <role-name>SiteAdministrator</role-name>
    <principal-name>SiteAdmin</principal-name>
</security-role-assignment>
```

During code construction, developers can freely choose role names for use in programs; at deployment time, roles created by the system administrator are mapped to the ones defined by the developer using the following mapping in web.xml.

System administrator–defined roles are listed below here:

```
<security-role>
    <role-name>SiteAdministrator</role-name>
</security-role>
<security-role>
    <role-name>PortalAdministrator</role-name>
</security-role>
<security-role>
    <role-name>NPOAdministrator</role-name>
</security-role>
```

The following is the mapping of system administrator–defined roles and roles used in the programs:

```
<servlet>
    ... rest of the declarations ...
    <security-role-ref>
        <role-name>SiteAdminRole</role-name>
        <role-link>SiteAdministrator</role-link>
    </security-role-ref>
    <security-role-ref>
        <role-name>PortalAdminRole</role-name>
        <role-link>PortalAdministrator</role-link>
    </security-role-ref>
    <security-role-ref>
        <role-name>NPOAdminRole</role-name>
        <role-link>NPOAdministrator</role-link>
    </security-role-ref>
</servlet>
```

The sample application uses three different roles, as illustrated in the preceding snippet. These three roles influence the application logic in how the Views are selected and processed, and how the resulting form data is handled. The sample application uses a special pattern to handle programmatic security, as illustrated by the following code:.

```
public class AdminLoginAction extends Action {
    public ActionForward execute( ActionMapping mapping,
    ActionForm form, HttpServletRequest req,
    HttpServletResponse res ) throws Exception {
        HttpSession session = req.getSession( true );
        if ( req.isUserInRole( "SiteAdminRole" ) ) {
            session.setAttribute( "GreaterCause.AdminRole",
                "SiteAdminRole" );
```

```
        }
        else if ( req.isUserInRole( "PortalAdminRole" ) ) {
            session.setAttribute( "GreaterCause.AdminRole",
                "PortalAdminRole" );
        }
        else if ( req.isUserInRole( "NPOAdminRole" ) ) {
            session.setAttribute( "GreaterCause.AdminRole",
                "NPOAdminRole" );
        }
        return mapping.findForward( "success" );
    }
}
```

The *AdminLoginAction* class is invoked by the Struts controller when access to the protected resource 2_SiteAdministratorServicesMainPage.jsp is attempted. The corresponding declaration in the struts-config.xml file is shown here:

```
<action path="/AdministratorServices"
        type="com.gc.prez.common.AdminLoginAction">
      <forward name="success"
        path="/2_SiteAdministratorServicesMainPage.jsp" redirect="false"/>
</action>
```

At first glance, it may seem that *AdminLoginAction* is redundant because it simply provides a mapping between the role names used in the web.xml file to the role names used in the application. Although not demonstrated in the *AdminLoginAction* class, this class has been designed based on the fact that many eCommerce applications have to rely on runtime variables and user entitlements for dynamically configuring a user-centric process flow; *isUserInRole()* is not adequate in such scenarios. *AdminLoginAction* provides a hook for evaluating other runtime parameters in deciding the most appropriate system behavior tailored to the user's environment rather than just the role name. The sample application leverages the information saved in the session to define a custom *hasAccess* tag to provide dynamic behavior in views (JSPs); this tag is used for controlling the formatting and processing of HTML forms, as shown here:

```
<gc:hasAccess role="SiteAdminRole">
    <html:link page="/PortalAllianceRegistration.do?action=Create">
        <bean:message key="SiteAdminServices.PortalRegistration"/>
    </html:link><br>
    <html:link page="/NPORegistration.do?method=ShowNPORegistrationForm">
        <bean:message key="SiteAdminServices.NPORegistration"/>
    </html:link><br><br>
</gc:hasAccess>
```

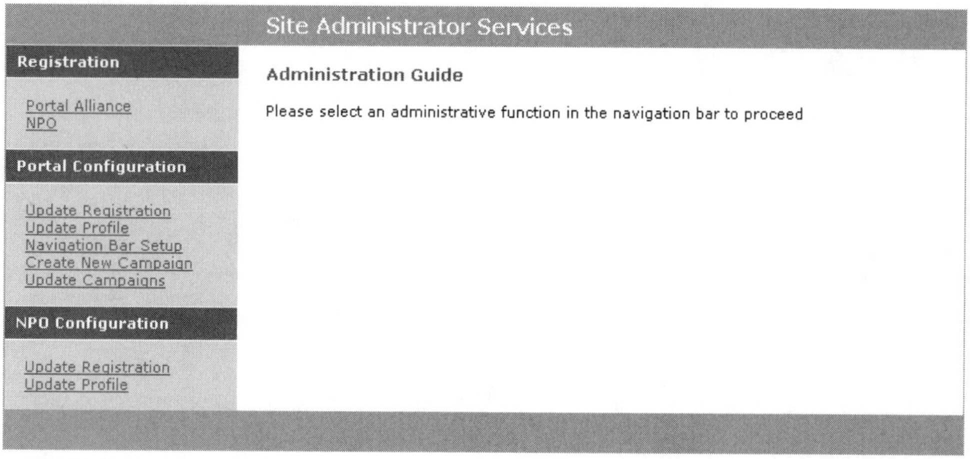

Figure 5-3 *Site Administrator Services*

This snippet is extracted from *2_AdministrativeServicesNavBar*, which is a highly dynamic navigation bar that is created based on a user's role. The `<gc:hasAccess>` tag will test the role, and if the role matches the one specified by the role attribute, then the body of the tag will be evaluated. The GreaterCause tag library containing the *hasAccess* tag is specified in the deployment descriptor as follows:

```
<taglib>
    <taglib-uri>/WEB-INF/GreaterCause.tld</taglib-uri>
    <taglib-location>/WEB-INF/GreaterCause.tld</taglib-location>
</taglib>
```

Using the `<gc:has Access>` tag, the *2_AdministrativeServicesNavBar* produces three different views for the three administrator roles, as illustrated in Figure 5-3, Figure 5-4, and Figure 5-5.

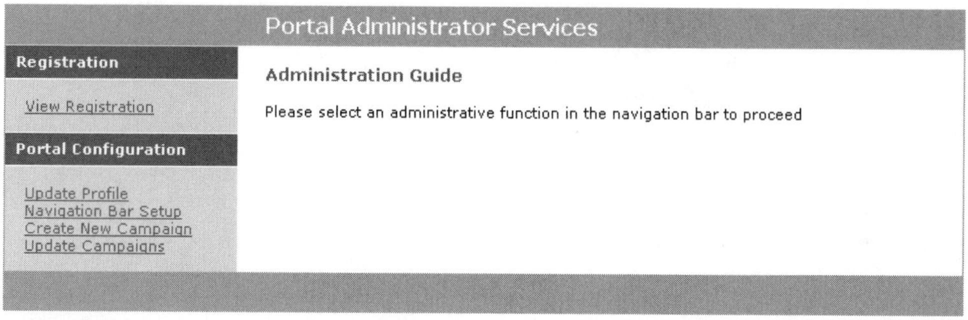

Figure 5-4 *Portal Administrator Services*

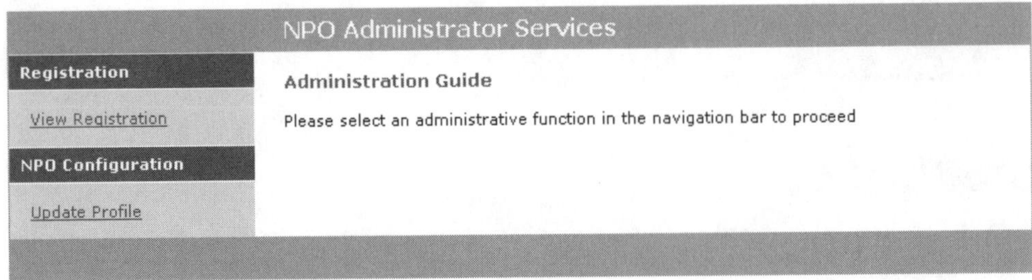

Figure 5-5 *NPO Administrator Services*

In the sample application, the various administrator-related functions are grouped together based on the `<auth-constraint>` specifications that list the authorized role names. To prevent any attempts by assailants to defeat the access mechanism tailored by the navigation bar, we specify the following constraints in the web.xml to prevent unauthorized access to protected resources:

```
<security-constraint>
    ... declarations to protect /AdministratorServices.do ...
</security-constraint>
<!-- Declarations to protect PortalAdministrator functions -->
<security-constraint>
    <display-name>Portal Alliance Administration</display-name>
    <web-resource-collection>
        <web-resource-name/>
        <description>Portal Alliance Management Functions</description>
        <url-pattern>/PortalAllianceRegistration.do</url-pattern>
        <url-pattern>/ManagePortalAlliance.do</url-pattern>
        <url-pattern>/CreateCampaignStep1.do</url-pattern>
        <url-pattern>/CreateCampaignStep2.do</url-pattern>
        <url-pattern>/UpdateCampaignsStep1.do</url-pattern>
        <url-pattern>/UpdateCampaignsStep2.do</url-pattern>
        <http-method>POST</http-method>
        <http-method>GET</http-method>
    </web-resource-collection>
    <auth-constraint>
        <role-name>SiteAdministrator</role-name>
        <role-name>PortalAdministrator</role-name>
    </auth-constraint>
</security-constraint>
<security-constraint>
    ... declarations to protect NPOAdministrator functions ...
</security-constraint>
```

The Java Servlet Specification Version 2.3, Chapter SRV.13 provides detailed information on the various elements of the deployment descriptor.

Realization of Site Administration Use Cases

The following subsections will provide the use case realization for use cases in the Site Administration package.

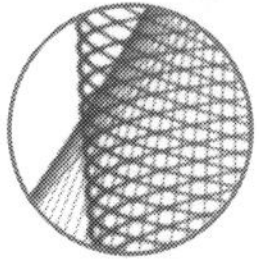

NOTE

The following subsections will provide readers with an opportunity to understand class interactions and dependencies visualized through class and sequence diagrams. Please refer to Chapter 1 for use case descriptions. Recurring solutions have been documented as patterns to enhance the readability and reuse of the GreaterCause implementation.

Manage NPO Profile Use Case

The task of updating the NPO Profile information is preceded by the registration process. However, since this is a much simpler implementation, it is being discussed before other use cases. Several concepts exposed in this section will create the foundation for realizing other use cases. Figure 5-6 illustrates a class diagram for realizing this use case; the semantics of this class diagram is explained using the multi-page pattern.

Pattern Discovery and Documentation

Object-oriented architectures contain repeatable solutions, also called patterns. Recognizing and documenting these patterns promotes reuse of solutions that otherwise may be implemented by another developer in a different way, thus reducing manageability and increasing complexity of the system. Patterns establish a vocabulary for the system, and permit efficient reuse of this vocabulary in the design and implementation phases. A problem solved by one developer can be reapplied in several other scenarios. Harvesting such reusable design patterns, applied within a context, will provide leverage for other parts of the solution because such patterns are proven to follow best practices and have endured the test of time. The advantage of using patterns is that it will make the software easier to understand by the development team, reduces the complexity of the system, and builds upon the success of other developers.

In later sections, I have attempted to document certain recurring solutions discerned in the course of developing the GreaterCause site administration services. The recurring solutions are documented to assist the readers in understanding how certain complex user interactions can be addressed using the Struts framework. Use of these proven techniques enables faster assimilation of Struts functionality into applications. Hopefully, these patterns will serve as templates for our readers, and a starting point from which to evolve.

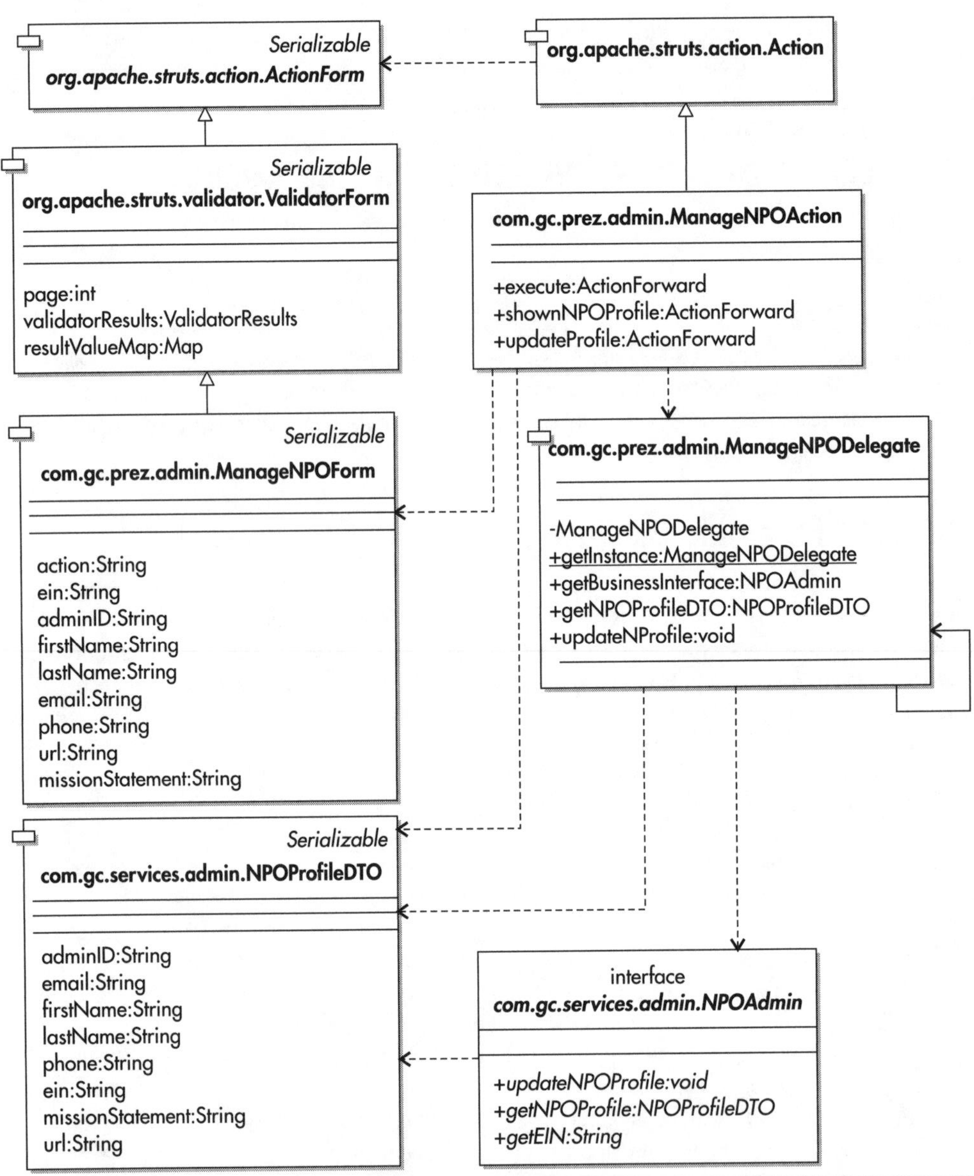

Figure 5-6 *Manage NPO Profile class diagram*

Multi-Page Pattern

This pattern is applicable when user interaction constitutes a series of forms. Functionally, it may be desirable to collect information from multiple pages into a single form-bean for accomplishing a unit of work. Using fewer form-beans keeps the number of form-beans to a minimum, and keeps related data together. It is easier to manage changes when page semantics are altered because the changes are localized to a single form-bean.

Structure The implementation of this pattern employs the *page* property of the form-bean. If the form-bean extends *ValidatorForm*, then it will inherit the *page* property from the *ValidatorForm*; if the form-bean extends the ActionForm, then this property will have to be defined in the form-bean. Figure 5-7 and Figure 5-8 illustrates the static and dynamic aspects of the multi-page pattern. Updating NPO profile is a two-step process when the site administrator impersonates an NPO administrator. First, as illustrated in Figure 5-9, the site administrator has to specify the EIN (for identifying a non-profit) it would like to impersonate; in the next step, the system allows the site administrator to update the profile information, as illustrated in Figure 5-10. The NPO administrator is taken directly to the update page without the intervening Enter EIN page because the system can identify the related EIN using the NPO administrator's login username. Figure 5-8 shows the usage of the *page* property in controlling the process flow within the request handler.

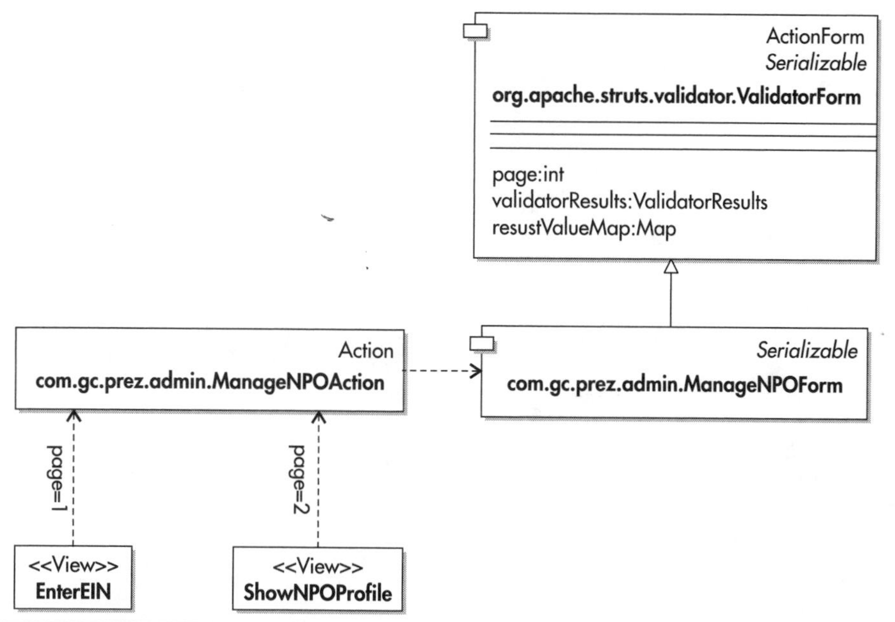

Figure 5-7 *Multi-page pattern*

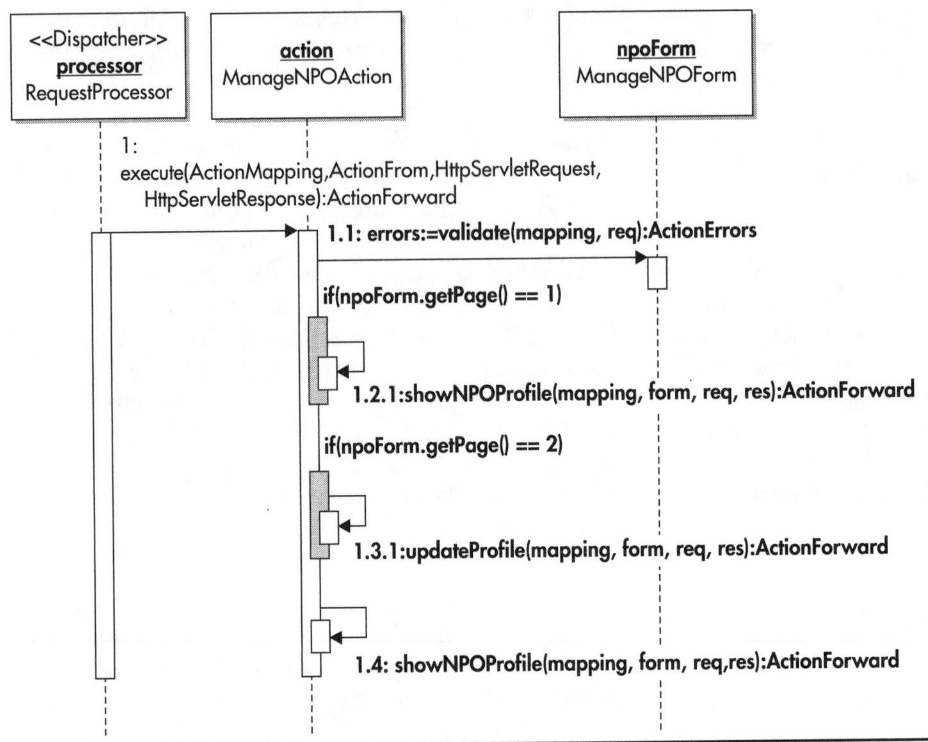

Figure 5-8 *Multi-page pattern sequence diagram*

Figure 5-9 *Enter EIN*

Site Administrator Services

Registration

Portal Alliance
NPO

Portal Configuration

Update Registration
Update Profile
Navigation Bar Setup
Create New Campaign
Update Campaigns

NPO Configuration

Update Registration
Update Profile

NPO Configuration > Update Profile

EIN 94-0385620
Administrator ID CALHisSoc

Contact Information

First Name
Last Name
Email
Phone

NPO Detail Page Info

URL
Mission Statement

Update

Figure 5-10 *Update Profile*

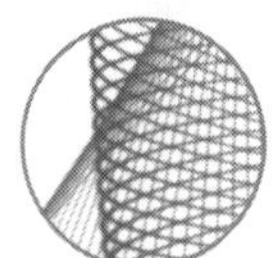

NOTE

All class diagrams using the stereotype <<View>>, do not show the intermediate Struts controller for the sake of simplifying the diagram. The controller will intercept the request resulting from a view and invoke the corresponding request handler. Also, note that with few exceptions, the view names used in pattern diagrams are labeled using their `<forward>` names of struts-config.xml file.

In the sample application, we use the *page* field (as a hidden field) in most forms for two reasons:

- The site administrator navigation scheme is different from the navigation scheme of the NPO administrator. The site administrator can impersonate an NPO administrator, and therefore has to specify the EIN as a precursor to most operations. The Enter EIN page has the *page* field set to 1.
- The validations performed by the *ValidatorForm.validate* method have to be advised which properties must be validated based on the navigation scheme chosen for different administrators. For example, the *ein* property is not required to be validated when the administrator is an NPO administrator. Please refer to the section "Factoring Validator into the Design Process" for further details.

Configuration Semantics The struts-config.xml declarations are shown in the following code. The site administrator is attached to an extra step *"/ManageNPOStep1"*, which is invoked from the navigation bar illustrated in the next subsection.

```
<form-bean name="ManageNPOForm" type="com.gc.prez.admin.ManageNPOForm"/>

<!-- Site Administration step invoked from navigation bar -->
<action path="/ManageNPOStep1" forward="/2_4B_EnterEIN.jsp"/>

<action path="/ManageNPOStep2"
    type="com.gc.prez.admin.ManageNPOAction"
    name="ManageNPOForm"
    scope="session"
    validate="false">
    <forward name="EnterEIN" path="/2_4B_EnterEIN.jsp"/>
    <forward name="ShowNPOProfile" path="/2_4_2_UpdateNPOProfile.jsp"/>
    <forward name="success" path="/2_SiteAdministratorServicesMainPage.jsp"/>
</action>
```

Please note that the *ActionMapping* identified by the path *"/ManageNPOStep2"* will have three possible *ActionForward*(s); the resulting views are discussed in the next section.

View Semantics The following snippet is from the dynamic navigation bar *2_Administration ServicesNavBar* that is included with all administrator JSPs. The navigation bar will invoke the ActionMapping identified by the path/render *"/ManageNPOStep1"* which will invoke the view 2_4B_EnterEIN.jsp shown next; in turn this view will use the *ActionMapping* identified by the path *"/ManageNPOStep2"*. The NPO administrator will use the *ActionMapping* identified by the path *"/ManageNPOStep2"*, which will invoke the view 2_4_2_UpdateNPOProfile.jsp shown later in this subsection.

```
<gc:hasAccess role="SiteAdminRole">
    ... rest of JSP ...
    <html:link page="/ManageNPOStep1.do"> <!-- Invoke 2_4B_EnterEIN.jsp -->
        <bean:message key="NPOAdminServices.UpdateProfile"/>
    </html:link><br><br>
    ... rest of JSP ...
</gc:hasAccess>

<gc:hasAccess role="NPOAdminRole">
    ... rest of JSP ...
        <html:link page="/ManageNPOStep2.do"> <!-- Invoke
                                               2_4_2_UpdateNPOProfile.jsp -->
            <bean:message key="NPOAdminServices.UpdateProfile"/>
        </html:link><br><br>
    ... rest of JSP ...
</gc:hasAccess>
```

The view 2_4B_EnterEIN.jsp will result in the invocation of the request handler *ManageNPOAction* using the *ActionMapping* identified by the path *"/ManageNPOStep2"* (refer to struts-config.xml shown earlier) with the *page* attribute property of the corresponding form-bean set to 1. The view 2_4B_EnterEIN.jsp is shown here:.

```
<html:form method="POST" action="/ManageNPOStep2.do" focus="ein">
    <table border="0" cellspacing="0" cellpadding="5">
        <tr>
            <td class="txt"><bean:message key="SiteAdminServices.EnterEIN"/></td>
            <td><html:text property="ein" size="14" maxlength="14"/></td>
            <html:hidden property="page" value="1"/>
        </tr>
        <tr>
            <td> </td>
            <td><html:submit><bean:message key="prompt.Submit"/>
                </html:submit></td>
        </tr>
    </table>
</html:form>
```

ActionMapping identified by the path *"/ManageNPOStep2"* will be responsible for invoking the request handler *ManageNPOAction.* This request handler will render the view 2_4_2_UpdateNPOProfile.jsp. This is discussed in the Request Handler section of this pattern. The view 2_4_2_UpdateNPOProfile.jsp can also invoke the request handler using the ActionMapping identified by the path *"/ManageNPOStep2"* (refer to struts-config.xml shown earlier) with the *page* property of the corresponding form-bean set to 2. The view 2_4_2_UpdateNPOProfile.jsp is shown here:

```
<html:form method="POST" action="/ManageNPOStep2.do" focus="firstName">
    <html:hidden property="page" value="2"/>
    ... rest of JSP ...
    <p align="center"><html:submit><bean:message key="prompt.Update"/></html:submit></p>
</html:form>
```

ActionForm Bean The action form-bean corresponding to ActionMapping identified by the path "*/ManageNPOStep2*" is shown here. A single form is used to store information gathered from two views, namely, 2_4B_EnterEIN.jsp and 2_4_2_UpdateNPOProfile.jsp.

```
public class ManageNPOForm extends ValidatorForm implements Serializable {
    public ManageNPOForm() {
    }
    /* EIN is collected from page 1 */
    public String getEin() {
        return ein;
    }
    public void setEin( String ein ) {
        this.ein = ein;
    }
```

```
    ... rest of the accessors ...
    //Form Data
    private String ein;
    private String adminID;
    private String firstName;
    private String lastName;
    private String email;
    private String phone;
    private String url;
    private String missionStatement;
    public void reset( ActionMapping mapping, HttpServletRequest req ) {
    }
    public ActionErrors validate( ActionMapping mapping,
    HttpServletRequest req ) {
        ActionErrors errors = new ActionErrors();
        /* NPO Administrator does not have to specify an EIN */
        if ( ( page == 1 ) && ( ( ein == null ) ||
           ( ein.trim().length() < 1 ) ) ) {
            errors.add( "ein", new ActionError( "error.ein.required" ) );
        }
        /* Call the validate method of ValidatorForm */
        else if ( page == 2 ) {
            errors = super.validate( mapping, req );
        }
        return errors;
    }
}
```

Request Handler This request handler is created from the ActionMapping identified by the path *"/ManageNPOStep2". The page* attribute property will identify the current page, which will also decide the resulting *ActionForward* shown earlier. Note that for the NPO administrator, the initial invocation of the request handler will have the *page* attribute property set to the value 0 because no HTML form with a *page* parameter has been processed yet; the first view displayed to the NPO administrator will be the profile page with the *page* attribute property set to 2. The semantics of the corresponding request handler is illustrated using the following code fragment. Please refer to Figure 5-8 for a high-level sequencing diagram.

```
public class ManageNPOAction extends Action {
    public ActionForward execute( ActionMapping mapping,
    ActionForm form, HttpServletRequest req,
    HttpServletResponse res ) throws Exception {
        ManageNPOForm npoForm = ( ManageNPOForm )form;
        ActionErrors errors = npoForm.validate( mapping, req );
        /* Ensure EIN is present on EnterEIN page (First page for
         * site administrator) */
        if ( npoForm.getPage() == 1 ) {
                if ( !errors.empty() ) {
```

```
                saveErrors( req, errors );
                return mapping.findForward( "EnterEIN" );
            }
            /* Show profile information if EIN is provided
             * (page 2 for updating profile information)*/
            return showNPOProfile( mapping, form, req, res );
        }
        /* The Profile page is identified by page == 2 */
        if ( npoForm.getPage() == 2 ) {
            if ( !errors.empty() ) {
                saveErrors( req, errors );
                return mapping.findForward( "ShowNPOProfile" );
            }
            return ( updateProfile( mapping, form, req, res ) );
        }
        /* 'page' property is set to 0 for NPO Administrator,
         * and this step is executed */
        return showNPOProfile( mapping, form, req, res );
    }
    public ActionForward showNPOProfile( ActionMapping mapping,
        ActionForm form, HttpServletRequest req,
        HttpServletResponse res ) throws Exception {
        ... rest of the code ...
        return mapping.findForward( "ShowNPOProfile" );
    }
    public ActionForward updateProfile( ActionMapping mapping,
        ActionForm form, HttpServletRequest req,
        HttpServletResponse res ) throws Exception {
        ... rest of the code ...
        return mapping.findForward( "success" );
    }
}
```

Register Portal-Alliance Use Case

A site administrator can create and update the registration information for a portal-alliance. However, the portal-alliance administrator can only view this information. Figure 5-11 illustrates the class diagram for realizing this use case; the semantics of this class diagram is explained using the multi-action pattern.

Multi-Action Pattern Using the Action Class Strategy

A multi-action pattern can be used for enabling a request handler to process different actions (a.k.a. commands) submitted by one or more forms. The sample application defines three actions: create, update, and view. If different forms are utilized for each of these actions,

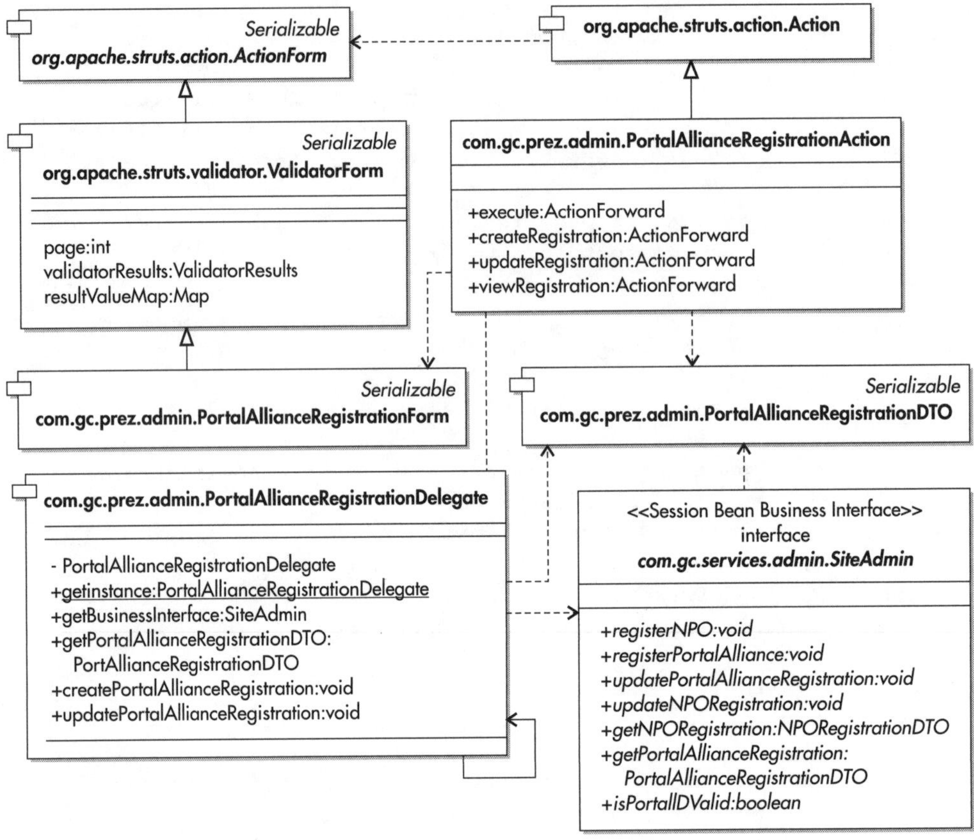

Figure 5-11 *Register portal-alliance class diagram*

then related fields will be spread across, or duplicated across, multiple forms, which creates redundancy and defeats modularity; in this scenario, a change in the form will require retrofitting several forms. The multi-action pattern enables creation of multiple views from a single JSP based on the action chosen by the user, while allowing the same request handler to service all variations of the view (in this case, a JSP).

Structure Both, dynamic view creation and request processing are synergistic functions. The participating view must indicate the initiated "action," and the request handler must save this knowledge in a JavaBean (which is usually the form-bean) for controlling conditional processing. The intent projected by the state of the *action* property in the form-bean will subsequently influence the view generated from a single JSP. The Portal-Alliance Registration use case is realized using a multi-action pattern in conjunction with a multi-page pattern. Figures 5-12 and 5-13 illustrate the static and dynamic aspects of the multi-action pattern. Figure 5-13 shows the usage of the *action* property in controlling the process flow within the request handler.

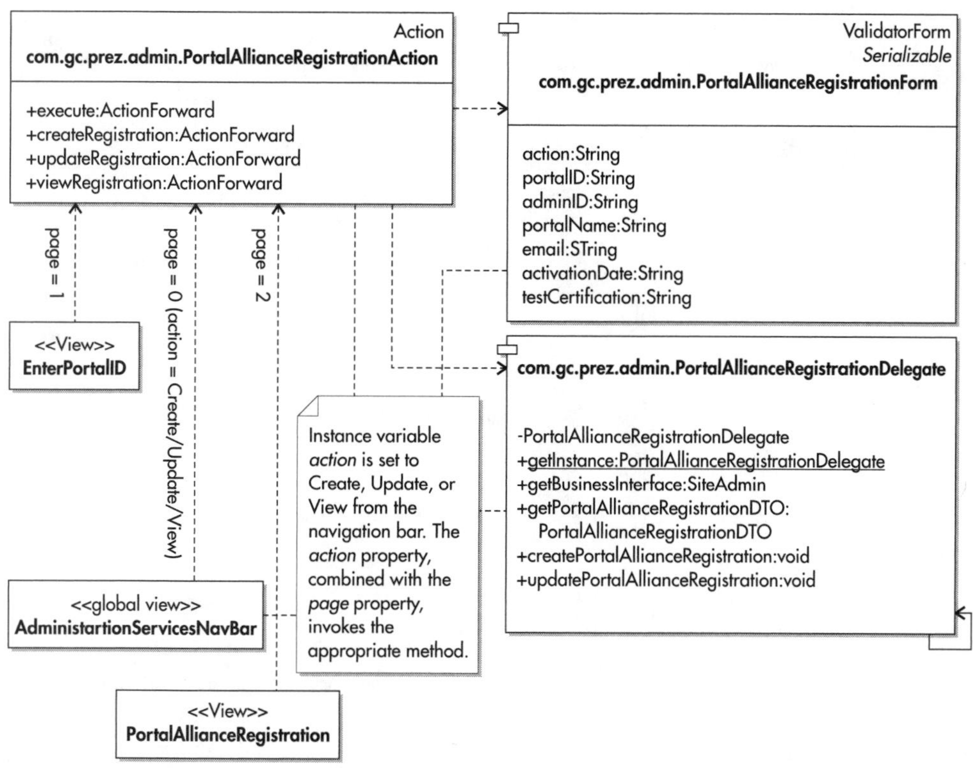

Figure 5-12 *Multi-action form pattern*

Configuration Semantics The struts-config.xml declarations are shown in the following code. In this pattern, we will use a single *Action* class and a corresponding *ActionForm*. The *ActionForm* extends *ValidatorForm*, which provides the *page* property for muti-page interaction, as explained in the section "Multi-Page Pattern."

```
<action path="/PortalAllianceRegistration"
        type="com.gc.prez.admin.PortalAllianceRegistrationAction"
        name="PortalAllianceRegistrationForm"
        scope="session"
        validate="false">
    <forward name="ShowPage"
path="/2_1_PortalAllianceRegistration.jsp"/>
    <forward name="EnterPortalID" path="/2_3A_EnterPortalID.jsp"/>
    <forward name="success"
path="/2_SiteAdministratorServicesMainPage.jsp"/>
</action>
```

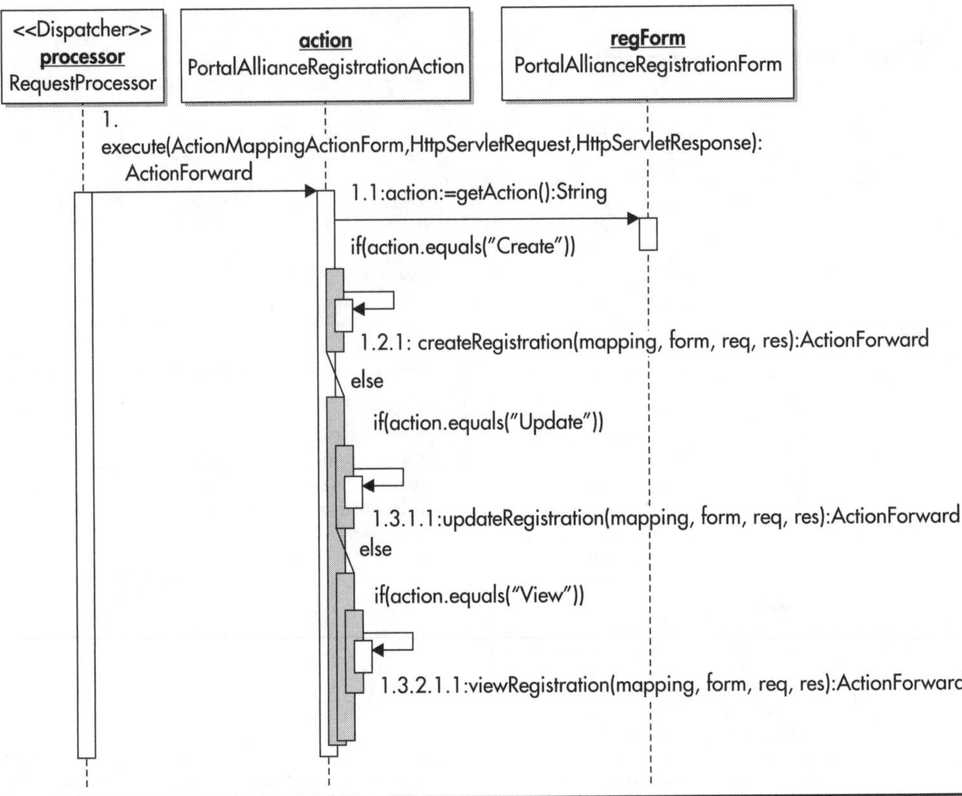

Figure 5-13 *Multi-action form pattern sequence diagram*

Please note that the *ActionMapping* identified by the path *"/PortalAllianceRegistration"* will have three possible *ActionForward*(s); the resulting views are discussed in the next section.

View Semantics The following snippet is from the dynamic navigation bar 2_Administration ServicesNavBar that is included with all administrator JSPs. Observe that all requests are directed to same URL, *"/PortalAllianceRegistration"*, which is the identifier for the *ActionMapping* object that will be used by the framework for invoking the associated request handler *PortalAllianceRegistrationAction.* Because the *"Update"* action by the site administrator requires a Portal ID, the request handler will invoke the view 2_3A_EnterPortalID.jsp. For the *"View"* action by the portal-alliance administrator, the request handler will use the login username to identify the associated Portal ID. Observe that the request time *action* parameter is used for setting the *action* property in the corresponding form-bean shown later.

```
<gc:hasAccess role="SiteAdminRole">
    <html:link page="/PortalAllianceRegistration.do?action=Create">
        <bean:message key="SiteAdminServices.PortalRegistration"/>
    </html:link><br>
```

```
</gc:hasAccess>
<gc:hasAccess role="SiteAdminRole">
    <html:link page="/PortalAllianceRegistration.do?action=Update">
        <bean:message key="SiteAdminServices.UpdatePortalRegistration"/>
    </html:link><br>
</gc:hasAccess>
<gc:hasAccess role="PortalAdminRole">
    <html:link page="/PortalAllianceRegistration.do?action=View">
        <bean:message key="PortalAdminServices.ViewRegistration"/>
</gc:hasAccess>
```

The view 2_3A_EnterPortalID.jsp will invoke the request handler *PortalAllianceRegistrationAction* using the *ActionMapping* identified by the path "*/PortalAllianceRegistration*" (refer to struts-config.xml shown earlier) with the *page* property of the corresponding form-bean set to 1. The view 2_3A_EnterPortalID.jsp is shown here:

```
<html:form method="POST" action="/PortalAllianceRegistration.do" focus=portalID">
    <html:hidden property="page" value="1"/>
    <table border="0" cellspacing="0" cellpadding="5">
        <tr>
            <td class="txt"><bean:message
                        key="SiteAdminServices.EnterPortalID"/></td>
            <td><html:text property="portalID" size="16" maxlength="16"/></td>
        </tr>
        <tr>
            <td> </td>
            <td><html:submit><bean:message key="prompt.Submit"/></html:submit>
            </td>
        </tr>
    </table>
</html:form>
```

The view 2_1_PortalAllianceRegistration.jsp will invoke the request handler using the *ActionMapping* identified by the path "/ *PortalAllianceRegistration"* (refer to struts-config.xml shown earlier) with the *page* attribute property of the corresponding form-bean set to 2. The *action* property of the form beanform-bean *PortalAllianceRegistrationForm* is checked for the values *Create*/*Update*/*View*; the `<logic:equal>` custom tag will conditionally display parts of the JSP based on the value of the *action* property. The view 2_1_PortalAllianceRegistration.jsp.jsp is shown here:

```
<html:form method="POST" action="/PortalAllianceRegistration.do"
            focus="portalID">
    <html:hidden property="page" value="2"/>
        <logic:equal name="PortalAllianceRegistrationForm"
                     property="action" scope="session" value="Create">
```

```
            ... display the registration creation part ...
            <html:submit>
                <bean:message key="prompt.Register"/>
            </html:submit></td>
        </logic:equal>
        <logic:equal name="PortalAllianceRegistrationForm"
                   property="action" scope="session" value="Update">
            ... display the registration update part ...
            <html:submit>
                 <bean:message key="prompt.Update"/>
            </html:submit>
        </logic:equal>
        <logic:equal name="PortalAllianceRegistrationForm"
                   property="action" scope="session" value="View">
            ... display the registration view part ...
            <html:submit>
                <bean:message key="prompt.Back"/>
            </html:submit>
        </logic:equal>
</html:form>
```

ActionForm Bean The action form-bean corresponding to ActionMapping identified by the path "*/PortalAllianceRegistration*" is shown here. The form has the *action* and the *page* property that is used for controlling the application flow. The *page* is inherited from ValidatorForm.

```
public class PortalAllianceRegistrationForm extends ValidatorForm
implements Serializable {
    public PortalAllianceRegistrationForm() {
    }
    public String getAction() {
        return action;
    }
    public void setAction( String action ) {
        this.action = action;
    }
    ... rest of the accessors ...
    private String action;
    private String portalID;
    private String adminID;
    private String portalName;
    private String email;
    private String activationDate;
    private String testCertification;
    public void reset( ActionMapping mapping,
    HttpServletRequest req ) {
```

```
        ... rest of the code ...
    }
    public ActionErrors validate( ActionMapping mapping,
    HttpServletRequest req ) {
        ... rest of the code ...
        return errors;
    }
}
```

Request Handler This request handler is created from the ActionMapping identified by the path *"/PortalAllianceRegistration"*. The *page* property is used to identify the HTML form being currently processed. Please review the entire code in the accompanying source distribution to see how the *action* property is used in conjunction with the *page* property.

The following code fragment demonstrates how the request handler *PortalAllianceRegistrationAction* uses the same form to provide different views for different user actions. In this example, the site administrator can create and update the Portal Alliance Registration, whereas a portal-alliance administrator can only view the registration information. Please refer to Figure 5-13 for a high-level sequence diagram.

```
public class PortalAllianceRegistrationAction extends Action {
    public ActionForward execute( ActionMapping mapping,
    ActionForm form, HttpServletRequest req,
    HttpServletResponse res ) throws Exception {
        PortalAllianceRegistrationForm regForm =
           ( PortalAllianceRegistrationForm )form;
        String action = regForm.getAction();
        if ( action.equals( "Create" ) )
        { return ( createRegistration( mapping, form, req, res ) ); }
        else if ( action.equals( "Update" ) ) {
            return ( updateRegistration( mapping, form, req, res ) );
        }
        else if ( action.equals( "View" ) )
        { return ( viewRegistration( mapping, form, req, res ) ); }
        else { return null; }
    }
    public ActionForward createRegistration( ActionMapping mapping,
    ActionForm form, HttpServletRequest req,
    HttpServletResponse res ) throws Exception {
        ... rest of the code ...
        return mapping.findForward( "success" );
    }
    public ActionForward updateRegistration( ActionMapping mapping,
    ActionForm form, HttpServletRequest req,
    HttpServletResponse res ) throws Exception {
        ... rest of the code ...
```

```
        return mapping.findForward( "success" );
    }
    public ActionForward viewRegistration( ActionMapping mapping,
    ActionForm form, HttpServletRequest req,
    HttpServletResponse res ) throws Exception {
    ActionForm form, HttpServletRequest req,
    HttpServletResponse res ) throws Exception {
        ... rest of the code ...
        return mapping.findForward( "success" );
    }
}
```

Manage Portal-Alliance Profile Use Case

The development of this use case has been combined with the Perform UI Customization use case by making use of the multi-action pattern discussed in the preceding section. Figure 5-14 illustrates the static model used in the realization of this use case.

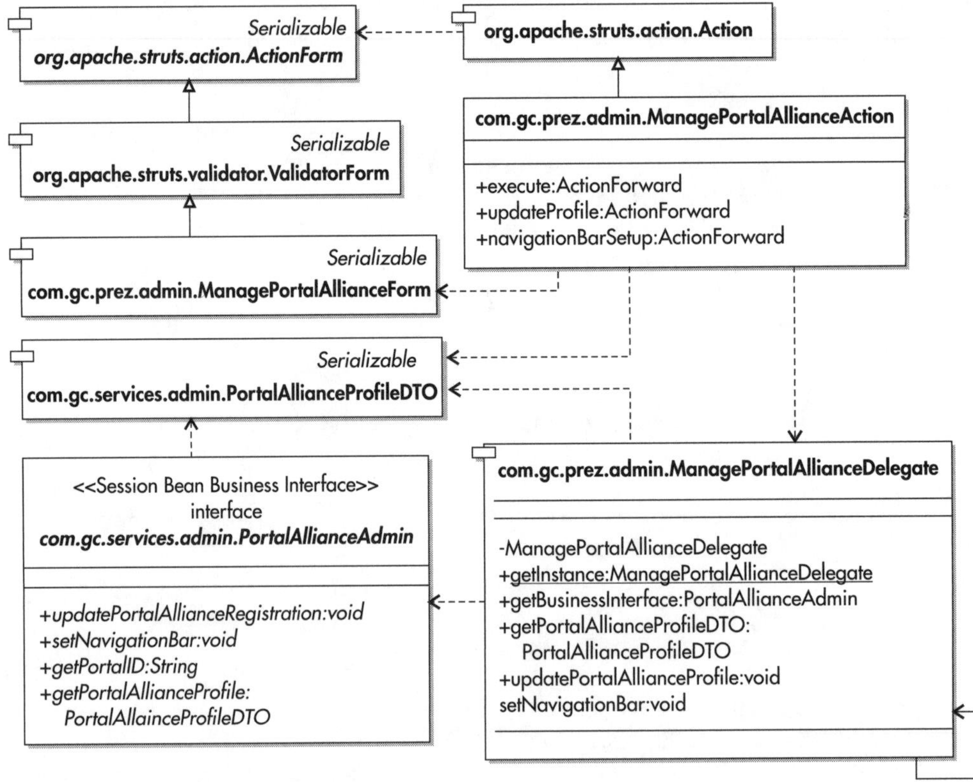

Figure 5-14 *Manage portal-alliance class diagram*

Multi-Action Pattern Using Action Class Strategy

The implementation here is only slightly different from the one used in the "Register Portal-Alliance Use Case" section. Here we define two actions—*updateProfile* and *navigationBarSetup*— to realize the use cases 'Manage Portal-Alliance Profile' and Perform UI Customization, respectively. The only difference in this implementation is that the actions are associated with different views, as depicted later in the upcoming "Configuration Semantics" section.

Structure Figures 5-15 and 5-16 illustrates the static and dynamic aspects of the multi-action pattern. Figure 5-16 shows the usage of *page* and *action* properties in controlling the process flow within the request handler

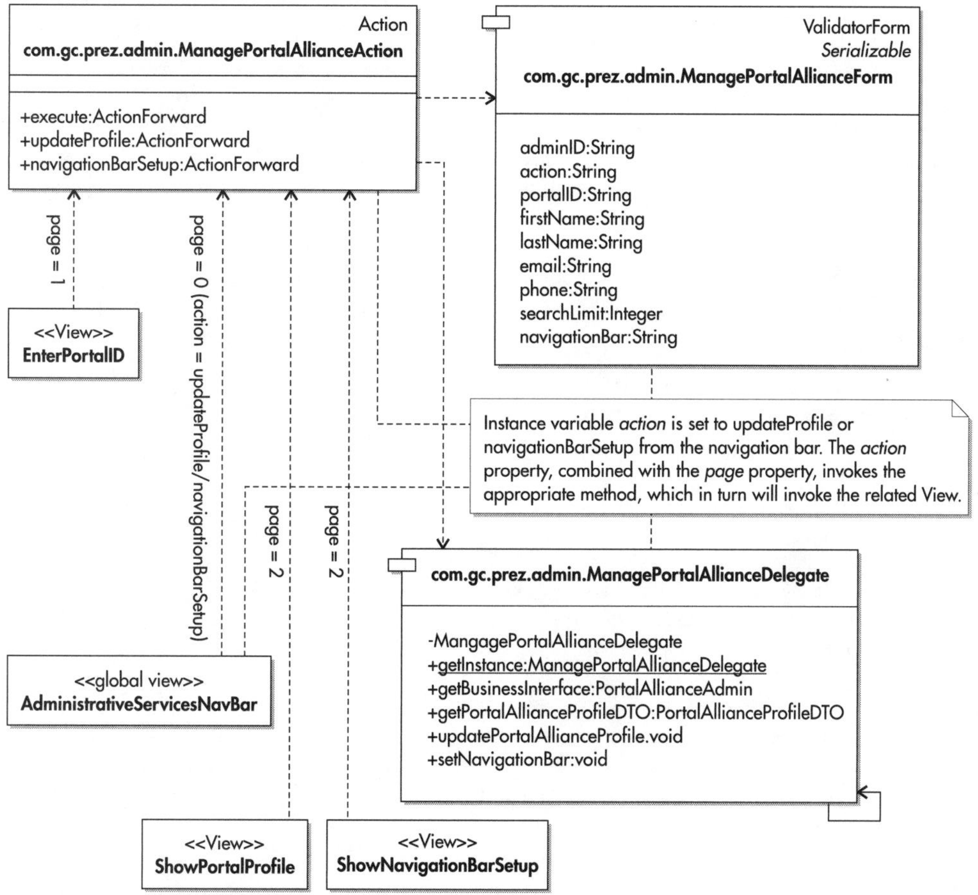

Figure 5-15 *Multi-action pattern*

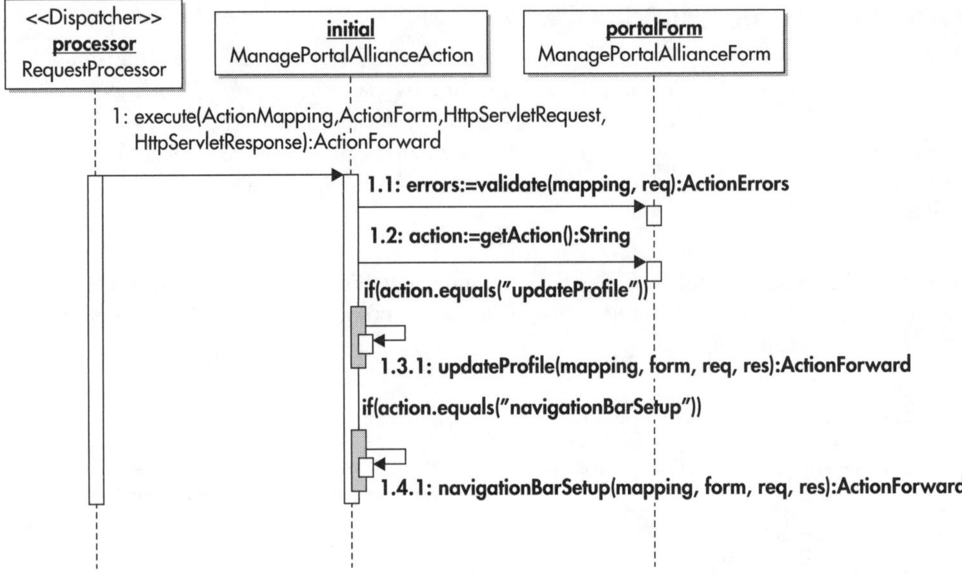

Figure 5-16 *Multi-action pattern sequence diagram*

Configuration Semantics The struts-config.xml declarations are shown here. In this pattern, we will use a single *Action* class and a corresponding *ActionForm*. The *ActionForm* extends *ValidatorForm*, which provides the *page* property for mutlti-page interaction:

```
<action path="/EnterPortalID"
    name="ManagePortalAllianceForm"
    scope="session"
    validate="false"
    forward="/2_3B_EnterPortalID.jsp"/>

<action path="/ManagePortalAlliance"
    type="com.gc.prez.admin.ManagePortalAllianceAction"
    name="ManagePortalAllianceForm"
    scope="session"
    validate="false">
    <forward name="EnterPortalID" path="/2_3B_EnterPortalID.jsp"/>
    <forward name="ShowPortalProfile" path="/2_3_2_UpdatePortalProfile.jsp"/>
    <forward name="ShowNavigationBarSetup" path="/2_3_3_PortalNavBar.jsp"/>
    <forward name="success" path="/2_SiteAdministratorServicesMainPage.jsp"/>
</action>
```

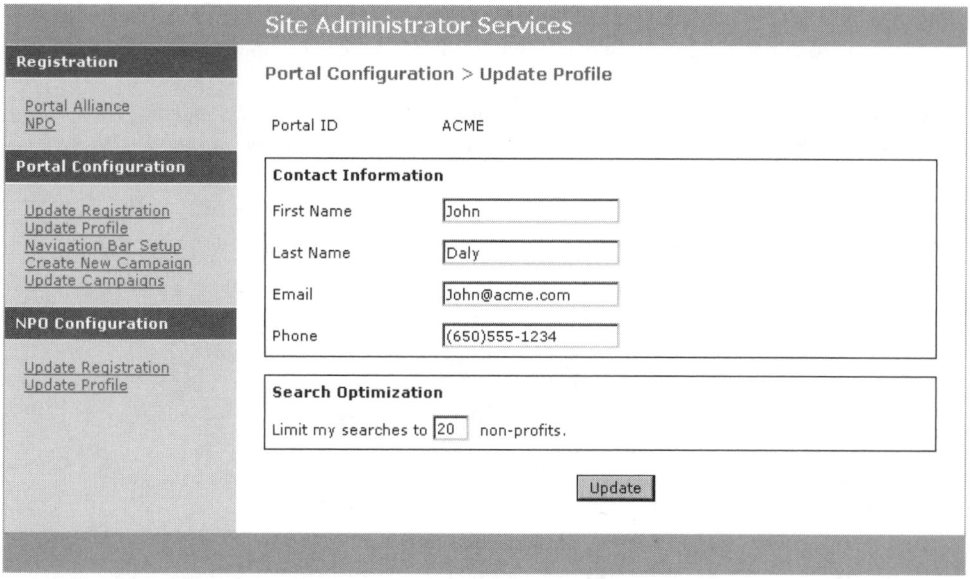

Figure 5-17 *Update portal-alliance profile*

Note that the *ActionMapping* identified by the path *"/ManagePortalAlliance"* will have four possible *ActionForward*(s). The *ShowPortalProfile* `<forward>` declaration is selected for updateProfile action, which will result in the view illustrated in Figure 5-17; and the *ShowNavigationBarSetup* `<forward>` declaration is selected for *navigationBarSetup* action, which will result in the view illustrated in Figure 5-18 . The rest of the semantics are

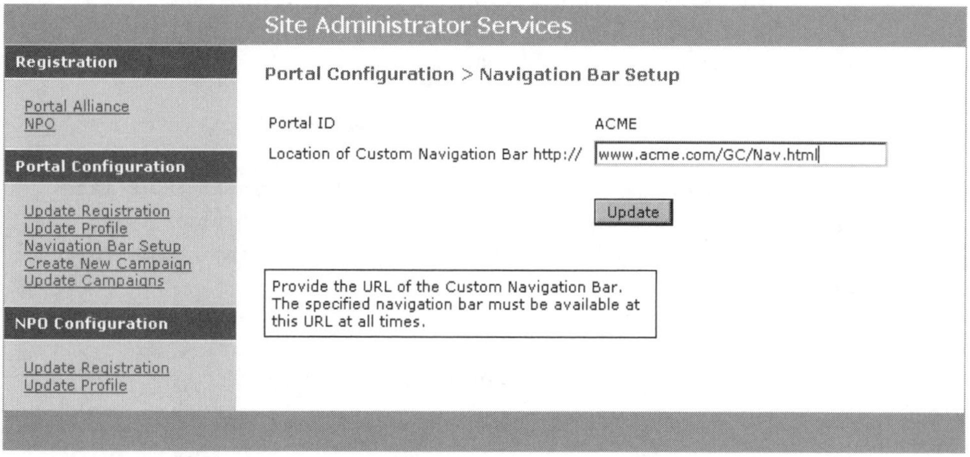

Figure 5-18 *Update navigation bar URL*

similar to the one demonstrated in the "Register Portal-Alliance Use Case" section. Readers are encouraged to review the implementation provided in the accompanying CD-ROM.

Request Handler The request handler in this case has to track the page sequence, that is the value of the *page* property of two different views, and the *action* property of these views; this makes the request handler slightly complex to implement. The semantics of the request handler is illustrated using the following code fragment. Please refer to Figure 5-16 for a high-level sequence diagram.

```
public class ManagePortalAllianceAction extends Action {
    public ActionForward execute( ActionMapping mapping,
    ActionForm form, HttpServletRequest req,
    HttpServletResponse res ) throws Exception {
        ManagePortalAllianceForm portalForm =
                ( ManagePortalAllianceForm )form;
        ActionErrors errors = portalForm.validate( mapping, req );
        String action = portalForm.getAction();
        /* First page for Site Administrator */
        if ( !errors.empty() && portalForm.getPage() == 1 ) {
            saveErrors( req, errors );
            return mapping.findForward( "EnterPortalID" );
        }
        /* Second page for updating profile */
        if ( ( !errors.empty() ) && ( portalForm.getPage() == 2 )
           && ( action.equals( "updateProfile" ) ) ) {
            saveErrors( req, errors );
            return mapping.findForward( "ShowPortalProfile" );
        }
        /* Second page for navigation bar setup */
        if ( ( !errors.empty() ) && ( portalForm.getPage() == 2 ) &&
        ( action.equals( "navigationBarSetup" ) ) ) {
            saveErrors( req, errors );
            return mapping.findForward( "ShowNavigationBarSetup" );
        }
        /* Page number is 0, i.e. request handler was invoked from
         * navigation bar by portal-alliance administrator using the
           "Update Profile" or the Navigation Bar Setup" link*/
        if ( action.equals( "updateProfile" ) ) {
            return ( updateProfile( mapping, form, req, res ) );
        }
        if ( action.equals( "navigationBarSetup" ) ) {
            return ( navigationBarSetup( mapping, form, req, res ) );
        }
        return null;
```

```
    }
    public ActionForward updateProfile( ActionMapping mapping,
    ActionForm form, HttpServletRequest req, HttpServletResponse res )
    throws Exception {
        ... rest of the code ...
    }
    public ActionForward navigationBarSetup( ActionMapping mapping,
    ActionForm form, HttpServletRequest req,
    HttpServletResponse res ) throws Exception {
        ... rest of the code ...
    }
}
```

Register NPO Use Case

A site administrator can create and update the registration information for a non-profit, while the NPO administrator can only view this information. Figure 5-19 illustrates the class diagram for realizing this use case; the semantics of this class diagram are explained in the following section.

Multi-Action Pattern Using *DispatchAction* Class Strategy

The multi-action pattern discussed in the section "Register Portal-Alliance Use Case" was implemented using an *Action* subclass. The Struts framework invokes the *execute* method on a request handler that extends the *Action* class. In this section, we will implement the multi-action pattern using the *DispatchAction* subclass. When a request handler extends the *DispatchAction* class, it must provide a *parameter* attribute in the `<action>` declaration of the struts-config.xml file, whose value is the name of a request time parameter that will be used to identify method names to be called in the *DispatchAction* subclass. This is depicted shortly in the "Configuration Semantics" section. The advantage of being able to specify method names other than the standard *execute* method is that the request handler methods can be directly coupled to user actions, embedded within the HTML form, rather than having to route all actions through the *execute* method. In the following subsections, we will look at an implementation that is identical in terms of functionality to the Register Portal Alliance Use Case but differs in implementation.

Structure Figures 5-20, 5-21, and 5-22 illustrates the static and dynamic aspects of the multi-action pattern using the *DispatchAction* class strategy. Figure 5-21 shows the setting of the *action* property as a result of the method call specified in the navigation bar using the request time parameter *method* (refer to the subsection "View Semantics" for more information); Figure 5-22 shows how the *action* property is used to control the process flow within the request handler.

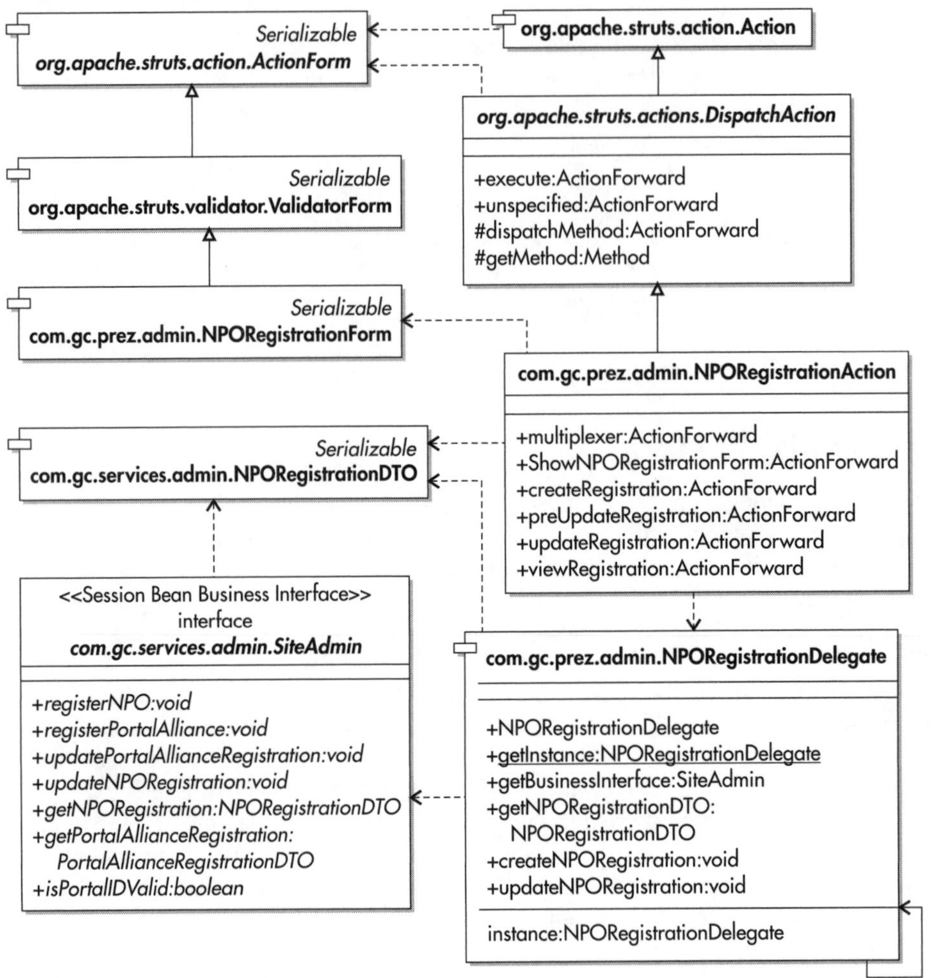

Figure 5-19 *Register NPO class diagram*

Configuration Semantics The struts-config.xml declarations are shown here. Observe the *parameter* attribute specification that identifies the request time parameter *method* to be used for identifying the request handler method that will be called instead of the *execute* method.

```
<action path="/NPORegistration"
    type="com.gc.prez.admin.NPORegistrationAction"
    name="NPORegistrationForm"
    scope="session"
    parameter="method"
```

```
    validate="false">
    <forward name="ShowPage" path="/2_2_NPORegistration.jsp"/>
    <forward name="EnterEIN" path="/2_4A_EnterEIN.jsp"/>
    <forward name="success" path="/2_SiteAdministratorServicesMainPage.jsp"/>
</action>
```

View Semantics Again, the following snippet is from the dynamic navigation bar 2_AdministrationServicesNavBar that is included with all administrator JSPs. Observe that all requests are directed to same URL *"/NPORegistration"*, which is the identifier for the *ActionMapping* object that will be used by the framework for invoking the associated request handler *NPORegistrationAction*. However, in this case the *execute* method of the request handler is not invoked; instead, the method to be invoked is specified by the request time parameter

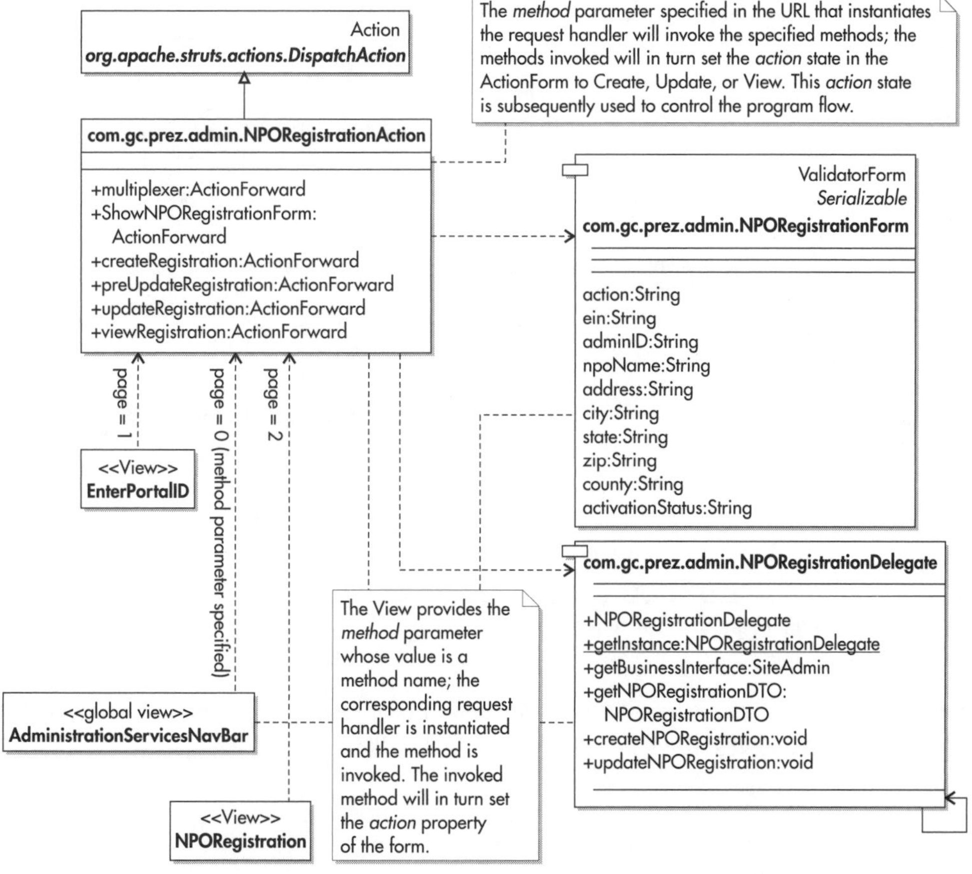

Figure 5-20 *Multi-action pattern using dispatch action class strategy*

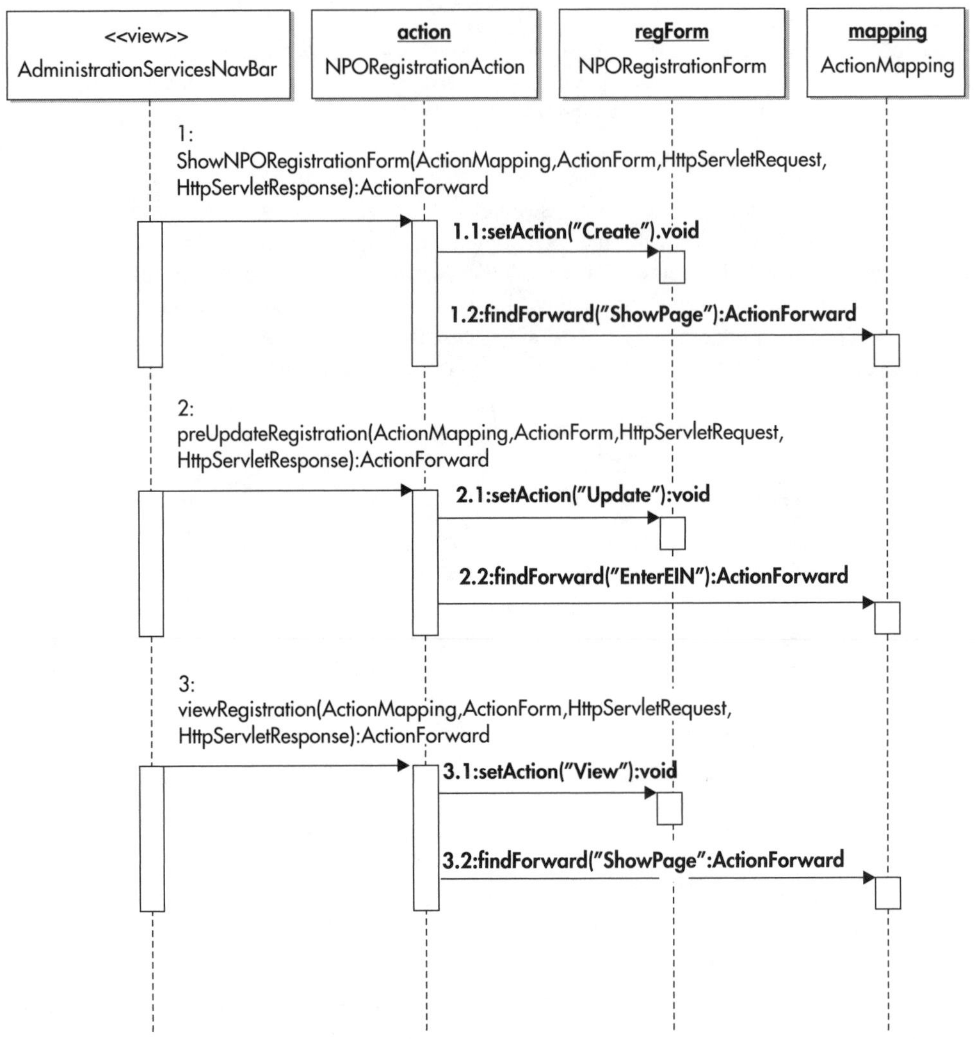

Figure 5-21 *Multi-action pattern sequence diagram*

method, as shown next. Each of the methods shown in the following snippet is responsible for setting the corresponding *action* property; this was illustrated in Figure 5-21.

```
<gc:hasAccess role="SiteAdminRole">
    <html:link page="/NPORegistration.do?method=ShowNPORegistrationForm">
        <bean:message key="SiteAdminServices.NPORegistration"/>
    </html:link><br><br>
</gc:hasAccess>

<gc:hasAccess role="NPOAdminRole">
    <html:link page="/NPORegistration.do?method=viewRegistration">
```

```
        <bean:message key="NPOAdminServices.ViewRegistration"/>
    </html:link><br><br>
</gc:hasAccess>

<gc:hasAccess role="SiteAdminRole">
    <html:link page="/NPORegistration.do?method=preUpdateRegistration">
        <bean:message key="SiteAdminServices.UpdateNPORegistration"/>
    </html:link><br>
</gc:hasAccess>
```

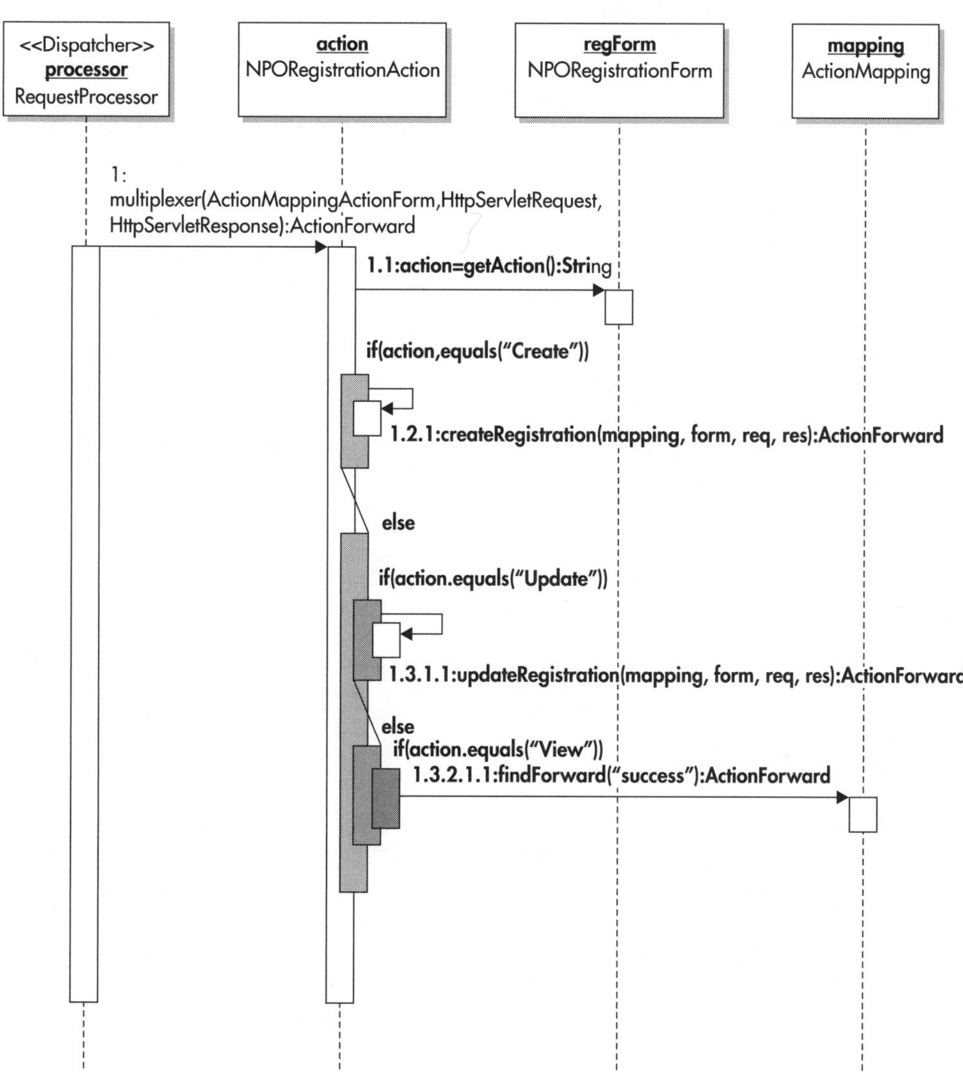

Figure 5-22 *Multi-action pattern sequence diagram*

In the preceding snippet, a selection on the navigation bar will first invoke a method that will set the desired action and then exit with an *ActionForward* pertinent to that action. For example, the *ShowNPORegistration* method will execute the following code:

```
public ActionForward ShowNPORegistrationForm( ActionMapping mapping,
    ActionForm form, HttpServletRequest req,
    HttpServletResponse res ) {
        NPORegistrationForm regForm = ( NPORegistrationForm )form;
        regForm.setAction( "Create" );
        saveToken( req );
        return mapping.findForward( "ShowPage" );
}
```

Comparing the *DispatchAction* subclass strategy with the *Action* subclass strategy, it is obvious that while this strategy reduces the complexity in the request handler, it introduces extra methods for displaying the initial view (the process start-up view). Applications with complex navigation schemes can benefit from this strategy at the cost of coupling the method invocations to the request time *method* parameter specified in the HTML form; however, it does take away the need to specify the *action* parameter at request time, as shown in the section View Semantics for the Multi-Action Pattern Using the Action Class Strategy.

The views participating in this use case, namely, 2_4A_EnterEIN.jsp and 2_2_NPORegistration .jsp, both invoke the method *multiplexer* of the request handler *NPORegistrationAction* (again, using the request time *method* parameter); this method has similar functionality as the *execute* method of the *PortalAllianceRegistrationAction* of the Register Portal Alliance Use Case. All other semantics of the *DispatchAction* subclass strategy are similar to the *Action* subclass strategy, readers are urged to review the implementation provided with the accompanying source distribution for additional details.

Realization of Search NPO Use Cases

The following subsections will explain the use case realization for the use cases in the Search NPO package. Please refer to Chapter 1 for use case descriptions.

Search NPO Use Case

The search facility is a generic facility that can seamlessly plug into the navigation scheme of any functionality desiring to use the NPO search function. Plugging of a search function into the navigation scheme of other functions is accomplished by using a combination of three techniques:

- The request handler calling the search function does so by rendering a search function-related view that transfers control to the request handler of the search facility.
- The search facility's request handler remembers the request handler that invoked the search facility.
- After the search is completed, the search facility transfers the control back to the calling request handler by rendering.

This use case is realized using the class structure depicted in Figure 5-23. The complete semantics will be are explained later in the section "Create the Campaign Use Case." Observe that the *SearchAndListNPOAction* is subclassed from *DispatchAction.*

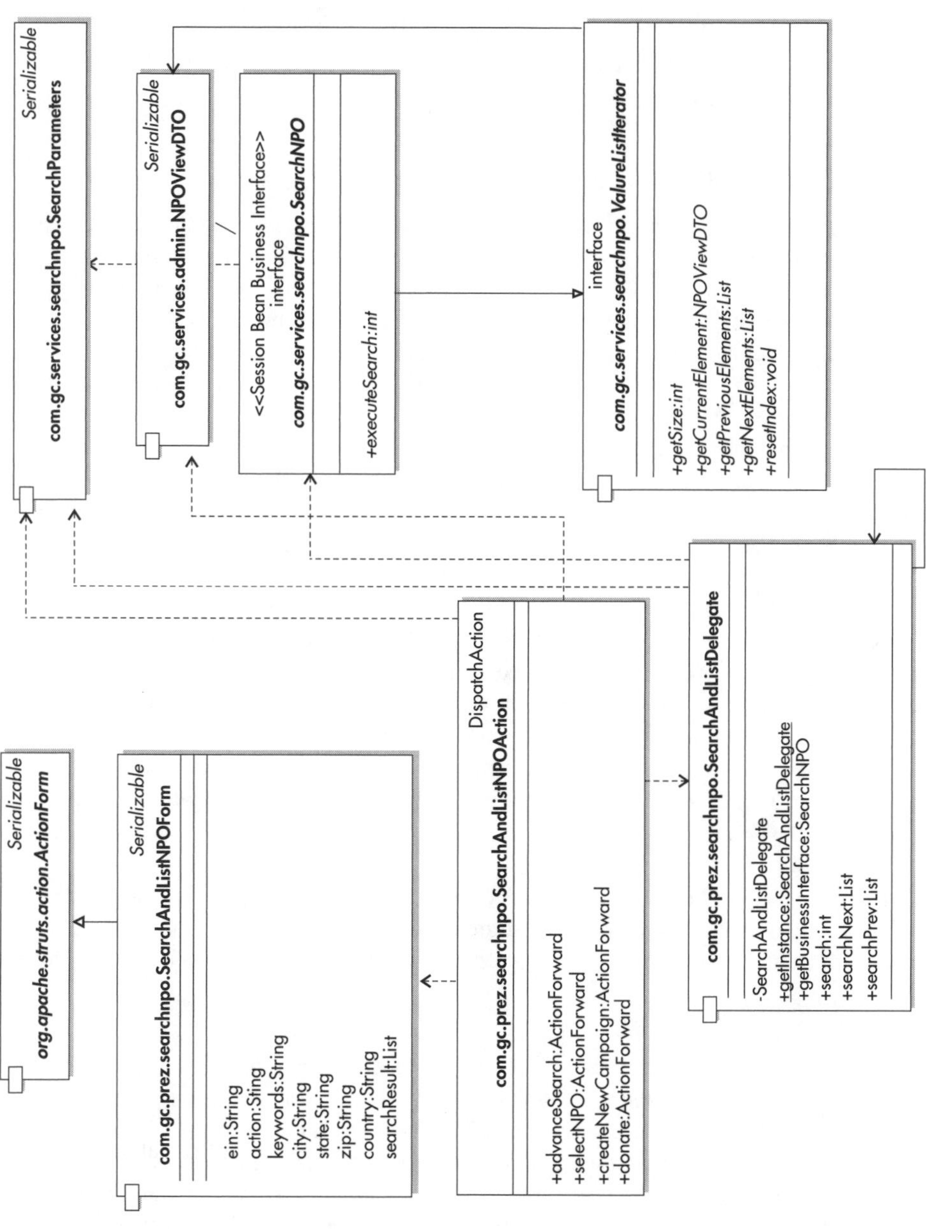

Figure 5-23 *Search NPO class diagram*

SearchAndListNPOForm uses a *Collection* object *searchResult*, which is a coarse-grained object consisting of *NPOViewDTO* objects. The business tier uses the value list handler pattern [Core] to provide this collection; this pattern is explained in Chapter 7.

Realization of Manage Campaigns Use Cases

The following subsections provide the use case realization for use cases in the Manage Campaigns package. Please refer to Chapter 1 for use case descriptions.

Create the Campaign Use Case

The campaign management function requires the ability to search and select an NPO for which a campaign has to be created. In order to accomplish this, the Create Campaign function will chain itself to the *Search* function. The Shared Request Handler pattern discussed in this section is used in demonstrating how we can accomplish this using the Struts framework. Figure 5-24 illustrates a class diagram for realizing this use case.

Shared Request Handler Pattern

A use case may include or depend on other use cases. Often a common set of functionality is shared between several use cases. A navigation scheme can be conditionally altered by injecting new services in the process flow. In the sample application, the search-related functionality (search parameter page and search result page) and the associated request handlers can be invoked by both the NPO administrators as well as the donors. An NPO administrator (or a Site admin as stand-in) will require search services for creating campaigns based on NPOs selected using the search process. A donor will require the search service to find a desired NPO prior to making a donation. In both cases, the same search functionality is invoked. Upon invocation, the search facility will provide a search parameters page, whose submission will provide a list of NPOs from which the administrators or donors can select the desired NPO. Selection of an NPO during the campaign creation process will take the administrator to a page for entering campaign details, whereas selection of an NPO during the donation process will take a donor to the donation cart.

Structure Figure 5-25 illustrates the class diagram of the Shared Request Handler pattern. There are several dynamic views to demonstrate the campaign creation function, as such, the associated sequence diagrams are discussed progressively through the section.

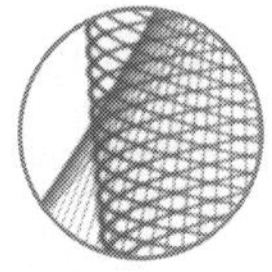

NOTE

From Figure 5-25, we observe that the Multi-Page pattern will be a foundational for implementing the Shared Request Handler pattern. We would have had significant difficultly implementing Shared Request Handler pattern without this foundational pattern. This demonstrates that the process of harvesting and documenting pattern is a continuous process. Over time, creating large-scale solutions implies looking at the catalog of design patterns whose implementation is already proven and the vocabulary well understood, and applying these pattern within the context of the problem domain to create a highly modular, scalable, maintenable, and extensible solution.

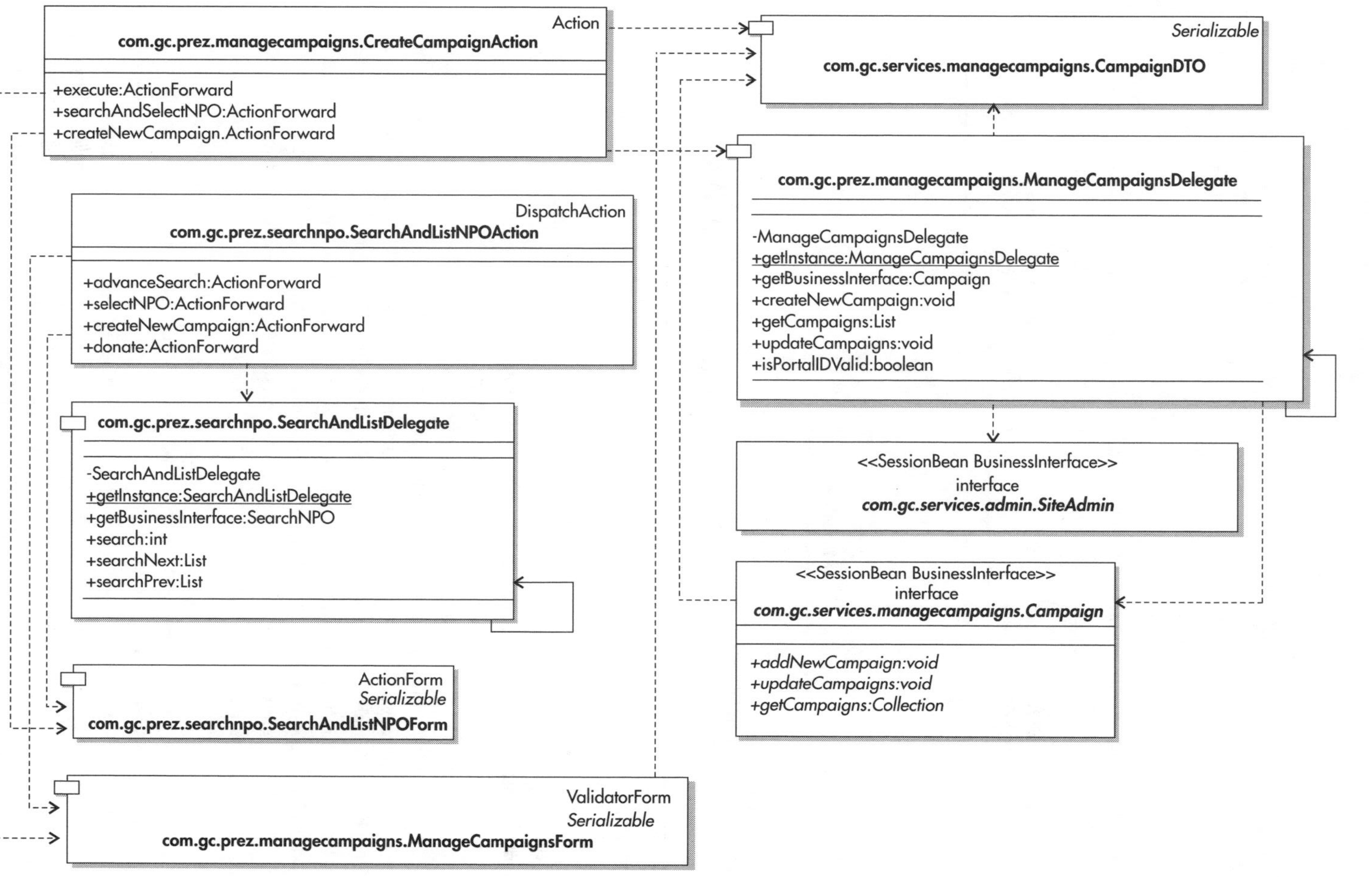

Figure 5-24 *Create Campaign class diagram*

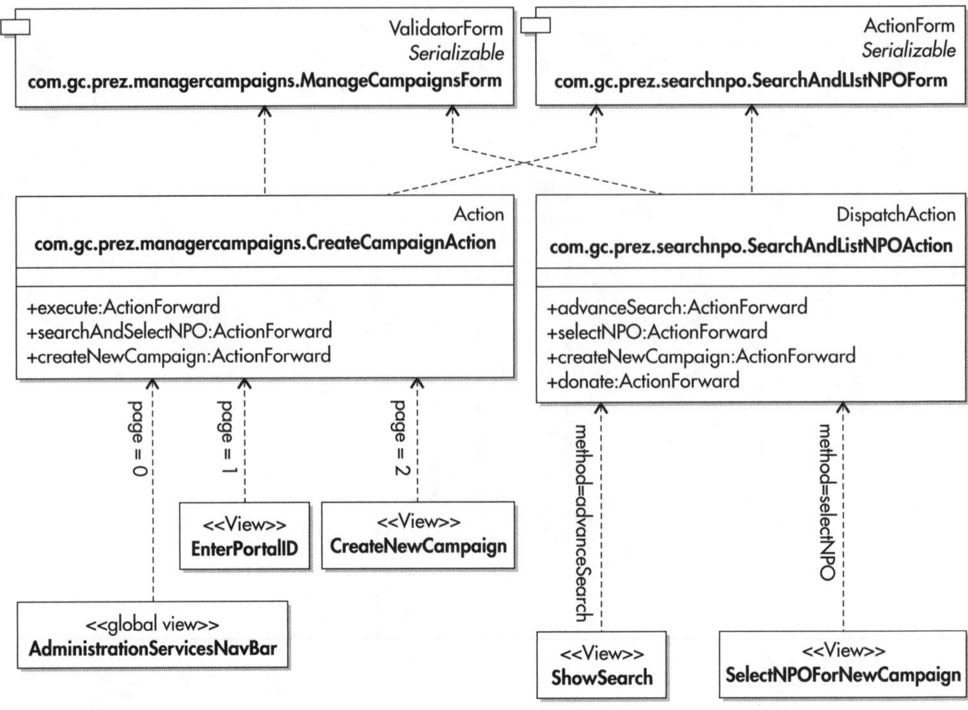

Figure 5-25 *Shared Request Handler Pattern*

Configuration Semantics The struts-config.xml declarations are shown in this section. The Create Campaign use case employs the multi-page pattern. The view associated with page 1 is 2_3C_EnterPortalID.jsp, and the view associated with page 2 is 2_3_4_2_CampaignDetails.jsp; this is shown in the following struts-config.xml declaration. However, please note that the views 2_3C_EnterPortalID.jsp and 2_3_4_2_CampaignDetails.jsp need intervening views provided by the search function to search and select the NPO. Therefore, we should transfer control to the search function from the Create Campaign function. *CreateCampaignAction* request handler accomplishes this by creating an *ActionForward* with *name="ShowSearch"* for displaying the view 2_3_4_NewCampaignSearch.jsp after successfully processing the view 2_3C_EnterPortalID.jsp and before processing the view 2_3_4_2_CampaignDetails.jsp.

```
<!-- Use Case: Create Campaigns (Use Case Package: Manage Campaigns)-->
<action path="/CreateCampaignStep1" forward="/2_3C_EnterPortalID.jsp"/>
<action path="/CreateCampaignStep2"
    type="com.gc.prez.managecampaigns.CreateCampaignAction"
    name="ManageCampaignsForm"
    scope="session"
    validate="false">
    <forward name="EnterPortalID" path="/2_3C_EnterPortalID.jsp"/>
```

```
    <forward name="ShowSearch" path="/2_3_4_NewCampaignSearch.jsp"/>
    <forward name="CreateNewCampaign" path="/2_3_4_2_CampaignDetails.jsp"/>
    <forward name="success" path="/2_SiteAdministratorServicesMainPage.jsp"/>
</action>
```

The view 2_3_4_NewCampaignSearch.jsp includes a generic search parameter view G_AdvancedSearchForNPO.jsp whose HTML form's *action* parameter attribute has the URL "/SearchAndListNPO.do?method=advanceSearch". Submitting this form will cause the search parameter page to invoke *ActionMapping* identified by the path *"/SearchAndListNPO"*, which in turn will be used for invoking the *SearchAndListNPOAction.advanceSearch* method of the request handler, therefore accomplishing a transfer of control from the campaign function to the *SearchAndListNPOAction* request handler. This transfer of control also includes transfer of application state from the *action* property stored in the forms *ManageCampaignsForm* to the *action* property of *SearchAndListNPOForm*. The *action* property informs the *SearchAndListNPOAction* request handler, whose function must be returned control when the search function exits after completing NPO selection. The *action* property provides a kind of callback facility when the *SearchAndListNPOAction* request handler is ready to transfer control back to the calling request handler. For example, in the sample application, when the *action* property is set to *createNewCampaign*, the *SearchAndListNPOAction* request handler will return control to the campaign function's next view (page 2 of campaign process) using the `<forward>` specification identified by the name="CreateNewCampaign"; the *action* property can also be set to "Donate", in which case the SearchAndListNPOAction request handler will return control to the donate function's next view using the `<forward>` specification identified by the name="Donate". This is shown here by the forward declarations "Create New Campaign" and "Donate". Note that the *SearchAndListNPOAction* is subclassed from *DispatchAction.*

```
<!-- Use Case: Search NPO (Use Case Package: Search NPO) -->
<action path="/SearchAndListNPO"
    type="com.gc.prez.searchnpo.SearchAndListNPOAction"
    name="SearchAndListNPOForm"
    scope="session"
    parameter="method"
    validate="false">
    <forward name="ShowSearchForCampaign" path="/2_3_4_NewCampaignSearch.jsp"/>
    <forward name="ShowSearchForDonation" path="P_3_DonorServicesAndSearch.jsp"/>
    <forward name="SelectNPOForNewCampaign" path="/2_3_4_1_SelectNPO.jsp"/>
    <forward name="SelectNPOForDonation" path="/P_3_1_SelectNPO.jsp"/>
    <forward name="CreateNewCampaign" path="/2_3_4_2_CampaignDetails.jsp"/>
    <forward name="Donate" path="/P_3_1_1_DonationCart.jsp"/>
    <forward name="failure" path="/2_SiteAdministratorServicesMainPage.jsp"/>
</action>
```

In the preceding struts-config.xml declaration, observe that the views selected by the *SearchAndListNPOAction* are specific to the calling function (Create Campaign or Donor Search); the *"ShowSearchFor..."* and "selectNPOFor ..." `<forward>` specifications are associated with caller-specific views that embed a generic search form G_AdvancedSearchForNPO.jsp, and a generic select NPO form G_NPOSearchList.jsp, respectively. This embedding of search-related forms inside of other views is necessary to maintain the look and feel of the calling function and provide a consistent user experience.

View Semantics The following snippet is from the dynamic navigation bar 2_AdministrationServicesNavBar that is included with all administrator JSPs. This is just another case of multi-page pattern where the site administrator has an extra step "/CreateCampaignStep1"; this will invoke the view 2_4B_EnterEIN.jsp shown next:

```
<gc:hasAccess role="SiteAdminRole">
    <html:link page="/CreateCampaignStep1.do">
        <bean:message key="PortalAdminServices.CreateNewCampaign"/>
    </html:link><br>
</gc:hasAccess>
<gc:hasAccess role="PortalAdminRole">
    <html:link page="/CreateCampaignStep2.do">
        <bean:message key="PortalAdminServices.CreateNewCampaign"/>
    </html:link><br>
</gc:hasAccess>
```

The view 2_3C_EnterPortalID.jsp will invoke the request handler *CreateCampaignAction* using the *ActionMapping* identified by the path *"/CreateCampaignStep2"* (refer to struts-config .xml shown earlier) with the *page* attribute property of the corresponding form-bean set to 1. The request handler *CreateCampaignAction* may also be directly invoked from the navigation bar using the *ActionMapping* identified by the path *"/CreateCampaignStep2"* when the user is a portal-alliance administrator. The view 2_3C_EnterPortalID.jsp is shown next; the corresponding page is shown in Figure 5-26, and the multi-page pattern semantics are depicted in Figure 5-27.

```
<html:form method="POST" action="/CreateCampaignStep2.do" focus="portalID">
<html:hidden property="page" value="1"/>
<table border="0" cellspacing="0" cellpadding="5">
        <tr>
            <td class="txt"><bean:message
                key="SiteAdminServices.EnterPortalID"/></td>
            <td><html:text property="portalID" size="16" maxlength="16"/></td>
        </tr>
        <tr>
            <td> </td>
            <td><html:submit><bean:message key="prompt.Submit"/></html:submit>
            </td>
        </tr>
    </table>
</html:form>
```

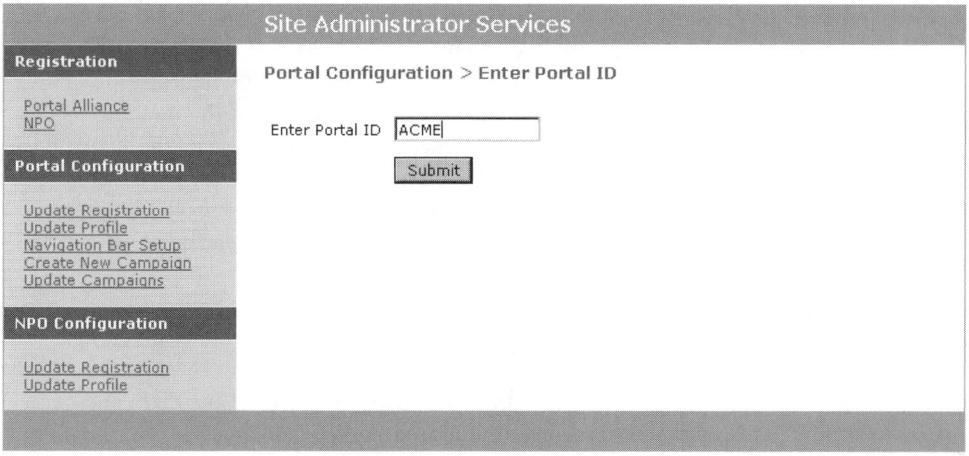

Site Administrator Services

Registration

Portal Alliance
NPO

Portal Configuration

Update Registration
Update Profile
Navigation Bar Setup
Create New Campaign
Update Campaigns

NPO Configuration

Update Registration
Update Profile

Portal Configuration > Enter Portal ID

Enter Portal ID ACME

Submit

Figure 5-26 *Enter Portal ID page*

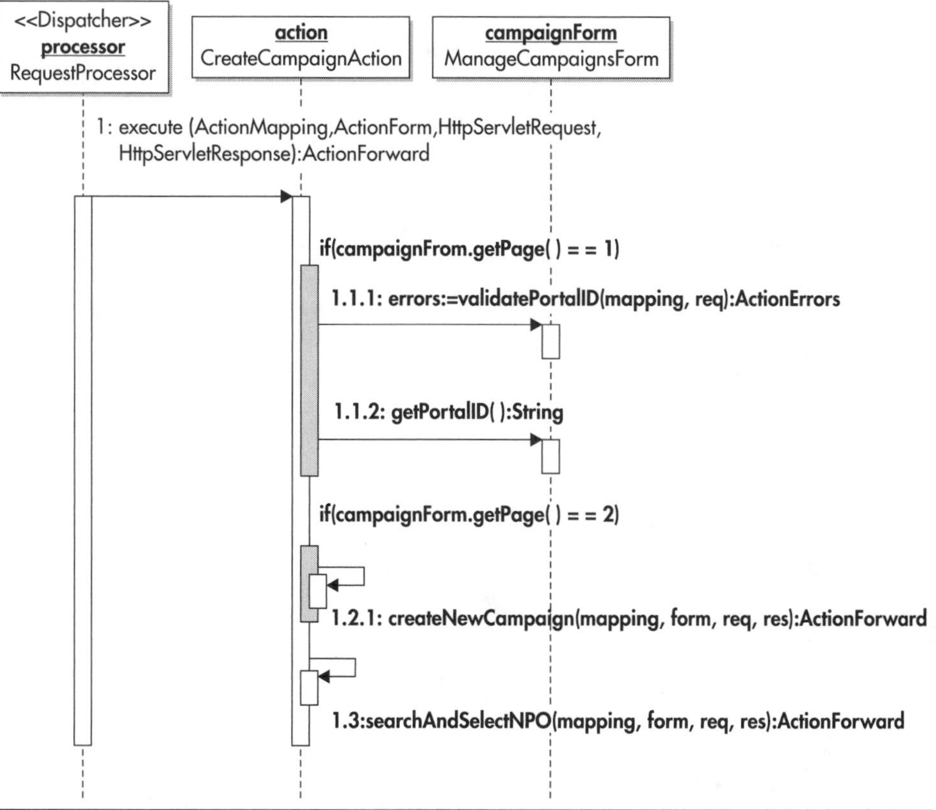

Figure 5-27 *Multi-page Pattern sequence diagram*

Once invoked, the *CreateCampaignAction* request handler will in turn invoke the search facility–related view 2_3_4_NewCampaignSearch.jsp using the `<forward>` specification identified by name="ShowSearch" in the method *SearchandSelectNPO*; the corresponding page is shown in Figure 5-28. Figure 5-29 is a sequence diagram for the method *CreateCampaignAction.searchAndSelectNPO* that depicts the flow of events for invoking the search facility page 2_3_4_ NewCampaignSearch.jsp. Observe that this page has an embedded view /G_AdvancedSearchForNPO.jsp that will invoke the *SearchAndListNPOAction* request handler. This is how the Create New Campaign function manages to transfer control to the search function.

As mentioned earlier, the view 2_3_4_NewCampaignSearch.jsp includes the search function–related view G_AdvancedSearchForNPO.jsp. A condensed version of G_AdvancedSearchForNPO.jsp is shown next. When this form is submitted, it will result in the invocation of the *SearchAndListNPOAction* request handler. The *SearchAndListNPOAction* request handler is subclassed from *DispatchAction*, therefore the method invoked for this request handler is the one specified by the request time parameter *method* specified in the query portion of HTML form's *action* attribute URL.

```
<html:form method="POST"
    action="/SearchAndListNPO.do?method=advanceSearch"
    focus="keywords">
    ... rest of the JSP containing search parameters...
</html:form>
```

After successfully processing the parameters of the view 2_3_4_NewCampaignSearch.jsp, the request handler will list the results of the search by invoking the view 2_3_4_1_SelectNPO.jsp; the corresponding page is shown in Figure 5-29. The *SearchAndListNPOAction* request handler *SearchandListNPOAction* invokes this view by creating the *ActionForward* object related to the `<forward>` specification identified by *name="SelectNPOForNewCampaign"* (refer to

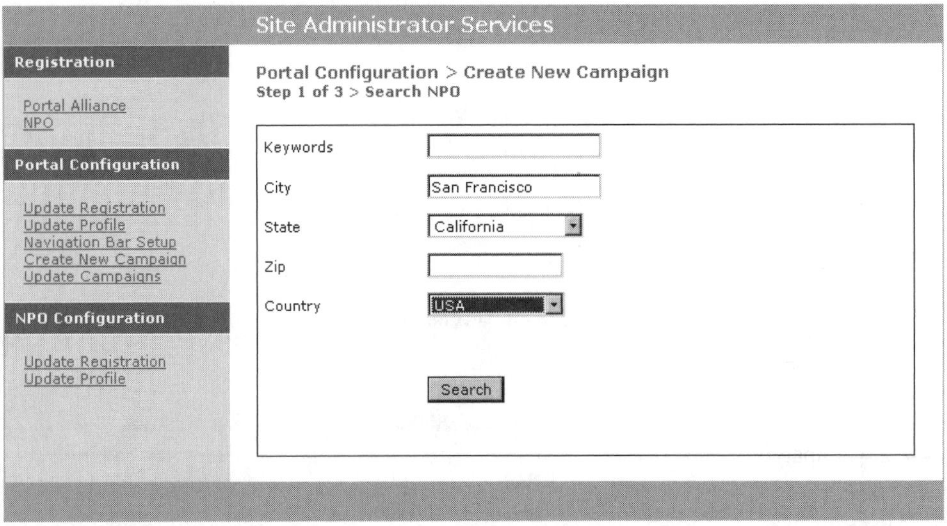

Figure 5-28 *Enter Search Parameters page*

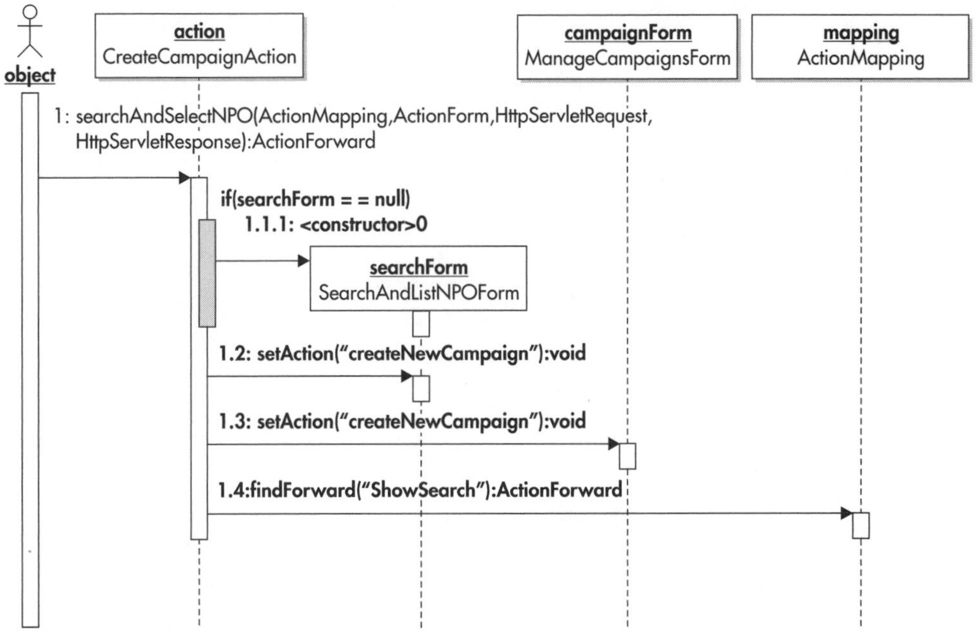

Figure 5-29 *Invoke the search facility view using ActionForward*

struts-config.xml declarations specified in the preceding discussion). This view is selected because the state maintained in the *SearchAndListForm* form-bean identifies that the search is being performed on behalf of the Create Campaign function and therefore the look-and-feel of this function is desired.

The view 2_3_4_1_SelectNPO.jsp includes the generic view G_NPOSearchList.jsp for selecting an NPO from the selection list; the corresponding page is shown in Figure 5-30.

The specification *action="/SearchAndListNPO.do?method=selectNPO"* in the following HTML form (generated with view 2_3_4_1_Select.jsp) will use the *ActionMapping* object identified by the path "*/SearchAndListNPO*" to invoke SearchAndListNPOAction. The selection is applied to the corresponding form-bean, and the controller then calls the method *SearchAndListNPOAction .selectNPO()* of the request handler; this method is identified by the request time parameter *method* specified in the query portion of HTML form's *action* attribute URL.

```
<html:form method="POST"
    action="/SearchAndListNPO.do?method=selectNPO">
    ... rest of the JSP for displaying search results...
</html:form>
```

The *SearchAndListNPOAction.selectNPO* method will re-invoke the calling *CreateCampaignAction* by exiting with an *ActionForward* that invokes the next view 2_3_4_2_CampaignDetails.jsp (with the *page* property set to 2) in the campaign creation process using the `<forward>` declaration identified by name="*CreateNewCampaign*". This is how the search function manages to transfer control back to the Create Campaign function.This is shown in the Figure 5-31.

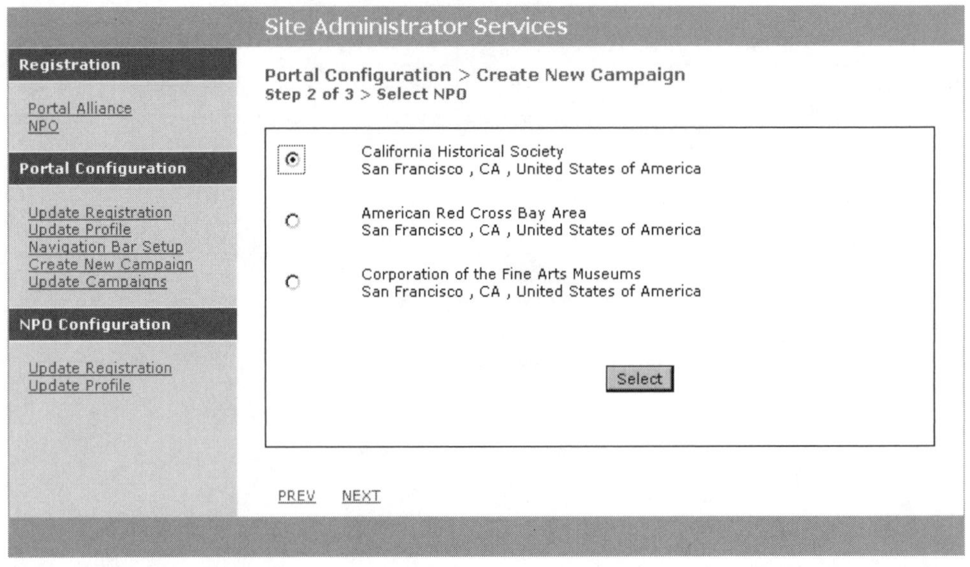

Figure 5-30 *Select NPO from the selection list*

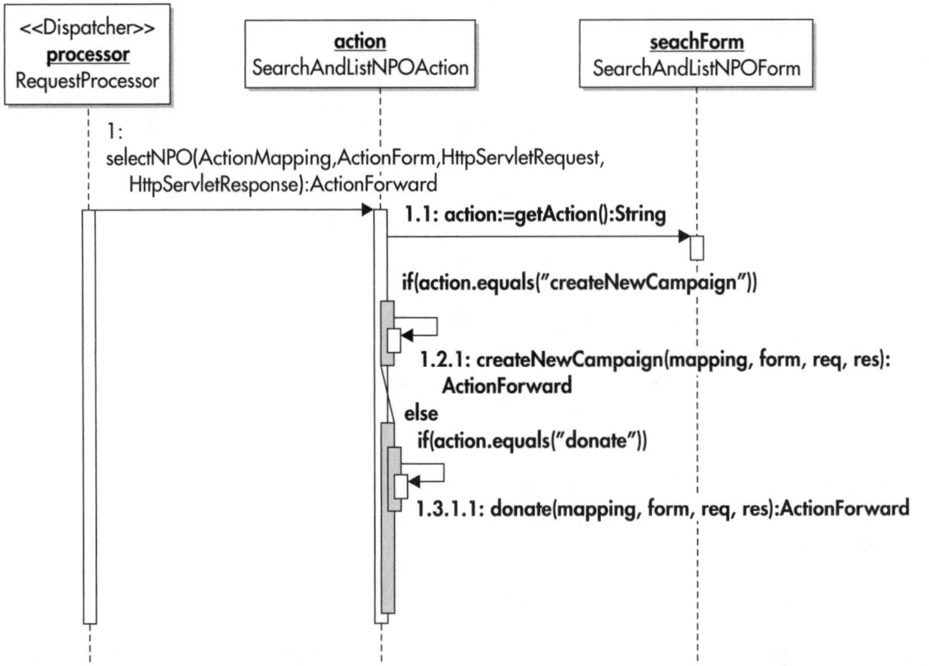

Figure 5-31 *Transfer control to the caller*

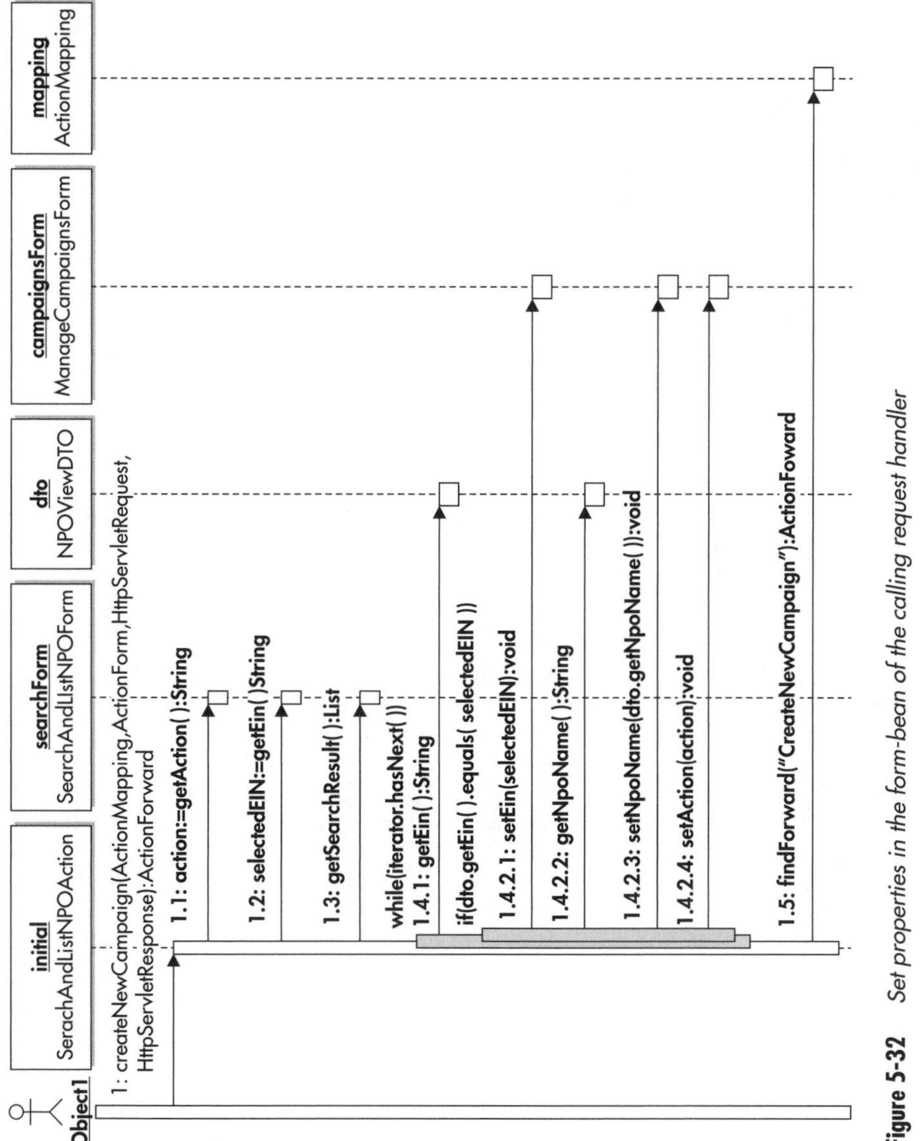

Figure 5-32 *Set properties in the form-bean of the calling request handler*

The *SearchAndListNPOAction.selectNPO* method, prior to exiting, will first transfer the information on the selected NPO to the form-bean associated with the calling request handler. This is illustrated in Figure 5-32. The resulting page (based on 2_3_4_2_CampaignDetails.jsp) is shown in Figure 5-33. The rest of the process is similar to the multi-page pattern.

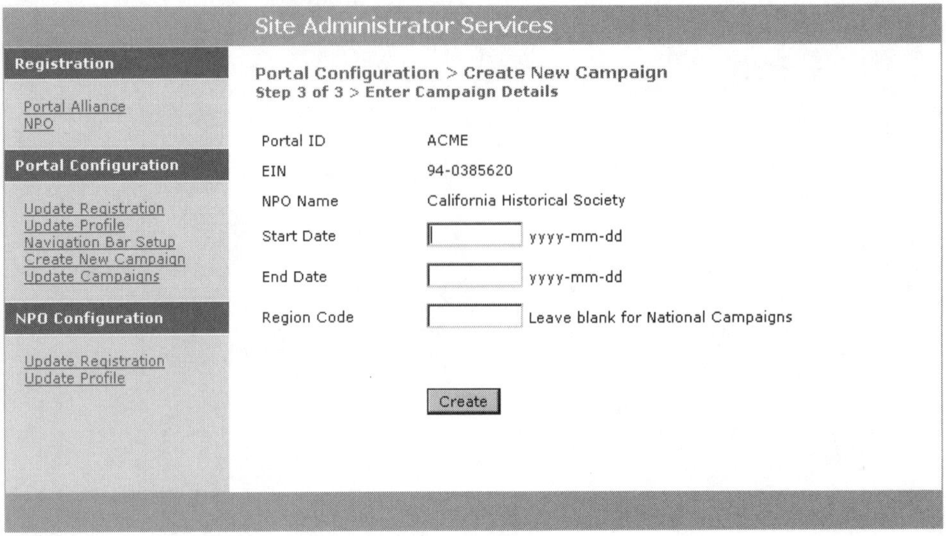

Figure 5-33 *Create New Campaign page*

Successful submission of the Campaign page will result in the creation of a campaign for the corresponding Portal ID. This is illustrated in Figure 5-34, which shows the flow of events for the final step in campaign creation.

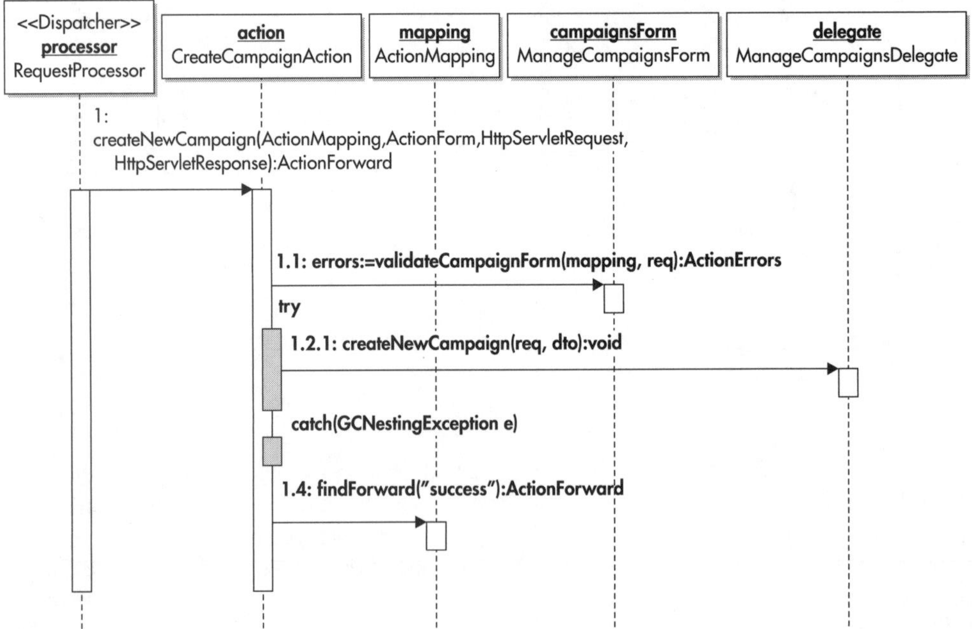

Figure 5-34 *Final step in campaign creation*

Request Handler In the following abridged version of the *CreateCampaignAction* request handler, when the *searchAndSelectNPO* method is called from the *execute* method, the request handler initializes the *action* property of the search form-bean *SearchAndListNPOForm* with a value that informs the *SearchAndListNPOAction* of the *ActionForward* that it will have to create when the search function has completed selecting the desired NPO. The *CreateCampaignAction* request handler transfers control to the search function by creating an *ActionForward* relating to the `<forward>` specification identified by *name="ShowSearch"*. This is illustrated using the following code fragment:

```
public class CreateCampaignAction extends Action {
    public ActionForward execute( ActionMapping mapping,
    ActionForm form, HttpServletRequest req,
    HttpServletResponse res ) throws Exception {
        /* The logic here is similar to multi-page pattern */
... rest of the code ...
    }

    public ActionForward searchAndSelectNPO( ActionMapping mapping,
    ActionForm form, HttpServletRequest req,
    HttpServletResponse res ) {
        ManageCampaignsForm campaignForm = ( ManageCampaignsForm )form;
        /* Find or create a new search form-bean */
        SearchAndListNPOForm searchForm =
        ( SearchAndListNPOForm )req.getSession().getAttribute(
                    "SearchAndListNPOForm" );
        if ( searchForm == null ) {
            searchForm = new SearchAndListNPOForm();
            req.getSession().setAttribute( "SearchAndListNPOForm", searchForm );
        }
        /* Store information on the calling module in search form-bean */
        searchForm.setAction( "createNewCampaign" );
        campaignForm.setAction( "createNewCampaign" );
        /* Display the search page for transferring control to the
         * search function */
        return mapping.findForward( "ShowSearch" );
    }
    /* Process page 2 after the NPO is selected by the search facility */
    public ActionForward createNewCampaign( ActionMapping mapping,
    ActionForm form, HttpServletRequest req,
    HttpServletResponse res ) throws Exception {
        ...rest of the code...
        /* The logic here is similar to multi-page pattern */
        return mapping.findForward( "success" );
    }
}
```

In the following *SearchAndListNPOAction* request handler, the *advanceSearch* method will set the *searchResult* property of the *SearchAndListNPOForm*; this property is a *Collection* object consisting of *NPOViewDTO* objects the *SearchAndListNPOAction.selectNPO* method will invoke the view of the calling function that was responsible for instantiating the search service; before transferring control to the Create Campaign view, the request handler will transfer information about the selected EIN from the search form-bean to the campaign form-bean.

```
public class SearchAndListNPOAction extends DispatchAction {
    public ActionForward advanceSearch( ActionMapping mapping,
    ActionForm form, HttpServletRequest req,
    HttpServletResponse res ) throws Exception {
        SearchAndListNPOForm searchForm = ( SearchAndListNPOForm )form;
...rest of the code...
        int resultCount =
        SearchAndListDelegate.getInstance().search( req, searchParameters );
        /* Get a Collection object from the business tier */
if ( resultCount > 0 ) {
            searchForm.setSearchResult(
            ( SearchAndListDelegate.getInstance() ).searchNext(
                      req, Constants.PageSize ) );
        }
        ...rest of the code...
        /* Show custom selection view related to the calling function */
        if ( action.equals( "createNewCampaign" ) ) {
            return mapping.findForward( "SelectNPOForNewCampaign" );
        }
        else if ( action.equals( "donate" ) )
        { return mapping.findForward( "SelectNPOForDonation" ); }
        else { return null; }
    }
    /* Based on action property value, transfer control to the caller */
    public ActionForward selectNPO( ActionMapping mapping,
    ActionForm form, HttpServletRequest req,
    HttpServletResponse res ) {
        SearchAndListNPOForm searchForm = ( SearchAndListNPOForm )form;
        String action                   = searchForm.getAction();
        ...rest of the code...
        /* Invoke post-search page of the calling function */
        if ( action.equals( "createNewCampaign" ) ) {
            return createNewCampaign( mapping, form, req, res );
```

```
        }
        else if ( action.equals( "donate" ) ) {
            return donate( mapping, form, req, res ); }
        else { return null; }
    }
    /* Initialize calling function's form-bean with selected NPO */
    public ActionForward createNewCampaign( ActionMapping mapping,
    ActionForm form, HttpServletRequest req, HttpServletResponse res ) {
        SearchAndListNPOForm searchForm = ( SearchAndListNPOForm )form;
        String action                   = searchForm.getAction();
        ManageCampaignsForm campaignsForm = ( ManageCampaignsForm )
             req.getSession().getAttribute( "ManageCampaignsForm" );
        String selectedEIN = searchForm.getEin();
        Iterator iterator =
        ( ( Collection )searchForm.getSearchResult() ).iterator();
        while ( iterator.hasNext() ) {
            NPOViewDTO dto = ( NPOViewDTO )iterator.next();
            if ( dto.getEin().equals( selectedEIN ) ) {
                /* Transfer the information on selected NPO
                 * to campaign form-bean */
                campaignsForm.setEin( selectedEIN );
                campaignsForm.setNpoName( dto.getNpoName() );
                campaignsForm.setAction( action );
                req.getSession().removeAttribute( "SearchAndListNPOForm" );
                break;
            }
        }
        saveToken( req );
        return mapping.findForward( "CreateNewCampaign" );
    }
    public ActionForward donate( ActionMapping mapping,
    ActionForm form, HttpServletRequest req, HttpServletResponse res ) {
        ... donor search function related code ...
    }
}
```

Update Campaigns Use Case

A site administrator or a portal-alliance administrator can modify existing campaigns by altering the start and end dates of the campaigns. The implementation of this use case employs the multi-page pattern. Figures 5-35 and 5-36 illustrate the static and dynamic aspects of the Update Campaigns use case.

The use of nested indexed properties in realizing this use case is explained in Chapter 4, which demonstrates the ability to map request time parameters to properties of JavaBean

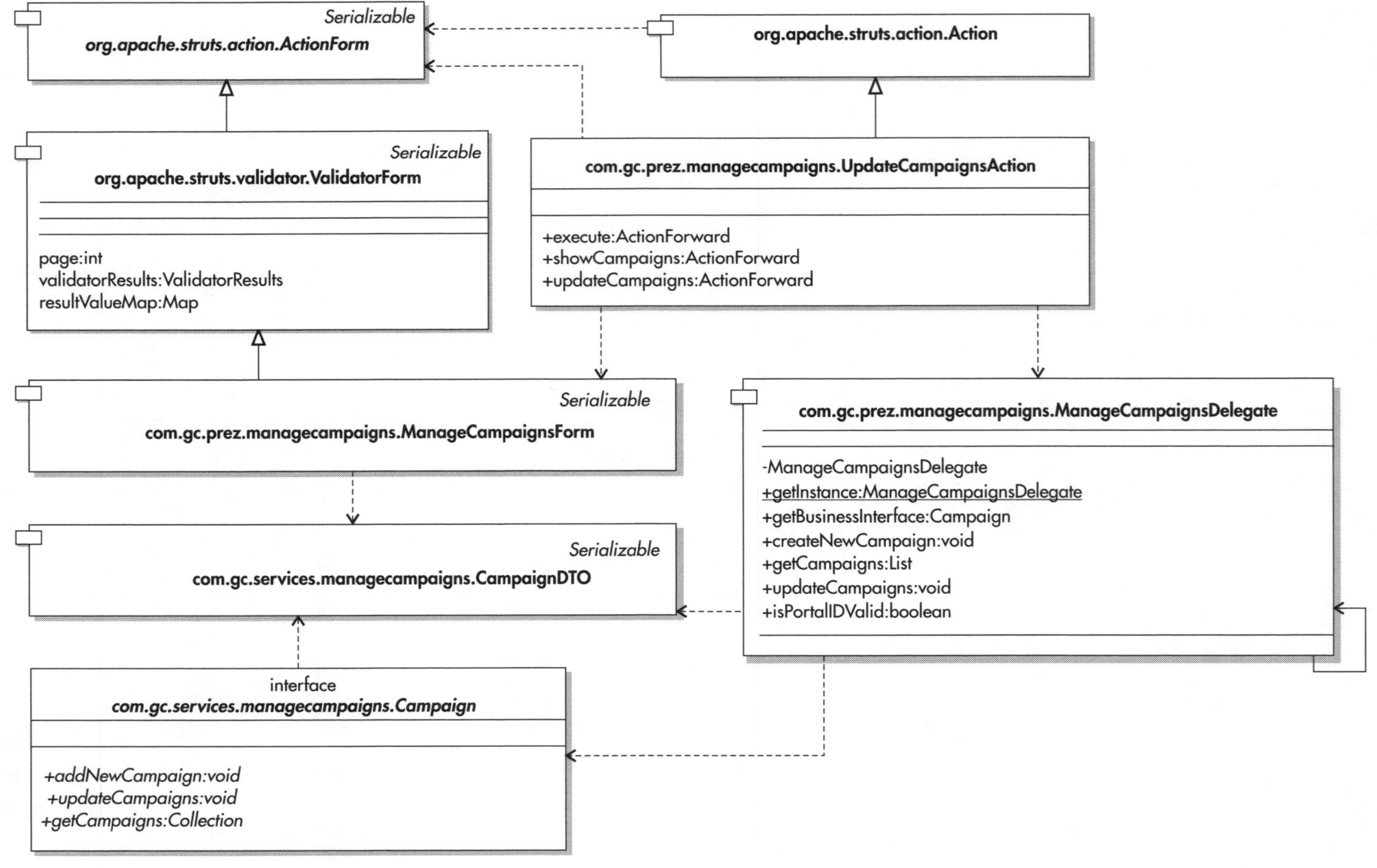

Figure 5-35 *Update Campaigns class diagram*

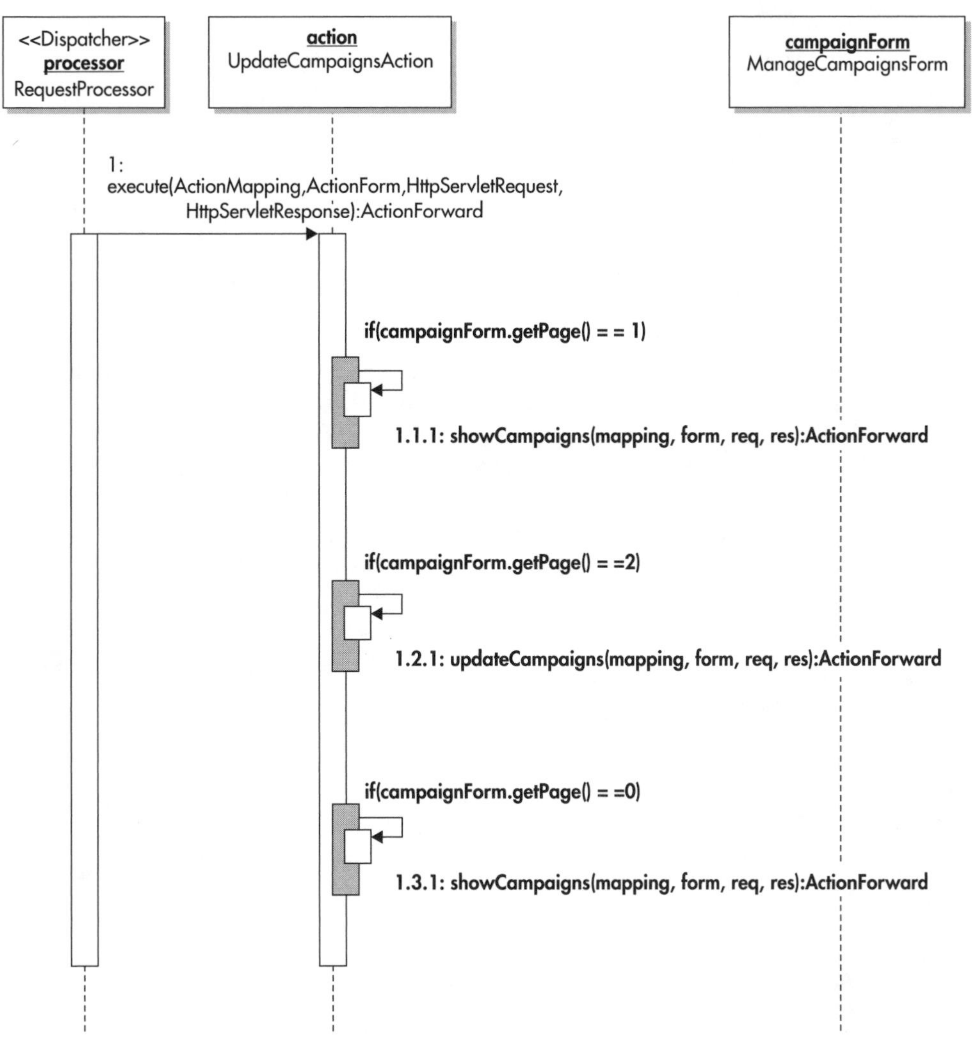

Figure 5-36 *Update Campaigns sequence diagram*

objects contained in a *Collection* object. The declarations in the struts-config.xml file are depicted here:

```
<action path="/UpdateCampaignsStep1" forward="/2_3_5_EnterRegionCode.jsp"/>

<action path="/UpdateCampaignsStep2"
```

```
    type="com.gc.prez.managecampaigns.UpdateCampaignsAction"
    name="ManageCampaignsForm"
    scope="session"
    validate="false">
    <forward name="EnterRegionCode"
             path="/2_3_5_EnterRegionCode.jsp"/>
    <forward name="ShowUpdateCampaigns"
             path="/2_3_5_1_UpdateCampaigns.jsp"/>
    <forward name="success"
             path="/2_SiteAdministratorServicesMainPage.jsp"/>
</action>
```

The *ActionMapping* identified by the path *"/UpdateCampaignsStep1"* will render the view 2_3_5_EnterRegionCode.jsp; the corresponding page is shown in Figure 5-37. In turn, this view will use the *ActionMapping* identified by the path *"/UpdateCampaignsStep2"* to invoke the *UpdateCampaignsAction* request handler which in turn will render the view 2_3_5_1_UpdateCampaigns.jsp using the `<forward>` specification identified by name= "ShowUpdateCampaigns". The corresponding page is shown in Figure 5-38. Readers are urged to review the implementation provided in the accompanying source distribution.

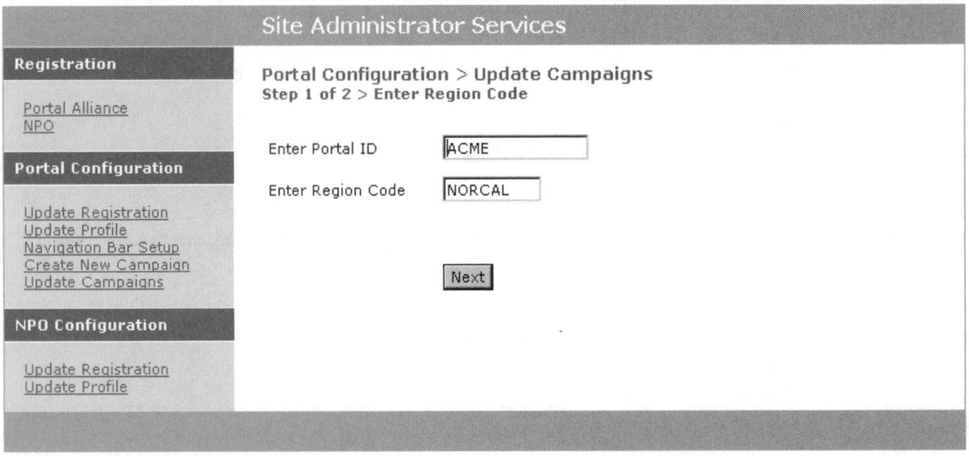

Figure 5-37 *Enter region code page*

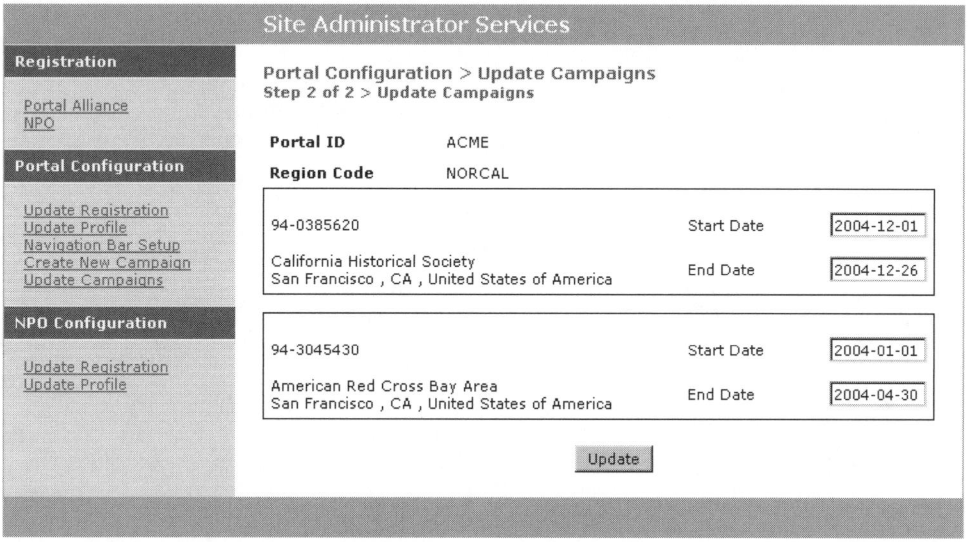

Figure 5-38 *Update Campaigns page*

Summary

In this chapter, we followed the iterative approach for realizing use cases that is pervasive in this book. The solution abstracted and documented several Struts-related implementation patterns for creating a consistent implementation vocabulary; this allows the developers to implement recurring problems in a consistent manner, therefore improving readability and maintainability of the code. The Struts-related patterns employed form-beans and request handlers, and utilized the standard J2EE design patterns for realizing client-side semantics. Struts-related patterns made use of the ValidatorForm's page property for providing wizard-like behavior; when used in conjunction with other properties, we were able create a wide range of process flows within a single request handler, and use a single JSP for providing varying HTML forms.

References

[Core] *Core J2EE Patterns* by Deepak Alur et al. (Prentice-Hall, 2001)
[Gof] *Design Patterns* by Erich Gamma et al. (Addison-Wesley, 1995)

CHAPTER

6

Domain Model Design and Implementation

IN THIS CHAPTER:

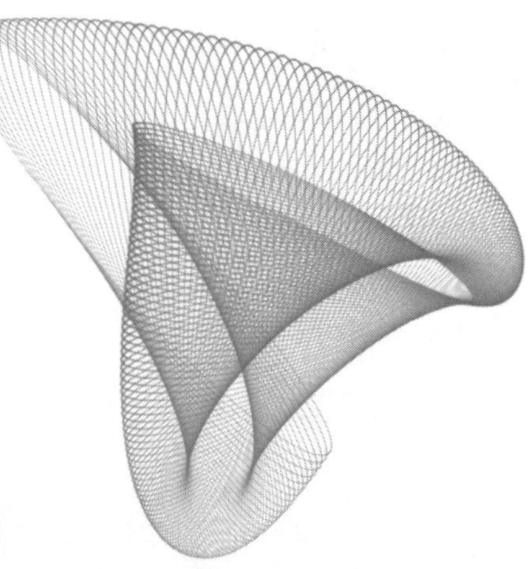

In Chapter 5, the business tier interfaces exposed to the presentation tier enabled us to create an implementation for realizing the use cases identified by the packages GreaterCause Site Administration, Manage Campaigns, and Search NPO. The business tier interfaces, explained in detail in Chapter 7, employ the session façade pattern that is implemented using either stateless or stateful session beans. These session beans encapsulate business logic, which in turn employs domain entities. Domain entities are real-world things and concepts that are part of the problem domain. Domain modeling is the task of discovering these entities and defining their relationships in the context of the problem domain. The discovery of domain entities and their implementation is the focus of this chapter. Basic EJB concepts like home, remote, and local interfaces are not covered in any detail in this chapter. Readers are urged to review the basic material from excellent tutorials and examples available at java.sun.com. The EJB 2.0 specification also has a wealth of material; rather than reproduce this information, we suggest specific sections to read from the EJB 2.0 specification in the context of the material being discussed.

Discovering Domain Objects

Domain modeling involves identifying objects that represent the persistent state of the system. This does not imply that there exists a one-to-one mapping between domain objects and entity beans (or any other object persistence technology). This is because domain objects may represent a conceptual thing that may require services of other entities. The domain objects encapsulate logic that acts upon the domain objects. This logic is aware of the relationships between domain objects and the rules enforced for manipulating the state of the object. Therefore, one must clearly distinguish between logic that resides in the domain objects and the logic that resides in the business tier (business tier is the topic of Chapter 7).

From the Site Administration and Manage Campaigns use case packages described in Chapters 1 and 2, we infer the following requirements for the persistence state of the application.

- The Site Administrator will create the registration information for portal-alliances and NPOs, a portal-alliance administrator will modify the portal-alliance profile, and an NPO administrator will modify the NPO profile. A *PortalAlliance* and *NPO* object can provide the encapsulation for accessing and manipulating registration and profile information.
- Portal-alliance and NPO administrators are authorized to access and modify related portal-alliance or NPO profiles. An *Admin* object can provide us with this association. Although each administrator can be embedded in the *PortalAlliance* or the *NPO* domain object, we have chosen to separate the *Admin* object with the anticipation that in the future the *Admin* object may have many-to-one relationship with either the *PortalAlliance* or the *NPO* domain object.
- Campaigns are created by the portal-alliance administrator. A portal-alliance administrator creates portal-specific campaigns, i.e., each Portal-Alliance domain object is associated with a Campaign domain object. Each campaign will also be associated with an *NPO* object. A Portal-Alliance object can encapsulate the access mechanisms for portal-alliance–specific campaigns.

From the preceding discussion, we define the domain model shown in Figure 6-1. We assume that readers have the knowledge of UML and object-oriented analysis and design, therefore we do not explain those concepts here. Normally, the practice adopted during domain modeling is to first create an analysis-level class diagram, which we continue to refine as we walk through our requirements expressed in the use cases, and consulting with domain experts to validate the domain model. The problem domain of our sample application is limited in scope, as such we have gone straight to the design-level domain model. We also assume that the domain objects will be implemented as entity beans with container-managed persistence. We continue our discussion on the domain model and its implementation in the section "Implementing the Domain Model." Please note that although the methods on each of the domain objects are identified in Figure 6-1, in reality these methods are discovered incrementally during analysis, design, and implementation of the domain objects, as well as during the design and implementation of business objects that employ the services of these domain objects. Generalization relationships, associations, and multiplicity are discovered in a similar fashion.

Relationships in the Domain Model

The following is a discussion of relationships, roles, and multiplicity identified on the domain model in Figure 6-1.

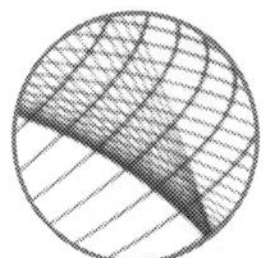

TIP

When creating the domain model, we need to capture all the relationships, roles, and the multiplicity for each side of the relationship. This information is essential for configuring the deployment descriptors. Deployment descriptors are discussed later in the chapter.

- **Admin-NPO** The relationship between *Admin* and *NPO* objects is represented by an association Admin-NPO. This relationship is unidirectional, implying that the Admin interface can access NPO and not the other way around. This directionality is manifested by the *getNpo* and *setNpo* accessor methods in the Admin interface. These accessors are defined in the deployment descriptor using the *cmr-field-name* element whose value is "npo". The relationship is supported in the database using a foreign key field in the ADMIN table to reference the NPO object. We observed in Chapter 5 that an NPO administrator's login username is used for determining the associated *NPO* object. Using the Admin-NPO relationship, the corresponding *getNpo* accessor is used for retrieving the associated *NPO* object. Domain objects will be accessed in the business tier session beans described in Chapter 7.
- **Admin-PortalAlliance** The relationship between *Admin* and *PortalAlliance* objects is represented by an association Admin-PortalAlliance. This relationship is unidirectional, implying that the Admin interface can access PortalAlliance and not the other way around. This directionality is manifested by the *getAlliance* and *setAlliance* accessor methods in the Admin interface. These accessors are defined in the deployment descriptor using the *cmr-field*-name element whose value is "alliance". The relationship is supported in the database using a foreign key field in the ADMIN table to reference the *PortalAlliance* object. We observed in Chapter 5 that a Portal-Alliance administrator's login username is used for determining the associated *PortalAlliance* object. Using the

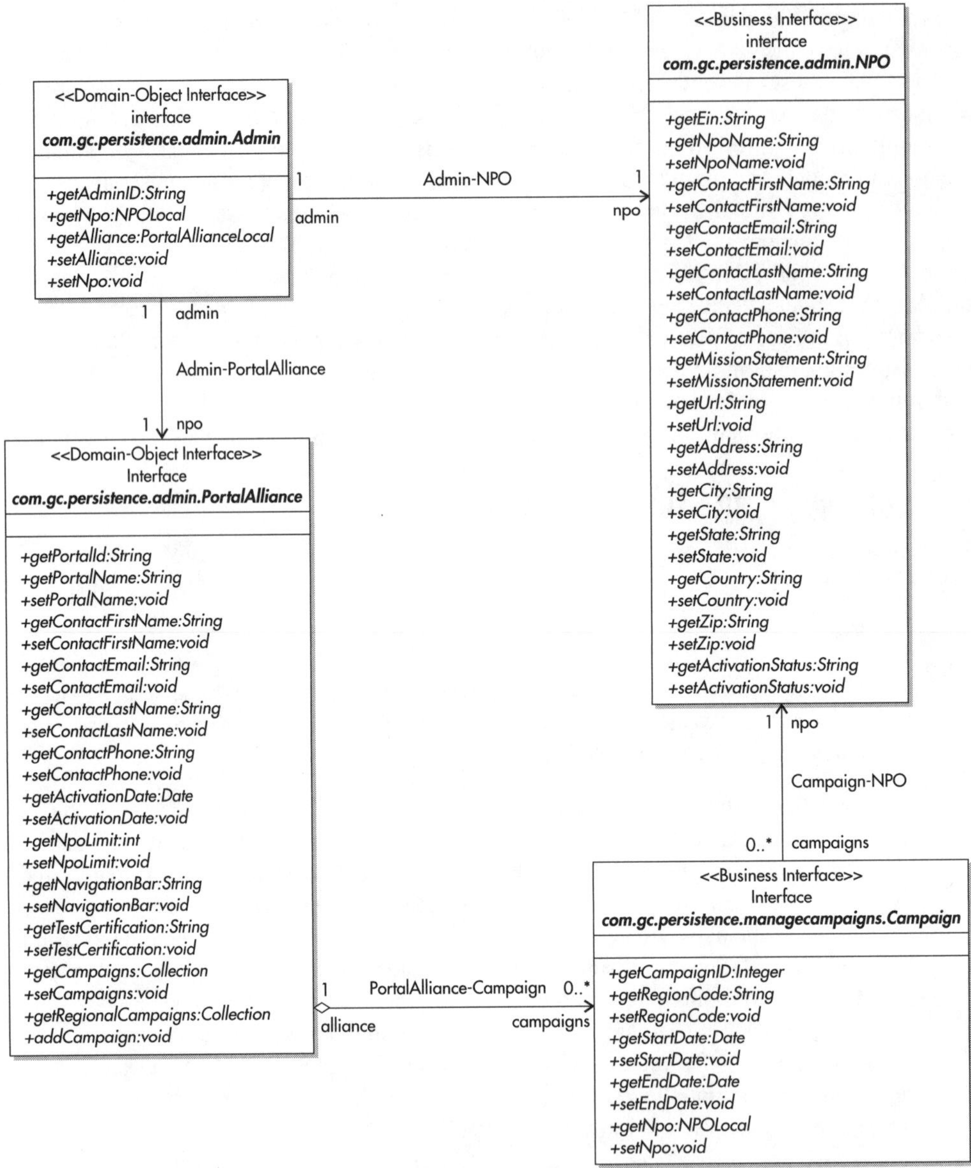

Figure 6-1 *Domain model for Site Administration and Manage Campaigns use case packages*

Admin-PortalAlliance relationship, the corresponding *getAlliance* accessor is used for retrieving the associated *PortalAlliance* object.

- **PortalAlliance-Campaign** The relationship between *PortalAlliance* and *Campaign* objects is represented by an aggregation relationship PortalAlliance-Campaign. This relationship is unidirectional, implying that the PortalAlliance interface can access

Campaigns and not the other way around. This type of relationship represents a "has-a" relationship, meaning that the *PortalAlliance* object has objects of the type *Campaign*. This directionality is manifested by the *getCampaigns* and *setCampaigns* accessor methods in the PortalAlliance interface. These accessors are defined in the deployment descriptor using the *cmr-field-name* element (for container-managed relationship) whose value is "campaigns". The aggregation relationship is implemented as a Collection. This is apparent from the *getCampaigns* accessor method that returns a Collection. The corresponding *cmr-field*-type element in the ejb-jar.xml deployment descriptor also declares the *Collection* type. The relationship is supported in the database using a foreign key field in the CAMPAIGN table to reference the *PortalAlliance* object. This relationship is utilized for retrieving a Collection of Campaigns associated with a given Portal-Alliance.

- **Campaign-NPO** The relationship between Campaign and NPO objects is represented by an association Campaign-NPO. This relationship is unidirectional, implying that the Campaign interface can access NPO and not the other way around. This directionality is manifested by the *getNpo* and *setNpo* accessor methods in the Campaign interface. These accessors are defined in the deployment descriptor using the *cmr-field-name* element whose value is "npo". The relationship is supported in the database using a foreign key field in the CAMPAIGN table to reference the NPO object. This relationship is utilized for retrieving the NPO associated with a given Campaign.

Creating the Data Model

More often than not, projects may be forced to use an existing data model, perhaps from a legacy system. In this situation, there is no other option but to start with the existing data model and build your domain model around it. A comprehensive analysis should be undertaken to map domain objects to existing database schema and determine if the new application's processes fit into the model. It's a challenging architectural feat—you must be careful not to bring over the legacy tables wholesale because the tables may contain columns that may not belong in the context of the domain model. However, in the context of our sample application, we can start designing the data model from scratch. For the domain model of Figure 6-1, we define the data model using the ER diagram of Figure 6-2. Please note that the data model of Figure 6-2 uses IDEF1X notation. Using this notation, an optional non-identifying relationship is drawn as a dashed line with a solid dot on the child end and a diamond on the parent end.

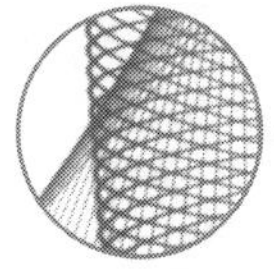

NOTE

In a non-defining relationship, the foreign key becomes a non-key attribute in the child entity.

The data model in Figure 6-2 contains the ADMIN table that maintains the relationship between the portal-alliance administrators and NPO administrators with their corresponding portal-alliance and NPO objects. Later we review the implementation that establishes these relationships using container-managed persistence (CMP) and container-managed relationships (CMR). The ADMIN table is related to the NPO table through an NPO_Admin relationship. The ADMIN table is also related to the PORTAL_ALLIANCE table through a PortalAlliance_Admin

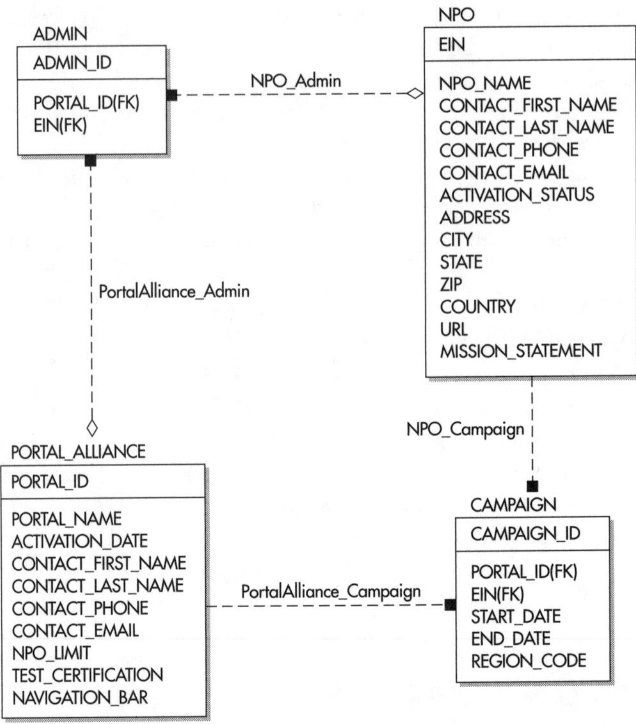

Figure 6-2 *Data model for Site Administration and Manage Campaigns use case packages*

relationship. Please note that both the profile and registration information for portal-alliances are kept in the PORTAL_ALLIANCE table; the same is true for the NPO table.

The PORTAL_ALLIANCE table is related to the CAMPAIGN table through PortalAlliance_Campaign relationship. This is an optional relationship, which means that a Campaign may or may not exist for a given Portal-Alliance. The CAMPAIGN table is related to the NPO table through a NPO_Campaign relationship. This relationship mandates that each campaign be associated with an NPO.

Once we have designed the data model and decided the table names and column names, we can implement the domain objects as entity beans with container-managed persistence. The table names and columns will be referred to in the deployment descriptors for the entity beans. The container will provide the implementation for getting and setting the values of the table columns using accessor methods for each column declared as container-managed. This concludes the initial setup required for arriving at a suitable domain-model and the corresponding persistence strategy. Note that for many-to-many relationships, you will probably want to use an associative table, but no such cases were present for our sample use cases.

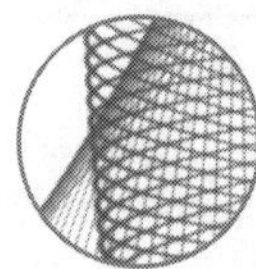

NOTE

The ID column in the CAMPAIGN table is populated using the sequence number generation facility of the database. This usage is associated with vendor-specific deployment descriptors, which we address later in this chapter.

Implementing the Domain Model

Before we begin our implementation of domain objects identified in Figure 6-1, we first examine a design pattern for simplifying the implementation of the entity bean interfaces. At this point, we suggest that you take a little detour to the section "Implementing the Business Interface Pattern" of Chapter 7. Business interface is an inappropriate stereotype for domain objects, as such, this same design pattern will be used with the stereotype <<Domain-Object Interface>>. We found that this business tier pattern used for session beans serves equally well for entity beans. A review of this pattern reveals several advantages:

- The Domain-Object interface (Admin, PortalAlliance, NPO, and Campaign interfaces shown in Figure 6-1) shows only the interface methods relevant to the business tier. The container callbacks defined in the javax.ejb.EntityBean interface and the javax.ejb. EJBLocalHome interface (assuming that we are using local home interface) appear on the bean implementation, for example, the AdminBean. The client can use only the Domain-Object interface.
- The analysis-level domain model contains only the Domain Object interfaces with their associated methods. We do not assume implementation aspects such as CMP at this time. This model directly maps to the interfaces described using Domain-Object interfaces. The analysis time artifacts can be used directly during development.
- The accessors for container-managed fields are declared as abstract methods on the *Bean* class (for example, *AdminBean*). The corresponding implementation is provided by container provider's tools. When using the Domain-Object interface, we do not have to declare these methods as abstract methods on the *Bean* class. When new properties are added or old ones removed, only the Domain-Object interface will change.

The following discussion focuses on the CMP semantics defined in the EJB 2.0 specification. For the most part, using CMP implies that the developer provides the accessors for container-managed fields. If CMR is being used, the developer provides the accessors for the CMR fields; other than that, all of the implementation is generated by the vendor tool using the configuration options specified declaratively in the deployment descriptors.

EJB 2.0 specification introduced local interfaces for EJBs. Local interfaces are used when the domain objects are collocated in the same JVM as the business objects utilizing them. This improves the performance significantly by eliminating the overhead associated with remote interfaces, while taking away location transparency. The objects that implement the local home interface and local interface are local java objects, therefore the arguments and results of the methods of the local home interface and local interface are passed by reference. Because the local programming model is relatively less expensive in terms of making method calls, it can support fine-grained access to components. For our sample application, we have chosen to implement all entity beans using local interfaces. While designing applications using local interfaces, one must be aware of the pass-by-reference semantics inherent in the local programming model. The remote programming model uses pass-by-value semantics and therefore offers a level of isolation from inadvertent modification to the data.

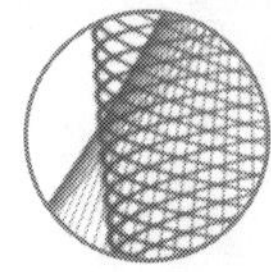

NOTE

According to the EJB 2.0 specification, in order to be the target of a container-managed relationship, an entity bean with container-managed persistence must provide a local interface.

Defining the Admin Interface

In this section, we complete the Admin Domain-Object interface and define the CMP and CMR fields for the *AdminBean*. Figure 6-3 shows the CMP- and CMR-related accessors defined on the Admin interface that the container will implement. Once the primary key for an entity bean has been set, no attempt should be made to change it using the *set* accessor methods. Therefore, the *set* accessor method for the primary-key is not provided on the Domain-Object interface, instead it is specified only on the AdminBean as an abstract method.

The following snippet shows the accessors defined in the Admin interface. It has accessors for the CMP field *adminID* and the CMR fields *alliance* and *npo*. The *adminID* provided by the presentation tier is used to identify the association between the remote user and the associated *NPO* entity bean or the *PortalAlliance* entity bean. According to the Register NPO use case and the Register Portal-Alliance use case, only NPO and Portal-Alliance administrators can change their respective NPO and Portal-Alliance profiles. The implementation for the accessor methods is supplied by the container. All accessors must be public and must be structured according to the *cmp-field* and *cmr-field* element specification in the ejb-jar.xml file. This is discussed later in this section.

```
package com.gc.persistence.admin;
public interface Admin {
    /* CMP field adminID */
    public String getAdminID();
    /* Because adminID is primary-key, setAdminID is
    * defined only in the bean class */
    /* CMR field alliance */
    public PortalAllianceLocal getAlliance();
    public void setAlliance(PortalAllianceLocal alliance);
    /* CMR field npo */
    public NPOLocal getNpo();
    public void setNpo(NPOLocal npo);
}
```

In order to create the *AdminBean* entity bean that implements the Admin interface, the local home interface shown in the following snippet exposes two *create* methods: one method is for creating an *AdminBean* object with a local reference to the corresponding NPO entity bean, and the other *create* method is used for creating an *AdminBean* object with a local reference to the corresponding *PortalAlliance* entity bean. The corresponding implementations are shown in the *AdminBean* class. The local home interface also exposes a set of *find* methods. The *findByPrimaryKey* method is implemented by the container based on the *prim-key-class* element in the deployment descriptor. The rest of the *find* methods use EJB QL (Query Language)

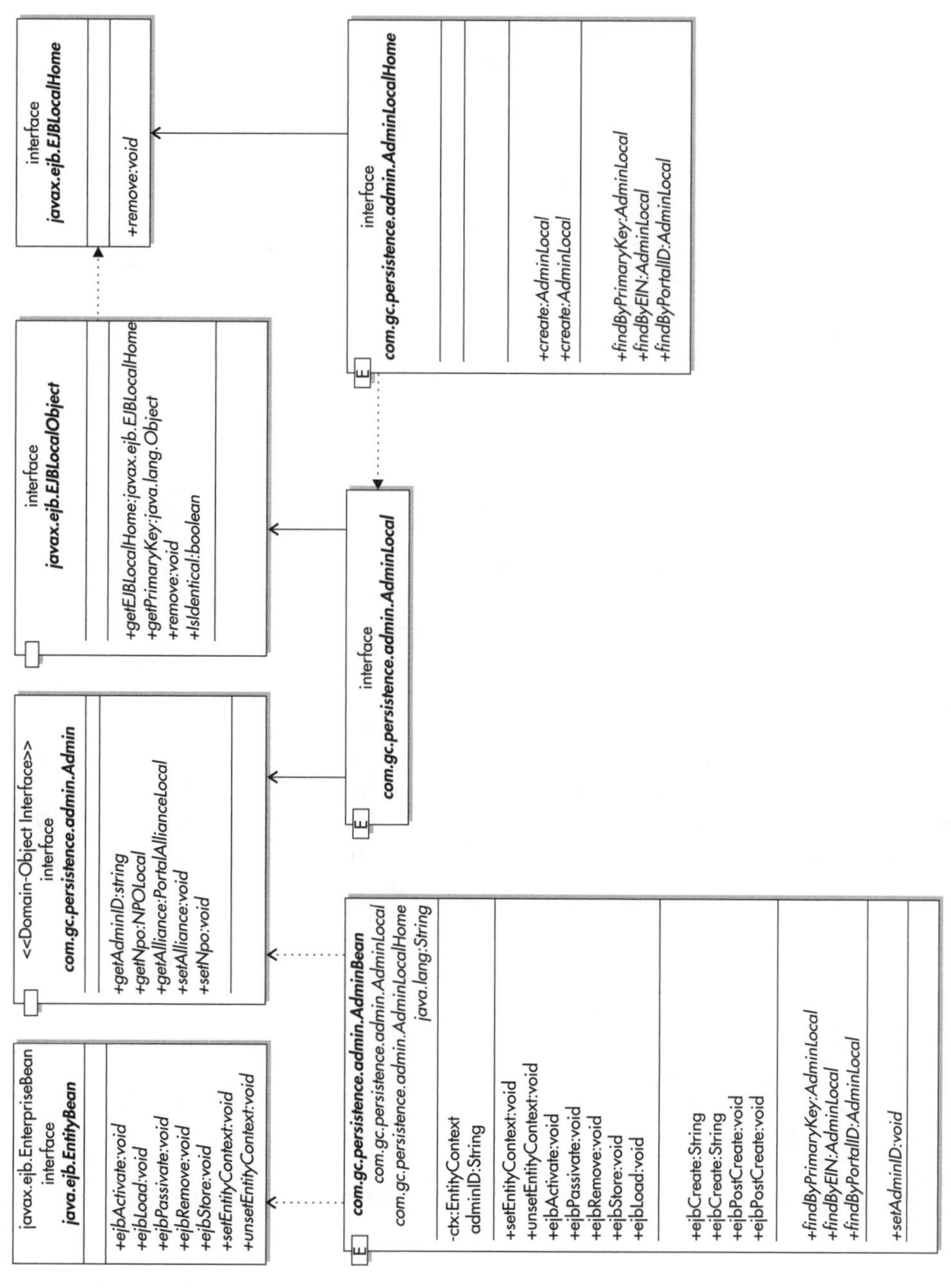

Figure 6-3 *Defining the AdminBean and the Admin interface*

queries and therefore these methods are implemented by the container based on the query elements specified in the deployment descriptors. Please note that we have deferred discussing deployment descriptors for the later part of this section. For a complete discussion on EJB QL, please refer to Chapter 11 of the EJB 2.0 specification.

```
package com.gc.persistence.admin;
public interface AdminLocalHome extends javax.ejb.EJBLocalHome {
    /* Create Methods */
    public AdminLocal create(String adminId, NPOLocal npo)
            throws CreateException;
    public AdminLocal create(String adminId, PortalAllianceLocal alliance)
            throws CreateException;
    /* Finder Methods */
    public AdminLocal findByPrimaryKey(String adminId)
            throws FinderException, ObjectNotFoundException;
    public AdminLocal findByEin(String ein)
            throws FinderException, ObjectNotFoundException;
    public AdminLocal findByPortalID(String portalID)
            throws FinderException, ObjectNotFoundException;
}
```

Observe that the finder methods throw *ObjectNotFoundException*. The CMP implementation raises this exception when the corresponding entity bean is not found in the persistent store. The business tier (which is the client in this case) must catch this exception instead of trying to catch *FinderException*. Chapter 7 explains the difference between these two exceptions in the section "Handling Exceptions in Transactions."

The *create* methods of the *AdminLocalHome* are delegated to the *ejbCreate* methods of the *EntityBean* by the container. The *ejbCreate* methods shown in the following code will set the appropriate CMP field. Observe that the CMR fields must be set only in the *ejbPostCreate* methods. The parameter list for *ejbCreate* and *ejbPostCreate* is identical. As you will see later in the discussion on deployment descriptor, the container persists the objects and relationships based on the abstract persistence schemas of entity beans and their container-managed relationships.

```
package com.gc.persistence.admin;
public abstract class AdminBean implements EntityBean, Admin {
    private EntityContext ctx;
    public String ejbCreate(String adminID, NPOLocal npo)
        throws CreateException{
        this.setAdminID(adminID);
        return null;
    }
    public String ejbCreate(String adminID, PortalAllianceLocal alliance)
        throws CreateException{
        this.setAdminID(adminID);
        return null;
    }
    public void ejbPostCreate(String adminID, NPOLocal npo)
        throws CreateException{
```

```
        this.setNpo(npo);
    }
    public void ejbPostCreate(String adminID, PortalAllianceLocal alliance)
        throws CreateException{
        this.setAlliance(alliance);
    }
    /* The set method for adminID appears only in the bean class definition because
    * it is the primary-key */
    public abstract void setAdminID(String adminID);
... other container callback methods ...
}
```

Instead of using the *setNpo* method (or the *setAlliance* method) in the *ejbPostCreate* method, we could have easily done the *set* in the business tier session beans. However, this will break the encapsulation. We must let the logic for CMR be part of the *AdminBean* creation process.

The bean developer must define the entity bean class as an abstract class. The container-managed persistent fields and container-managed relationships are exposed to the client through *get* and *set* accessor methods. These fields are not present in the bean class since these are virtual fields. The bean implementation produced by the container is aware of these fields through *cmp-field* and *cmr-field* element declarations in the ejb-jar.xml deployment descriptor. One must therefore follow the JavaBean naming convention for specifying the names for CMP and CMR fields in the deployment descriptor, that is, the name must begin with a lowercase letter.

Specifying the Deployment Descriptors

In this section, we configure various deployment descriptors associated with setting up the *SiteAdmin* bean with container-managed persistence and container-managed relationships. This section discusses the specifics of configuring the ejb-jar.xml file, vendor-specific weblogic-ejb-jar.xml, and weblogic-cmp-rdbms-jar.xml files. We first discuss the ejb-jar.xml deployment descriptor file.

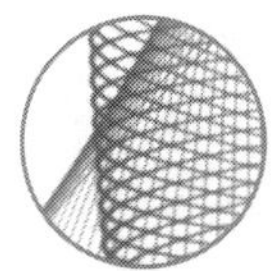

NOTE

The sample application GreaterCause was developed and tested on the WebLogic Server 7.0 (SP1); as such, all vendor-specific deployment descriptors discussed in this chapter will confirm to WebLogic Server 7.0.

```
<enterprise-beans><entity>
    <description>Admin Bean Description</description>

    <!-- Logical name of the EJB within the ejb-jar file -->
    <ejb-name>AdminEntityEJB</ejb-name>

    <!-- Specify abstract schema type for use in EJB QL -->
    <abstract-schema-name>Admin</abstract-schema-name>

    <local-home>com.gc.persistence.admin.AdminLocalHome</local-home>
```

```
    <local>com.gc.persistence.admin.AdminLocal</local>
    <ejb-class>com.gc.persistence.admin.AdminBean</ejb-class>
    <persistence-type>Container</persistence-type>
    <prim-key-class>java.lang.String</prim-key-class>
    <reentrant>False</reentrant>

    <!-- Describe the container-managed fields -->
    <cmp-field><field-name>adminID</field-name></cmp-field>

    <!-- Name of the primary key field; this field is mapped to the
    database schema in weblogic-cmp-rdbms-jar.xml file -->
    <primkey-field>adminID</primkey-field>

    <!-- Query for findByEin method in home interface; note the use
    of abstract schema type 'Admin' defined previously using
    abstract-schema-name element -->
    <query>
        <query-method>
            <method-name>findByEin</method-name>
                <method-params>
                    <method-param>java.lang.String</method-param>
            </method-params>
        </query-method>
        <ejb-ql>
             SELECT OBJECT(a)
             FROM Admin AS a
                     WHERE (a.npo.ein = ?1)
        </ejb-ql>
     </query>
    <!-- Query for findByPortalID method in home interface -->
     <query>
         <query-method>
             <method-name>findByPortalID</method-name>
             <method-params>
                 <method-param>java.lang.String</method-param>
             </method-params>
         </query-method>
         <ejb-ql>
             SELECT OBJECT(a)
             FROM Admin AS a
                     WHERE (a.alliance.portalID = ?1)
         </ejb-ql>
     </query>
</entity></enterprise-beans>
```

The *ejb-name* element specifies an EJB's logical name in the deployment descriptor. The name *AdminEntityEJB* is assigned to *AdminBean*. This name is used to reference the bean in several places within ejb-jar.xml, weblogic-ejb-jar.xml, and weblogic-cmp-rdbms-jar.xml.

The *prim-key-class* element contains the fully qualified name of an entity bean's primary key class. The definition of the primary key can be deferred to deployment time, in this case use *prim-key-class* as *java.lang.Object*. The *findByPrimaryKey* method of the local home interface uses this class name as method parameter type. Database-assisted key generation can also be supported by providing the object type of the key that is generated by the database; any primitives must be converted to the corresponding Java object types.

The *primkey-field* element specifies the *cmp-field* that contains the primary key. Once the primary key for an entity bean has been set, no attempt should be made to change it using the *set* accessor methods. Therefore *set* accessor methods are not provided on the Domain-Object interface. When the primary key is made of more than one CMP field, the composite key can be represented using a custom type. All fields in the primary key class must be declared public. The *primkey-field* element is not used when the primary key is a compound key, that is, it maps to multiple *cmp-field*s.

The container-managed persistent fields and container-managed relationship fields are specified in the deployment descriptor using the *cmp-field* and *cmr-field* elements, respectively. Java types assigned to *cmp-field* can be Java primitive types and Java serializable types. The names assigned to *cmp-fields* and *cmr-fields* must begin with a lowercase letter. The corresponding accessor methods defined in the bean class follow the JavaBean method naming convention, that is, the first letter of the name of the *cmp-field* or *cmr-field* is uppercased and prefixed by *get* or *set*. Note that all *cmp-field*s and *cmr-field*s are mapped to the database schema using the vendor-specific weblogic-cmp-rdbms-jar.xml file. We discuss this deployment descriptor later in this section.

The container-managed fields are virtual fields since they are not explicitly declared in the bean class. Instead, the bean developer declares an abstract set of *get* and *set* accessor methods for each container-managed field. These abstract methods are declared in the entity bean class. The corresponding implementation is generated by the container provider's tools at deployment time. For the purpose of our example, we have a slight deviation in that the abstract accessor methods are not made explicitly part of the entity bean class but rather these accessors are defined in a separate Domain-Object interface. In the case of the *AdminBean* class, the accessors are defined on the Admin interface, which is implemented by the *AdminBean* class and extended by the *AdminLocal* interface as shown previously in Figure 6-3. The advantages of doing this have been discussed in the section "Implementing the Domain Model."

The *query* element is used to specify queries for both the *finder* and *select* methods. The container will provide the implementation for methods declared in the *query* element. The container uses the query specified by the *ejb-ql* element as part of the method implementation. Queries are expressed using EJB QL (for a complete discussion on EJB QL, please refer to Chapter 11 of the EJB 2.0 specification). Input parameters to queries are designated by the question mark (?) prefix followed by an integer. This integer specifies the position of the parameter in the method declared in the deployment descriptor by the *query-method* element. For the *findByEin* method shown in the deployment descriptor in the preceding, there is only one method parameter of type *java.lang.String*.

As part of our discussion on ejb-jar.xml deployment descriptor file, we examine the *relationships* element declared in the descriptor file. The following snippet shows the descriptors required for configuring the relationship between *Admin* and *NPO* entity beans. Please note that the persistence mechanism is configured accordingly, and the mapping between the persistence layer and the EJBs is provided by a vendor-specific weblogic-cmp-rdbms-jar.xml deployment descriptor.

```
<!-- Define container-managed relationships -->
<relationships>
    <ejb-relation>
        <!-- Provide unique name for a relationship; this name is used in
        weblogic-cmp-rdbms-jar.xml for mapping the relationship to the
        database schema -->
        <ejb-relation-name>Admin-NPO</ejb-relation-name>

        <!-- Define the relationship in the context of role name 'admin' -->
        <ejb-relationship-role>
            <ejb-relationship-role-name>admin</ejb-relationship-role-name>
            <multiplicity>One</multiplicity>
            <relationship-role-source>
                <!-- Identify the EJB previously described
                using ejb-name element -->
                <ejb-name>AdminEntityEJB</ejb-name>
            </relationship-role-source>
            <cmr-field>
                <!-- get and set accessors are defined for this field;
                this also indicates the direction of the relationship -->
                <cmr-field-name>npo</cmr-field-name>
            </cmr-field>
        </ejb-relationship-role>

        <!-- Define the relationship in the context of role name 'npo' -->
        <ejb-relationship-role>
            <ejb-relationship-role-name>npo</ejb-relationship-role-name>
            <multiplicity>One</multiplicity>
            <relationship-role-source>
                <ejb-name>NPOEntityEJB</ejb-name>
            </relationship-role-source>
        </ejb-relationship-role>
    </ejb-relation>
</relationships>
```

Figure 6-1 shows the association Admin-NPO between *Admin* and *NPO* entity beans. We defined the accessors for this unidirectional relationship in the *Admin* interface using *getNpo* and *setNpo* CMR-related methods. Note that we have chosen the *role-name* as the *cmr-field* name. The following code fragment shows the accessors that form the Admin-NPO relationship.

```
public interface Admin {
    public NPOLocal getNpo();
    public void setNpo(NPOLocal npo);
}
```

To explain the associated deployment descriptors, we take a bottom-up approach. The basic structure that establishes a relationship is a container-managed-relationship field that is declared using the *cmr-field* element. In the preceding snippet for the *Admin* entity bean, we have the *Admin* bean declaring a *cmr-field* element *npo*, the corresponding accessors are declared in the *Admin* interface, and the weblogic-cmp-rdbms-jar.xml defines a *weblogic-rdbms-relation* element that provides a concrete schema of how this relationship will be physically persisted. For the Admin-NPO relationship, the corresponding *weblogic-rdbms-relation:column-map* (subordinate to *weblogic-rdbms-relations* element) element indicates that the ADMIN table column name EIN is a foreign key associated with the primary key column EIN of the NPO table. We will see usage of the *column-map* element shortly.

The *ejb-relationship-role* element is defined in the context of the role name associated with the *relationship-role-source* element. For our sample descriptor, the source is identified by the logical name assigned to the *AdminBean*, which is *AdminEntityEJB*, and the corresponding role name identified by the *ejb-relationship-role-name* is *admin*. The *relationship-role-source NPOEntityEJB* does not have a *cmr-field* because the association between Admin and NPO is undirected when traversing from NPO to Admin.

The *multiplicity* element describes the multiplicity of the role identified by the *ejb-relationship-role-name* element—it can take the value *One* or *Many*. A little digression is in order to explain this. The multiplicity of *0..** specified in Figure 6-1 for the *Campaign* entity bean side of the PortalAlliance-Campaign relationship will be specified as `<multiplicity> Many</multiplicity>`. This creates a collection-valued relationship. The *getCampaigns* method on the PortalAlliance entity bean will return a *Collection* object containing objects of the type *CampaignLocal* (which extends the Campaign domain-object interface. We discuss this again in the section "Defining the PortalAlliance Interface." You can refer to section 10.3.6 of the EJB 2.0 specification for a detailed discussion of collection-valued relationships, but this knowledge is not required for understanding the rest of this chapter.

Recapping the preceding discussion, we have successfully defined the bean classes, corresponding interfaces, and the *ejb-jar-xml* deployment descriptor that implements a one-to-one unidirectional relationship from Admin to NPO entity bean. The following discussion explains the vendor-specific deployment descriptor necessary for vendors to generate the concrete classes for the abstract bean classes we defined earlier. We begin by discussing the declarations in the weblogic-ejb-jar.xml file—a snippet of this file appears here in the context of *AdminBean* class:

```
<!-- Admin Entity Bean Definition -->
<weblogic-enterprise-bean>
```

```
    <ejb-name>AdminEntityEJB</ejb-name>
    <entity-descriptor>
        <entity-cache>
            <max-beans-in-cache>1000</max-beans-in-cache>
        </entity-cache>
        <persistence>
            <persistence-use>
                <type-identifier>WebLogic_CMP_RDBMS</type-identifier>
                <type-version>7.0</type-version>
                <type-storage>META-INF/weblogic-cmp-rdbms-jar.xml</type-storage>
            </persistence-use>
        </persistence>
    </entity-descriptor>
    <local-jndi-name>ejb/local/com.gc.persistence.admin.AdminLocalHome
    </local-jndi-name>
</weblogic-enterprise-bean>
```

The *ejb-name* element provides the logical name by which the bean declarations are identified in the ejb-jar.xml deployment descriptor. The *entity-descriptor:type-storage* element defines the location of the deployment descriptor weblogic-cmp-rdms-jar.xml for the RDBMS-based persistence mechanism. The *local-jndi-name* element provides the JNDI name for the entity bean. The EJB specification recommends prefixing JNDI names with "ejb/."

Moving forward, we look at how the persistence mechanism ties into container-managed entity beans using the weblogic-cmp-rdbms-jar.xml deployment descriptor. We use the Admin entity bean example for this purpose.

```
<weblogic-rdbms-bean>
    <ejb-name>AdminEntityEJB</ejb-name>
    <data-source-name>jdbc/gcOracleTxPool</data-source-name>
    <table-map>
        <table-name>ADMIN</table-name>
        <field-map>
                <cmp-field>adminID</cmp-field>
                <dbms-column>ADMIN_ID</dbms-column>
            </field-map>
    </table-map>
</weblogic-rdbms-bean>
```

The value of the *ejb-name* element is a logical name that refers to the bean configuration defined in the ejb-jar.xml deployment descriptor. The value of the *data-source-name* element specifies the JNDI name given to the connection pool while configuring the server. We discuss this configuration in Chapter 9.

The *table-map* element defines the mapping between the entity bean and the database table. The *table-name* element identifies the table name, and the *field-map* entries identify the mapping between a *cmp-field* and the corresponding table column. This mapping must be provided for all the *cmp-fields* defined for the entity bean. The *AdminBean* has only one *cmp-field*.

```
<weblogic-rdbms-relation>
    <relation-name>Admin-NPO</relation-name>
    <weblogic-relationship-role>
        <!-- This role name was defined in the ejb-jar.xml file -->
        <relationship-role-name>admin</relationship-role-name>
        <relationship-role-map>
            <column-map>
                <foreign-key-column>EIN</foreign-key-column>
                <key-column>EIN</key-column>
            </column-map>
        </relationship-role-map>
    </weblogic-relationship-role>
</weblogic-rdbms-relation>
```

We can draw a parallel between the *weblogic-rdbms-relation* element of the weblogic-cmp-rdbms-jar.xml and the *ejb-relation* element of the ejb-jar.xml file. While the *ejb-relation* element specified the *cmr-field* names, the *weblogic-rdbms-relation:column-map* specifies the column name of the ADMIN table that will be used to persist the relationship. The *foreign-key-column* element provides the column name of the foreign key in the ADMIN table, while the *key-column* element provides the column name of the primary key for the NPO table that will map to the foreign key of the ADMIN table.

This concludes the implementation and configuration of the AdminBean class and its corresponding interfaces and deployment descriptors. In the following section, we discuss the semantics for implementing a one-to-many relationship that involves a collection-valued *cmr-field*.

Defining the PortalAlliance Interface

In this section, we define the methods pertinent to the PortalAlliance domain-object interface. This interface has the standard accessor methods for the *cmr-field* "campaigns" except that in this case we are dealing with a collection-valued *cmr-field*. Also, a couple of convenience methods have been declared to work in conjunction with EJB QL for returning *Collection* objects.

Figure 6-1 shows that a PortalAlliance object can be associated with zero or more *Campaign* objects. The direction of relationship is from PortalAlliance to Campaign. The accessors associated for this relationship are created for the PortalAlliance interface as *getCampaigns* and *setCampaigns*. Observe that the *getCampaigns* accessor method returns a *Collection* object, whereas the *setCampaigns* accessor method specifies a collection-valued parameter. We strongly recommend that you refer to section 10.3.6 of the EJB 2.0 specification for details on collection-valued relationships. However, this knowledge is not required for understanding the rest of this chapter. A convenience method *addCampaign* is specified on the PortalAlliance domain object interface for adding a single *Campaign* object to this collection-valued relationship. Another convenience method *getRegionalCampaigns* is added for extracting the qualifying campaigns based on a *regionCode* parameter. The PortalAlliance interface is shown here:

```
public interface PortalAlliance {
    /* CMP Field Accessors */
    public String getPortalID();
    public String getPortalName();
    public void setPortalName(String portalName);
    ...other cmp-field accessor methods ...

    /* CMR Field Accessors */
    public Collection getCampaigns();
    public void setCampaigns(Collection campaigns);

    /* Other Convenience Methods */
    public Collection getRegionalCampaigns(String regionCode)
            throws FinderException;
    public void addCampaign(Campaign campaign);
}
```

As discussed before, the *cmp-field*'s and *cmr-field*'s accessor method implementation is provided by the container provider's tools; however, the bean class must provide implementation for the convenience methods *getRegionalCampaigns* and *addCampaign* that access the collection-valued *cmr-field.* The convenience methods are shown in the following code fragment:

```
public abstract class PortalAllianceBean
    implements EntityBean, PortalAlliance {
    private EntityContext ctx;

    /* Adding a new Campaign to a collection-valued relationship */
    public void addCampaign(Campaign campaign){
        Collection campaigns = getCampaigns();
        campaigns.add(campaign);
    }
    public Collection getRegionalCampaigns(String regionCode)
            throws FinderException{
        return ejbSelectRegionalCampaigns(getPortalID(),regionCode);
    }
    public abstract Collection ejbSelectRegionalCampaigns(String portalID,
        String regionCode) throws FinderException;
    ... other bean methods ...
}
```

There are two ways we can add a *Campaign* object for a given *PortalAlliance*, using either the container-implemented *setCampaigns* method, or the bean class implemented *addCampaign* method. When the *setCampaigns* method is used, the collection-valued parameter completely replaces existing relationships. The *setCampaigns* method therefore has the semantics of the *java.util.Collection*'s clear method, followed by *java.util.Collection*'s *addAll* method. For adding a new Campaign to the existing relationship set, we use the *addCampaign* method. This method first retrieves a container-managed collection on which the *java.util.Collection*'s add method is called. This has the effect of adding the new PortalAlliance-Campaign relationship in the CAMPAIGN table using the foreign-key PORTAL_ID specified for the CAMPAIGN table. Readers are recommended to review section 10.3.7 of the EJB 2.0 specification for further details on manipulating container-managed collections.

To obtain a filtered collection of objects based on a specific *regionCode*, we use the *getRegionalCampaigns* method on the local interface. This method delegates to *ejbSelectRegionalCampaigns* of the *PortalAllianceBean* class. This indirection is provided because the EJB specification does not permit exposing of the *ejbSelect<method>* method (where `<method>` is any given suffix that uniquely identifies the method name) to the client. The use of the *ejbSelect<method>* method is permitted only for an entity bean class. The *ejbSelect<method>* method was preferred in this case over the *ejbFind<method>* method because the *ejbFind<method>* method can only return an object (or collection) of type *PortalAllianceLocal* (the type corresponding to the interface itself), whereas the *ejbSelect<method>* method can return objects (or collection) of any *cmp-field* or *cmr-field* type; for the *ejbSelectRegionalCampaigns*, the desired collection is of type Campaigns. Observe that the *ejbSelectRegionalCampaigns* is declared as abstract as the actual implementation of the *ejbSelect<method>* method is provided by the container provider's tools. A corresponding EJB QL is provided in the ejb-jar.xml deployment descriptor using the query element, which is discussed in the following subsection.

Using EJB QL with Find and Select Methods

EJB QL is used for defining queries for accessing entity beans with container-managed persistence in a portable way. The queries created using EJB QL are specified in the ejb-jar.xml deployment descriptor using the *entity:query* element. The query element is specified for all *ejbFind<METHOD>*(s) (with the exception of *ejbFindByPrimaryKey*) and *ejbSelect<METHOD>*(s). The suffix *<METHOD>* is a stand-in for the name of the method. Only the finder methods are exposed to the entity bean clients through the beans home interface. *ejbSelect<METHOD>*(s) are used internally by the bean class, and declared as abstract method on an entity bean class. For container-managed persistence, the implementation for the *finder* and *select* methods are generated by the container provider's tools at deployment time.

One important distinction between *finder* and *select* methods is that the *finder* methods can only return a type that represents the entity bean's local or remote interface (depending on local or remote usage), or a type representing a collection of objects that implement the entity bean's local or remote interface, whereas *select* methods can return objects of any *cmp-field* or *cmr-field* type. Another important distinction is that the select methods execute in the transaction context determined by the transaction attribute of the invoking business method. The container is responsible for ensuring that changes to the states of all entity beans in the same transaction context as the select method are visible in the results of the select method.

Single-object *finder* methods and *select* methods should always return a single entity object, otherwise the container will throw the *FinderException*. Multi-object *finder* methods specify a result type as a *java.util.Collection* type. For remote interface types, the client must use the *PortableRemoteObject.narrow* method to convert the objects contained in a collection. Multi-object *select* methods specify a result type as a *java.util.Collection* type or *java.util.Set* type. For *Collection* type, the objects returned in the collection may contain duplicates if DISTINCT is not specified in the SELECT clause of the query. For *Set* type, SELECT DISTINCT is default when DISTINCT is not specified in the SELECT clause.

Specifying the Deployment Descriptors

We begin discussing deployment descriptors with an emphasis on collection-valued *cmr-fields* because of the one-to-many relationship between PortalAlliance and Campaign EJBs. Figure 6-1 shows the PortalAlliance-Campaign relationship, which is a *one-to-many* unidirectional relationship. We represent this relationship using the following deployment descriptor declarations. The *ejb-relationship-role* element is defined in the context of the role name associated with the *relationship-role-source* element. For the deployment descriptor shown in the following code, the source is identified by the logical name assigned to the *PortalAlliance* entity bean, which is *PortalAllianceEntityEJB*, and the corresponding role name identified by the *ejb-relationship-role-name* is *alliance*. The *relationship-role-source CampaignEntityEJB* does not have a *cmr-field* indicating that association between PortalAlliance and Campaign does not have directivity from Campaign to PortalAlliance.

```
<ejb-relation>
    <ejb-relation-name>PortalAlliance-Campaign</ejb-relation-name>
    <ejb-relationship-role>
        <ejb-relationship-role-name>alliance</ejb-relationship-role-name>
        <multiplicity>One</multiplicity>
        <relationship-role-source>
            <ejb-name>PortalAllianceEntityEJB</ejb-name>
        </relationship-role-source>
        <cmr-field>
            <cmr-field-name>campaigns</cmr-field-name>
            <cmr-field-type>java.util.Collection</cmr-field-type>
        </cmr-field>
    </ejb-relationship-role>
    <ejb-relationship-role>
        <ejb-relationship-role-name>campaigns</ejb-relationship-role-name>
        <multiplicity>Many</multiplicity>
        <relationship-role-source>
            <ejb-name>CampaignEntityEJB</ejb-name>
        </relationship-role-source>
```

```
    </ejb-relationship-role>
</ejb-relation>
```

In this snippet, observe that the *cmr-field-name* has the value *campaigns*. This value corresponds to the *getCampaigns* and *setCampaigns* accessor methods, and follows the JavaBean convention for naming accessor methods. The *cmr-field-type* specifies that the *get* and *set* methods will use a collection-valued object in their method signatures.

The following snippet from ejb-jar.xml depicts the *ejbSelectRegionalCampaign* method and query configurations..

```
<entity>
    ... other declarations appear here ...
    <abstract-schema-name>PortalAlliance</abstract-schema-name>
    <cmp-field><field-name>portalID</field-name></cmp-field>
    <cmp-field><field-name>portalName</field-name></cmp-field>
    ... rest of cmp-fields ...
    <primkey-field>portalID</primkey-field>
    <query>
        <query-method>
            <method-name>ejbSelectRegionalCampaigns</method-name>
            <method-params>
                <method-param>java.lang.String</method-param>
                <method-param>java.lang.String</method-param>
            </method-params>
        </query-method>
        <ejb-ql>
            SELECT OBJECT(c)FROM PortalAlliance AS p,
                IN (p.campaigns) c
                WHERE (p.portalID = ?1 AND c.regionCode = ?2)
        </ejb-ql>
    </query>
</entity>
```

The *getCampaigns* method on the PortalAlliance returns a collection as a result of one-to-many relationships existing between the *PortalAlliance* entity bean and *Campaign* entity beans. This is shown in Figure 6-2. The EJB 2.0 specification mandates that the iterator obtained over a collection in a container-managed relationship must be used within the transaction context in which the iterator was obtained. Therefore the *getCampaigns* method of the *PortalAlliance* entity bean is associated with the transaction attribute value of *Mandatory*. This constraint automatically enforces a requirement on the client to call the *getCampaigns* method of the PortalAlliance entity bean with a transaction attribute *Required*; this is because the client is going to iterate over the collection. Transactions are discussed in Chapter 7 in the section "Transaction Semantics for Enterprise Beans." The following snippet shows the transaction attribute declaration for the *getCampaigns* method in the ejb-jar.xml file.

```
<container-transaction>
    <method>
        <ejb-name>PortalAllianceEntityEJB</ejb-name>
        <method-name>getCampaigns</method-name>
    </method>
    <trans-attribute>Mandatory</trans-attribute>
</container-transaction>
```

The deployment descriptor files are included in their entirety in the accompanying source distribution. This concludes the discussion for implementing and configuring the *PortalAlliance* entity bean.

Defining the Campaign Interface

Figure 6-1 depicts the Campaign-NPO relationship between Campaign entity bean and the NPO domain-object interfaces entity bean. The relationship is unidirectional implying that only the *Campaign* bean has *cmr-field* accessor methods defined. The following code segment represents the methods required on the campaign interface:

```
public interface Campaign {
    public Integer getCampaignID();
    /* setCampaignID is specified only in the bean class */
    ... Other cmp-fields accessors ...
    /* Accessors for cmr-field npo */
    public NPOLocal getNpo();
    public void setNpo(NPOLocal npo);
}
```

Observe that the *getCampaignID* method returns an integer. This is because the CAMPAIGN_ID of the CAMPAIGN table, as shown in Figure 6-2, uses a database-generated key. For developing the sample application, we have used the Oracle database server, which provides a sequence generation facility. The vendor-specific implementation wraps the sequence number in an *Integer* object; this is discussed in the following section.

Specifying the Deployment Descriptors

The following declarations in the vendor-specific weblogic-ejb-jar.xml deployment descriptor are for configuring a primary key that employs automatic key generation:

```
<weblogic-rdbms-bean>
    <ejb-name>CampaignEntityEJB</ejb-name>
    <data-source-name>jdbc/gcOracleTxPool</data-source-name>
    <table-map>
        <table-name>CAMPAIGN</table-name>
        <field-map>
```

```
            <cmp-field>campaignID</cmp-field>
            <dbms-column>CAMPAIGN_ID</dbms-column>
        </field-map>
        ... Other field-map declarations ...
    </table-map>
    <automatic-key-generation>
        <generator-type>ORACLE</generator-type>
        <generator-name>CAMPAIGN_ID_SEQUENCE</generator-name>
        <key-cache-size>10</key-cache-size>
    </automatic-key-generation>
</weblogic-rdbms-bean>
```

The sequence CAMPAIGN_ID_SEQUENCE specified for the *generator-name* element is created using the following DDL:

```
CREATE SEQUENCE CAMPAIGN_ID_SEQUENCE
START WITH 10 INCREMENT BY 10 CACHE 20;
```

Providing key-cache-size optimizes access to the database because the container caches the sequence number and increments the sequence without requesting the next value from database for each entity creation. When using WebLogic with Oracle's sequence generator, the WebLogic document recommends using the same value for the *key-cache-size* element and INCREMENT; if these values differ, you will most likely experience duplicate key problems.

Summary

During domain modeling, we essentially discover classes from use cases. Most likely, the nouns and noun phrases provide an indication of entities that would be considered objects and attributes, and verbs and verb phrases will likely become operations and associations. The key abstractions from the problem domain must be identified at the outset, which forms the basis of the static model of the system. Business requirements are implemented on top of the domain model, therefore the domain model is a foundational artifact on which the business and presentation components are dependent. During domain modeling, we also identify the relationships between the domain objects. The type of relationship between entities and the multiplicity associated with roles on either side of the relationship will provide guidance for the creation of the database schema required to persist the corresponding entities. To arrive at an optimum design, we iterate and refine the model through the analysis phase. This optimization process can also continue through the design phase. To understand the object modeling process, we suggest that you read *Use Case Driven Object Modeling with UML* by Doug Rosenberg [Object Modeling], which further elaborates on this subject.

References

[Object Modeling] Use Case Driven Modeling with UML by Doug Rosenberg (Addison Wesley, 1999)

CHAPTER

7

Business Tier Design and Implementation

IN THIS CHAPTER:

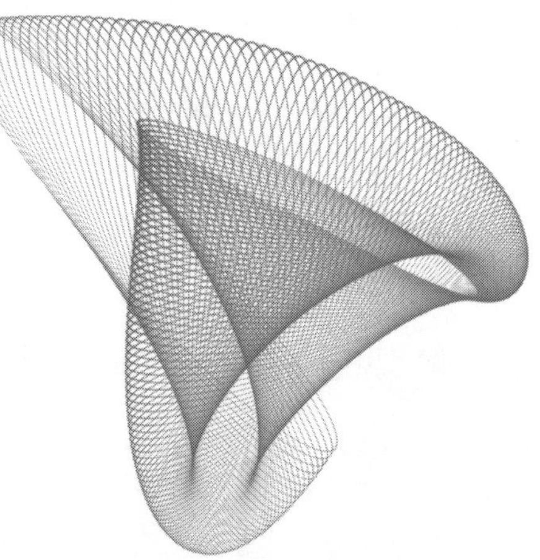

In Chapter 5, we looked at various design patterns applicable for the presentation tier along with implementation of the use case packages GreaterCause Site Administration, Manage Campaigns, and Search NPO. In this chapter, we discuss and implement several design patterns that are appropriate for the business tier. Emphasis in this chapter is on identification of appropriate design patterns in the context of our problem domain and applying these patterns for solving common problems during the design and development of the business tier. The patterns discussed in this chapter cover only those patterns that are relevant to realizing the above-mentioned use cases; for a comprehensive patterns list and related discussion, please refer to the references provided at the end of the chapter. A good understanding of this chapter will assist the readers in quickly assimilating other design patterns covered in the reference books and be able to discern their use in the context of different problem domains.

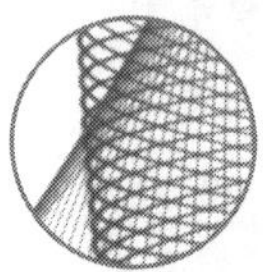

NOTE

It is assumed that the reader of this chapter has a basic understanding of EJBs and related technologies identified under J2EE framework. This chapter does not explain these technologies in great detail; instead it applies these technologies in the context of realizing the use cases identified in the preceding. We do discuss EJB usage and associated development and configuration semantics to provide the complete rationale behind our design decisions. For additional information on developing distributed systems using EJBs, please refer to tutorials available at java.sun.com.

Applying Design Patterns

In this section, we examine selected patterns that have been effectively used across most GreaterCause use cases. The Value List Handler pattern [Core] will be discussed in the section "Search NPO Use Case."

When designing distributed applications, appropriate partitioning of application logic across application tiers, coupled with efficient data transfer between tiers, is required to satisfy such concerns as scalability, performance, extensibility, and maintainability. A brief description of patterns follows; this is followed by a detailed discussion of the pattern usage in the context of the GreaterCause implementation.

- **Session Façade** This design pattern is used where there is a requirement to loosely couple the interactions between the client and the business logic residing on a server. This pattern minimizes the dependencies between the client tier and the business tier by providing a stable and simple interface to the business logic accessible by the client tier; it hides the complexities of the business processes within the methods of a session bean. This enables simpler client design and protects the client from the effects of business process changes in the business tier of the application.
- **Business Interface** This design pattern is used to provide a compile-time checking of method signatures for remote/local interface implementation in the EJB bean classes.

- **Data Transfer Object Pattern** This design pattern is used to transfer coarse-grained objects to and from the business tier and presentation tier, thus reducing overall network traffic and transferring more data in fewer remote call invocations.
- **EJB Home Factory Pattern** This design pattern is used to encapsulate the vendor-specific details required for looking up home interfaces; it also provides caching of home references for reuse.

Implementing the Session Façade Pattern

We first examine a scenario in which the presentation tier will try to implement the Register NPO Use Case by directly accessing the entity beans without the intervening business-tier objects, which are usually implemented using session beans. Register NPO Use Case is described in Chapter 1. The objective of this use case is to register an NPO, which includes creating the associated domain objects Admin and NPO (both are container-managed entity beans) for storing the administrator-related information and the NPO registration information, respectively. At the analysis level, the steps involved in implementing the Register NPO Use Case are depicted in the sequence diagram of Figure 7-1.

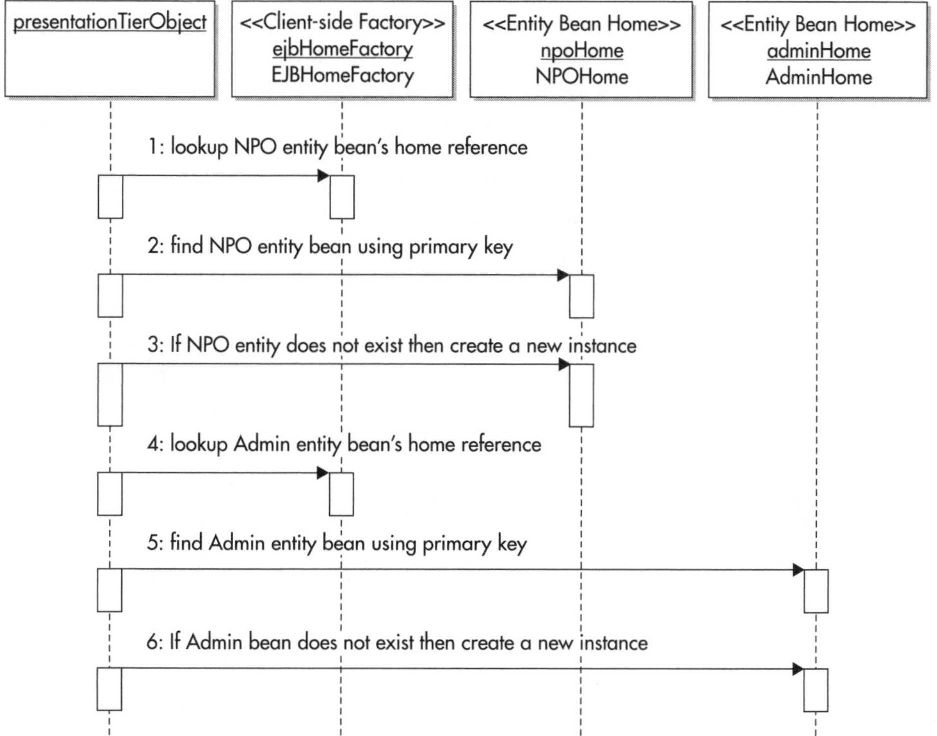

Figure 7-1 *Directly accessing domain objects from the presentation tier*

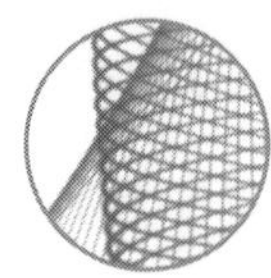

NOTE

Please note that the sequence diagrams illustrated in this chapter are analysis-level diagrams. They are used to provide a high-level understanding of the underlying interaction semantics.

In this scenario, the presentation tier will make several calls over the network (assuming remote reference usage) to achieve the objective of registering the NPO in the data store. The number of calls for registering the NPO creates network chatter that does not effectively use the network bandwidth. Also, in this scenario the presentation tier has embedded logic for accessing and manipulating the domain objects, which will increase the complexity of the presentation tier logic. As discussed in Chapter 4, the presentation tier must follow the MVC semantics. This implies that it must not concern itself with manipulating the model; the logic for manipulating the model must be abstracted into a different tier, which we call the business tier.

A best practice approach to addressing these inefficiencies uses a session bean for implementing the model portion of the problem domain. The business semantics are expressed in a session bean that also encapsulates access to domain objects, thus effectively hiding the complexity of accessing and manipulating domain objects implemented as entity beans. This implementation of the session bean is referred to as a Session Façade [Core]. When a session façade pattern is used, the presentation tier effectively makes a single network call to a method on the session bean with relevant arguments, which could potentially be a data transfer object (this is further explained in the section "Implementing the Data Transfer Object Pattern"); the façade method in turn deals with the complexities of business processes and data manipulation. The session façade isolates the presentation tier from the implementation aspects of the domain tier and the related business processes, thus providing a loosely coupled interaction semantics. Should the business tier logic change, or there is a change in the domain model, the presentation tier will usually remain unaffected. Figure 7-2 depicts the interaction between the presentation tier and the session façade.

The sequence diagram depicts that fewer calls are made by the presentation tier over the network instead of several calls as compared to Figure 7-1. In this scenario, the session façade is implemented by the *SiteAdmin* session bean.

From the preceding discussion, you will observe that the presentation tier is now limited in its responsibility while delegating most of the application logic to the session façade. By applying the session façade pattern, we have moved the business logic from the presentation tier to the business tier and introduced the MVC semantics for isolating the presentation tier from the intricacies of the domain model and the logic that manipulates the model. The session façade pattern is also extensively used when there is need to prevent the client from making fine-grained method calls to domain objects. Roughly speaking, the pattern could be used to wrap all the method calls required to get relevant data from entity beans in a single network call to the business tier. This pattern is usually used in conjunction with the Data Transfer Object pattern. The session bean implementing the session façade does not have to restrict itself to accessing domain objects; a session façade could in fact interact with other session beans for servicing the client request. This architecture is useful for solving complex business problems as well as promoting reuse and modularity.

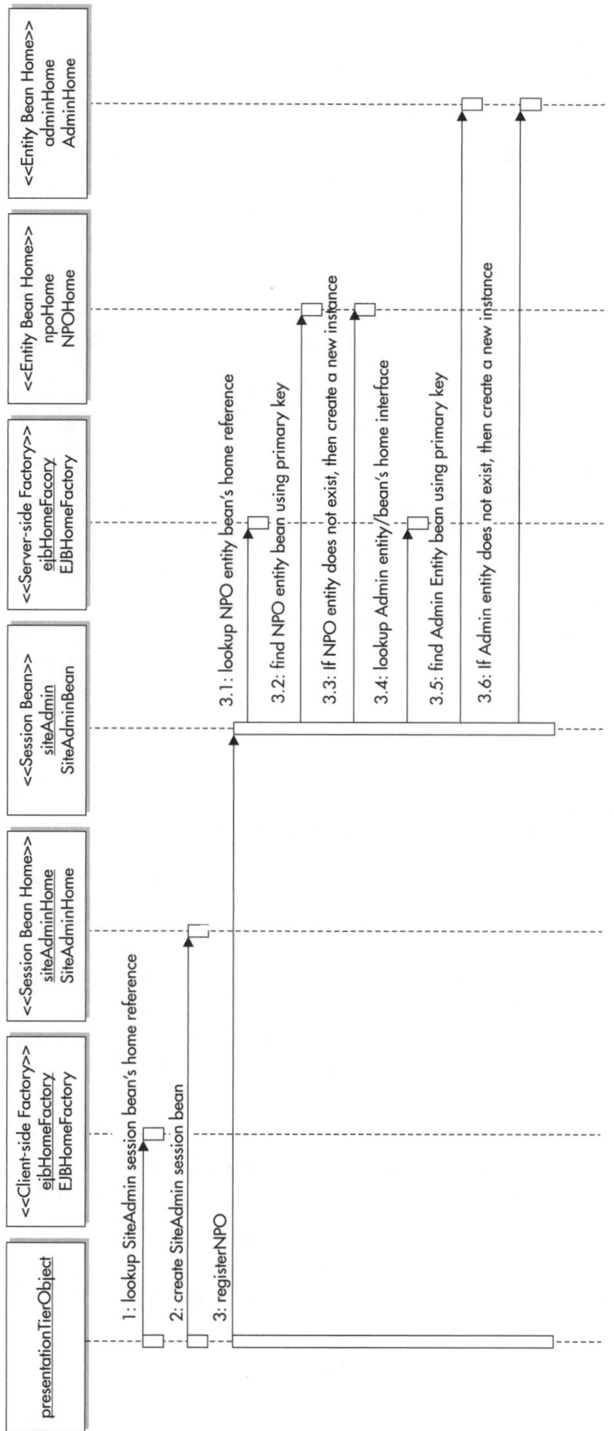

Figure 7-2 *Accessing business logic using Session Façade*

Optimization Note

For the reasons of scalability, you may want to consider using stateless session beans instead of stateful session beans. A *stateful* session bean requires that you maintain the conversational state for a client across method invocations; therefore a stateful bean cannot be assigned to another client. A *stateless* session bean does not maintain the conversational state and hence any free instance of the session bean from the bean pool may service any client. This provides better opportunities for the EJB container to scale the number of available instances of session beans for servicing the clients. However, using a stateless session bean may not be practical in certain situations; for example, the implementation of Search NPO use case (discussed in section "Search NPO Use Case") employed a stateful session bean to support the paging mechanism required by the presentation tier.

For small- to medium-sized applications, it may be tempting to implement all the use cases using a single session façade bean. This is not a recommended approach because this leads to unnecessary concentration of unrelated services into a single session bean. Instead, break up the business logic into manageable chunks based on application functionality and implement the use cases across multiple session beans as described in the following sections. This approach makes the application scalable, manageable, and modular. However, the architects must endeavor to keep the number of session façade beans to a manageable number.

Implementing the Business Interface Pattern

A session bean class or an entity bean class must implement all the methods defined on the remote interface. However, according to the EJB specification, the bean class is only required to implement the *javax.ejb.SessionBean* interface; therefore, at compile time, there is no checking to ensure that the methods of remote interface have been implemented by the bean class. It is only during the post-compilation process that the proprietary compliance checkers provided by EJB vendors will check that the bean class methods conform to the remote interface definition. The post-compilation checkers usually are very slow and are outside of the regular development environment.

An elegant solution for this problem is to define a special interface, called Business Interface [EJB Patterns], which the remote interface extends; this business interface is implemented by the bean class. Observe that by extending the remote interface with the business interface, the remote interface does not have to specify any business methods. As illustrated in Figure 7-3, *SiteAdminRemote* extends the required *EJBObject*, and it also extends the *SiteAdmin* business interface. The *SiteAdminBean* class implements the required *javax.ejb.SessionBean* interface (in the case of entity beans it is the *javax.ejb.EntityBean* interface) and it also implements the *SiteAdmin* business interface. During compilation, the *SiteAdminBean* class must have the implementation for methods defined by the *SiteAdmin* business interface, otherwise the compiler will flag this as an error; this makes it possible

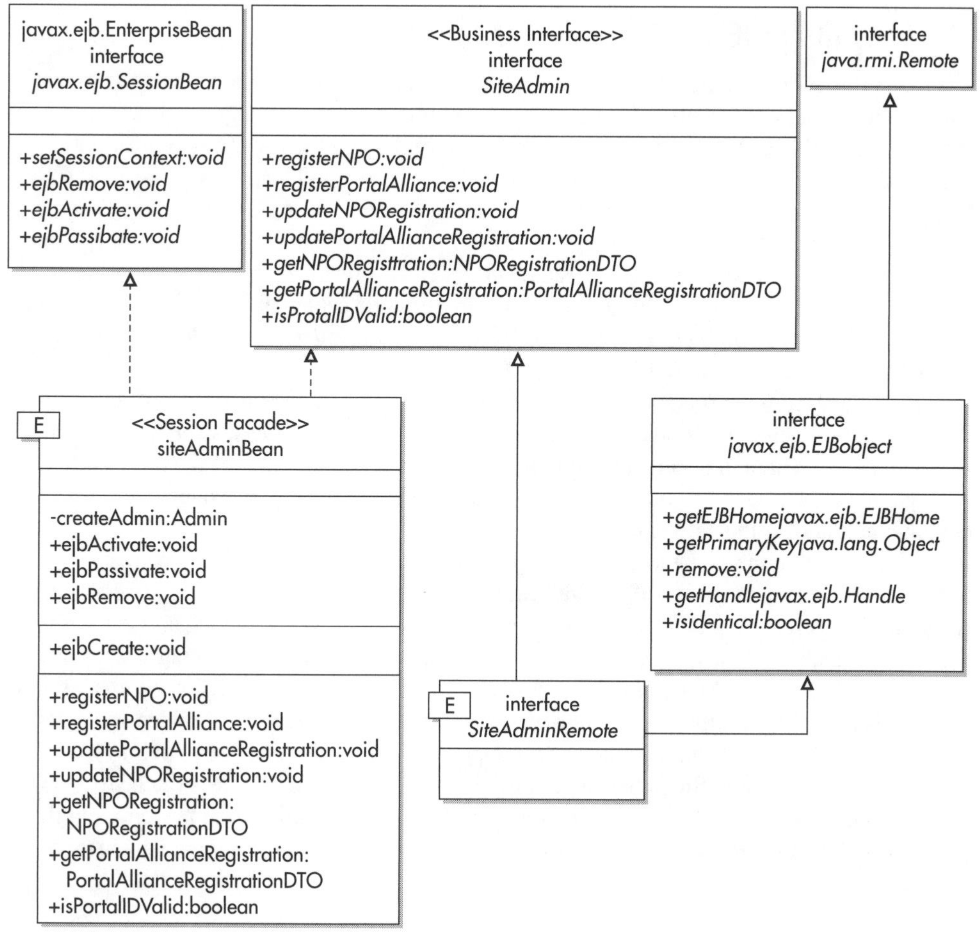

Figure 7-3 *Using the Business Interface for accessing an EJB*

to detect any mismatch between the method signatures on the business interface and the bean class. Using this solution, the EJB client can conveniently use the business interface instead of remote or local interface to interact with a session bean as shown by the SiteAdmin business interface in Figure 7-3.

The business interface differs slightly if it has to expose a remote interface or a local interface to the client. The EJB 2.0 specification specifies that all methods in a remote interface should throw a *RemoteException*, whereas the methods in a local interface must not throw a *RemoteException*. So if the remote interface extends a business interface, each method in the business interface must throw a *RemoteException*; as a result, this business interface cannot be used to extend the local interface.

This pattern provides a powerful mechanism for compile-time checking of method signatures defined in the remote/local interfaces that are being implemented by the EJB bean class. This pattern is sometimes called a *double-interface* pattern.

Implementing the Data Transfer Object Pattern

In a typical distributed application like GreaterCause, the presentation tier needs to interact with the business tier for getting information pertaining to the view being processed. For example, the Register NPO use case requires the view to show the registration information to the administrator; some of this information includes EIN, NPO Name, Address, and so on. One solution for requesting this data from the business tier is to have a session façade expose the methods *getEin()*, *getNpoName()*, *getAddress()*, and so on. The presentation tier will then call the appropriate method on the session bean to get the information for display purpose. This form of access is commonly referred to as fine-grained access in that the information required by the presentation tier is obtained incrementally using several calls to the business tier. This interaction is captured in Figure 7-4.

It is obvious from the sequence diagram in Figure 7-4 that there is a lot of traffic between the presentation tier and business tier. Each remote method call on the session bean is going across the wire, which in turn results in marshalling and unmarshalling of the objects EIN, NPO Name, Address, and so on. This level of object granularity is expensive when communicating over the network.

An elegant solution will be to make a single call to the session bean, which returns a serialized object that aggregates the fields required by the view, as shown in Figure 7-5. In this scenario, the presentation tier requests the session bean for registration data, and the session bean in turn makes all the necessary calls to the domain objects for assembling a serializable object; this object is called a *Data Transfer Object (DTO)* [EJB Patterns]. Further discussion on DTO is available at http://c2.com/cgi-bin/wiki?UseDataTransferObjects. This serializable object is used for exchanging data between the presentation and the business tiers. The use of DTO minimizes the traffic between the presentation tier and the business tier (EJB tier) in a distributed environment, and it reduces the complexity of the logic in the presentation tier. The DTO can be used to assemble data from several views (as in multipage interaction) when

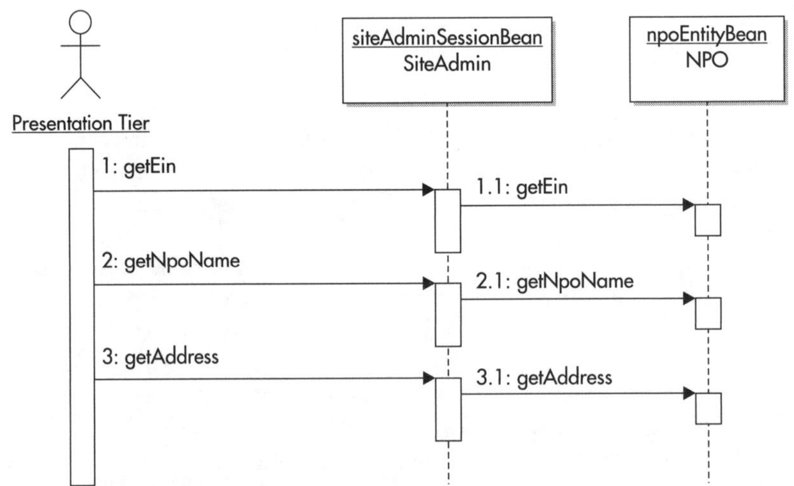

Figure 7-4 *Fine-grained access of business functionality*

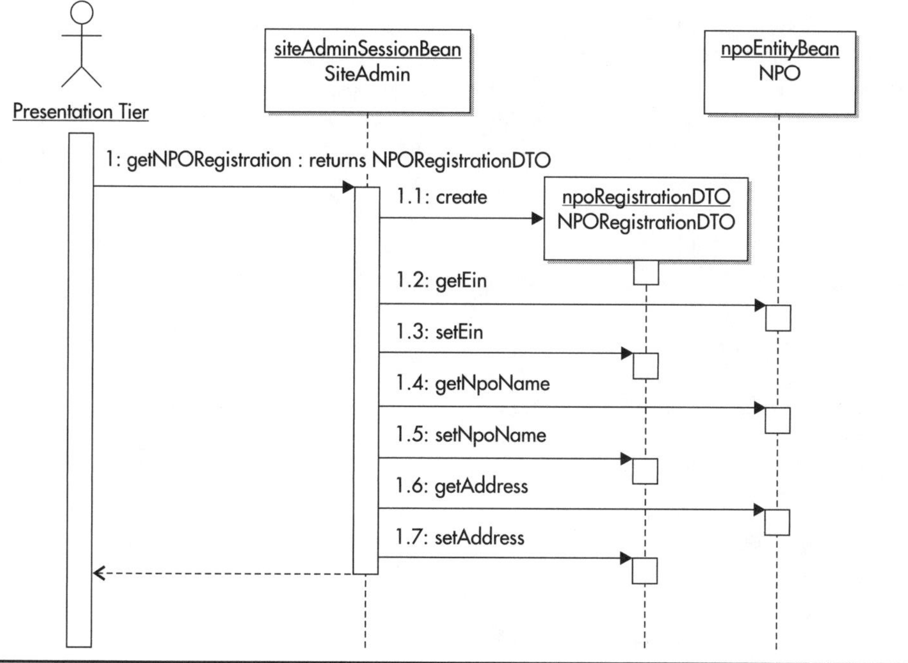

Figure 7-5 *Coarse-grained access using a DTO*

transporting data from the presentation tier to the business tier, or the DTO can be used to assemble data to be shown across several views when transporting data from the business tier to the presentation tier. Under certain circumstance one may require exchanging more than one DTO between different tiers; in such cases one can use a collection of DTO objects.

The data transfer objects are usually simple serializable JavaBean classes, as shown in the following code segment:

```
package com.gc.services.admin;
import java.io.Serializable;

public class NPORegistrationDTO implements Serializable{
    private String ein = null;
    private String npoName = null;
    private String adminID = null;
    private String address = null;
    private String city = null;
    private String state = null;
    private String zip = null;
    private String country = null;
    private String activationStatus = null;
    ... property accessors appear here ...
}
```

Depending on your implementation need, the DTOs can be mutable or immutable. *Immutable* DTOs are employed when the presentation tier should not update data values of the object, and therefore the DTO can only be used for display purposes. However, if the presentation tier requires the data to be updated, then *mutable* DTOs are employed, which allows the instance variables of the DTO to be changed. The changed DTO is sent back to the business layer for applying the changes to domain objects.

When the business tier receives an updated DTO, it needs a mechanism to identify the instance variables that have been changed. In the absence of this mechanism, the business layer may have to blindly update the domain objects with values from DTO, potentially updating unchanged attributes; avoiding such updates optimizes the database access performed by container-managed persistence EJB (CMP). A simple solution to recognize the changed value for an instance variable is to set a flag corresponding to the variable, as shown in the following code snippet:

```
package com.gc.services.admin;
import java.io.Serializable;

public class NPORegistrationDTO implements Serializable{
    private String _ein = null;
    private String _npoName = null;
    ... rest of the code ...
    /* Following members provide the index for the flags[] array */
    public static final int EIN = 0;
    public static final int NPO_NAME = 1;
    ... rest of the code ...
    private boolean[] flags = new boolean[9];
    public NPORegistrationDTO(){
        this.resetModifiers();
    }
    ... accessors are listed here ...
    public void setEin(String ein) {
        _ein = ein;
        flags[EIN] = true;
    }
    public void setNpoName(String npoName) {
        _npoName = npoName;
        flags[NPO_NAME] = true;
    }
    public boolean isFieldModified(int fieldIndex){
        /* Returns true if the corresponding setter method was called */
        return flags[fieldIndex] == true;
    }
    public void resetModifiers(){
        for (int index = 0; index <= flags.length-1; index++){
```

```
                flags[index] = false;
            }
        }
    }
```

In the business tier, the session bean simply needs to call the *isFieldModified* method to determine if the field has been updated by the presentation tier; this is illustrated in the following code segment. Please note that the variable *npo* corresponds to a domain object. Domain objects are discussed in Chapter 6.

```
public void updateNPORegistration(NPORegistrationDTO details){
    if (details.isFieldModified(NPORegistrationDTO.NPO_NAME) ) {
        npo.setNpoName(details.getNpoName());
    }
    ... check other attributes for modification ...
}
```

Proliferation of Data Transfer Objects

For a small-sized application like Greater Cause, only a handful of data transfer objects were needed to satisfy the requirements of the presentation tier. For large applications, the requirements of the presentation tier may require a large number of data transfer objects. To keep the number of DTOs manageable, one solution would be to create DTOs that have several common data elements; the flip side of this approach is that the data transfer object will contain more data than required for satisfying a presentation tier request; populating additional data also implies making unnecessary calls to the domain layer. Optionally, a data transfer object based on HashMapmay be appropriate in situations where an arbitrary amount of data needs to be transferred across tiers in a generic manner.

When Not to Use Data Transfer Objects

From the outset, the DTO pattern may be used between different tiers of the application—between the presentation and business tiers, and between the business and domain tiers. However, it is considered a bad practice to apply a data transfer object pattern for interactions with the domain tier.

Back in the days of EJB 1.*x*–based implementations, the DTO pattern surfaced due to the mandatory requirement that the calls to entity beans be remote even when the session or entity beans accessing them were co-located. To reduce the network overhead of these remote calls, the data transfer object pattern was applied in a fashion similar to the discussion in this section. Under this circumstance, if the same DTOs were used by both the presentation tier and the domain tier, then if the domain tier changed, the associated DTO changed and therefore the presentation tier was required to change, and vice versa. This tight coupling between the view and the domain objects will result in unnecessary dependency between tiers, which also undermines MVC semantics. Note that with the introduction of local interfaces in EJB 2.0, the method calls to entity beans are no longer required to be remote.

Implementing EJB Home Factory Pattern

The EJB specification standardizes the access mechanisms for locating the EJBs. A client locates a session or entity bean's home interface using JNDI. For example, the home interface for the *SiteAdmin* session bean (from the Register NPO Use Case) can be located using the following segment of code:

```
//Vendor specific code
Hashtable props = new Hashtable();
props.put(InitialContext.INITIAL_CONTEXT_FACTORY,
    "weblogic.jndi.WLInitialContextFactory");
props.put(InitialContext.PROVIDER_URL,
    "t3://localhost:7001");
InitialContext ctx = new InitialContext(props);
SiteAdminHome siteAdminHome = (SiteAdminHome)
    javax.rmi.PortalRemoteObject.narrow(
    ctx.lookup("ejb/com.gc.services.admin.SiteAdminHome"),SiteAdmin.class);
```

This code first packages the necessary vendor-specific values into a Hashtable and calls *PortalRemoteObject.narrow* with the corresponding JNDI name that was declared in the deployment descriptors. The preceding snippet has the following disadvantages:

- Each client accessing the EJB is providing vendor-specific code, and therefore the code is repeated in multiple places where access to EJBs is required.
- Getting the initial context and subsequently the home interface is a resource-intensive process, which will impact performance.

To overcome these limitations, the EJB Home Factory pattern [EJB Patterns] should be introduced as follows:

- Develop a helper class that hides all the vendor-specific details. In the sample application, this helper class is called *EJBHomeFactory*.
- Using a combination of Factory and Singleton [Gof] patterns, create a single instance of *EJBHomeFactory* that creates the *InitialContext* only once, and provides a suitable caching mechanism for home references.

The following code fragment shows the implementation for *EJBHomeFactory*:

```
public class EJBHomeFactory {
    private HashMap _ejbHomes;
    /* Singleton pattern */
```

```
    private static EJBHomeFactory _factory = new EJBHomeFactory();
    private static InitialContext _ctx = null;
    private EJBHomeFactory(){
        _ejbHomes = new HashMap();
    }
    public static EJBHomeFactory getFactory(){
        return _factory;
    }
    public static InitialContext getContext() throws NamingException{
        /* Check if initial context already exists */
        if (_ctx == null){
            /* Vendor specific parameters */
            Hashtable props = new Hashtable();
            props.put(
                InitialContext.INITIAL_CONTEXT_FACTORY,
                "weblogic.jndi.WLInitialContextFactory");
            props.put(InitialContext.PROVIDER_URL, "t3://127.0.0.1:7001");
            _ctx = new InitialContext(props);
        }
        return _ctx;
    }
    public EJBHome lookUpHome(Class homeClass) throws NamingException{
        EJBHome home = null;
        /* Check whether the reference for the EJB already exists in the
         * cache _ejbHomes */
        if ((home = (EJBHome)_ejbHomes.get(homeClass)) == null){
            home = (EJBHome)PortableRemoteObject.narrow(
                getContext().lookup("ejb/"+homeClass.getName()),homeClass);
            // Cache the reference for future use
            _ejbHomes.put(homeClass,home);
        }
        return home;
    }
}
```

The *EJBHomeFactory* has the *getFactory* method, which returns an instance of *EJBHomeFactory*. The convenience method *lookUpHome* creates the *InitialContext* only once using vendor-specific details in the *getContext* method. The *InitialContext* is used in the *PortableRemoteObject.narrow* method for looking up the home reference for the given JNDI name.

The following snippet illustrates usage of the EJB Home Factory class for accessing the home reference of the desired EJB. Note that the developers do not have to concern themselves with vendor-specific details. The home factory pattern provides a mechanism for caching home references while hiding vendor-specific details.

```
SiteAdminHome adminHome = (SiteAdminHome)EJBHomeFactory.getFactory().
            lookUpHome(SiteAdminHome.class);
```

The JNDI name for the home interface is described in the weblogic-ejb-jar.xml file, as shown here:

```
<weblogic-enterprise-bean>
   <ejb-name>SiteAdminEJB</ejb-name>
   <jndi-name>ejb/com.gc.services.admin.SiteAdminHome</jndi-name>
</weblogic-enterprise-bean>
```

Identifying Package Dependencies

The package structures shown in Figure 7-6 depict the dependencies between packages in the business tier. The package naming conventions used by the GreaterCause application in the business tier and the domain tier follow the following conventions:

Business Tier	Domain Tier
com.gc.services.admin	com.gc.persistence.admin
com.gc.services.managecampaigns	com.gc.persistence.managecampaigns
com.gc.services.searchnpo	

The basic premise of this book is use of object-oriented paradigm and a use case–driven approach. As such, we now examine how we have used the different patterns discussed in the preceding sections for realizing the use cases discussed in Chapter 1. In this chapter, we develop the use cases identified by the packages Site Administration, Manage Campaigns, and Search NPO. The intent of this endeavor is to assist the readers in understanding how to implement an architecture based on the patterns we just discussed; at the same time, we create static and dynamic models for representing our problem domain.

Moving Forward

The basic premise of this book is use of object-oriented paradigm and use case–driven approach. As such, we now examine how we have used the different patterns discussed in the preceding sections for realizing the use cases discussed in Chapter 1. In this chapter, we develop the use cases identified by the packages Site Administration, Manage Campaigns, and Search NPO. The intent of this endeavor is to assist the readers in understanding how to implement an architecture based on the patterns we just discussed, at the same time, we create static and dynamic models for representing our problem domain.

Realization of the Site Administration Use Case Package

The following subsections provide the use case realization for use cases in the Site Administration package. To avoid repetition, we cover only essential use cases that introduce new concepts; for the rest of the use cases, please refer to the implementation on the accompanying CD-ROM. In this section we apply all the business patterns we discussed earlier in this chapter. We also discuss the deployment descriptors required to configure the EJBs that will be created for realizing the Register NPO use case, along with the declarations that specify the transaction semantics for the various EJB methods. We conclude this section with a brief discussion on exceptions in the context of transactions.

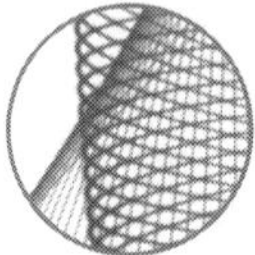

NOTE

The following subsections provide readers with an opportunity to understand class interactions and dependencies visualized through class and analysis-level sequence diagrams. Please refer to Chapter 1 for use case descriptions.

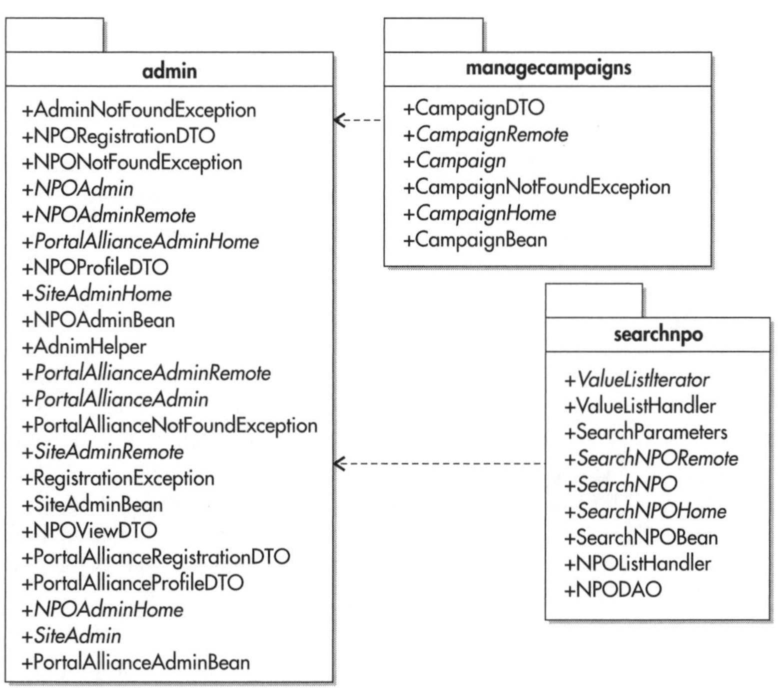

Figure 7-6 *Business Tier Package Diagram*

Register NPO Use Case

This section covers the implementation of Register NPO use case. The implementation details described here provide the necessary foundation for other use cases; and the same concepts are reapplied for implementing other use cases.

Discovering Business Interface Methods

The first step in realizing the use case is to identify the methods of the business interface necessary for realizing the use case. We identify the business interface methods by following the flow of events described for the use case. Since the Register NPO is an administration service, applying the business interface pattern described earlier in the section "Implementing the Business Interface Pattern," we define a business interface called *SiteAdmin.* This interface must provide a method called *registerNPO* for allowing the presentation tier to register NPO data. Using the data transfer object pattern, the presentation tier provides the required data in an object called *NPORegistrationDTO*. We can identify the attributes of this DTO from the wire frames identified during the use case elaboration process. The following code fragment shows the required attributes for the *NPORegistrationDTO* class that represent registration information:

```
public class NPORegistrationDTO implements Serializable {
    //Instance variables
    private String ein = null;
    private String npoName = null;
    private String adminID = null;
    private String address = null;
    private String city = null;
    private String state = null;
    private String zip = null;
    private String country = null;
    private String activationStatus = null;
    ... rest of the code ...
}
```

Since this DTO will go across the wire using RMI, ensure that it implements the Serializable interface. Once the registration information is created in the GreaterCause data store, the Register NPO use case will also need to maintain this information using the *updateNPORegistration* and *getNPORegistration* methods; these additional methods are added to the business interface as well. The following code fragment shows the business methods identified thus far in the business interface *SiteAdmin*:

```
public interface SiteAdmin {
    void registerNPO(NPORegistrationDTO detail) throws RemoteException,
        RegistrationException;
    void updateNPORegistration(NPORegistrationDTO details)
```

```
        throws RemoteException,NPONotFoundException, GCAppException;
    NPORegistrationDTO getNPORegistration(String ein, String adminID)
        throws RemoteException, NPONotFoundException,
        AdminNotFoundException, GCAppException;
}
```

The method signatures identified for the business interface shown were selected based on the design decision that we will be employing the services of a stateless session bean. Because the stateless session bean does not maintain any state information, the client must provide all the details necessary for the session bean to service the request; this design may complicate the client logic because the onus is on the client to maintain the application state. In the business interface of *SiteAdmin*, note two methods are used by the client for getting and updating the registration information; these methods are *getNPORegistration* and *updateNPORegistration*. The design of the client has accounted for the fact that both of these methods will be serviced by different session bean instances, therefore the client design will ensure that when *updateNPORegistration* is invoked, the corresponding parameters (that is, *NPORegistrationDTO*) will include the *ein* (EIN is the primary key for the NPO entity bean and is not updatable by the client) in addition to all the other information required by the session bean to service this request. Had we decided to use a stateful session bean instead of a stateless session bean, the update method would not require the *ein* because the session bean would be aware of the parameters that were supplied when *getNPORegistration* was invoked for constructing the *NPORegistrationDTO*. This is further clarified by the sequence diagrams shown in Figure 7-8, 7-9, and 7-10.

Please observe that the business methods declared in the business interface also declare the possible exceptions the business methods may throw to the presentation tier. In addition to the application exceptions, the business methods must also throw *RemoteException*; this is because the remote interface for the session bean will be extended from this business interface. Recall from the discussion in the section "Implementing the Business Interface Pattern" that the business methods must throw *RemoteException* if they are to be exposed through a remote interface as required by the EJB 2.0 specification.

Implementing Business Interface

In this section, we discuss the implementation aspects of the business interface *SiteAdmin* defined in the preceding section. Figure 7-7 shows the class diagram for realizing the Register NPO use case. You will find additional methods on the *SiteAdminBean* class pertaining to other use cases, which you should ignore for now. Figure 7-7 shows the interactions between various business tier components. The *SiteAdmin* interface employs the Business Interface pattern; the *SiteAdminBean* class employs the Session Façade pattern; and the *NPORegistrationDTO* class employs the Data Transfer Object pattern. The *SiteAdminBean* class employs the services of the *EJBHomeFactory* class for getting references to domain tier entities such as Admin and NPO entity beans. For brevity, Figure 7-7 does not show application-specific exceptions and the usage of EJBHomeFactory.

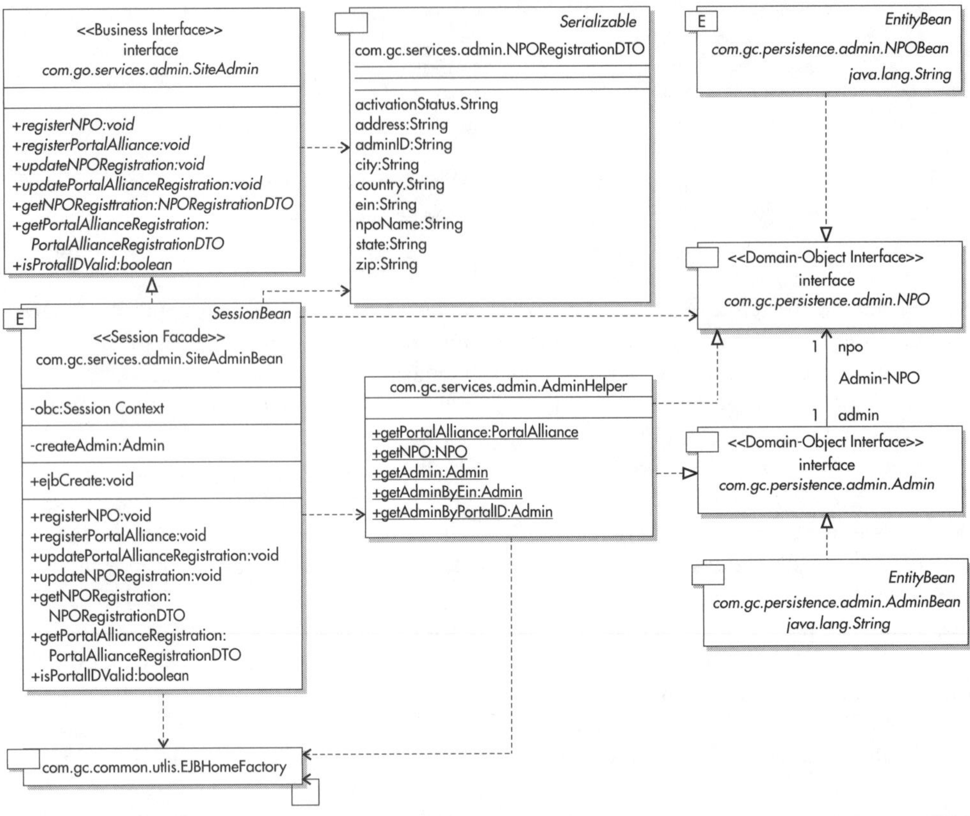

Figure 7-7 *Register NPO class diagram*

Figure 7-8 depicts the creation of domain objects Admin and NPO using the DTO supplied by the presentation tier, whereas Figure 7-9 depicts the creation of DTO using the information from the domain objects Admin and NPO. From the sequence diagram, it is apparent that the session façade *SiteAdmin* is responsible for handling all the complexities of creating and managing domain objects while the presentation tier need only make a single call to the session façade. For brevity, certain steps are removed from the sequence diagrams and the reader is requested to check the accompanying CD-ROM for the complete source code.

SiteAdmin Session Bean Deployment Descriptors

The session bean *SiteAdminBean* defined in the preceding section needs to be configured for deployment in an EJB container. We use deployment descriptors for providing the configuration information.

There is essentially more than one deployment descriptor associated with the deployment of a session bean. The ejb-jar.xml file contains standard declarations as dictated by the EJB specification. Additionally, the vendor will provide other deployment descriptors that are

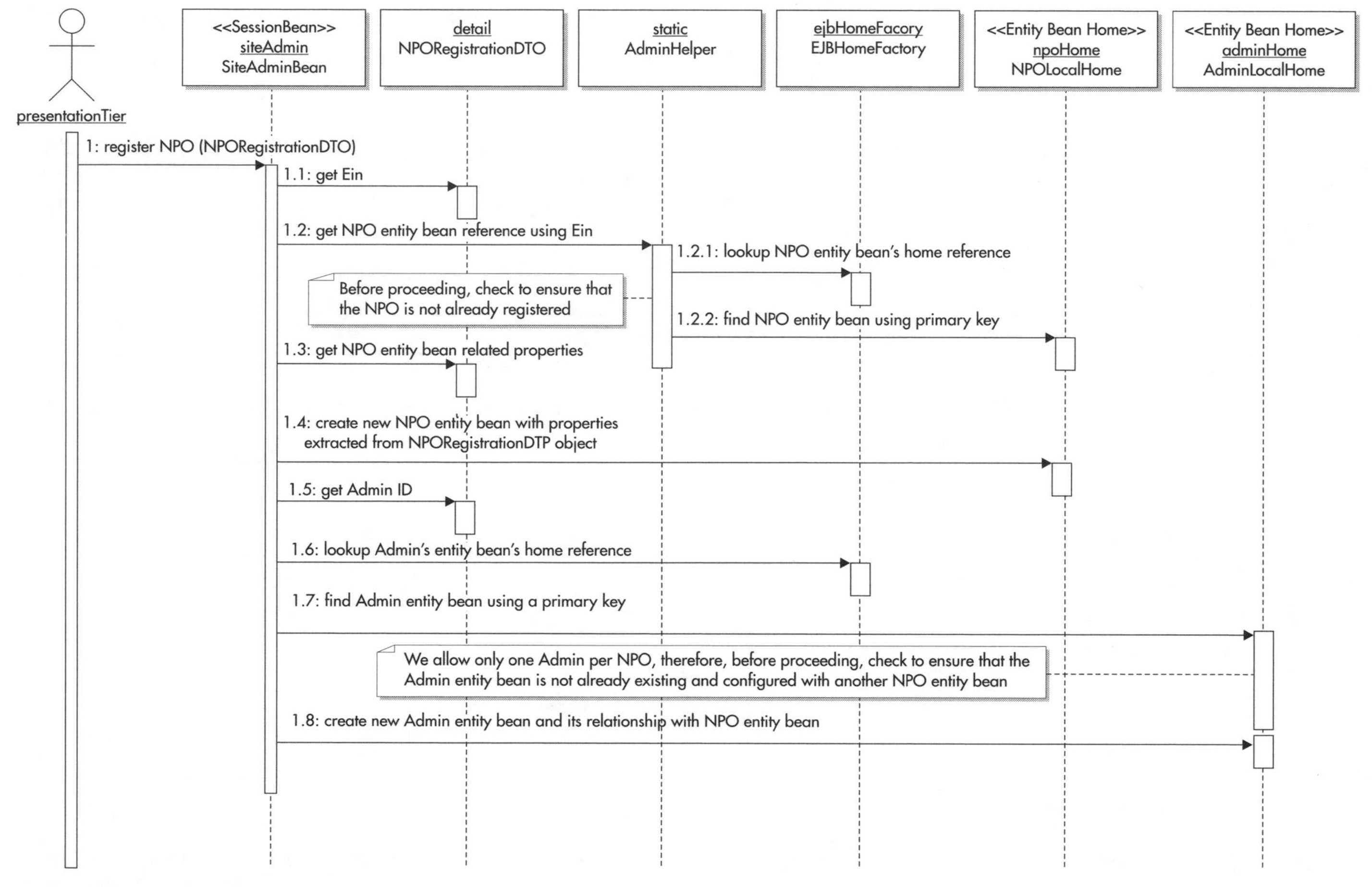

Figure 7-8 *Sequence diagram for registerNPO*

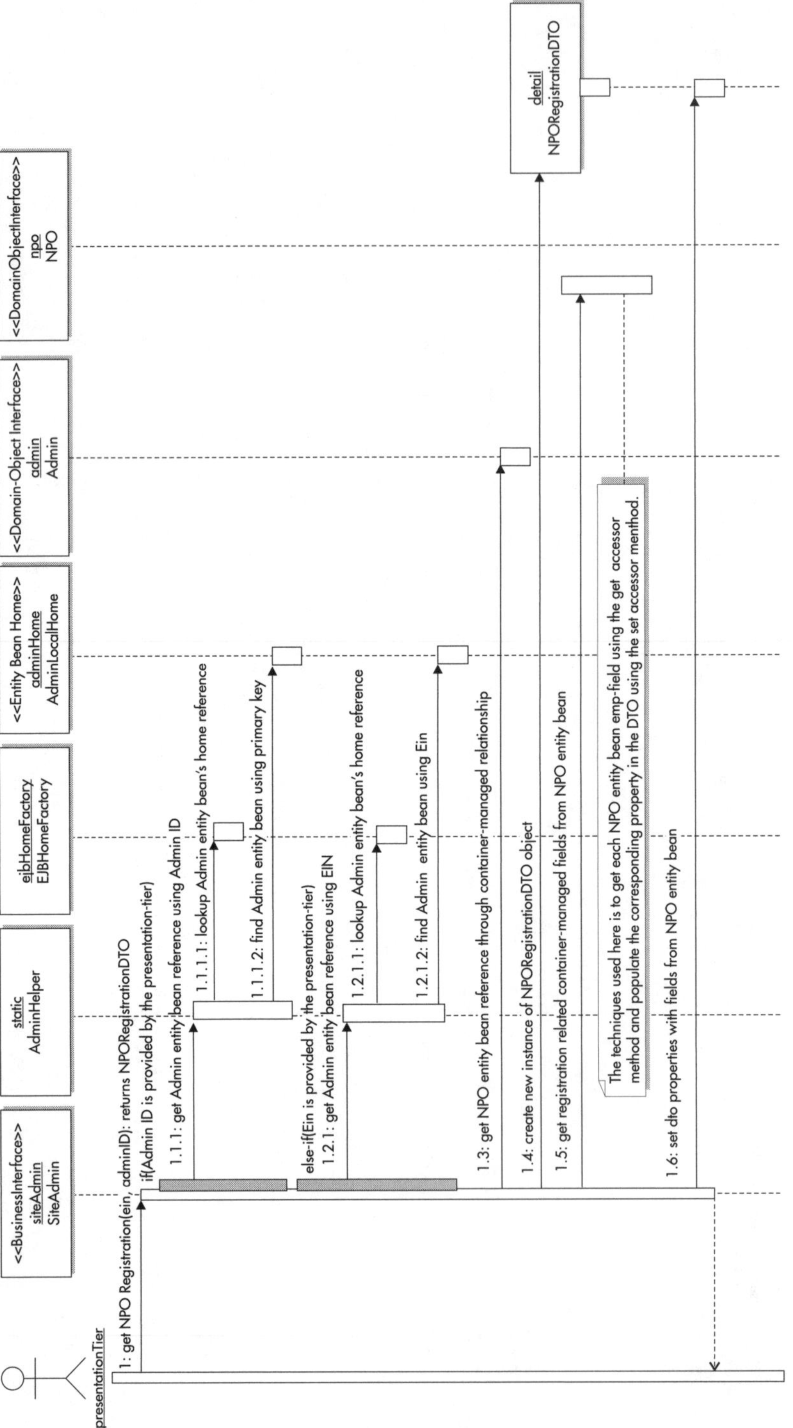

Figure 7-9 *Sequence diagram for getNPORegistration*

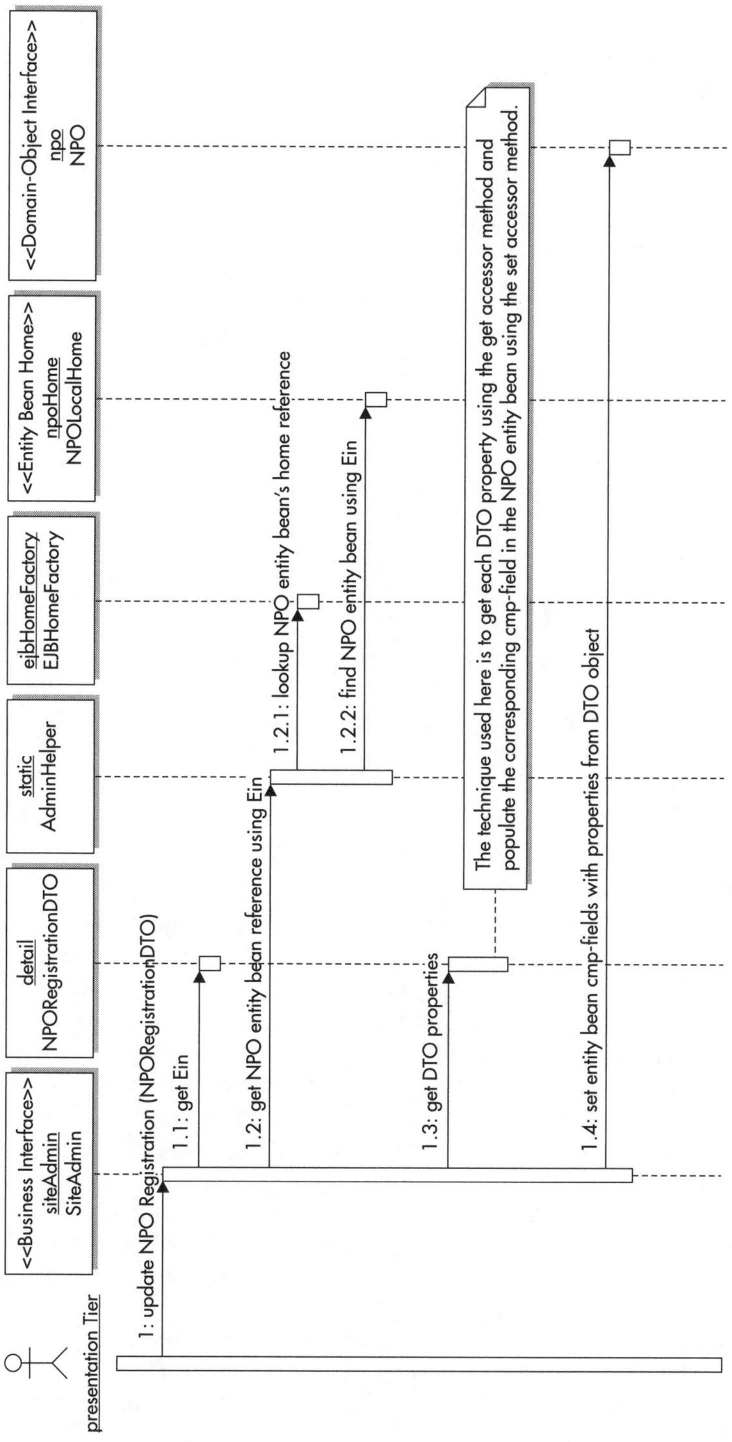

Figure 7-10 *Sequence diagram for updateNPORegistration*

proprietary in nature. We first discuss the ejb-jar.xml deployment descriptor and the associated semantics. Following snippet provides configuration information for the *SiteAdmin* session bean.

```
<session >
   <description>Site Admin Definitions</description>
   <ejb-name>SiteAdminEJB</ejb-name>
   <home>com.gc.services.admin.SiteAdminHome</home>
   <remote>com.gc.services.admin.SiteAdminRemote</remote>
   <ejb-class>com.gc.services.admin.SiteAdminBean</ejb-class>
   <session-type>Stateless</session-type>
   <transaction-type>Container</transaction-type>
   <!-- Referencing NPO Entity Bean -->
   <ejb-local-ref>
      <ejb-ref-name>com.gc.persistence.admin.NPOLocalHome</ejb-ref-name>
      <ejb-ref-type>Entity</ejb-ref-type>
      <local-home>com.gc.persistence.admin.NPOLocalHome</local-home>
      <local>com.gc.persistence.admin.NPOLocal</local>
      <ejb-link>NPOEntityEJB</ejb-link>
   </ejb-local-ref>
   <!-- Referencing Admin Entity Bean -->
   <ejb-local-ref>
      <ejb-ref-name>com.gc.persistence.admin.AdminLocalHome</ejb-ref-name>
      <ejb-ref-type>Entity</ejb-ref-type>
      <local-home>com.gc.persistence.admin.AdminLocalHome</local-home>
      <local>com.gc.persistence.admin.AdminLocal</local>
      <ejb-link>AdminEntityEJB</ejb-link>
   </ejb-local-ref>
</session>
```

Using the *ejb-name* element, we assign a logical name to the session bean. This logical name must be unique within the ejb-jar.xml file. This name is referenced in other constructs such as the subelements of the *container-transaction* element and *ejb-relation* element (refer to the element *ejb-name* in these constructs). The session EJB is further described using the *home*, *remote*, and *ejb-class* elements that provide the fully qualified class names for the home interface, remote interface, and the bean class, respectively. The *session-type* element is used for specifying whether the bean is stateful or stateless. Changing the *session-type* element's values without properly analyzing the impact of the current implementation could produce unpredictable results. The *transaction-type* element specifies the bean's transaction type, which could be either *Bean*, implying that the bean is providing transaction demarcation, or *Container*, implying that the container is providing the transaction demarcation based on the transaction attributes specified as part of the container-transaction element in the ejb-jar.xml file. The transaction-type element must not be specified for entity beans because all entity beans must use container-managed transaction demarcation.

Recall that when a client accesses an EJB in a container, it uses the following code that employs vendor-specific properties for correctly creating an *InitialContext*. Note that this vendor-specific code is required only when you are accessing EJBs from outside the container.

```
//Vendor specific code
Hashtable props = new Hashtable();
props.put(InitialContext.INITIAL_CONTEXT_FACTORY,
    "weblogic.jndi.WLInitialContextFactory");
props.put(InitialContext.PROVIDER_URL,
    "t3://localhost:7001");
InitialContext ctx = new InitialContext(props);
SiteAdminHome siteAdminHome = (SiteAdminHome)
    javax.rmi.PortalRemoteObject.narrow(
    ctx.lookup("ejb/com.gc.services.admin.SiteAdminHome"),SiteAdmin.class);
```

The access mechanism shown here is not required when an EJB is accessing another EJB. The session bean *SiteAdminBean* references NPO and Admin entity beans as part of the implementation of Register NPO use case. The EJB 2.0 specification simplified the access mechanisms when an EJB in a container is accessing another EJB within the same or a different container. To reference an EJB from another EJB, you do not need to specify any JNDI initialization parameters; instead you acquire default JNDI *InitialContext* as follows:

```
Context initialContext = new InitialContext();
```

When default JNDI *InitialContext* is used, the lookup mechanism will take the following form. In this form, the *java:comp/env/* string specifies the default environment naming context.

```
NPOHome npoHome = (NPOHome)
        initialContext.lookup("java:comp/env/"+NPOHome.class);
```

The *NPOHome.class* is mapped by the container to the value of the *ejb-ref-name* element within the deployment descriptors; the value of the *ejb-ref-name* element is subsequently used by the container to get the descriptors of the corresponding EJB. The *ejb-ref-name* element has a sibling *ejb-link* element (defined under the parent *ejb-local-ref* element); this *ejb-link* element provides the link to the original definition of the entity bean; the value of this element is the logical name given in the *ejb-name* element of the corresponding entity bean where it was originally defined. Since the *NPO* entity bean is described in the same ejb-jar.xml file for our sample application, we can simply provide the value *NPOEntityEJB* for the *ejb-link* element.

For the session bean deployment descriptors being discussed in this section, notice that the *ejb-ref-name* element occurs under the *ejb-local-ref* element; these constructs assist the container in accessing the *NPO* and *Admin* entity beans. This concludes the discussion on the deployment descriptors for the *SiteAdmin* session bean. The JNDI name for the session bean is defined in a vendor-specific deployment descriptor; since we have used the WebLogic Server, the corresponding deployment descriptor is the weblogic-ejb-jar.xml file.

```
<!-- SiteAdmin Definition -->
<weblogic-enterprise-bean>
    <ejb-name>SiteAdminEJB</ejb-name>
    <jndi-name>ejb/com.gc.services.admin.SiteAdminHome</jndi-name>
</weblogic-enterprise-bean>
```

The *ejb-name* element refers to the *ejb-name* defined in the ejb-jar.xml file. The *jndi-name* element represents the JNDI name to be used for accessing the session bean. The EJB 2.0 specification recommends prefixing the JNDI names with "ejb/."

Transaction Semantics for Enterprise Beans

The EJB Specification greatly simplified declarative transaction management. Without this, the developer had to explicitly manage the transactions with fairly complex Java Transaction Service (JTS), which is based on OMG's Object Transaction Service (OTS) API. Explicit transaction management is prone to errors, especially for those who are new to transactional application development. Including transaction semantics in business applications increases the code complexity, which results in high maintenance cost; a change in the transactional behavior will force a change to business logic. The EJB specification allows declarative transaction management through deployment descriptors. The transaction semantics are introduced at the time of deployment, which introduces flexibility in manipulation of transactional behavior of the application without resorting to code changes. For this chapter, we use container-managed transaction demarcation where the container demarcates the transactions based on the instructions provided through the deployment descriptor.

The bean provider may also choose to use programmatic transaction demarcation; this is called bean-managed transaction demarcation. With bean-managed transaction demarcation, the enterprise bean demarcates transactions using the *javax.transaction.UserTransaction* interface. Accesses to container-managed resources, between *UserTransaction.begin()* and *UserTransaction.commit()*, are part of this transaction. Please refer to the EJB specifications or Mastering Enterprise JavaBeans [JavaBeans] for detail information on using programmatic bean-managed transaction demarcation.

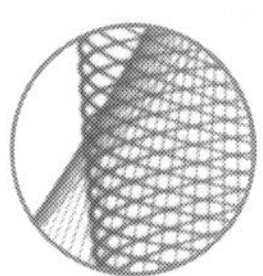

NOTE

The EJB architecture supports flat transactions, implying that a transaction cannot have other nested (child) transactions. We assume that the reader has prior knowledge of what a transaction is and the associated ACID properties.

Scope of a Transaction When using container-managed transaction demarcation, the scope of a transaction is controlled by the transaction attribute specified for the EJB's methods. Following briefly discusses these transaction attributes so that we can understand its impact in the context of our implementation.

Transaction Attributes A *transaction attribute* is a value associated with a method of a session or entity bean's home or component interface that specifies how the Container must manage transactions for a method when a client invokes the method via the enterprise bean's home or component interface (i.e., local or remote interfaces). EJB specification supports the following values for the transaction attribute when using container-managed transaction demarcation for EJBs:

- *NotSupported* When the transaction attribute is set to *NotSupported*, the container invokes the related enterprise bean method with an unspecified transaction context. When a client is associated with a transaction context, the container suspends the client's transaction context until the enterprise bean's business method returns. This means that the transaction context is not propagated to the bean method. After completion of the bean method's execution, the client's transaction context is resumed. This attribute value is specified when the bean method needs to access a resource that cannot or should not participate in a transaction.

- ***Required*** When the transaction attribute is set to *Required*, the container must invoke the related enterprise bean method with a valid transaction context. If the client invokes the enterprise bean's method with a transaction context, the same transaction context is propagated to the bean's method. If the client is not associated with a transaction context, the container automatically starts a new transaction before calling the business method. This option is selected when the bean method is changing the state of the application; for example, creating one or more entity beans or updating the value of entity beans, and so on. This option is not necessary if the bean method is just reading the contents from the data store, and the application is not concerned with holding stale data. The *Required* attribute value is the most widely used option in EJB declarations for injecting transactional semantics into method calls. The *registerNPO* method of the *SiteAdminBean* session bean is declared with the *Required* transaction attribute because the use case requires the creation of a new Admin entity bean and NPO entity bean. Both beans must be successfully created and their relationship established in the same transaction for the transaction to succeed.
- ***Supports*** When the transaction attribute is set to *Supports*, the container invokes the related enterprise bean method as follows:
  - If the client call is associated with a transaction context, the semantics applicable are similar to the *Required* case.
  - If the client call is not associated with a transaction context, the semantics applicable are similar to the *NotSupported* case.
- ***RequiresNew*** When the transaction attribute is set to *RequiresNew*, the container invokes the related enterprise bean method with a new transaction context. This transaction context is propagated to methods of other enterprise beans. When the client invokes the enterprise bean while the client is already associated with a transaction context, then that transaction is suspended. The bean method starts a new transaction and completes its execution under this new transaction. When the bean method returns, the Container resumes the client's transaction. This option is usually selected if the bean's method cannot participate in the callers transaction context.
- ***Mandatory*** When the transaction attribute is set to *Mandatory*, the container must invoke the related enterprise bean method in a client's transaction context. If the client calls with a transaction context, the container performs the same steps as described in the *Required* case; if the client calls without a transaction context, the container throws the *javax.transaction.TransactionRequiredException* for a remote client, or *javax.ejb.TransactionRequiredLocalException* for a local client.
- ***Never*** When the transaction attribute is set to *Never*, the container invokes the related enterprise bean method without a transaction context. If the client calls with a transaction context, the container throws *java.rmi.RemoteException* for a remote client,

or *javax.ejb.EJBException* for a local client. If the client calls without a transaction context, the container performs the same steps as described in the *NotSupported* case.

Transaction Attributes for *SiteAdmin* Session Bean Methods

The transaction attributes for each EJB are defined in deployment descriptors. The descriptors have the flexibility for providing a single transaction attribute for all the methods using the * notation, as shown here:

```
<container-transaction>
    <method>
        <ejb-name>SiteAdminEJB</ejb-name>
        <method-name>*</method-name>
    </method>
    <trans-attribute>Required</trans-attribute>
</container-transaction>
```

This representation specifies that all methods of *SiteAdminEJB* will have the transaction attribute of *Required*. This implies that all the *SiteAdminEJB* method invocations are always under a transaction context even if the bean method is simply reading the data from data store. The transaction attribute must be set to *Required* for those methods that affect the persistent state of the application. For example, the transaction attribute is set to *Required* for the *registerNPO* and *updateNPORegistration* methods of the *SiteAdmin* session bean because these methods change the persistent state of the application. Transaction attributes for individual methods of the SiteAdminBean can be specified as follows.

```
<container-transaction>
    <method>
        <ejb-name>SiteAdminEJB</ejb-name>
        <method-name>registerNPO</method-name>
    </method>
    <method>
        <ejb-name>SiteAdminEJB</ejb-name>
        <method-name>updateNPORegistration</method-name>
    </method>
    <trans-attribute>Required</trans-attribute>
</container-transaction>
```

Handling Exceptions in Transactions

The EJB 2.0 specification introduces conceptual difference between application exceptions and system exceptions. The EJB developer must understand this difference in addition to the relationship between exceptions and transaction semantics.

An application exception is an exception defined in the *throws* clause of a method of the enterprise bean's home and component interfaces (remote and local interfaces), other than *java.rmi.RemoteException* or *javax.ejb.EJBException*. An application exception is a direct or indirect subclass of *java.lang.Exception*; it must not be defined as a subclass of *java.lang.RuntimeException* or *java.rmi.RemoteException*. Application exceptions are used to inform the client about abnormal conditions in the business logic; clients catching such exceptions are expected to recover from the exception and to provide alternative business logic to deal with the situation, provide information to the user about corrective action, or fail gracefully with appropriate logging of the exception and instructions for the client. In our sample application, all the exceptions subclassed from *GCAppException* are application exceptions. The container also throws application exceptions such as *javax.ebj.CreateException*, *javax.ejb.RemoveException*, *javax.ejb.FinderException*, and so on.

On the other hand, system-level exceptions are created as a result of situations that prevent EJB methods from completing successfully; for example, failure to obtain a database connection, JNDI exceptions, unexpected *RemoteException* from invocation of other enterprise beans, *RuntimeException*, JVM errors, and so on. The bean methods must not try to catch these *RuntimeException*s but let them propagate to the container. When a bean method is processing a checked exception and discovers that it cannot recover from the exception, the bean method should throw the *javax.ejb.EJBException*; *EJBException* is a subclass of *RuntimeException*, and therefore it does not have to be listed in the *throws* clause of business methods. The *Container* catches all non-application exceptions, logs the exception, marks the transaction for rollback, and subsequently throws a *RemoteException* (for clients using remote interfaces) or *EJBException* (for clients using local interfaces). The following code fragment has been excerpted from the *getNPORegistration* method of the *SiteAdmin* session bean:

```
try {
    NPOLocalHome npoHome =
   (NPOLocalHome) EJBHomeFactory.getFactory().lookUpLocalHome(
       NPOLocalHome.class);
    ... Rest of the code ...
} catch (NamingException ne) {
    throw new EJBException(
    "Unable to locate local reference to NPO:", ne);
}
```

NamingException is thrown by the container during JNDI lookup; since this signifies a configuration issue, the application will throw an *EJBException* and not an application exception because the client is not expected to recover from this exception.

According to the EJB 2.0 specification, when a system exception is encountered in the business method of an EJB, the container must either mark the transaction for rollback (this is true when the method runs in the context of the caller's transaction), or roll back the transaction started by the container (this is true when the method runs in the context of a transaction that the container started immediately before dispatching the business method). When the container discards an instance of a bean because of a system exception, the container releases all the connections to the resource managers that the instance acquired through resource factories declared in the enterprise bean environment such as JDBC DataSource references, JMS connection factories, JavaMail connection factories, URL connection factories, and so on; the container cannot release "unmanaged" resources that the instance may have acquired directly.

When the business method encounters an application exception, and if the exception is deemed unrecoverable, it is the EJB developer's responsibility to identify and mark the transaction for rollback using *setRollbackOnly()* on *EJBContext*; this marks the transaction for rollback. The *setRollbackOnly* method can be invoked only when bean methods are participating in a transaction context. Observe from the following code fragment that the *setRollbackOnly* method is invoked prior to throwing the *RegistrationException*, which is an application exception; the intent here is to mark the transaction for rollback because the NPO entity bean has already been created. Please note that the code shown is slightly modified for explaining the concepts; the actual code can be found in *SiteAdminBean* implementation.

```
try {
    AdminLocalHome adminHome =
       (AdminLocalHome) EJBHomeFactory.getFactory().lookUpLocalHome(
        AdminLocalHome.class);
    admin = adminHome.create(adminID, (NPOLocal) npo);
} catch (CreateException ce) {
    ctx.setRollbackOnly();
    throw new RegistrationException("error.CannotCreateAdmin",
         "Unable to Register Admin with AdminID:" + adminID, ce);
} catch (NamingException ne) {
  /* setRollbackOnly() not required because the EJBException is a system exception */
    throw new EJBException("Unable to locate local reference to Admin:", ne);
}
```

The following is a brief discussion of standard application exceptions for entity beans. We discuss this in the context of marking transaction for rollbacks.

- ***CreateException*** This exception is thrown by the container when using container-managed persistence, or this exception can be thrown by the bean developer in the *ejbCreate* or *ejbPostCreate* method. The transaction may or may not be marked for rollback, although it is advisable that the bean developer should mark the transaction for rollback to leave the database in a consistent state. When bean-managed transaction is in effect, the session bean method can determine the status of the transaction using the *getStatus* method on the *javax.transaction.UserTransaction* interface; when container-managed transaction is in effect, the session bean method can determine the status of the transaction using the *getRollbackOnly* method of the *javax.ejb.EJBContext*.
- ***DuplicateKeyException*** This exception is a subclass of *CreateException*. It is thrown by the *ejbCreate* method to indicate to the client that the requested entity bean could not be created because an entity bean with the same key already exists. Normally, the *ejbCreate* method will not mark the client's transaction for rollback; it is left to the client to take corrective measures.
- ***FinderException*** This exception indicates an application-level error occurring in the find methods on the home interface of an entity bean. The bean provider throws this exception to flag an error in the *ejbFind* method; this exception is not used to indicate entity not found conditions; for entity not found conditions, the bean provider uses the *ObjectNotFoundException*, which is discussed next. Typically, the bean provider will not mark the client's transaction for rollback; it is left to the client to take corrective measures.
- ***ObjectNotFoundException*** This exception indicates that the requested entity was not found by the *ejbFind* method. This exception can be thrown only by a finder method that

returns a single object. Finder methods that return a collection object do not use this exception; such methods return an empty collection to indicate that no matching objects were found. The EJB container typically does not mark the transaction for rollback. The container or the bean provider does not mark the client's transaction for rollback when *ObjectNotFoundException* is encountered; it is left to the client to take corrective measures.

- ***RemoveException*** This exception is thrown by the container when using container-managed persistence, or this exception can be thrown by the bean developer in *ejbRemove*. The client receiving this exception does not generally know if the entity bean was removed or not. The transaction may or may not be marked for rollback, although it is advisable that the bean developer should mark the transaction for rollback to leave the database in a consistent state. When bean-managed transaction is in effect, the bean method can determine the status of the transaction using the *getStatus* method on the *javax.transaction.UserTransaction* interface; when container-managed transaction is in effect, the bean method can determine the status of the transaction using the *getRollbackOnly* method of *javax.ejb.EJBContext*.

Realization of the Manage Campaigns Use Case Package

The following subsections describe use case realization for use cases in the Manage Campaigns package. Please refer to Chapter 1 and Chapter 2 for use case descriptions of this package.

Create Campaigns Use Case

In this section, we define and implement the components necessary for the implementation of the Create Campaigns use case. In this section we will implement a one-to-many relationship existing between a *PortalAlliance* entity bean and *Campaign* entity beans (refer to Figure 7-10) using a collected-valued container-managed relationship *PortalAlliance-Campaign*. This discussion is continuation of the material discussed in Chapter 6.

Discovering Business Interface Methods

In this use case, we define the *Campaign* business interface. We pick up the development of this use case from where Chapter 5 left off. There are numerous calls from the presentation tier for satisfying this use case because the process of creating a campaign involves several user interactions; these user interactions include checking existence of a Portal-Alliance (provided by the site administrator) for which campaigns are to be created, followed by search and selection of the desired NPO for which a campaign needs to be created; finally the campaign information is stored in the data store for the given Portal-Alliance. Please refer to Chapters 1 and 2 for complete details of this use case; Chapter 5 exhaustively explains the various user interaction within the context of the Struts framework and the associated Shared Request Handler Pattern. Although we have been progressively building this use case from use case analysis and implementing the presentation tier, nothing precludes us from developing the Create Campaign business-tier functionality in parallel with presentation-tier development;

you will recall that the business delegate pattern used in the presentation tier offers the point of integration between the presentation tier and the business tier. Once the development of the presentation tier and business tier is accomplished, the integration between the two tiers is achieved using the business delegate (presentation tier side) and session façade (business tier side) with the intervening service locator for getting the references to business-services in the business tier.

We begin by identifying the methods required on the new *Campaign* business interface. The presentation tier will need the method *addNewCampaign* on the new business interface to add campaign details. The following code segment shows the method in the business interface.

```
public interface Campaign {
    void addNewCampaign(CampaignDTO campaign)
         throws RemoteException ,NPONotFoundException,
         AdminNotFoundException,PortalAllianceNotFoundException,
         GCAppException;
}
```

Observe that this method will require *CampaignDTO* to carry the campaign information across tiers. *CampaignDTO* has complete information on the campaign being created, as well as the Portal ID with which the campaign is to be associated. Refer to the accompanying CD-ROM for *CampaignDTO* implementation. However, before the campaign creation process can proceed, the site administrator has to ensure that the corresponding portal ID is valid and active in the system (from the use cases you will recall that only site administrator has to specify the portal ID; for portal-alliance administrator the portal ID is detected by *AdminID* association). We must add a method to support checking of the portal ID in support of site administrator process flow.

```
public interface SiteAdmin {
    ... rest of the methods ...
    boolean isPortalIDValid(String portalID)
    throws GCAppException, RemoteException;
}
```

Implementing Business Interface

In Chapter 5, we took the approach of developing each package as a separate subsystem. Building upon this approach, we create all campaign-related components with their own package. Figure 7-11 illustrates a class diagram for realizing this use case.

For realizing the Create Campaign use case, we have several interacting classes and patterns that work harmoniously to provide a cohesive solution. The *CampaignBean* class implements the Session Façade pattern, whose *Campaign* business interface is exposed to the clients. The DTO pattern is implemented using the *CampaignDTO* JavaBean. The *Campaign* domain object (this is different from the *Campaign* session façade and is discussed in Chapter 6) is used for persisting campaign data.

The *addNewCampaign* method on the *CampaignBean* will first retrieve references to the *PortalAlliance* entity bean and *NPO* entity bean; it then creates a new instance of the

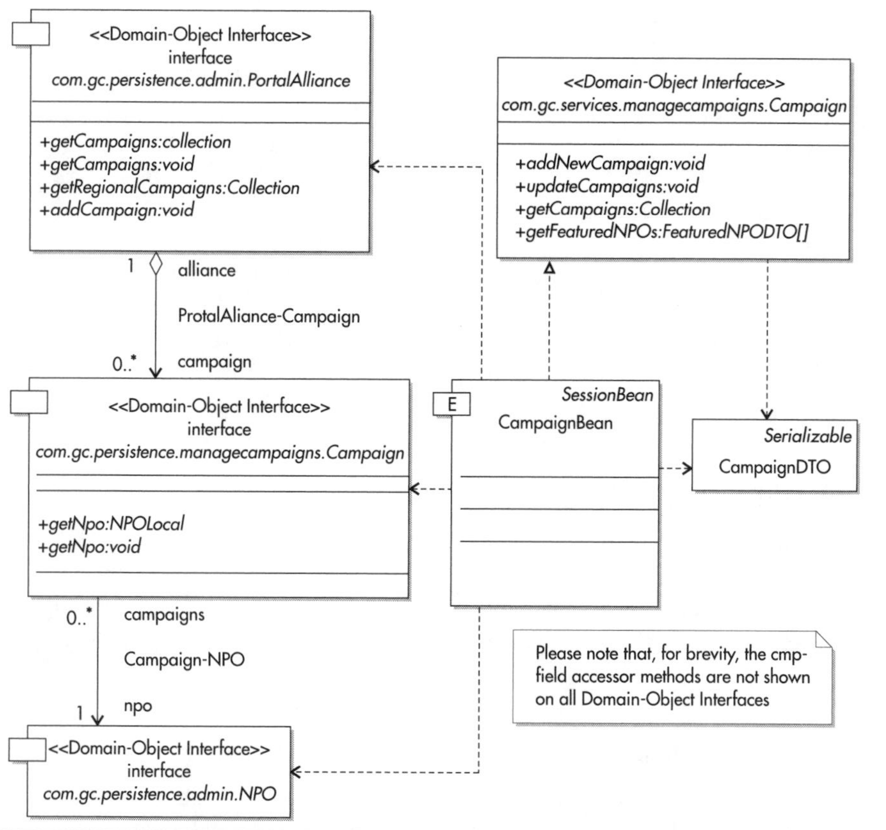

Figure 7-11 *Create Campaign class diagram*

Campaign entity bean with the information provided by the *CampaignDTO*; subsequent to this, the convenience method *addCampaign* on the *PortalAlliance* domain-object interface is invoked to add the newly created campaign entity bean to the collection-valued container-managed relationship *PortalAlliance-Campaign* as shown in Figure 7-11. The *PortalAlliance* entity bean and related methods are explained in detail in Chapter 6.

The domain model of Figure 6-1 shows the relationship between the *Campaign* entity bean and the *PortalAlliance* entity bean. Although a campaign can only be related to a single *PortalAlliance*, a *PortalAlliance* can have 0 or more (0.*) campaign(s). With the same token, a campaign can only be associated with a single *NPO*, while for a given *NPO* there may be 0 or more campaign(s).

In order to persist these relationships, we must first establish a relationship between the campaign and the *NPO* entities. Because there should always be an *NPO* for each campaign (multiplicity of '1' for the *npo* role provides this constraint), the *Campaign* entity bean ensures this linkage by accepting a reference to the *NPO* bean in its create method, as shown here:

```
try{
    ... Rest of the Code ...
```

```
    Campaign newCampaign =
        campaignHome.create(startDate, endDate,
        campaign.getRegionCode(), (NPOLocal)npo);
    ... Rest of the Code ...
}
```

This code segment creates the *newCampaign* object. Observe that during campaign creation, the primary key value *CampaignID* is not being provided since the CampaignID is system generated. Once the campaign entity bean is created, it has to be related to the PortalAlliance entity bean. This is accomplished by calling the *addCampaign* convenience method available on the *PortalAlliance* domain-object interface of the *PortalAlliance* entity bean, as shown in the following code. Please refer to Chapter 6 for additional details.

```
portalAlliance.addCampaign(newCampaign);
```

Update Campaigns Use Case

In this section, we identify and implement the components needed for the realization of the Update Campaigns use case. A large part of this use case was developed in Chapter 5 to address the needs of the presentation tier. The presentation tier expects a collection of CampaignDTO object, which it uses for creating a dynamic view; subsequently the user updates various campaigns, and the presentation tier repackages the updated CampaignDTO(s) and sends it back to the business tier.

Discovering Business Interface Methods

We continue to add to the *Campaign* business interface discussed in the preceding section; this is to ensure that logically related functionality is encapsulated within the same interface and to avoid unnecessary proliferation of business interfaces. We also use the same CampaignDTO that was used as part of the Create Campaign use case. Therefore, we have most of the essential classes and interfaces already available to us for realizing this use case.

The following interface methods are added to the Campaign interface for realizing the Update Campaigns use case.

```
public interface Campaign {
    ... Other Methods ...
    /* Method takes a Collection of type CampaignDTO from the Presentation Tier*/
    void updateCampaigns(Collection campaigns )
         throws RemoteException , CampaignNotFoundException, GCAppException;

    /* Method provides a Collection of type CampaignDTO to the Presentation Tier*/
    Collection getCampaigns(String portalID, String adminID, String regionCode)
         throws RemoteException , PortalAllianceNotFoundException,
         CampaignNotFoundException, AdminNotFoundException, GCAppException;
}
```

Implementing the Business Interface

Since we are reusing the same business interface and associated components that were used in the realization of the Create Campaigns use case, the class diagram represented by Figure 7-11 is still relevant for the following discussion.

We now examine some interesting aspects of the *getCampaigns* business method of the *Campaign* session bean.

```
public Collection getCampaigns(String portalID,String adminID,
  String regionCode)
... Rest of the Code ...
  if (adminID != null) {
      /* This branch applicable only for Portal-Alliance Administrator
       * because the Portal ID association is derived from adminID */
      Admin admin = getAdmin(adminID); //Get Admin Entity bean
      portalAlliance = admin.getAlliance(); //Get PortalAlliance Entity bean
  } else if (portalID != null) {
      /* This branch applicable only for Site Administrator
       * because the portalID is explicitly provided by administrator */
       /* Get PortalAlliance Entity bean */
       portalAlliance = getPortalAlliance(portalID);
  }
  /*Collection of Campaign Entity bean references */
  Collection campaigns = null;
  try {
   if (regionCode == null)
      campaigns = portalAlliance.getCampaigns();
   else
      campaigns = portalAlliance.getRegionalCampaigns(regionCode);
  } catch (FinderException fe) {
    ... rest of the code ...
  }
... code for verification appear here ...
   /* Finally create a Collection of DTOs */
   ArrayList results = new ArrayList();
   Iterator itr = campaigns.iterator();
   while (itr.hasNext()) {
      Campaign campaign = (Campaign) itr.next();
      // Get the cmr-field npo (i.e. the NPO Entity bean related to the Campaign)
      NPO npo = campaign.getNpo();
      CampaignDTO theCampaignDTO =
      new CampaignDTO(npo.getEin(), portalAlliance.getPortalID());
      theCampaignDTO.setCity(npo.getCity());
      theCampaignDTO.setCampaignID(campaign.getCampaignID());
      theCampaignDTO.setCountry(npo.getCountry());
      theCampaignDTO.setEndDate(campaign.getEndDate().toString());
      theCampaignDTO.setNpoName(npo.getNpoName());
      theCampaignDTO.setRegionCode(campaign.getRegionCode());
      theCampaignDTO.setStartDate(campaign.getStartDate().toString());
      theCampaignDTO.setState(npo.getState());
```

```
        results.add(theCampaignDTO); //Add to the Collection of DTOs
    }
    return results;
}
```

In this snippet, observe that the *portalID* is provided by the presentation tier when the user is a site administrator, whereas an *adminID* is provided by the presentation tier when the use is a portal-alliance administrator. The code also demonstrates retrieval of the Campaign entity bean collection for the cmr-field *campaigns* (the *campaigns* cmr-field is specified in the deployment descriptor subordinate to the *ejb-relation* element) and subsequent packaging of DTOs in a *Collection* object for use by the presentation tier.

In Chapter 6, we observed that the PortalAlliance entity bean has a helper *getRegionalCampaigns* method; this convenience method has been specially designed to accommodate the filtering of campaign entities based on a given region code; please refer to Chapter 6 for a complete discussion on how EJB QL is being used to accomplish this filtering.

In the preceding code snippet, we observed the packaging of DTOs for the presentation tier; the following code snippet for the *updateCampaigns* method of the campaign session bean illustrates the use of collection of updated DTOs received from the presentation tier, and its effect on the current transaction.

```
public void updateCampaigns(Collection campaigns)
    throws CampaignNotFoundException, GCAppException {
    ...  Other Code for checking pre-conditions ...
    Iterator itr = campaigns.iterator();
    while (itr.hasNext()) {
        CampaignDTO campaignDTO = (CampaignDTO) itr.next();
       /* Stateless bean expects that the client remember and
        * resend the Campaign ID */
        if (!campaignDTO.isFieldModified(CampaignDTO.CAMPAIGN_ID)){
            ctx.setRollbackOnly();
            throw new GCAppException("error.MustProvideCampaignID",
                   "Campaign ID must be provide to update campaign");
            }
            // Get reference to the Campaign entity bean
            Campaign campaign =
                getCampaign((Integer) campaignDTO.getCampaignID());
            // Set all cmp-fields that need to be changed in the Campaign entity bean
            if (campaignDTO.isFieldModified(CampaignDTO.START_DATE))
                campaign.setStartDate(Date.valueOf(campaignDTO.getStartDate()));
            if (campaignDTO.isFieldModified(CampaignDTO.END_DATE))
                campaign.setEndDate(Date.valueOf(campaignDTO.getEndDate()));
            if (campaignDTO.isFieldModified(CampaignDTO.REGION_CODE))
                campaign.setRegionCode(campaignDTO.getRegionCode());        }
    }
}
```

From this snippet, it is apparent that the stateless nature of the session bean expects that DTOs sent to the client, using the *getCampaigns* method, must be cached by the client. Once the DTOs are updated by the client, the client must send the complete DTOs back to the campaign session bean's *updateCampaigns* method and ensure that the primary key *campaignID* is present in all DTOs for the updates to be successful. Please observe that failure to get a *campaignID* on any of the DTOs will result in marking of the transaction for rollback.

The campaign updates are expected to be low volume, therefore we did not hesitate using collection-valued *portalAlliance.getCampaigns()* or *portalAlliance.getRegionalCampaigns(regionCode)* methods within the *getCampaigns* method of the *CampaignBean*. Normally, high-volume read only data must be extracted using patterns like DAO (Data Access Object) [Core] that directly queries the database rather than obtaining a collection of references to the entity bean. EJBs are heavy-weight objects requiring system resources for their creation, life-cycle management, and network overhead involved in their access. However, for updating high volume data, one should not circumvent entity beans since the business logic for ensuring data integrity and consistency resides in the entity bean methods; directly manipulating data would be breaking away from the object-oriented encapsulation technique, which will lead to manageability and modularity issues.

Figure 7-12 depicts the implementation of the *updateCampaigns* business method defined in the campaign bean's business interface.

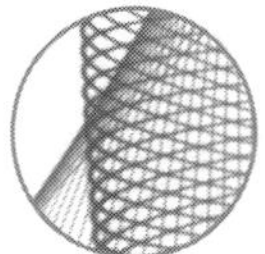

NOTE

For marshalling tabular data from a JDBC ResultSet to the client without the hassle of converting it to DTOs and then back to tabular list on the client side, a special technique is demonstrated in the book EJB Design Patterns *[EJB Patterns]; the design pattern employed is called Data Transfer Rowset.*

Campaign Session Bean Deployment Descriptors

The declarations in the deployment descriptors for the campaign session bean are similar to descriptors we discussed in the section "*SiteAdmin* Session Bean Deployment Descriptors."

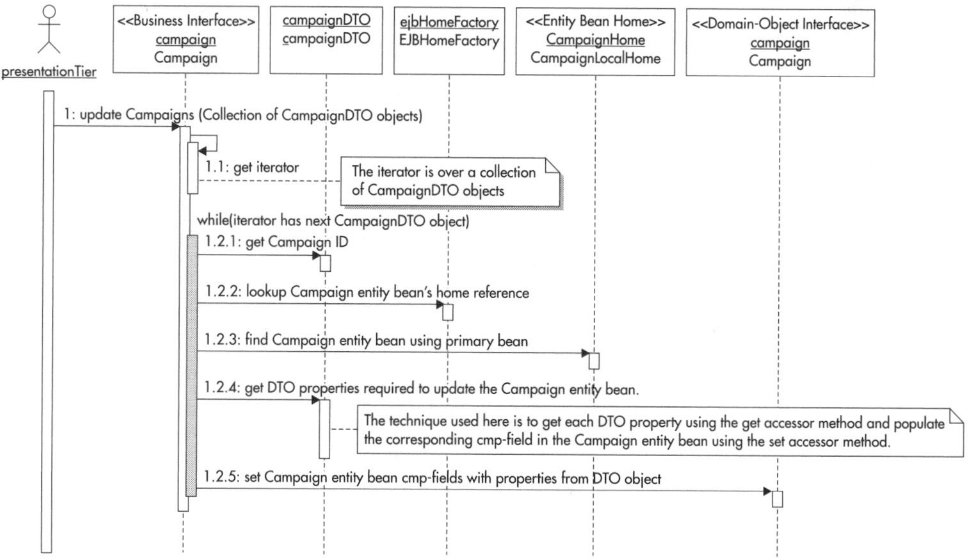

Figure 7-12 *Sequence diagram for updateCampaigns*

This section discusses the transaction-related deployment descriptors for the campaign session bean.

The *addNewCampaign* and *updateCampaigns* methods modify the application state by adding or changing the *Campaign* entity beans, therefore these methods are specified with the transaction attribute value of *Required*. The *getCampaigns* method on the *PortalAlliance* entity bean returns a collection as a result of a one-to-many relationship existing between the *PortalAlliance* entity bean and *Campaign* entity beans. The EJB 2.0 specification mandates that the iterator obtained over a collection in a container-managed relationship must be used within the transaction context in which the iterator was obtained; therefore the *getCampaigns* method of the *PortalAlliance* entity bean (discussed in Chapter 6) is associated with the transaction attribute value of *Mandatory*; this constraint automatically enforces a requirement on the *getCampaigns* method of the campaign session bean to call the *getCampaigns* method of the *PortalAlliance* entity bean with a transaction attribute *Required*. The following segment shows the appropriate configuration semantics for the *Campaign* session bean and *PortalAlliance* entity bean.

```
<container-transaction>
   <method>
       <ejb-name>CampaignEJB</ejb-name>
       <method-name>addNewCampaign</method-name>
   </method>
   <method>
       <ejb-name>CampaignEJB</ejb-name>
       <method-name>updateCampaigns</method-name>
   </method>
   <method>
       <ejb-name>CampaignEJB</ejb-name>
       <method-name>getCampaigns</method-name>
   </method>
   <method>
        <ejb-name>CampaignEJB</ejb-name>
        <method-name>getFeaturedNPOs</method-name>
   </method>
   <trans-attribute>Required</trans-attribute>
</container-transaction>

<container-transaction>
     <method>
         <ejb-name>PortalAllianceEntityEJB</ejb-name>
          <method-name>getCampaigns</method-name>
     </method>
     <trans-attribute>Mandatory</trans-attribute>
</container-transaction>
```

Realization of the Search NPO Use Case Package

The following subsections describe realization of use cases in the Search NPO package. Please refer to Chapter 1 and Chapter 2 for description of this package.

Search NPO Use Case

In this section, we look into the design and implementation of the Search NPO use case. The search function uses a stateful session bean for incrementally providing the result of the search to the presentation tier. The NPO data is retrieved using the Value List Handler pattern; the rationale for using this pattern is explained in the following discussion.

Discovering Business Interface Methods

From the use case, it is apparent that the presentation tier will be providing a search criteria to the business tier. If we were to use the collection-valued approach for retrieving entity beans, we would get references to a large number of entity beans; entity beans are heavy-weight objects demanding system resources for their construction and access. Since we are doing a read-only operation on the NPO data, it is convenient to access them directly using a DAO pattern [Core] that may use JDBC to access the NPO table data. Most often, the users will prefer some form of paging mechanism to browse through the result; this is convenient from the user perspective and from the perspective of keeping network traffic to a minimum by reducing the amount of data that goes across the network. One approach is to provision the result set with a single call to the database tier and then incrementally supply the results to the client. A design pattern that readily meets our requirement is the Value List Handler pattern [Core]; in this section, we discuss how this pattern is implemented for realizing the Search NPO use case.

We begin by creating a business interface that contains a search function that accepts the search criteria provided by the presentation tier and returns an integer to signal the presentation tier if it found any corresponding data. The following code segment shows the definition of the business method *executeSearch* on the business interface *SearchNPO*:

```
public interface SearchNPO {
    int executeSearch(SearchParameters searchDetails)
    throws RemoteException, GCAppException;
}
```

The ValueListHandler class implements the following ValueListIterator interface. The ValueListIterator defines the methods required for navigating the result set.

```
public interface ValueListIterator {
    /* Returns the number of items in the collection */
    public int getSize()
        throws IteratorException, RemoteException;

    /* Returns the current element based on the current index of iterator */
    public NPOViewDTO getCurrentElement()
```

```
        throws IteratorException, RemoteException;

    /* Returns the requested number of elements occurring before the current position
     * of the iterator */
    public List getPreviousElements(int count)
        throws IteratorException, RemoteException;

    /* Returns the requested number elements occurring after the current position
     * of the iterator */
    public List getNextElements(int count)
        throws IteratorException, RemoteException;

    /* Repositions the iterator position to the beginning of the result list */
    public void resetIndex()
        throws IteratorException, RemoteException;
}
```

The methods described in this interface satisfy the navigational semantics necessary to implement the Search NPO use case. The *ValueListHandler* class provides a default implementation of *ValueListIterator*. Please check the accompanying CD-ROM for the complete source code of this class. Figure 7-13 illustrates the usage of the Value List Handler pattern in the context of the client requests.

Implementing the Business Interface

The presentation tier imposes upon the *SearchNPO* session bean the need to maintain state information; therefore the *SearchNPO* bean is implemented as a stateful session bean. The *SearchNPOBean* implements the *SearchNPO* business interface, which in turn extends the *ValueListIterator*; the existence of all required methods in the SearchNPOBean will therefore be guaranteed at compile time. For servicing client requests, the *SearchNPO* session bean instantiates the *NPOListHandler* class, which is a subclass of *ValueListHandler*, and delegates navigation-related operations, such as *getNextElements* and *getPreviousElements* to *NPOListHandler*. The implementation of *NPOListHandler* is specific to accessing the NPO table using the *NPODAO* object. The *NPODAO* object uses JDBC for accessing the data. Please check the accompanying CD-ROM for complete source code.

Figure 7-14 shows the class diagram for realizing the Search NPO use case.

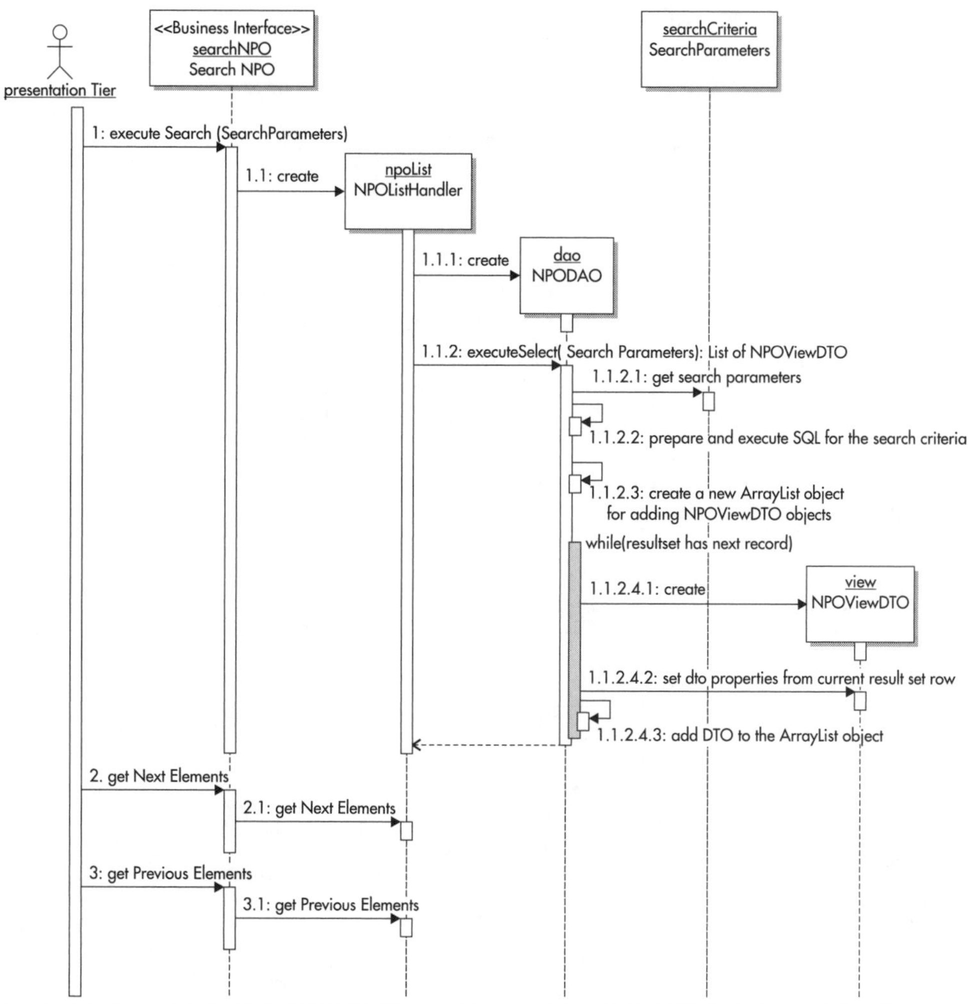

Figure 7-13 *Value List Handler Pattern Usage*

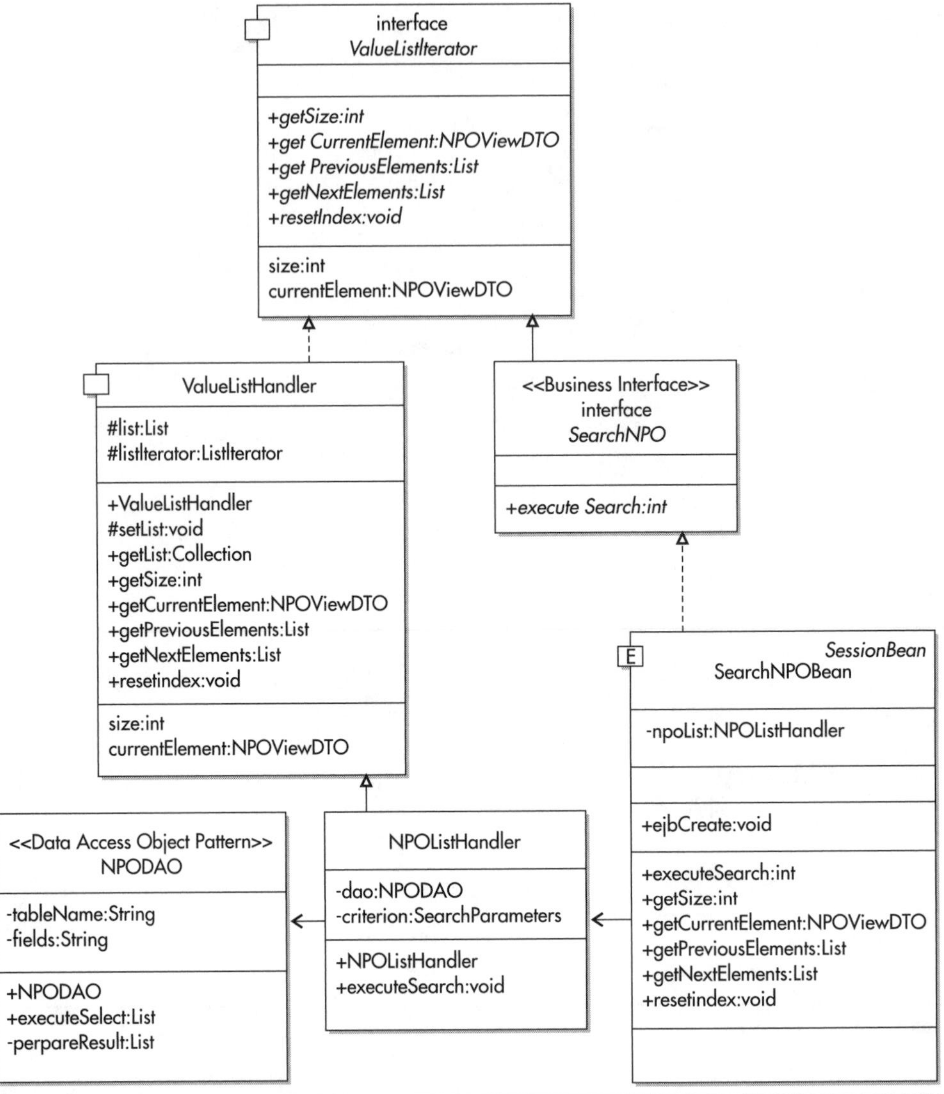

Figure 7-14 *Search NPO class diagram*

Summary

In this chapter, we looked at the implementation of various design patterns and their appropriate usage in the context of the GreaterCause application. Design patterns implemented in this chapter make the application modular, scalable, and extensible. The implementation of design patterns discussed in this book provide reusable solutions for interaction between components in various application tiers; the patterns provide a consistent design vocabulary, making it easier to develop software that is implemented based on best practices; this increases understandability and maintainability of the design artifacts and the corresponding code.

This chapter also covered the transactional semantics and attributes associated with EJBs, and the responsibilities of the bean developer to ensure transactional integrity. The emphasis on use cases is even more evident in this chapter; we developed our solutions based on the use cases identified in Chapters 1 and 2; this was done in a manner similar to Chapter 5, where presentation-tier objects were developed based on a use case–driven approach.

The knowledge gained from this chapter can be complemented by referring to the EJB specification for getting a thorough understanding of bean lifecycle management, container-managed relationships, EJB QL, transaction support, message-driven beans, and declarative and programmatic security. We also recommend reading *Mastering Enterprise JavaBeans* (2nd Edition) by Ed Roman et al., and *EJB Design Patterns: Advanced Patterns, Processes, and Idioms* by Floyd Marinescu.

References

[Core] *Core J2EE Patterns* by Deepak Alur et al. (Prentice Hall, 2001)
[Gof] *Design Patterns* by Erich Gamma et al. (Addison-Wesley, 1995)
[EJB Patterns] *EJB Design Patterns* by Floyd Marinescu (Wiley, 2002)
[JavaBeans] *Mastering Enterprise JavaBeans, Second Edition* by Ed Roman et al. (Wiley, 2002)

CHAPTER

8

Web Services for Application Integration

IN THIS CHAPTER:

Introduction to Web Services

Web Services Architecture

Development Methodologies and Supporting Tools

Introduction to Web Services Description Language

Introduction to Simple Object Access Protocol

GreaterCause B2B Integration

Workshop SOAP:style Semantics

Summary

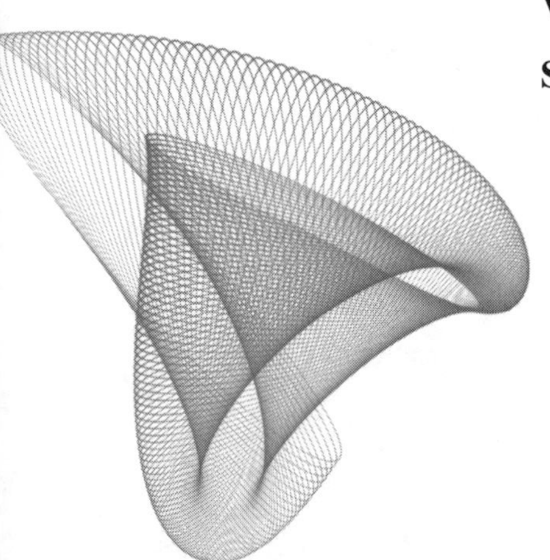

In this chapter, we introduce the Web services technology and the associated standards. We bring to light key aspects of the WSDL and SOAP specification such that readers are able to discern the relationships between WSDL constructs and the corresponding SOAP message constructs. The evolution of systems integration and emergence of Web services as a new way of integrating disparate applications and systems are discussed. The chapter's emphasis is on WSDL, SOAP, and other aspects of Web services technology.

The concepts learned in this chapter are subsequently applied in the creation of a Web service, in the context of our sample application using BEA-provided IDE called WebLogic Workshop. This is covered in the section "GreaterCause B2B Integration," which discusses the integration requirements, the rationale for selecting an appropriate architecture, followed by complete Web service implementation. Web services are built on a stack of technologies in which XML plays an important role in the overall architecture. This chapter does not talk about XML technologies nor the pertinent APIs. To learn more about XML, a good place to begin is http://java.sun.com/xml, http://www.xml.org (hosted by OASIS) and http://www.w3.org/TR/REC-xml (XML specification).

Introduction to Web Services

Software technology emerged from linkage of programming statements into object code and linkage of object code into monolithic programs (applications). Monolithic programs were developed using many different programming languages and operating systems–specific system linkers. Early requirements for process and data integration gave birth to a new business: the systems integration. Systems integration, after years of evolution, arrived at Enterprise Application Integration (EAI). EAI space created a host of new technologies, tools, and processes, and in some cases development methodologies. EAI competitions also created confusing terminologies such as data-centric EAI, process-centric EAI, message-centric EAI, and object broker EAI. Each EAI segment tried to address part of the old "systems integration" problem, but in nonintegrated and broken ways, such as data, process, objects, and messages. Although, traditional EAI made a great improvement in building "integrated solutions," the artificial marketing-driven separation of integration as a whole failed to converge the EAI technology into a uniform eBusiness application construction platform.

On the other hand, the necessity of conducting business on the World Wide Web created an extremely complex set of requirements for building eBusiness applications. Constructing eBusiness applications requires the integration of business functions that are embedded in thousands of applications, each implemented in different programming languages, object models, messaging systems, databases, and operating system platforms. The integration itself is dynamically driven by the business rules and requirements, that is, it is the business rules that decide what business function, and therefore application, should be executed next. Traditional EAI failed because it did not allow for the diversity of things to be integrated in a standard manner and did not deal with business functions at all.

Taking a low-level tour of a single execution thread in an eBusiness application, that is, performing a business function, one may discover that a specific application interface (legacy, CORBA, J2EE, .NET, or just pure Java) has to be invoked within the required application context.

The application context (with or without transaction) may include the application adapter, the messages/parameters that need to be sent to the application, and the application execution engine. The execution engine may be a proprietary application server, a CORBA server, a J2EE server, a .NET server, or it may just be a stand-alone JVM. The execution context may include a Web server (Apache, Tomcat, IIS, and so on). The execution itself may result in generating some new information that needs to be fetched into the next thread of execution in order to perform the next business function. With traditional EAI, extensive development had to take place to develop the adapters and the required messages. The business rules have to be coded either in the applications, adapters, or messages, or all of these entities. Changes to the business rules require changes in execution order, applications, adapters, messages, and other contextual information.

One of the complex spaces that never standardized in the traditional EAI approach was the messaging mechanism. In fact, the proliferation of messaging models resulted in creation of several messaging systems by many EAI vendors. Each messaging system suggests its own way of adapter development, communication models, and protocols. The emergence of XML not only unified the application-messaging paradigm, but it has created significant opportunities for infrastructure vendors to simplify, in a cost-effective manner, the construction of eBusiness applications. Although XML can be used in many different ways, in the context of Web services it can be thought as the "language of the Internet." By "language of the Internet" we mean the XML representation of the information or messages exchanged between the applications. Web services are computer programs that are accessible through the Web. In a typical Web services scenario, a business application sends a request, represented as XML, to a Web service at a given URI. The remote service receives the request, processes it, and returns a response. The XML-based request and response messages are based on a standard format called Simple Object Access Protocol (SOAP). The SOAP specification defines bindings for using SOAP in combination with HTTP and HTTP extension framework; however, SOAP can be potentially used with a variety of other protocols.

Web services cover the RPC model that is epitomized by the EJB or CORBA models and hold the promise of knocking down barriers among operating systems, programming languages, and geography, all in a secure, standards-based manner. Web services and consumers of Web services are typically businesses, making Web services predominantly business-to-business transactions. An enterprise can be the provider of Web services and also the consumer of other Web services. For example, an automobile parts distributor could be in the consumer role when it uses a Web service to check the availability of specific automobile parts, and in the provider role when it supplies prospective customers with different vendors' prices for the automobile parts.

Web services combine the best aspects of component-based development and the Web—delivering true distributed "peer-to-peer" computing. Web services can vary in function from simple operations, like the retrieval of a stock quote, to complex business systems that access and combine information from multiple sources. Web services also can be thought of as the building blocks in the move to distributed computing on the Internet. Enterprise class Web services are usually loosely coupled, asynchronous, and coarse-grained. Loose coupling allows Web service providers to change an implementation without disrupting users. Asynchronous Web services tend to be more scalable than Web services based on Remote Procedure Call (RPC).

There are probably as many definitions of Web service as there are companies building them, but almost all definitions have the following in common:

- Web services expose useful functionality to Web users through a standard Web protocol. In most cases, the protocol used is SOAP.
- Web services provide a way to describe their interfaces in enough detail to allow a user to build a client application to talk to them. This description is usually provided in an XML document called a Web Services Description Language (WSDL) document.
- Web services are registered in directories so that potential users can find them easily. This is done with Universal Discovery, Description, and Integration (UDDI).

A *Web service* is a software system identified by a URI, whose public interfaces and bindings are defined and described using XML. Its definition can be discovered by other software systems. These systems may then interact with the Web service in a manner prescribed by its definition, using XML-based messages conveyed by Internet protocols.

Once a Web service is defined and implemented, it needs to be described with a WSDL file and registered in UDDI. By exposing existing applications such as XML, Web services will allow users to build new, more powerful applications. For example, a user might develop a purchasing application to automatically obtain price information from a variety of vendors, and allow the user to select a vendor, submit the order, and then track the shipment until it is received. The vendor application, in addition to exposing its services on the Web, might in turn use Web services of other businesses to check the customer's credit, charge the customer's account, and set up the shipment with a shipping company. In the next sections, we discuss the three essential Web services building blocks: SOAP, WSDL, and UDDI. SOAP and WSDL are also covered in detail in later sections. The SOAP specification is available at http://www.w3.org/ TR/SOAP, the WSDL specification is available at http://www.w3.org/TR/wsdl, and the UDDI specification is available at www.uddi.org.

What Is SOAP?

SOAP is a lightweight protocol for exchange of information in a decentralized, distributed environment. It is an XML-based protocol that consists of three parts: an envelope that defines a framework for describing what is in a message and how to process it, a set of encoding rules for expressing instances of application-defined data types, and a convention for representing remote procedure calls and responses.

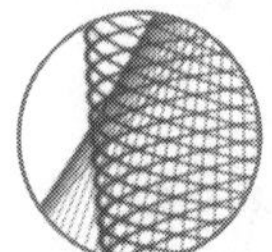

NOTE

From an architectural perspective, making encoding an integral part of the message makes SOAP language neutral.

SOAP is defined as a communications protocol, but unlike DCOM or CORBA, it does not support object activation and does not rely on any naming service. The XML schema for SOAP messages (http://schemas.xmlsoap.org/soap/envelope) specifies a standard structure that needs to be supported by any compliant SOAP implementation.

When using CORBA, the IDL had to be compiled to client- and server-side implementation language in order to produce proper stubs and skeletons. When using SOAP, developers will not have to concern themselves with encoding rules because the vendor-provided tools handle serialization (analogous to parameter marshalling in CORBA) and deserialization (analogous to parameter demarshalling in CORBA) of application-defined datatypes.

SOAP defines two separate styles of messages—the RPC-oriented (messages containing parameters and return values) and document-oriented (messages containing documents). The SOAP RPC defines a convention that can be used to represent remote procedure calls and responses. In an RPC-oriented style, a SOAP request containing a callable function (an operation exposed by a Web service) with associated function parameters is sent from the client to the server. The server returns a response with the results of the executed function. Most current implementations of SOAP are based on RPC-style Web service because programmers who are used to developing COM or CORBA applications easily understand the RPC style.

RPC and document-style Web services are discussed in the section "Introduction to Web Services Description Language."

The SOAP specification defines HTTP bindings that describe how a SOAP message can be carried in HTTP messages, with or without the HTTP extension framework. The HTTP binding is optional, but almost all SOAP implementations support it because it's the only standardized protocol for SOAP. For this reason, there's a common misconception that SOAP requires HTTP. Implementation may support SMTP, FTP, RMI/IIOP, or a proprietary messaging protocol, but most current Web services use HTTP because it is ubiquitous. Since HTTP is a core protocol of the Web, most organizations have a network infrastructure that supports HTTP and people who understand how to manage it. Security, monitoring, and load-balancing infrastructure for HTTP are also readily available.

Generally, Developers who use SOAP don't write SOAP messages directly—instead they use a SOAP toolkit to automate their development. For example, vendor tools like CapeClear, PolarLake, Apache Toolkit, and BEA WebLogic Workshop provide facility for automatically generating SOAP interfaces, for existing EJB, Java, CORBA, and .NET components. These server-side interfaces are exposed to the SOAP client as Web services. A practical example of this scenario using the BEA WebLogic Workshop is discussed in the section "GreaterCause B2B Integration," where the vendor tool handles the Web service protocols, allowing the developers to focus on the business logic embedded in the EJB. By the same token, the Microsoft SOAP Toolkit 2.0 translates COM function calls to SOAP.

SOAP Security

Early in its development, SOAP was seen as an HTTP-based protocol, so the assumption was made that HTTP security would be adequate for SOAP. After all, there are thousands of Web applications running today using HTTP security. When SOAP expanded to become a more general-purpose protocol running on top of a number of transports, security became a bigger issue. For example, HTTP provides means for authenticating which user is making a SOAP call, but how does that identity get propagated when the message is routed from HTTP to an SMTP transport? SOAP was designed as a building-block protocol, so fortunately there are already new specifications in the works. The idea is to build on SOAP so it can provide additional security features for Web services. The WS-Security specification describes enhancements to SOAP messaging to provide quality of protection through message integrity, message confidentiality, and single message authentication. It's a mechanism for accommodating a wide variety of security models and encryption technologies—this and related specifications are available at http://xml.coverpages.org/ws-security.html. The section "Introduction to Simple Object Access Protocol" presents additional discussion on SOAP.

What Is WSDL?

WSDL stands for Web Services Description Language. A WSDL document contains XML constructs for describing network services as collections of communication endpoints capable of exchanging messages. It also provides a recipe for automating the details involved in application communication. A WSDL file describes SOAP messages and how the messages are exchanged. In other words, WSDL is to SOAP what IDL is to CORBA. Since WSDL is XML, it is readable and editable; however, in most cases, it is generated and consumed by software tools. WSDL specifies, in XML notation, what a request message must contain and what the response message will look like. The notation that a WSDL file uses to describe messages is based on the XML schema standard, which makes the Web services both programming-language neutral and accessible from a wide variety of platforms.

In addition to describing request and response messages, WSDL defines the location of the Web service and the communication protocol used for accessing the service. This means that the WSDL file defines everything required to communicate with a Web service. Fortunately, there are several tools available to read a WSDL file and generate the code required to communicate with a Web service. The existing SOAP toolkits include tools to generate WSDL files from existing program interfaces (such as CORBA IDL, EJB, and .NET components). Like CORBA IDL tools, these tools can generate proxies and stubs used by Web services clients. The WSDL specification can be found at http://www.w3.org/TR/wsdl. The section "Introduction to Web Services Description Language" discusses the details of the WSDL.

What Is UDDI?

Universal Discovery, Description, and Integration can be seen as the yellow pages of Web services. As with traditional yellow pages, one can search for a company that offers the required services, read about the service offered, and contact someone for more information. If the Web service is designed and planned to be accessible by many clients, it should be registered with the UDDI. A UDDI directory entry is an XML document that describes a business and the services it offers. There are three parts to an entry in the UDDI directory. The "white pages" describe the company offering the service—name, address, contacts, and so on. The "yellow pages" include industrial categories based on standard taxonomies such as the North American Industry Classification System and the Standard Industrial Classification. The "green pages" describe the interface to the service in enough detail for someone to write an application to use the Web service. Services are defined through a UDDI document called a Type Model, or tModel. In many cases, the tModel contains a WSDL document that describes a SOAP-based Web service, but the tModel is flexible enough to describe almost any kind of service.

One of the primary potential uses of Web services is for business-to-business integration. For example, a company might expose a movie ticket purchasing Web service that allows its consumers to send requests over the Internet. If a travel agency wanted to purchase movie tickets over the Internet, it would need to search for all vendors who sell movie tickets. To do this, the travel agency will require a directory of all businesses that expose Web services. This directory is called Universal Description, Discovery, and Integration, or UDDI.

Like a typical yellow-pages directory, UDDI provides a database of businesses searchable by the type of business. You typically search using business taxonomy such as the North American Industry Classification System (NAICS) or the Standard Industrial Classification (SIC). You could also search by business name or geographical location. Going back to our example, the travel agency could search UDDI for NAICS and some identifier, perhaps "entertainment." This search would return a list of companies registered with UDDI that sell movie tickets.

Web services exposing functionality for use by other businesses are registered with UDDI. Services are grouped by a type. The service type has a unique identifier and comes from a pool of well-known service types that are registered with UDDI. These service types are called tModels in UDDI terminology. Each tModel has a name, description, and a unique identifier. This unique identifier is a Universal Unique Identifier (UUID) and is called the tModelKey. By having a pool of well-known service types, UDDI makes it possible to find out how to do electronic business with a company. The UDDI directory may be searched in several ways. For example, one can search for providers of a service in a specified geographic location or for business of a specified type. The search may result in information such as contacts, links, and technical data that can be used to evaluate against service requirements.

Web Services Architecture

Let's observe the Web services architecture in the context of a distributed computing environment. The basic requirements for a network node to play the role of requestor or provider in XML messaging–based distributed computing are the ability to build and/or parse a SOAP message and the ability to communicate over a network. There are two important actors in the SOAP model. One actor is the network node that plays the role of requestor, which might be a Web service executing on a network computer (node) requesting the service of another Web service. The other actor is another network node that plays the role of a provider: this is a Web service executing on a network computer (node) providing the service. Note that a provider of a service may in turn make several requests to other providers to complete a request; by the same token the requestor of a Web service could be a Web service trying to satisfy other requests. So a Web service may play the role of both the provider and the requester. Since SOAP messages are represented in XML, there has to be some mechanism on both the client and the server side to build and/or parse a SOAP message. These functions in most cases can be provided by a SOAP server running in an HTTP server. The SOAP server implements the functionality expressed by the SOAP specification. Given this summary, a service-oriented architecture of Web services environment is illustrated in Figure 8-1.

Figure 8-1 illustrates Web-service1 hosted in a SOAP server and running in an HTTP server at http://www.business1.com. Web-service2 is hosted in a SOAP server running in an HTTP

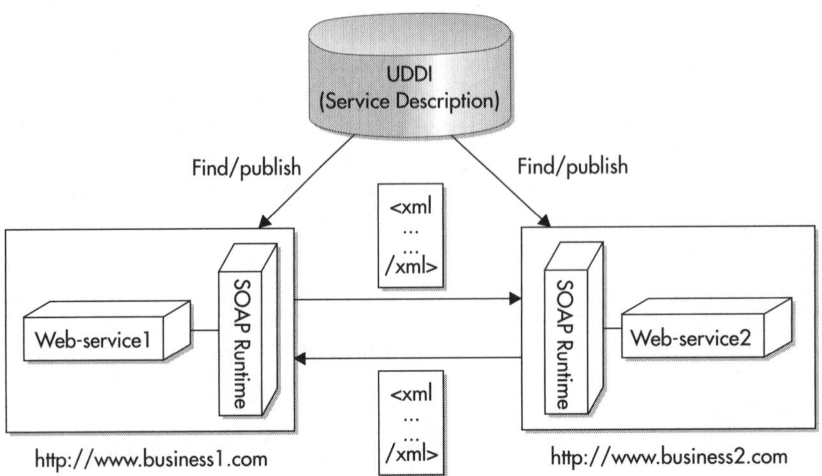

Figure 8-1 *Service-oriented architecture: peer-to-peer pattern*

server at http://www.business2.com. The UDDI services are also exposed as Web services according to the UDDI standards, but for simplicity's sake we do not show this in the diagram.

The following discussion summarizes this architecture by tracing a request-response transmission between the requestor (assuming Web-service1 is in the role of the requestor) and the provider (assuming Web-service2 is in the role of the provider) of Figure 8-1. The service requestor could very well be a requestor that may not be a Web service, however, to demonstrate a service-centric architecture we assume that several Web services may need to interact for fulfilling the original service request.

1. Web-service1 (the requestor) creates a SOAP message that invokes the operation exposed by Web-service2 (the provider). The XML payload in the body of the message can be a RPC-style or a document-style message. We discuss these two styles of messaging when discussing WSDL in the section "Introduction to Web Services Description Language." The Web-service1 presents this message together with the network address of the Web-service2 to the SOAP infrastructure (SOAP client runtime). The SOAP client runtime interacts with an underlying network protocol (such as HTTP) to send the SOAP message over the network. The network infrastructure delivers the message to Web-service2's SOAP runtime which is the SOAP server.
2. The SOAP server routes the request message to Web-service2. The SOAP runtime is responsible for converting the XML message into programming language–specific objects if required by the Web-service2 implementation. This conversion is governed by the encoding schemes specified within the message. Web-service2 is responsible for processing the request message and formulating a response. The response is also a SOAP message. The response SOAP message is presented to the SOAP runtime with Web-service1 as the destination.

3. The response message is received by the networking infrastructure on the Web-service1's node. The message is routed through the SOAP infrastructure; the SOAP runtime will potentially convert the XML message into objects corresponding to the target programming language, that is the implementation language of Web-service1.
4. The response message is then presented to the Web-service1.

In this architecture, the granularity is at the service level and not the object or component level; component in this context means EJB, .NET, CORBA, or Java bean components and objects that are not executable entities unless they are packaged, according to their component model, into a coarser-grained entity known as a container; the containers ultimately execute in their respective application servers (J2EE, .NET, CORBA). From granularity perspective, a Web service is analogous to a container. Services are the entities known at the network level (distribution) that expose their public interfaces as contracts to the outside world. Interacting services can be hosted on any operating system platform and can be implemented in any programming language.

SOAP provides semantic constructs like the SOAP *Header* element, which adds more flexibility to this service-oriented architecture. For example, using the flexibility and extensibility of XML, a *Header* element can be modified by an intermediary service along the message path and passed to the next service. The semantics of header entries are only known between the sender and the receiver, a receiver cannot forward the *Header* element to the next application in the SOAP message path; however, the recipient may insert a similar *Header* element but in that case, the contract is between that application and the recipient of the *Header* element. The header entries assist in adding extra semantics to the message being delivered. For example, a *Header* element may provide a transaction ID that is not part of the application code but instead part of an infrastructure component; by adding a header entry with a transaction ID, the transaction manager on the receiving side can extract the ID and use it without affecting the SOAP construct that represents a remote procedure call. Therefore, the header part of a message can include information pertinent to extended Web services functionality, such as transaction context, security, orchestration information, or message routing information.

Figure 8-1 showed the software agents participating in the basic architecture. The Web Services Architecture document specifies an extended architecture that describes Web services support for message exchange patterns (MEPs) that group basic messages into higher-level interactions, details how support for features such as security, transactions, orchestration, privacy, and others may be represented in SOAP messages, and describes how additional features can be added to support business-level interactions.

In a service-oriented architecture, many different kinds of interactions between service requester and service provider are possible. *One-way* interaction is comprised of a message sent from a requestor to a provider, *Conversational* interaction comprises several messages exchanged between a requestor and a provider, and *Many-to-Many* interaction comprises a message sent from a requestor to many providers, or a service provider responds to many requestors. These interactions can be defined by a choreography language. More information is available at www.w3.org/TR/ws-arch.

Development Methodologies and Supporting Tools

At the time of writing this book, Web services–related technologies are still growing. It is predictable that several related specifications will be added to the existing specifications. For example, Microsoft is working on some of these supporting Web services–related specifications. These specifications will extend the Web services environment by including infrastructure services that will define operational management functions such as ability to route messages among many servers and dynamic configuration of servers. These services are specified in the WS-Routing specification and the WS-Referral specification. More information about these specifications is available at http://msdn.microsoft.com/library/en-us/dnglobspec/html/ws-routing.asp and http://msdn.microsoft.com/library/en-us/dnglobspec/html/ws-referral.asp.

Dealing with protocol-specific constructs and programming models makes it difficult to develop Web services. Fortunately numerous vendors offer Web service development tools; companies like CapeClear, Polarlake, BEA, IBM, IONA, and others provide visual tools for editing XML, and automatic creation of Web service interface from existing legacy components like Java classes, EJBs, CORBA, and .NET components. Most of these tools allow development, deployment, and maintenance of Web services–based applications.

Web services are good candidates for widely used legacy systems. Message-oriented middleware (MOM) and transaction managers like IBM MQSeries, Microsoft MSMQ, Tibco Rendezvous, BEA MessageQ, and BEA Tuxedo offer out-of-the-box Web services interfaces, ready for plugging into a larger business solutions.

Web services can

- Create new business opportunities and value-add for customers, by exposing services over the Internet.
- Revitalize and/or reuse existing applications with new, powerful, and integrated business solutions.
- Increase developer productivity by simplifying the task of distributed systems development.
- Provide a standards-based solution, which in turn provides a portable and extensible solution, therefore "future proofing" the investment in integration technologies.

Although it is outside the scope of this book to discuss specific development paradigms for Web services, we briefly discuss a development methodology recommended by Object Management Group (OMG). OMG proposes a model-driven architecture (MDA), which tries to simplify the challenging problem of dealing with multiple industry standards and competing middleware architectures and information models/vocabularies. MDA tries to simplify this problem by unifying these diverse technologies using information models/designs and mapping these models to one or more implementation technologies (middleware, databases, languages, and so on). MDA also raises the level of abstraction at which these applications and integration scenarios can be designed and implemented, which is a key requirement to managing software integration complexity. MDA defines a software architecture that complements existing middleware, and modeling tools, and allows integration and interoperability to be addressed across the application life cycle and not just between individual objects or components. MDA provides an open, vendor-neutral approach to the challenge of interoperability, building upon and leveraging the UML, Meta-Object Facility (MOF), and Common Warehouse Meta-Model (CWM) standards. MDA allows a developer to design a model of an application or a component only once, and automatically map this model to several technologies. Additional information about MDA is available at http://www.omg.org/mda.

Other methodologies may be used by some mainstream tool vendors. For example, Polarlake's "Transactional XML." Transactional XML suggests a programming model where XML is at the center of the architecture. Transactional XML has the following modes:

- **Web services** Exposing existing IT assets, and providing mechanisms for discovering and interacting with those assets. Typically, a Web service exposes the assets as a series of remote procedure calls. These services fit into the larger eCommerce context using XML integrations .
- **XML services** Similar to Web services, without the notion of request-response model implicit in Web services.
- **XML integrations** Creating process flows from combinations of Web services and XML services.
- **XML applications** Creating new applications from a combination of XML integrations and services.

This methodology is useful in composing coarse-grained solutions by aggregating fine-grained solutions. It promotes modularity and reuse. Further information is available at www.polarlake.com.

From an application and component architecture perspective, Web service adds a new way of integrating the existing legacy applications, components, and systems into larger solutions. Note that applications and components themselves will still be designed, developed, and deployed using their respective mainstream object models, specifically J2EE, .NET, and CORBA. For example, one may use a tool to generate Web service interface from an exiting CORBA application, or one can implement a new Web service, by first implementing its business logic using any mainstream object model and then generating the required WSDL.

The Web services standard can be broken into three parts:

- **SOAP** The communication protocol
- **WSDL** The service description
- **UDDI** A directory through which one can query for an existing Web service

The following sections visit WSDL and SOAP standards. The method used to describe these standards is broken into two steps. The first step introduces the standard using its formal definition. In this step we provide an abstract summary of the formal specification developed by W3C. In the second step, we provide an example of how the standard applies to a real-world problem.

Introduction to Web Services Description Language

WSDL was originally designed by IBM, Microsoft, and Ariba to provide a standard mechanism for describing Web services. This work was then submitted to the W3C for standardization and has grown to encompass a large number of vendors. Similar to CORBA IDL, WSDL was designed to meet the needs of distributed systems. WSDL is a standard format for describing Web service interfaces. Using WSDL, tools can automate the generation of proxies for Web services in a language-independent and platform-independent way. Like CORBA IDL, a WSDL file is a contract between client and server.

Note that WSDL has been designed such that it can express bindings to protocols other than SOAP. In this chapter, we examine WSDL as it relates to SOAP over HTTP.

Summary of the WSDL Formal Specification

The elements within a WSDL document can be divided into two groups: the service interface definition and service implementation definition. A service interface definition is an abstract or reusable service definition that may be referenced by multiple service implementation definitions. This is analogous to defining an abstract interface in a programming language and having multiple concrete implementations. The service interface contains three elements that comprise the reusable portion of the service description, including `<types>`, `<message>`, `<portType>`, and `<binding>` elements. The service implementation definition describes how a particular service interface is implemented by a given service provider, and it also describes its location so that a requestor can interact with it. In WSDL, a Web service is modeled as a `<service>` element. It contains a collection of `<port>` elements—the `<port>` element associates a URL (endpoint) with a `<binding>` element from the service interface definition. This discussed in more detail below.

WSDL documents use the following elements for defining network services:

- **Types** Machine- and language-independent type definitions are specified by the `<types>` element. This element provides data type definitions used in messages using some type system. For maximum interoperability and platform neutrality, WSDL prefers the use of XSD as the canonical type system.
- **Message** Abstract, typed definition of the data being transmitted. A message consists of logical parts, each of which is associated with a type-definition within some type system or encoding scheme. A message can be thought of as an operation/method parameter.
- **Operation** Abstract description of an action supported by the service. An operation element, including its sub-elements, collectively define a signature (operation name, input parameters, and output parameters). There are four forms of primitive operations based on the nature of the interaction: one-way, request-response, notification, and solicit-response.
- **PortType** Abstract interface (set of operations) supported by one or more endpoints. An interface refers to one or more operations, input messages, and output messages. Like the CORBA IDL interface, a `<portType>` element including its sub-elements collectively define a group of operations.

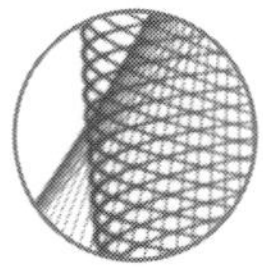

NOTE

Recapping this discussion, the `<portType>` is an abstract interface that consists of abstract `<operation>`(s). `<operation>` has parameters defined by abstract `<message>`(s). Each `<message>` parameter is defined within the `<types>` element.

- **Binding** Specifies concrete protocol and data format specifications for the `<operation>`(s) and `<message>`(s) defined by a particular `<portType>`. A `<portType>` is abstract and not realizable unless associated with a `<binding>`. Similar to a Java class that implements an Interface, a `<binding>` provides the implementation details for the `<portType>`.
- **Port** Specifies an address for a binding, thus defining a single communication endpoint. It is actually defining the network address (IP) of the machine that is hosting the service.
- **Service** Specifies a collection of related ports that make up the service. This has the effect of packaging all the previously discussed elements into a single service offering.

We recap these definitions with a WSDL document in the next subsection. One way of looking at a WSDL file is that it determines what gets sent over the wire. WSDL, in addition to defining the "interface contract," also specifies the transport protocol for interacting with the service interface. WSDL also specifies whether SOAP messages employ RPC- or document-style semantics. An RPC-style message looks like a function call with zero or more parameters, and employs the request-response semantics, whereas a document-style message is used for exchanging an XML document. We elaborate further on this in later sections.

A Closer Look at a Sample WSDL File

WSDL is very verbose. To understand each element of a WSDL construct, we use a very simple example. We take a bottom-up approach starting with a Java class with a single method. We examine the automatically generated WSDL representation of our simple Java class. As noted earlier, developers will usually use a tool for generating the WSDL; in our case we have employed the BEA WebLogic Workshop for building this simple Web service example. Think of WSDL as our contract on the Internet to the outside world—in this section we generate WSDL for the simple service *MyService* shown here:

```
public class MyService {
    public int foo(int arg) {
        return arg;
    }
}
```

This Java class contains a method *foo()*, which accepts an integer parameter and returns the same value. A WSDL document needs to be created for describing *foo()* within the context of a Web service. The following WSDL has been generated using the BEA WebLogic Workshop tool; as such, some of the URIs used in this document are BEA specific. The WSDL document shown can be used by any SOAP client to access *MyService*'s (the Web service) *foo()* method.

Observe the complexity of representing a simple service using WSDL. We discuss each element of the following WSDL document later in this section.

```
<?xml version="1.0" encoding="UTF-8"?>
<definitions xmlns="http://schemas.xmlsoap.org/wsdl/"
xmlns:conv="http://www.openuri.org/2002/04/soap/conversation/"
xmlns:cw="http://www.openuri.org/2002/04/wsdl/conversation/"
xmlns:http="http://schemas.xmlsoap.org/wsdl/http/"
 xmlns:jms="http://www.openuri.org/2002/04/wsdl/jms/"
 xmlns:mime="http://schemas.xmlsoap.org/wsdl/mime/"
 xmlns:s="http://www.w3.org/2001/XMLSchema"
xmlns:s0="http://www.openuri.org/"
 xmlns:soap="http://schemas.xmlsoap.org/wsdl/soap/"
 xmlns:soapenc="http://schemas.xmlsoap.org/soap/encoding/"
 xmlns:xm="http://www.bea.com/2002/04/xmlmap/"
 targetNamespace="http://www.openuri.org/">
     <types>
          <s:schema attributeFormDefault="qualified"
                    elementFormDefault="qualified"
                    targetNamespace="http://www.openuri.org/">
               <s:element name="foo">
                    <s:complexType>
                         <s:sequence>
                              <s:element minOccurs="1" maxOccurs="1"
                                              name="arg" type="s:int"/>
                         </s:sequence>
                    </s:complexType>
               </s:element>
               <s:element name="fooResponse">
                    <s:complexType>
                         <s:sequence>
                              <s:element minOccurs="1" maxOccurs="1"
                                              name="fooResult" type="s:int"/>
                         </s:sequence>
                    </s:complexType>
               </s:element>
               <s:element name="int" type="s:int"/>
          </s:schema>
     </types>
     <message name="fooSoapIn">
          <part name="parameters" element="s0:foo"/>
     </message>
     <message name="fooSoapOut">
          <part name="parameters" element="s0:fooResponse"/>
     </message>
     <message name="fooHttpGetIn">
          <part name="arg" type="s:string"/>
     </message>
     <message name="fooHttpGetOut">
          <part name="Body" element="s0:int"/>
```

```
</message>
<message name="fooHttpPostIn">
     <part name="arg" type="s:string"/>
</message>
<message name="fooHttpPostOut">
     <part name="Body" element="s0:int"/>
</message>
<portType name="MyServiceSoap">
     <operation name="foo">
          <input message="s0:fooSoapIn"/>
          <output message="s0:fooSoapOut"/>
     </operation>
</portType>
<portType name="MyServiceHttpGet">
     <operation name="foo">
          <input message="s0:fooHttpGetIn"/>
          <output message="s0:fooHttpGetOut"/>
     </operation>
</portType>
<portType name="MyServiceHttpPost">
     <operation name="foo">
          <input message="s0:fooHttpPostIn"/>
          <output message="s0:fooHttpPostOut"/>
     </operation>
</portType>
<binding name="MyServiceSoap" type="s0:MyServiceSoap">
     <soap:binding transport="http://schemas.xmlsoap.org/soap/http"
                    style="document"/>
     <operation name="foo">
          <soap:operation soapAction="http://www.openuri.org/foo"
                          style="document"/>
          <input>
               <soap:body use="literal"/>
          </input>
          <output>
               <soap:body use="literal"/>
          </output>
     </operation>
</binding>
<binding name="MyServiceHttpGet" type="s0:MyServiceHttpGet">
     <http:binding verb="GET"/>
     <operation name="foo">
          <http:operation location="/foo"/>
          <input>
               <http:urlEncoded/>
          </input>
          <output>
               <mime:mimeXml part="Body"/>
          </output>
```

```
            </operation>
        </binding>
        <binding name="MyServiceHttpPost" type="s0:MyServiceHttpPost">
            <http:binding verb="POST"/>
            <operation name="foo">
                <http:operation location="/foo"/>
                <input>
                    <mime:content type="application/x-www-form-urlencoded"/>
                </input>
                <output>
                    <mime:mimeXml part="Body"/>
                </output>
            </operation>
        </binding>
        <service name="MyService">
            <port name="MyServiceSoap" binding="s0:MyServiceSoap">
                <soap:address
                        location="http://server1:7001/WS_MyService/MyService.jws"/>
              </port>
            <port name="MyServiceHttpGet" binding="s0:MyServiceHttpGet">
<http:address
                  location="http://server1:7001/WS_MyService/MyService.jws"/>
            </port>
            <port name="MyServiceHttpPost" binding="s0:MyServiceHttpPost">
                <http:address
                    location="http://server1:7001/WS_MyService/MyService.jws"/>
            </port>
        </service>
</definitions>
```

You will probably agree that for the simple service depicted by class *MyService*, one will not want to manually define WSDL. Developing Web services without the use of advanced tools is not recommended. Once the WSDL is created, the vendor tool can help create stubs and proxies, and the Web service can be subsequently used by a SOAP client written in any programming language. The wide availability of tools to automate development of Web services from existing server-side components allows the developer to focus on developing business services rather than develop any infrastructure components. Developing a Web service requires two steps:

1. Implement the business logic in a server-side component. This is discussed in Chapter 7.
2. Expose the business component interface as a Web service using WSDL. This is the subject of this section.

WSDL data typing is based on "XML Schema: Datatypes" (XSD), which is now a W3C recommendation. There are different versions of this document (1999, 2000, and 2001), and declaring it as one of the namespace attributes in the `<definitions>` element specifies which version is used in our WSDL file. For instance the declaration, *xmlns:s="http://www.w3*

.org/2001/XMLSchema", makes all the predefined types, specified in the XMLSchema 2001 version, available to the *MyService* WSDL definition. This namespace is referred by other constructs using the *s* prefix, as in *s:int*, which makes a reference to the predefined type *int* defined in the XMLSchema.

WSDL Namespaces

Several namespaces have been declared in the root element `<definitions>`. These namespace declarations provide a shorthand for each namespace used in the document. For instance *xmlns:xsd* defines a shorthand *xsd* for the namespace http://www.w3.org/ 2001/XMLSchema. This enables references to this namespace later in the document simply by prefixing (or "qualifying") a name with *xsd:* as in *xsd:int*, which is a qualified type name. Normal scoping rules apply for the shorthand prefixes. For example, a prefix defined in an element only holds within that element.

The purpose of namespaces is to avoid naming conflicts. It is similar to namespace in C++ or in the Java programming language. Two separate Java packages may define the same variable or method names. An importer of these packages can refer to a name, unambiguously, if package qualification is used. In our example, all types in the *conv* namespace can be referenced by using *conv:typename. conv:* is a shorthand for http://www.openuri.org/2002/04/soap/conversation/.

Note that URIs are used as namespaces because they guarantee uniqueness. The location pointed to by the URI does not have to correspond to a real Web location. The *targetNamespace* attribute declares a namespace to which all element names declared within the *MyService* WSDL will belong. In the sample WSDL file, the *targetNamespace* specified in `<definitions>` is http://www.openuri.org/.

In the sample GreaterCause example discussed later, you will observe that the targetNamespace is www.GreaterCause.com, and the corresponding datatypes as seen by the clients of the Web service will use com.GreaterCause.www as package prefix.

Types

The `<types>` element may be omitted if there are no data types that need to be declared. For those who programmed CORBA IDL, this section resembles IDL type definitions that are used by the IDL operation definitions. For maximum interoperability and platform neutrality, WSDL prefers the use of XSD as the canonical type system, and treats it as an intrinsic type system. This is apparent from the use of the namespace *xmlns:s="http://www.w3.org/2001/XMLSchema"* in our sample WSDL.

```
<types>
    <s:schema ...>
        <s:element name="foo">
            <s:complexType>
                <s:sequence>
                    <s:element minOccurs="1" maxOccurs="1"
                               name="arg" type="s:int"/>
                </s:sequence>
            </s:complexType>
        </s:element>
        <s:element name="fooResponse">
```

```
            <s:complexType>
                <s:sequence>
                    <s:element minOccurs="1" maxOccurs="1"
                               name="fooResult" type="s:int"/>
                </s:sequence>
            </s:complexType>
        </s:element>
        <s:element name="int" type="s:int"/>
    </s:schema>
</types>
```

The type names *"arg"* and *"fooResponse"* are defined within the body of the <types> element using the <s:element> element. These definitions are subsequently used within the <message> element to define the parameters—this is done using the *name* and *element* attributes of its subordinate <part> element.

Messages

A <message> element defines the parameters for an operation/method. Each <part> child element in the <message> element corresponds to a parameter that is passed to the operation. Input parameters are defined in a single <message> element, separate from output parameters, which have their own <message> elements. Parameters that are both input and output have their corresponding <part> elements in both input and output <message> elements. By convention, the name of a return <message> element ends in *Response*, as in *fooResponse* to correspond to the method *foo*. Each <part> element has a *name* and *type* attribute, just as a *method* parameter has both a name and a type, where the attribute *element* refers to the element we described using the <element> construct in the <types> section. When used for document exchange (in contrast to RPC operations), WSDL allows the use of <message> elements to describe the document to be exchanged. The message-typing attribute *element* refers to an XSD element using a *QName* (prefixed by *s0:*). The message-typing attribute *type* refers to an XSD *simpleType* or *complexType* using a *QName* (prefixed by *s:*). Prefix *s0:* refers to *targetNamespace="http://www.openuri.org/*, which is the namespace associated with this WSDL, and therefore references the elements with name *foo* and *fooResponse* from the <types> section. Prefix *s:* refers to *xmlns:s= "http://www.w3.org/2001/XMLSchema* and the related XSD type system. A message binding describes how the abstract content is mapped into a concrete format. We cover a more complex scenario when discussing the sample application's (GreaterCause) Web service implementation in the section "Web Service Implementation."

```
<message name="fooSoapIn">
    <part name="parameters" element="s0:foo"/>
</message>
<message name="fooSoapOut">
    <part name="parameters" element="s0:fooResponse"/>
</message>
<message name="fooHttpGetIn">
```

```
    <part name="arg" type="s:string"/>
</message>
<message name="fooHttpGetOut">
    <part name="Body" element="s0:int"/>
</message>
<message name="fooHttpPostIn">
    <part name="arg" type="s:string"/>
</message>
<message name="fooHttpPostOut">
    <part name="Body" element="s0:int"/>
</message>
```

The WSDL tool generated <message> elements for three separate bindings—fixed XML, HTTP *Get*, and HTTP *Post* as follows:

- **For XML binding** *fooSoapIn, fooSoapOut*
- **For HTTP *Get* binding** *fooHttpGetIn, fooHttpGetOut*
- **For HTTP *Post* binding** *foorHttpPostIn, fooHttpPostOut*

The message names provide a unique name for messages defined within the enclosing WSDL document, while the part name provides a unique name among all parts within the enclosing message.

Port Types

A <portType> element defines one or more abstract operations using <operation> elements. For our simple service, *MyService* the tool produces three separate contracts as follows. Notice that the messages bound to the various operations have been defined in the current namespace (prefixed by *s0:*) using the <message> elements discussed in the preceding subsection.

```
<portType name="MyServiceSoap">
    <operation name="foo">
        <input message="s0:fooSoapIn"/>
        <output message="s0:fooSoapOut"/>
    </operation>
</portType>
<portType name="MyServiceHttpGet">
    <operation name="foo">
        <input message="s0:fooHttpGetIn"/>
        <output message="s0:fooHttpGetOut"/>
    </operation>
</portType>
<portType name="MyServiceHttpPost">
    <operation name="foo">
        <input message="s0:fooHttpPostIn"/>
```

```
        <output message="s0:fooHttpPostOut"/>
    </operation>
</portType>
```

The port type name attribute provides a unique name among all port types defined within the enclosing WSDL document. *MyServiceSoap* allows access to *MyService* using standard fixed XML format (document-style messages). *MyServiceHttpGet* allows access to *MyService* using a standard HTTP *Get* call, and *MyServiceHttpPost* allows access to *MyService* using a standard HTTP *Post* call. These abstract operations (contracts) will "bind" to their corresponding concrete protocols and associated data formats using the `<binding>` element discussed in the next section. The `<operation>` element can have one, two, or three child elements, namely, the `<input>`, `<output>`, and `<fault>` elements. These constructs specify how SOAP messages are constructed; this is discussed further in the section "Introduction to Simple Object Access Protocol." WSDL has four transmission primitives or message exchange patterns that an endpoint can support.

- **One-way** The endpoint receives a message. Only the `<input>` element is specified for the corresponding WSDL construct. This is used for creating asynchronous services. In this scenario, the client application that invokes the Web service never receives a response, including any exceptions.
- **Request-response** The endpoint receives a message, and sends a correlated message. This model is used in the GreaterCause example. In this scenario, the `<input>`, `<output>`, and an optional `<fault>` element specify the abstract message format.
- **Solicit-response** The endpoint sends a message, and receives a correlated message. In this scenario, the `<input>`, `<output>` and an optional `<fault>` element specify the abstract message format. Specification precedes `<input>` and `<fault>` specifications.
- **Notification** The endpoint sends a message. Only the `<output>` element is specified for the corresponding WSDL construct.

WSDL refers to these primitives as operations. Although request-response or solicit-response can be modeled abstractly using two one-way messages, it is useful to model these as primitive operation types. These primitives represent message exchange patterns. Although the request-response or the solicit-response operations are semantically related, they may be implemented as part of one or two actual network communications. The primitives are merely an abstract representation. It is the binding that will specify how the messages are actually sent. WSDL only defines bindings for one-way and request-response primitives.

Bindings

The purpose of the `<binding>` element is to specify how each `<operation>`, with corresponding parameters, and the correlated response is sent over the wire using the SOAP message format. The immediate child elements of the `<binding>` element are used to specify the concrete grammar for the input, output, and fault messages. In *MyService* WSDL snippet shown below, the `<soap:binding>` element specifies the protocol (using the *transport* attribute) and data format (using *style* attribute) for each <operation> scoped within the parent <binding> element. Each binding must specify exactly one protocol. SOAP allows each operation to be realized using a different invocation style. Let's examine the binding *MyServiceSoap*, which specifies document-style message exchange; this is the first <binding> element in the following snippet. The binding *MyServiceSoap* references the corresponding *portType* that it binds using the *type* attribute.

```
<binding name="MyServiceSoap" type="s0:MyServiceSoap">
    <soap:binding transport="http://schemas.xmlsoap.org/soap/http"
                  style="document"/>
    <operation name="foo">
        <soap:operation soapAction="http://www.openuri.org/foo"
                        style="document"/>
        <input>
            <soap:body use="literal"/>
        </input>
        <output>
            <soap:body use="literal"/>
        </output>
    </operation>
</binding>
<binding name="MyServiceHttpGet" type="s0:MyServiceHttpGet">
    <http:binding verb="GET"/>
    <operation name="foo">
        <http:operation location="/foo"/>
        <input>
            <http:urlEncoded/>
        </input>
        <output>
            <mime:mimeXml part="Body"/>
        </output>
    </operation>
</binding>
<binding name="MyServiceHttpPost" type="s0:MyServiceHttpPost">
    <http:binding verb="POST"/>
    <operation name="foo">
        <http:operation location="/foo"/>
        <input>
            <mime:content type="application/x-www-form-urlencoded"/>
        </input>
        <output>
            <mime:mimeXml part="Body"/>
        </output>
    </operation>
</binding>
```

For binding *MyServiceSoap*, the *transport* attribute in the WSDL fragment instructs the SOAP runtime to use HTTP as the transport because it is set to http://schemas.xmlsoap.org/ soap/ http. The transport attribute also instructs it to use document-oriented messages, because the *style* attribute of the `<soap:binding>` element is set to *"document"*; the value of the *style* attribute is the default attribute for each contained `<soap:operation>` element. The `<operation>` element with name=*"foo"* specifies binding information for the operation *foo* defined in the *portType* element. The following snippet is a mapping of the *MyServiceSOAP* binding construct to its corresponding SOAP message (wire format):

```
<SOAP-ENV:Envelope
  xmlns:SOAP-ENV="http://schemas.xmlsoap.org/soap/envelope/"
  SOAP-ENV:encodingStyle="http://schemas.xmlsoap.org/soap/encoding/">
   <SOAP-ENV:Body>
       <m:foo xmlns:m="http://www.openuri.org/">
           <arg>2222</arg>
       </m:foo>
   </SOAP-ENV:Body>
</SOAP-ENV:Envelope>
```

The `<soap:body>` element specifies how the message parts appear inside the SOAP *Body* element. When the operation *'style'* attribute is *'rpc'*, each part is a parameter or a return value and appears inside a wrapper element within the body (refer to section 7.1 of the SOAP specification). This wrapper element in named identically to the operation name. Each message part appears under the wrapper, represented by an accessor named identically to the corresponding parameter of the call. If the operation *'style'* attribute is *'document'*, there are no additional wrappers, and the message parts appear directly under the SOAP *Body* element. A comparison between *'rpc'* and *'document'* style messages is discussed in the section "Workshop *SOAP:style* Semantics."

The mandatory *'use'* attribute indicates whether the message parts (the parameters of *foo*) are encoded using some encoding rules, or whether the parts define the concrete schema of the message. If the *'use'* attribute is set to *'encoded'*, each message part references an abstract type using the *'type'* attribute. In our example, the use is set to *"literal"* meaning that each part of the message (that is, *foo*'s parameters) references a concrete definition using the *'element'* or *'type'* attribute specified in the message elements. Note that WSDL includes a binding for HTTP 1.1's *GET* and *POST* verbs in order to describe the interaction between an HTTP client and an HTTP server. For details on serialization rules for message parts, please refer to the SOAP specification at http://www.w3.org/TR/SOAP/.

Observe the use of `<http:urlEncoded/>` in the binding *MyServiceHttpGet*. The *urlEncoded* element indicates that all message parts are encoded into the HTTP request URI using the standard URI-encoding rules.

Services

The services element contains `<port>` elements, each of which refers to a `<binding>` element discussed previously. A port defines an endpoint; it specifies the location of the Web service and the associated binding. In our sample *MyService* WSDL, the following construct is created for identifying the *MyService* Web service:

```
<service name="MyService">
  <port name="MyServiceSoap" binding="s0:MyServiceSoap">
    <soap:address
        location="http://server1:7001/WS_MyService/MyService.jws"/>
  </port>
  <port name="MyServiceHttpGet" binding="s0:MyServiceHttpGet">
    <http:address
        location="http://server1:7001/WS_MyService/MyService.jws"/>
  </port>
  <port name="MyServiceHttpPost" binding="s0:MyServiceHttpPost">
    <http:address
        location="http://server1:7001/WS_MyService/MyService.jws"/>
  </port>
</service>
```

MyServiceSoap defines the endpoint for *MyService*. The tool generated three separate bindings (XML, HTTP *GET*, and HTTP *POST*), and defined a corresponding port for each binding. Note that all locations point to *MyService*, implying that the same service can be called by three different clients, each associated with a different binding. Each port provides semantically equivalent behavior. The SOAPAction attribute of the HTTP header specifies the URI of the end point servicing the SOAP request.

Introduction to Simple Object Access Protocol

Similar to the WSDL definition, we visit the SOAP constructs, which are important in context of service-centric architecture. Especially, we discuss the constructs that add flexibility to a service-centric architecture and provide mechanisms for better B2B implementation.

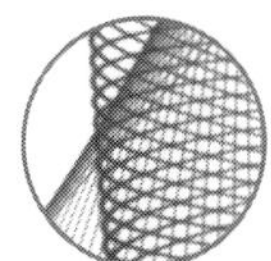

NOTE

A SOAP message is an XML document that consists of a mandatory SOAP envelope, an optional SOAP header, and a mandatory SOAP body. This XML document is referred to as a SOAP message as per the SOAP specification.

A SOAP message contains the following:

- **Envelope** The envelope is the root element of the XML document representing the message. The element must be present in a SOAP message and may contain namespace declarations and additional attributes. The envelope contains an optional SOAP header, and a mandatory SOAP body.
- **Header** The header is a generic mechanism for adding features to a SOAP message in a decentralized manner without prior agreement between the communicating parties. SOAP defines certain header attributes that can be used to indicate who should deal with a given feature and whether it is optional or mandatory. The *Header* element is optional in a SOAP message. If present, the element must be the first immediate child

element of a SOAP *Envelope* element. It may contain a set of header entries, each being an immediate child element of the SOAP *Header* element. The child elements must be namespace-qualified. The header entries are an extensibility feature that are leveraged to provide semantic information to nodes along a message path; it may also carry information necessary for infrastructure components that provide transactional and security semantics.

- **Body** The body is a container for mandatory information intended for the ultimate recipient of the message. The *Fault* element is subordinate to the *Body* element, and is used for reporting errors. The *Body* element must be present in a SOAP message. When the *Header* element is present, the *Body* element must directly follow the *Header* element; otherwise the *Body* element must be the first immediate child element of the *Envelope* element. This element may contain a set of body entries, each being an immediate child element of the *Body* element.

For the *MyService* example, a SOAP request message that accesses the operation *foo(2222)* exposed by *MyService* will take the following form:

```
<SOAP-ENV:Envelope
  xmlns:SOAP-ENV="http://schemas.xmlsoap.org/soap/envelope/"
  SOAP-ENV:encodingStyle="http://schemas.xmlsoap.org/soap/encoding/">
   <SOAP-ENV:Body>
       <m:foo xmlns:m="http://www.openuri.org/">
           <arg>2222</arg>
       </m:foo>
   </SOAP-ENV:Body>
</SOAP-ENV:Envelope>
```

The correlated SOAP response received back from the service will take the following form:

```
<SOAP-ENV:Envelope
  xmlns:SOAP-ENV="http://schemas.xmlsoap.org/soap/envelope/"
  SOAP-ENV:encodingStyle="http://schemas.xmlsoap.org/soap/encoding/">
   <SOAP-ENV:Body>
       <m:fooResponse xmlns:m="http://www.openuri.org/">
           <fooResult>2222</fooResult>
       </m:fooResponse>
   </SOAP-ENV:Body>
</SOAP-ENV:Envelope>
```

In the following subsection, we examine SOAP message constructs that are architecturally significant in designing a Web service.

SOAP Envelope

The SOAP envelope defines the overall framework for expressing what is in a message, who should deal with the message, and whether parts of the message are optional or mandatory.

The SOAP *encodingStyle* global attribute (specified using the namespace declaration *SOAP-ENV:encodingStyle="http://schemas.xmlsoap.org/soap/encoding/"*) can be used to indicate the serialization rules used in a SOAP message. This attribute may appear on any element, and is scoped to that element's contents and all child elements not themselves containing such an attribute. There is no default encoding defined for a SOAP message. The attribute value is an ordered list of one or more URIs; these URIs identify the serialization rules that can be used to deserialize the SOAP message indicated in the order of most specific to least specific.

SOAP Header

The SOAP header provides an extension mechanism for adding additional semantics to a SOAP message when such information cannot be ordinarily added to the SOAP body, or it is inappropriate to add such information to the SOAP body. When a SOAP message follows a message path—that is, it travels from the originator to its final destination—it can potentially pass through a set of SOAP intermediaries that fall along the message path. A SOAP intermediary is an application that is capable of both receiving and forwarding SOAP messages. The role of a recipient of a *Header* element is similar to that of accepting a contract in that it cannot be extended beyond the recipient; this is because the meaning of the header is understood only between the sender and the recipient. This does not preclude the recipient from adding a *Header* element when it forwards the message to another node; in this case the contract is between the sender application and the recipient of that *Header* element. Examples of extensions that can be implemented as header entries are security context, transaction context, and so on.

For example, an originating service constructs a *Header* element targeted for an authentication service along the message path; the authentication service performs authentication, and if the authentication is successful, it forwards the SOAP message to the next destination in the message path. The SOAP global attribute *'actor'* can be used to indicate the recipient of a *Header* element. The value of the SOAP *'actor'* attribute is a URI. Omitting the *'actor'* attribute implies that the recipient is the ultimate destination of the SOAP message. When the SOAP *'actor'* attribute is set to the special URI http://schemas.xmlsoap.org/soap/actor/next, it indicates that the *Header* element is intended for the very first SOAP application that Connection header field in HTTP. The SOAP *Header* element has a significant architectural feature. It can be used to build a complex B2B system where numerous Web services are collaborating to realize a set of complex business functions. The SOAP *mustUnderstand* global attribute indicates whether a header entry is mandatory or optional for the recipient to process. If the *mustUnderstand* attribute has the value "1", the recipient of the header entry must either obey the semantics and process the header entry correctly or must fail processing the message. In the following representation of a SOAP message, the *Header* element contains a header entry *Transaction*; this header entry's meaning is known only to the receiving application that may be capable of dealing with the transactional context of the caller.

```
<SOAP-ENV:Envelope
  xmlns:SOAP-ENV="http://schemas.xmlsoap.org/soap/envelope/"
  SOAP-ENV:encodingStyle="http://schemas.xmlsoap.org/soap/encoding/"/>
   <SOAP-ENV:Header>
```

```
        <t:Transaction
            xmlns:t="some-URI"
            SOAP-ENV:mustUnderstand="1">
                1234
        </t:Transaction>
    </SOAP-ENV:Header>
    <SOAP-ENV:Body>
         ... body entries ...
    </SOAP-ENV:Body>
</SOAP-ENV:Envelope>
```

SOAP Body

According to the SOAP specification, the SOAP *Body* element provides a simple mechanism for exchanging mandatory information intended for the ultimate recipient of the message. Typical uses of the *Body* element include marshalling RPC calls and error reporting. All immediate child elements of the *Body* element are called body entries and each body entry is encoded as an independent element within the SOAP *Body* element. SOAP defines one body entry called the fault entry used for reporting errors. The encoding rules for body entries are as follows:

- A body entry is identified by its fully qualified element name, which consists of the namespace URI and the local name. Immediate child elements of the SOAP *Body* element may be namespace-qualified.
- The SOAP *encodingStyle* attribute may be used to indicate the encoding style used for the body entries.

The following example illustrates a SOAP message in which the function *foo exposed* by the Web service is being accessed; the function takes an integer value as parameter. You will recall from our WSDL discussion how WSDL will be used in the creation of stubs and proxies that will understand the semantics embedded in this SOAP message.

```
<SOAP-ENV:Envelope
  xmlns:SOAP-ENV="http://schemas.xmlsoap.org/soap/envelope/"
  SOAP-ENV:encodingStyle="http://schemas.xmlsoap.org/soap/encoding/"/>
   <SOAP-ENV:Header>
        ... header entries ...
   </SOAP-ENV:Header>
   <SOAP-ENV:Body>
       <m:foo xmlns:m="http://www.openuri.org/">
           <arg>2222</arg>
       </m:foo>
   </SOAP-ENV:Body>
</SOAP-ENV:Envelope>
```

SOAPFault

The SOAP *Fault* element defines the following four sub-elements:

- **faultcode** Intended for use by software to provide an algorithmic mechanism for identifying the fault.
- **faultstring** Intended to provide a human readable explanation of the fault and is not intended for algorithmic processing.
- **faultactor** Intended to provide information about who caused the fault to happen within the message path.
- **detail** Intended for carrying the application-specific error information related to the *Body* element. It must be present if the contents of the *Body* element could not be successfully processed. The absence of the detail element in the *Fault* element indicates that the fault is not related to processing of the *Body* element. This can be used to distinguish whether the *Body* element was processed or not in case of a fault situation where the problem could be with the server process and not the *Body* element itself.

The following demonstrates the use of the *Fault* element. If we call the *MyService* Web service, whose *foo* operation expects an integer value, with a bad string like *"garbageString", we receive the following SOAP response:*

```
<SOAP-ENV:Envelope
    xmlns:SOAP-ENV="http://schemas.xmlsoap.org/soap/envelope/"
    SOAP-ENV:encodingStyle="http://schemas.xmlsoap.org/soap/encoding/"/>
    <SOAP-ENV:Body>
         <SOAP-ENV:Fault>
            <faultcode>SOAP-ENV:ServiceError</faultcode>
            <faultstring>Invalid request</faultstring>
            <detail>Error deserializing arguments. 'garbageString' is not
                 a valid encoding for type java.lang.Integer</detail>
        </SOAP-ENV:Fault>
    </SOAP-ENV:Body>
</SOAP-ENV:Envelope>
```

GreaterCause B2B Integration

To understand the B2B requirement for the Web service required by the GreaterCause application, let's recap the use cases. Once the portal provider is registered in the GreaterCause.com site by the site administrator, a portal-alliance is formed between GreaterCause.com and the portal provider. This relationship allows the portal provider to provide a pass-through or gateway component, also called a portlet, on the portal page for redirecting portal users to the GreaterCause.com site. This portlet is responsible for displaying the list of available campaigns, such as NPOs featured by the portal provider.

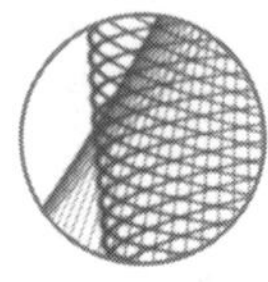

NOTE

A portlet can be implemented as part of the portal infrastructure provided by vendors, or as part of a JSP using a custom tag. It is left to the readers to decide how a portlet is integrated into a portal page. In the following discussion, we assume that the portlet is housed in a JSP page using a custom tag.

The campaigns for featuring selected NPOs are created by the portal administrator using the Create Campaign functionality offered by the GreaterCause.com site. This Create Campaign Use Case was discussed in Chapters 1 and 2, and developed in Chapters 1, 2, 5, and 7. Note that the campaigns are created and stored in the GreaterCause data store; these portal-domain–specific featured NPOs must be extracted by the respective portal domains and displayed in the portlet. The campaign list is obtained only once and cached locally by the portal domain; the portlet is subsequently populated from the local cache. The solution discussed in the chapter is part of the realization of the Cache Featured-NPOs use case discussed in Chapter 1. To access the list of featured-NPOs from the GreaterCause data store, the portlet can make a call to the *FeaturedNPOQueryService* Web service for retrieving the list of campaigns related to the portal domain, which it can subsequently caches in the *ServletContext* (the Application Scope). This is an oversimplification of the caching strategy; there are several caching strategies possible for handling caching of campaigns. *FeaturedNPOQueryService* is a Web service that exposes a method called *getFeaturedNPOs*. This method returns an array of *FeaturedNPODTO* objects; we have used an array because the SOAP encoding does not support the Collection API. The B2B scenario uses the request-response message interaction. The corresponding interaction semantics are depicted in Figure 8-2.

WebLogic Web services implement the Java API for XML-based RPC (JAX-RPC) as part of a client JAR that client applications can use to invoke both WebLogic and non-WebLogic Web services. Although the knowledge of JAX-RPC is not essential for implementing Web services when using vendor-provided tools, you can refer to http://java.sun.com/xml/jaxrpc/index.html to read more on this subject. The generated client includes a proxy for invoking the operations of a Web service. Because the GreaterCause Web service is called *FeaturedNPOQueryService*, the client JAR created for accessing the Web service uses the

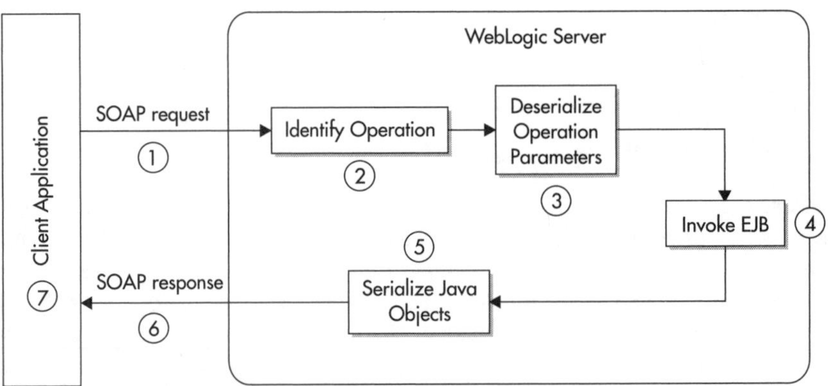

Figure 8-2 *Request-response–based interaction*

a factory class *FeaturedNPOQueryService_Impl* to get the related stub implementation *FeaturedNPOQueryServiceSoap_Stub* using this stub which the Web service method is called. Before proceeding with implementation details, let's review the architecture provided by WebLogic for servicing client requests. The request-response message exchange pattern of Figure 8-2 is explained here.

1. The client application sends a SOAP message by invoking the Web service method on *FeaturedNPOQueryServiceSoap* interface. This interface is implemented by the *FeaturedNPOQueryServiceSoap_Stub*. Based on the URI in the request, the server identifies the Web service and passes the XML payload to the Web service.
2. The *FeaturedNPOQueryService* Web service identifies the operation to be performed. For *FeaturedNPOQueryService*, the server-side components generated for the Web service embed a reference to the stateless session bean *Campaign* on which the identified operation must be called. The implementation of the *Campaign* bean and pertinent use case is explained in Chapter 7.
3. The *FeaturedNPOQueryService* Web service transforms the parameters in the SOAP *Body* using the appropriate encoding scheme to Java objects; this may require using appropriate deserializer class. For non-built-in data types, a deserializer class is created as part of Web service creation process. For our sample application, the *FeaturedNPODTO* deserializer class is automatically created by the vendor tool. This is discussed in the implementation section to follow.
4. The *FeaturedNPOQueryService* Web service invokes the appropriate method that accesses the *Campaign* bean. The *Campaign* bean's method processes the request and creates a response.
5. The *FeaturedNPOQueryService* Web service converts the response object from Java to XML using the appropriated serializer class for the array of *FeaturedNPODTO* objects; this serialized array of *FeaturedNPODTO* objects is packaged into a SOAP message response.
6. The *FeaturedNPOQueryService* Web service sends the SOAP message response back to the client application that invoked the Web service.
7. The client SOAP runtime transforms the response value in the SOAP *Body* using the appropriate encoding scheme to Java objects; this may require using an appropriate deserializer class. For non-built-in data types, a deserializer class is created as part of Web service creation process. For our sample application, the *FeaturedNPODTO* array deserializer class is automatically created by the vendor tool. This is discussed in the implementation section to follow.

The view (JSP) containing the portlet uses *FeaturedNPOQueryService*'s client-side jar file, generated automatically by the vendor tool; which employs a WSDL document for defining the correct SOAP message semantics between the client and the server. Now that we have an understanding of the overall architecture and the interaction semantics between the client view and the GreaterCause.com domain, let's explore the *FeaturedNPOQueryService* Web service's implementation.

Web Service Implementation

Without using a tool like BEA WebLogic Workshop, developing a Web service in Java implies writing a large amount of code to interface with a SOAP library and possibly with WSDL or UDDI. Tools like BEA WebLogic Workshop automate the creation of Web services, handle all the SOAP protocol coding, and allow the developers to focus on implementing the business logic. For example, in the case of the *FeaturedNPOQueryService* Web service, we have implemented only the necessary EJB and left the generation of WSDL, the Web service client-side proxies, and server-side components to the Workshop. Therefore our implementation responsibility is reduced to proper use of EJB programming model.

This section of the document describes step-by-step the design and implementation of *FeaturedNPOQueryService* using BEA WebLogic Workshop. We test this service using a simple JSP. Readers who would like to create *FeaturedNPOQueryService* should follow the instructions for installing WebLogic platform provided in Chapter 9. The focus of our discussion is creation and consumption of a Web service, as such we spend very little time explaining the tool itself; information regarding Workshop is available at www.bea.com; a user manual also accompanies the download, and is accessible from the Workshop's Help menu option.

Design Considerations

In this section, we briefly discuss some design aspects for implementing server-side components. Let's recap our requirement: the *FeaturedNPOQueryService* must expose a single *getFeaturedNPOs* method (contract) to the outside world. The method *getFeaturedNPOs* accepts two parameters, a *PortalID* and a *RegionCode*, both of *String* type; the Web service returns an array of type *FeaturedNPODTO*; this array consists of all the global campaigns, and regional campaigns for the region specified in the method signature.

- **Deciding between synchronous or asynchronous operation** The synchronous interaction employ the RPC-oriented semantics; in this scenario a SOAP message sent to a Web service is paired with a response from the Web service. Using the asynchronous interaction semantics the client does not expect a response from the Web service; the back-end components return void, also in-out parameters cannot be specified in the operation signature. The web-services.xml deployment descriptor uses the invocation-style attribute for the operation element for specifying this behavior; you can specify either "one-way" or "request-response"; the default value is "request-response". From the requirements, it is apparent that we will be using the default "request-response" style for a synchronous Web service.
- **Deciding the type of back-end component** The *FeaturedNPOQueryService* uses the stateless session bean for providing the core implementation. The *Campaign* EJB was developed as part of the GreaterCause application in Chapter 7. This EJB employs the Session Façade pattern whose operation *getFeaturedNPOs* implements the required business logic and implements the necessary semantics for interacting with pertinent CMP Entity beans; the return value is implemented using the Data Transfer Object pattern. The J2EE component architecture used for creating the *Campaign* bean provides a solid foundation on which we can build the *FeaturedNPOQueryService* Web service; the use of EJB automatically provides several features such as security

management, resource pooling, container managed transactions, and persistence services. Alternately, one can use Java classes, or a JMS message consumer or producer, such as a message-driven bean; for these alternate implementations and associated design rationale, please consult vendor documentation.

Although the Web services cannot use stateful session beans, one can mimic a conversational Web service by creating a persistent unique ID and associate it with the conversational state stored in a data store using JDBC or Entity beans.

- **Deciding between RPC-oriented or document-oriented** Document-oriented Web service operation can support only one parameter of any supported data type; this style uses literal encoding. RPC-oriented Web service operation has no restrictions on the number of parameters. The *FeaturedNPOQueryService* employs document-oriented semantics.
- **Data types** Built-in data types are specified by the JAX-RPC specification. Using these data types offers automatic conversion between XML and the corresponding Java representation. For Web service operations that employ non-built-in data types as parameters and return values, one must create the serialization class that converts the data between its XML and Java representation. For our *FeaturedNPOQueryService*, the data type mapping and accompanying serializer classes are automatically generated by the vendor tool. For manually assembling serializer classes, please refer to the vendor documentation.

FeaturedNPOQueryService Implementation Using BEA WebLogic Workshop

Constructing and deploying Web services using the BEA WebLogic Workshop involves several steps. These are summarized here, followed by additional details on how the vendor tool assists in accomplishing these steps.

1. Set up the development environment.
2. Create the stateless EJB that will expose its method through the Web service. Deploy the EJB.
3. Create the Web service that exposes the stateless EJB business method.
4. Create serialization classes that convert Java objects to its XML representation and vice versa.
5. Generate client proxies for accessing the Web service. Build a test client and verify the working of the Web service.
6. Deploy the Web service to a production server.

Setting Up the Development Environment BEA WebLogic Server 7.0 provides templates for creating server domains that are preconfigured for offering different test and development environments. Using the Domain Configuration Wizard we must first create the WebLogic Workshop domain (for detailed insructions please refer to Chapter 9). This domain has support for the Workshop IDE that creates JAX-RPC– compliant client and server runtime components. The runtime components created by the Workshop IDE interpose between the client call on the Web service and the server-side component servicing the request.

The Workshop IDE is installed with the WebLogic server installation. Workshop requires that a Workshop domain server be up and running for creating Web services. You can configure Workshop to use a specific server as shown in Figure 8-3. After starting the workshop IDE, choose Tools/Preferences, select the paths tab and provide the werver-related information. Observe that the domain directory selected is the *workshopDomain* directory created by the Domain Configuration Wizard. The startWebLogic.cmd script in $(workshopDomain) directory configures the environment for use with the Workshop IDE. If a server pertaining to the domain identified in Figure 8-3 is already running, Workshop will indicate this by a green light at the bottom of the screen; the server can be started using the Tools option in the menu bar.

Creating the Stateless EJB In Chapter 6 and 7, we created the *Campaign* entity bean and the *Campaign* stateless session bean. We simply add an additional *getFeaturedNPOs* method on the stateless session bean. This method returns an array of *FeaturedNPODTO* objects. We have used an array because the SOAP encoding does not support the *Collection* API. In the .jws class file (to be discussed shortly), we associate this method and associated Home and Remote interfaces with the method exposed by the Web service. For assisting the tool in identifying the Home and Remote interfaces, copy the client jar for the EJB to the ${workshopDomain}\applications\ GreaterCauseWebService\WEB-INF\lib directory.

Please refer to Chapter 9 for additional information on creating GreaterCauseEJBClient.jar file and setting up of Data Source for accessing the database server. Please ensure that the GreaterCause application is deployed before attempting to access the Web service. The GreaterCauseEJBClient.jar is supplied with the download and can also be generated using the Ant build script explained in Chapter 9.

Creating the Web Service Web services are organized by projects in Workshop; therefore, create a new project under any name; say GreaterCauseWebService. This name is subsequently used by Workshop for hot deploying a web application _appsdir_GreaterCauseWebService_ dir that is accessible by HTTP clients for testing the Web Service.

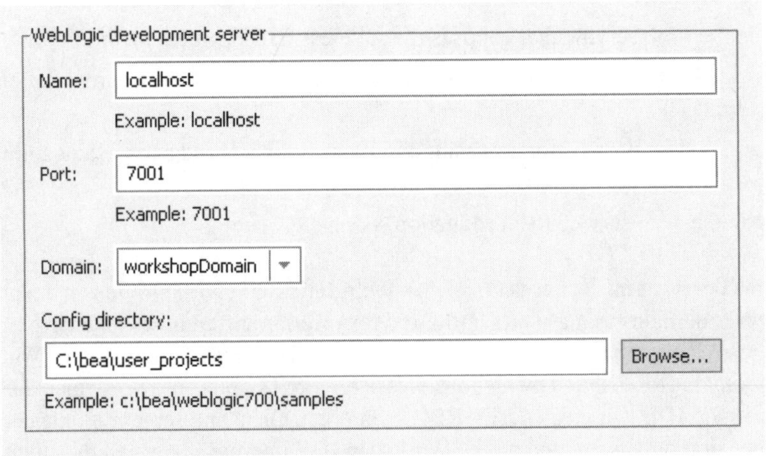

WebLogic development server
Name: localhost
Example: localhost
Port: 7001
Example: 7001
Domain: workshopDomain
Config directory:
C:\bea\user_projects
Browse...
Example: c:\bea\weblogic700\samples

Figure 8-3 *Selecting the WebLogic server*

Create New File

This action will create a new file in the current project.
Type of file to create:

Web service
Creates a new JWS file that implements a web service.

Java
Creates a new Java file.

JavaScript
Creates a new JavaScript file.

Text
Creates a blank text file.

File name: FeaturedNPOQueryService
File extension: jws

Create in folder: \ (project root directory)
Note: To create a file in a different folder, cancel this dialog, right-click the desired folder in the project tree, and choose New File.

Help OK Cancel

Figure 8-4 *Setting up* FeaturedNPOQueryService

We are now ready to create Web services under this project. From the menu, select File | New | New Web Service; provide a name for the Web service, as shown in Figure 8-4; call this service *FeaturedNPOQueryService*.

Workshop creates a .jws file under the ${workshopDomain}\applications\GreaterCauseWebService. This is the main class file that will create a link between the Web service seen by the outside world to the server component actually providing the service; a control interface CampaignControl.ctrl (an EJB Control for this example) is used within this .jws class file to provide additional information about the server-side component interfaces and the corresponding JNDI names. Workshop uses a set of custom tags based on Javadoc technology to inject specialized behavior and information, in classes and interfaces, required by Workshop in the generation of a Web service. These tags begin with *@jws:* and are not explained in the following discussion because they are fairly intuitive in what they represent; for complete details please refer to the vendor documentation. Figure 8-5 illustrates the directory structure once the project directory for *GreaterCauseWebService* is created.

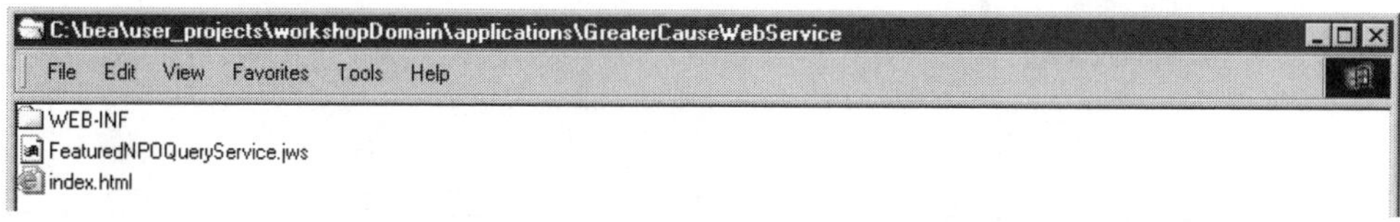

Figure 8-5 *Project directories used by Workshop*

Workshop hot deploys a web module in the WebLogic server; this module is named _appsdir_GreaterCauseWebService_dir, it has the context *GreaterCauseWebService*, and its path is defined as ${workshopDomain}\applications\GreaterCauseWebService; this is illustrated in Figure 8-6. This can be verified by accessing the WebLogic console using http://localhost:7001/console; in the left hand frame select workshopDomain | Deployments | Web Applications | _appdir_GreaterCauseWebServe_dir.

This testing module is used by Workshop to provide a console and test environment for the Web service before it is deployed; this is shown in Figure 8-7. The test page, also called the test view, is launched using the menu option Debug | Start, or Debug | Restart. The test page should be launched only after a Web service is successfully configured as explained in the subsequent steps.

Workshop provides the design view for enabling creation of the EJB control and the corresponding .jws class file, as shown in Figure 8-8. The *getCampaigns* method was created selecting the Add Method option available on the Add Operation drop-down. The Web service is going to expose this method to the outside world. The variable *"campaign*" represents the *CampaignControl*; this control interface was created using the Add EJB Control option (Figure 8-9) available on the Add Control drop-down; the control shows all the business methods exposed by the *Campaign* session bean.

The Add EJB Control provides the dialog box shown in Figure 8-9.

Once the EJB control is configured, the CampaignControl.ctrl file defines the following interface. We use *CampaignControl* in the FeaturedNPOQueryService.jws class file, as shown in Figure 8-10.

```
import weblogic.jws.*;
import weblogic.jws.control.*;
/**
 *   @jws:ejb home-jndi-name="ejb/com.gc.services.managecampaigns.CampaignHome"
 *   @editor-info:ejb home="GreaterCauseClient.jar" bean="GreaterCauseClient.jar"
 */
public interface CampaignControl
  extends com.gc.services.managecampaigns.CampaignHome,    // home interface
          com.gc.services.managecampaigns.CampaignRemote, // bean interface
           weblogic.jws.control.SessionEJBControl         // control interface
{ }
```

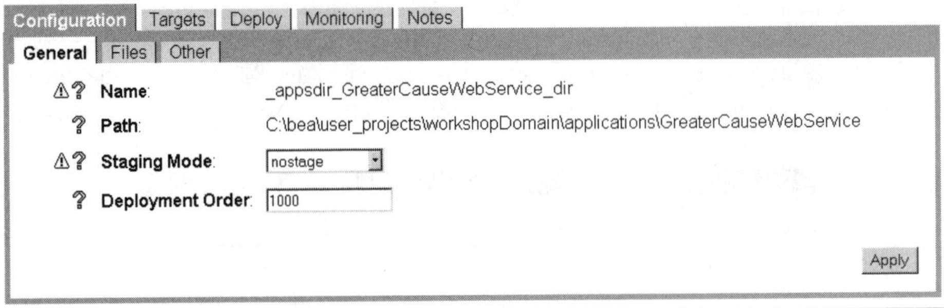

Figure 8-6 *Testing module deployed by Workshop*

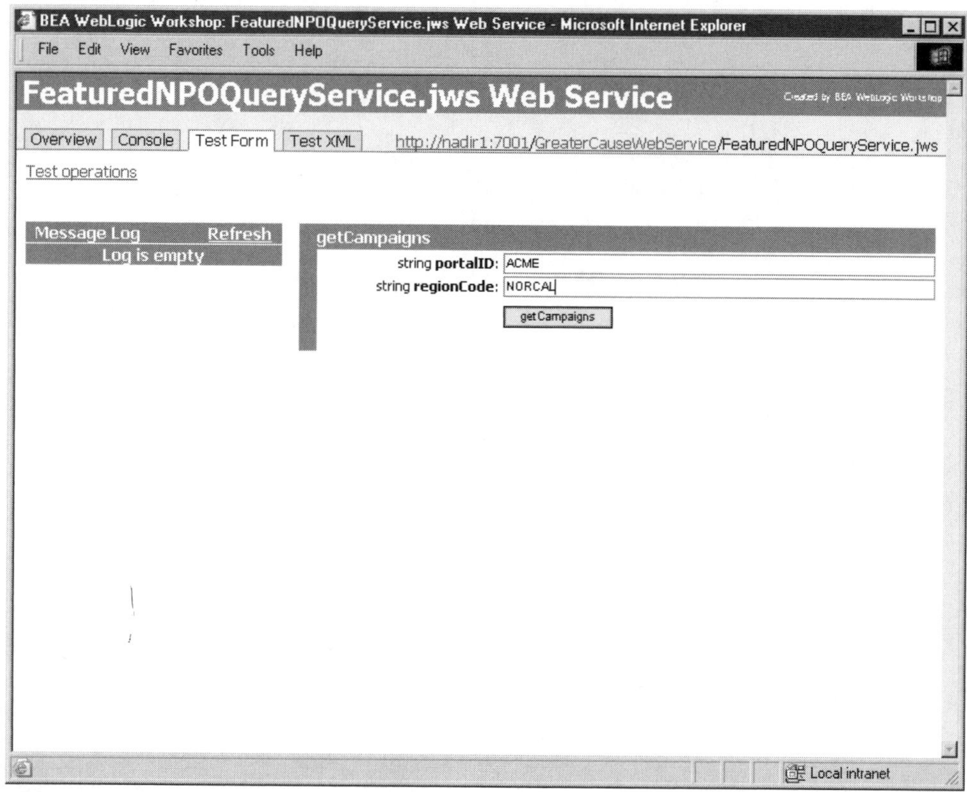

Figure 8-7 *Launching the test environment*

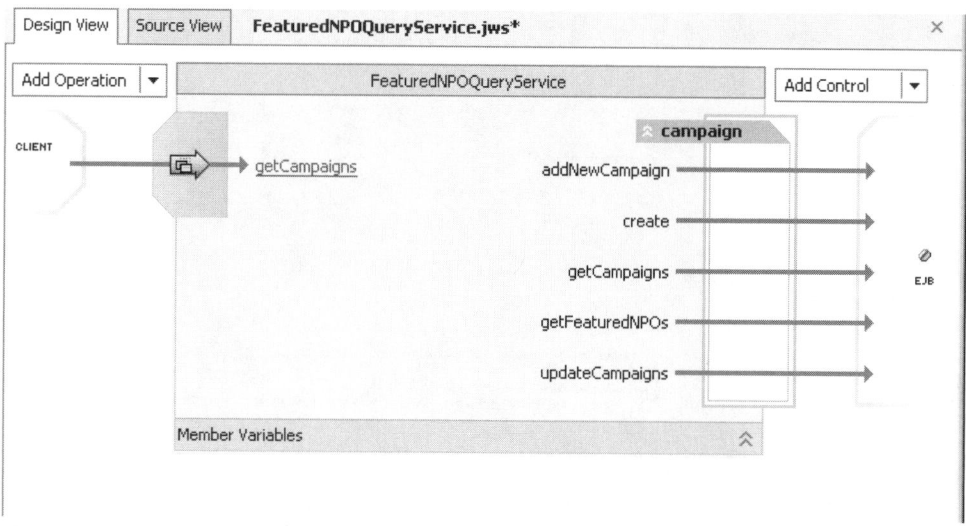

Figure 8-8 *Design view*

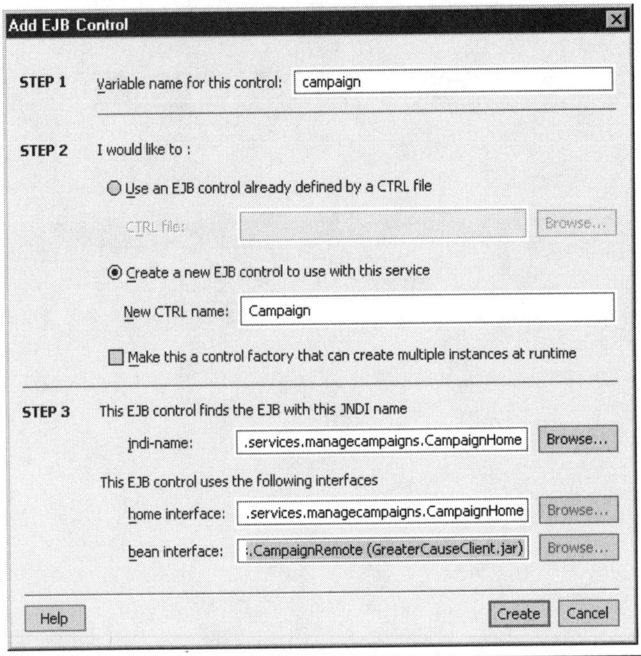

Add EJB Control

STEP 1 Variable name for this control: campaign

STEP 2 I would like to :

Use an EJB control already defined by a CTRL file

CTRL file: Browse...

Create a new EJB control to use with this service

New CTRL name: Campaign

Make this a control factory that can create multiple instances at runtime

STEP 3 This EJB control finds the EJB with this JNDI name

jndi-name: .services.managecampaigns.CampaignHome Browse...

This EJB control uses the following interfaces

home interface: .services.managecampaigns.CampaignHome Browse...

bean interface: :.CampaignRemote (GreaterCauseClient.jar) Browse...

Help Create Cancel

Figure 8-9 *Configure CampaignControl.ctrl file*

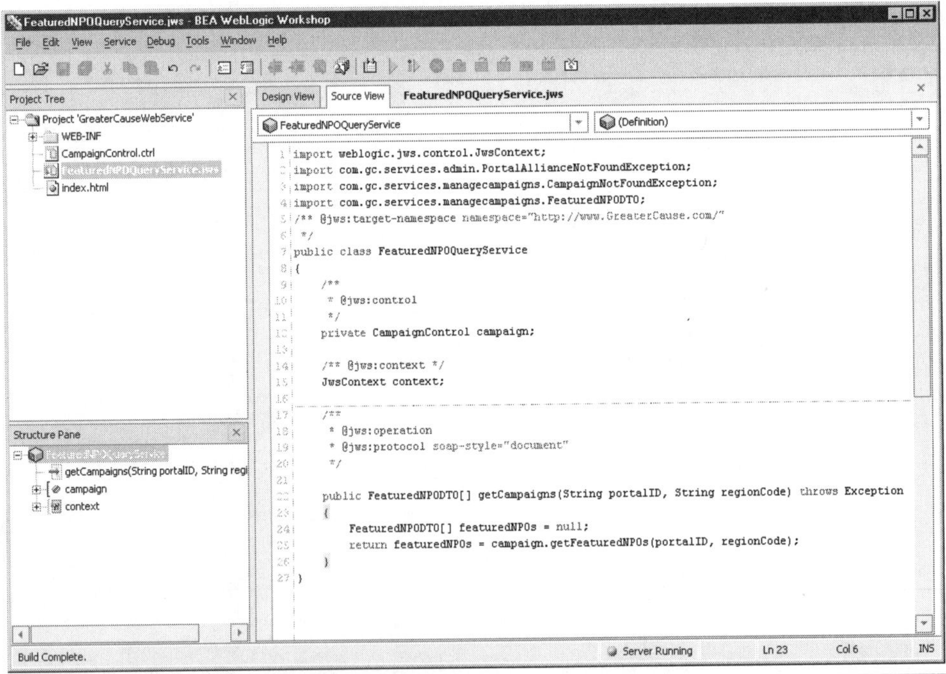

Figure 8-10 *Source view for FeatureNPOService.jws*

Figure 8-10 shows the source view of the .jws file that ties the various components of the *FeaturedNPOQueryService* Web service. The .jws file and the control file are used for creating the client runtime and the server runtime classes and interfaces.

With the .jws completed, we are now ready to generate the client-side proxies and the server-side components that will provide access to the *getCampaignNPOs* method on the *Campaign* session bean. Use the menu option Debug | Build (or Debug | Start).At this time access the WebLogic console using http://localhost:7001/console; in the left hand frame select workshopDomain | Deployments | EJB. Note that Workshop has hot deployed a new ejb module GreaterCauseWebService.FeaturedNPOQueryService_EJB whose ejb-jar file path is *${workshopDomain}\mySever\.jwscompile_jwsdir_GreaterCauseWebService\EJB\FeaturedNPOQueryServiceEJB.jar*. Peeking inside the FeaturedNPOQueryServiceEJB.jar at the specified directory will show that there are two server-side stateless EJBs that provide infrastructure support for interacting with the Web service; these EJBs have various environment entries, specified in ejb-jar.xml deployment descriptor, that are Web service–specific. One of the environment entries, *ServiceURI*, for the *RemoteDispatcherBean* provides the URI for the test view; this URI is /GreaterCauseWebService/FeaturedNPOQueryService.jws; this URI, as discussed earlier, is automatically invoked by selecting Debug | Start (or Debug | Restart) in the Workshop IDE.

At this stage, we can quickly test the Web service by using the test form in the test view, and providing the Portal ID and Region Code. The resulting array, represented in XML, is depicted in Figure 8-11. The WSDL associated with the *FeaturedNPOQueryService* is shown in Appendix D. This array will be embedded in the SOAP response message when the Web service is accessed.

Optionally, one can use the "Test XML" tab to hand code the parameters sent as part of the SOAP *Body* element. The resulting SOAP request message and response message are shown in their entirety in Figure 8-12. Please note that to avoid naming conflict for clients using the *FeaturedNPODTO* class, the Web service defines the namespace http://www.GreaterCause.com as the namespace for the result set. All serializer classes use this namespace as the package name for the *FeaturedNPODTO* class. More on serialization classes in the following subsection.

Unhandled exceptions in the .jws class file will result in SOAP *Fault* to be sent back to the client. You must add an appropriate *try/catch* block in the .jws file for exception handling. One of the techniques used for propagating server-side errors is to convert the exception to a meaningful code or a message and send it in the response. Recall that the *SOAP:style="rpc"* declaration allows specification of out or in-out parameters for an operation; for synchronous request-response message pattern using RPC-oriented style, an out parameter can hold the application-level errors. Out and in-out parameters must implement the *javax.xml.rpc.holders.Holder* interface as shown in the following code; for standard data type, use one of the JAX-RPC Holder classes or the built-in Holder classes provided by the server vendor.

```
public String someMethod(String param1, javax.xml.rpc.holders.IntHolder param2) {
    param2.value = 100;
    return param2;
}
```

Optionally, a *javax.xml.rpc.soap.SOAPFaultException* (or a subclass) can be thrown to ensure that the client application receives appropriate information of a server-side exception.

Figure 8-11 *XMLized* FeaturedNPODTO *array*

Creating Serialization Classes When the data types of the parameters and return values in a Web service are of built-in data types, the server automatically converts the data between Java object and its XML representation. Built-in SOAP data types are defined by the namespace http://schemas.xmlsoap.org/soap/encoding; additional details are available in Section 5 of the SOAP specification. Serialization classes are required only for non-built-in data types. Creating non-built-in data types involves several steps. However, we have let the tool do all the work described in each of these steps.

1. Create the XML schema data type representation to describe the structure of the non-built-in data type.
2. Create the Java data type representation to represent the XML in terms of a Java object.
3. Write the serialization class that performs conversion of Java objects to XML and vice versa.
4. Create the data type mapping file that contains information about the non-built-in data type's Java class, serializer, deserializer, and so on.

   The mapping file shown below in created as part of the *Java Proxy* generation process (explained in the next section) and is available in the proxy jar file

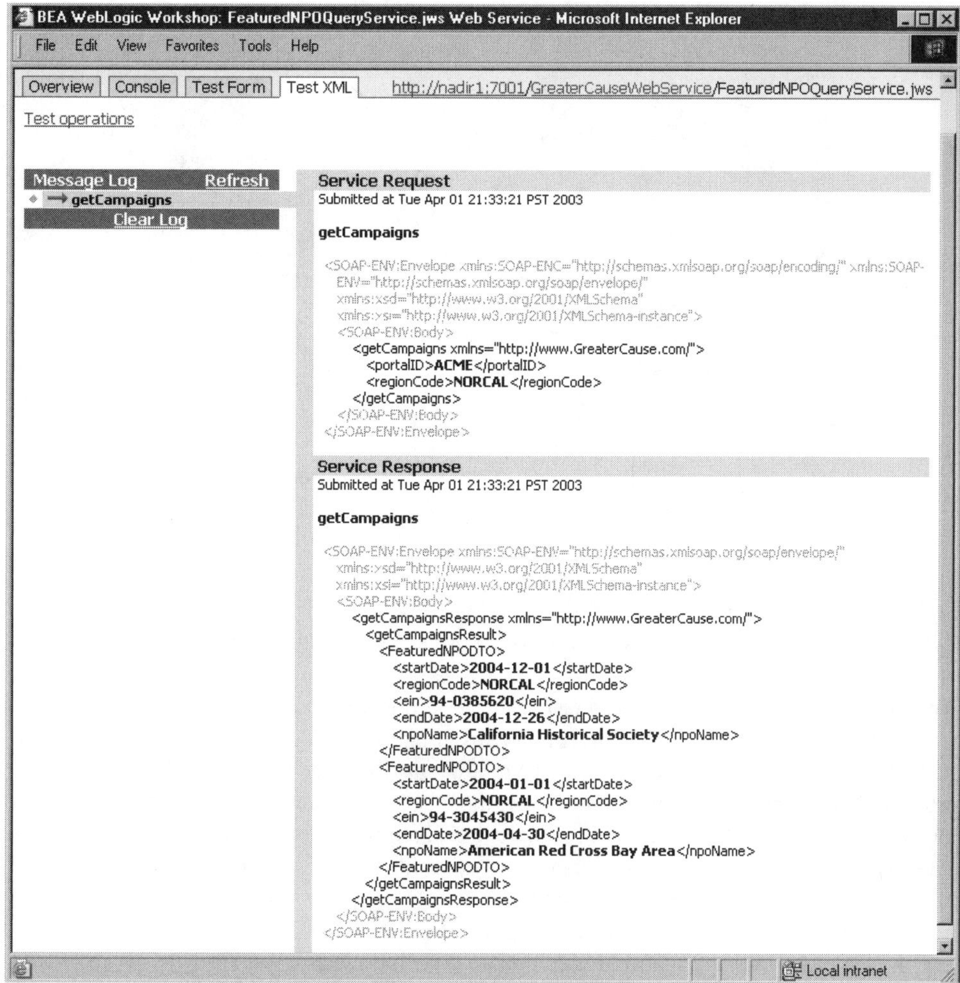

Figure 8-12 *SOAP request and response*

(FeaturedNPOQueryService.jar) under the name FeaturedNPOQueryService.xml. Please note that this mapping is created only when @jws:protocol soap-style="document" is specified in the FeaturedNPOQueryService.jws class file (this is the default). A different mapping is generated when soap-style="rpc" is specified.

```
<type-mapping>
  <type-mapping-entry
      deserializer="com.GreaterCause.www.ArrayOfFeaturedNPODTOSequenceCodec"
      class-name="com.GreaterCause.www.FeaturedNPODTO[]"
      xmlns:p1="http://www.GreaterCause.com/" type="p1:ArrayOfFeaturedNPODTO"
```

```
        serializer="com.GreaterCause.www.ArrayOfFeaturedNPODTOSequenceCodec">
    </type-mapping-entry>
    <type-mapping-entry
        deserializer="com.GreaterCause.www.GetCampaignsResponseCodec"
        class-name="com.GreaterCause.www.GetCampaignsResponse"
        xmlns:p2="http://www.GreaterCause.com/" type="p2:getCampaignsResponse"
        serializer="com.GreaterCause.www.GetCampaignsResponseCodec">
    </type-mapping-entry>
    <type-mapping-entry
        deserializer="com.GreaterCause.www.FeaturedNPODTOCodec"
        class-name="com.GreaterCause.www.FeaturedNPODTO"
        xmlns:p3="http://www.GreaterCause.com/" type="p3:FeaturedNPODTO"
        serializer="com.GreaterCause.www.FeaturedNPODTOCodec">
      </type-mapping-entry>
      <type-mapping-entry deserializer="com.GreaterCause.www.GetCampaignsCodec"
          class-name="com.GreaterCause.www.GetCampaigns"
          xmlns:p4="http://www.GreaterCause.com/" type="p4:getCampaigns"
          serializer="com.GreaterCause.www.GetCampaignsCodec">
      </type-mapping-entry>
    </type-mapping>
```

The required components for handling non-built-in data types are provided as part of the Java Proxy creation process, which is discussed in the following section.

Generating Client Runtime and Building a Test Client Before we can compile the client code, we need to obtain the client runtime. In order to do this, use the menu option Debug | Start to launch the Web service's personalized page (the test view); as discussed earlier, this page provides testing and other supporting functions. Select the Overview tab and click Java Proxy; this will download the proxy classes required for making calls to the Web service; this client JAR file is name FeaturedNPOQueryService.jar. The client jar file includes service-specific classes, stubs, and interfaces required by the client to invoke the Web service. The classes, stubs, and interfaces are based on the implementation of the JAX-RPC API.

If the GreaterCause application is deployed, you can use a simple JSP FeaturedNPOQueryService.jsp to test our Web service; the FeaturedNPOQueryService.jar is installed in the web module's WEB-INF\lib directory. All of the WebLogic proxy classes belong to the weblogic.jws.proxies package, therefore this package is referenced in the import attribute of the page directive.

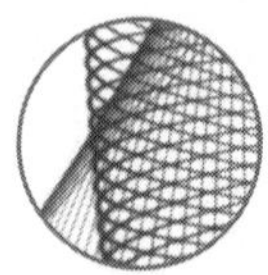

NOTE:

Once you have generated FeaturedNPOQueryService.jar (Java Proxy), add it to GreaterCause/build/archives directory of the source distribution. The Ant build process explained in Chapter 9 will ensure that this jar file is added to the WEB-INF\lib directory. Please follow the instructions in Chapter 9 for correctly setting the domain directory in the GC.Properties file used by the Ant build script.

The view FeaturedNPOQueryService.jsp, shown here, generates the response shown in Figure 8-13. All of the WebLogic proxy classes belong to the weblogic.jws.proxies package, therefore this package is referenced in the import attribute of the page directive.

```
<%@ page contentType="text/html;charset=UTF-8" language="java"
    import="weblogic.jws.proxies.FeaturedNPOQueryService_Impl,
            weblogic.jws.proxies.FeaturedNPOQueryServiceSoap,
            java.rmi.RemoteException,
            com.GreaterCause.www.FeaturedNPODTO"
%>
<html><body>
<% try {
    FeaturedNPOQueryService_Impl webservice = new FeaturedNPOQueryService_Impl();
    FeaturedNPOQueryServiceSoap webserviceProxy =
        webservice.getFeaturedNPOQueryServiceSoap();
    FeaturedNPODTO[] npoList =
        (FeaturedNPODTO[])webserviceProxy.getCampaigns("ACME","NORCAL");
    for (int i=0; i < npoList.length; i++) {
       FeaturedNPODTO dto = (FeaturedNPODTO) npoList[i]; %>
       NPO Name: <%= dto.getNpoName() %><br>
       Region Code <%= dto.getRegionCode() %><br>
       EIN: <%= dto.getEin() %><br>
       Start Date: <%= dto.getStartDate() %><br>
       End Date: <%= dto.getEndDate() %><p>
<%  }
}
catch (RemoteException ex) {
    ... rest of the code ...
} %>
</body></html>
```

For using the proxy jar outside of the WebLogic server, or for stand-alone Java clients, you need another jar file containing supporting classes. This jar is downloadable by using the Proxy Support Jar link on the Web service's page.

Deploying to a Production Server To deploy the *FeaturedNPOQueryService* on the production server, change the hostname element's value from *localhost* to the production machine in the

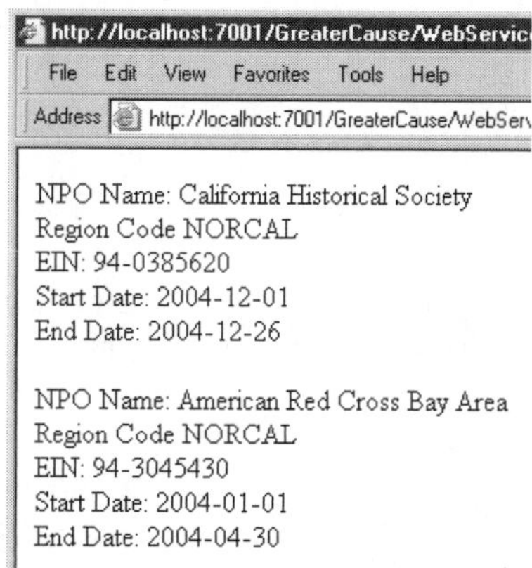

Figure 8-13 FeaturedNPOQueryService *response*

weblogic-jws-config.xml file located in the WEB-INF directory. Compile the Web application as an EAR file and deploy the EAR file on the production server.

```
<config>
   <protocol>http</protocol>
   <hostname>localhost</hostname>
   <http-port>7001</http-port>
   <https-port>7002</https-port>
   <jws>
       <class-name>FeaturedNPOQueryService</class-name>
       <protocol>http</protocol>
   </jws>
    <jws>
       <class-name>FeaturedNPOQueryServiceSecure</class-name>
       <protocol>https</protocol>
   </jws>
</config>
```

Note the use of https protocol in the protocol element for *FeaturedNPOQueryServiceSecure*. For the Web service to use SSL, make sure that the WSDL specifies https instead of http.

Workshop SOAP:style Semantics

For FeaturedNPOQueryService, we employed *SOAP:style="document"*; this is illustrated in the following WSDL fragment. The corresponding SOAP request and response messages were shown in Figure 8-12.

```
<operation name="getCampaigns">
    <soap:operation style="document"
        soapAction="http://www.GreaterCause.com/getCampaigns"/>
    <input>
        <soap:body use="literal"/>
    </input>
    <output>
        <soap:body use="literal"/>
    </output>
</operation>
```

Recall that the request-response operation is an abstract notion; therefore the vendor implementation will dictate whether messages are sent within a single HTTP request-response, or as two independent HTTP requests. WebLogic Web service deployment descriptor allows you to specify an operation:invocation-style attribute that can take the values *"one-way"* or *"request-response"*; for *FeaturedNPOQueryService*, we use *invocation-style="request-response". Note that the XML document "getCampaignsResponse*" in the SOAP body in Figure 8-12 is converted to its Java equivalent by the deserialization mechanisms generated by the vendor tool; please refer to section "Creating Serialization Classes" for the type-mapping construct created by the tool. Document-oriented Web service operations use literal encoding, which implies that the message elements described in WSDL reference a concrete schema using the *type* attribute.

If we had employed *SOAP:style="rpc"*, the resulting SOAP messages will follow the representation stated in section 7.1 of the SOAP specification; the data types marshalled across the wire follow a set of encoding rules described in Section 5 of the SOAP specification, which has the namespace identifier "http://schemas.xmlsoap.org/soap/encoding/" (also called SOAP encoding). Changing *SOAP:style* to *"rpc"* will yield the following response:

```
<SOAP-ENV:Envelope xmlns:SOAP-ENC="http://schemas.xmlsoap.org/soap/encoding/"
   xmlns:SOAP-ENV="http://schemas.xmlsoap.org/soap/envelope/"
   xmlns:xsd="http://www.w3.org/2001/XMLSchema"
   xmlns:xsi="http://www.w3.org/2001/XMLSchema-instance">
   <SOAP-ENV:Body
      SOAP-ENV:encodingStyle="http://schemas.xmlsoap.org/soap/encoding/">
      <m:getCampaignsResponse xmlns:m="http://www.GreaterCause.com/"
         xmlns:types="http://www.GreaterCause.com/encodedTypes">
         <getCampaignsResult SOAP-ENC:arrayType="types:FeaturedNPODTO[2]"
            xsi:type="SOAP-ENC:Array">
            <item>
               <startDate xsi:type="xsd:string">2004-12-01</startDate>
               <regionCode xsi:type="xsd:string">NORCAL</regionCode>
               <ein xsi:type="xsd:string">94-0385620</ein>
               <endDate xsi:type="xsd:string">2004-12-26</endDate>
               <npoName
               xsi:type="xsd:string">California Historical Society</npoName>
            </item>
            <item>
               <startDate xsi:type="xsd:string">2004-01-01</startDate>
               <regionCode xsi:type="xsd:string">NORCAL</regionCode>
               <ein xsi:type="xsd:string">94-3045430</ein>
               <endDate xsi:type="xsd:string">2004-04-30</endDate>
               <npoName
               xsi:type="xsd:string">American Red Cross Bay Area</npoName>
            </item>
         </getCampaignsResult>
      </m:getCampaignsResponse>
   </SOAP-ENV:Body>
</SOAP-ENV:Envelope>
```

Because other encoding schemes are possible for representing data types, the SOAP *'encodingStyle'* attribute can be used to indicate the encoding style of the method call and the response. Using SOAP for RPC is orthogonal to the SOAP protocol binding (please refer to the Sample WSDL discussed previously for FeaturedNPOQueryService). When using HTTP as the protocol binding, an RPC call maps to an HTTP request and an RPC response maps to an HTTP response.

Summary

Web services open a new possibility for integration and development of next generation Web applications. Web services do not suggest any development paradigm nor introduce a new programming language. Web services leverage on top of highly scalable and industry proven server-side technologies like J2EE, .NET, and CORBA. Web services provide the basis for flexible and scalable service-oriented architecture. With Web services, building B2B and business process automation solutions are easier and less expensive than traditional approaches. Web services simplify the task of integration by leveraging on flexibility of XML and its maturing stack of tools and technologies. Making XML as the standard format for messaging between distributed components not only fills the gap left by the EAI technology, but it removes interoperability and portability issues.

We believe that Web services will soon become the backbone for building small to very complex distributed and transactional business systems. Currently there are large numbers of vendors providing tools and technologies that automate Web services development and deployment. Web service development and deployment processes are mainly influenced by the existence of mature server-side technologies (J2EE, .NET, and CORBA). To adopt Web services, organization-specific development methodology should be applied. Due to service-centric nature of Web service, there is a need for Web service assembler tools using which a total business solution can be packaged and deployed from existing services.

CHAPTER

9

Application Assembly and Deployment

IN THIS CHAPTER:

Installing and Configuring Struts

Configuring the WebLogic Domain

Configuring GreaterCause Users

Deploying the GreaterCause Application

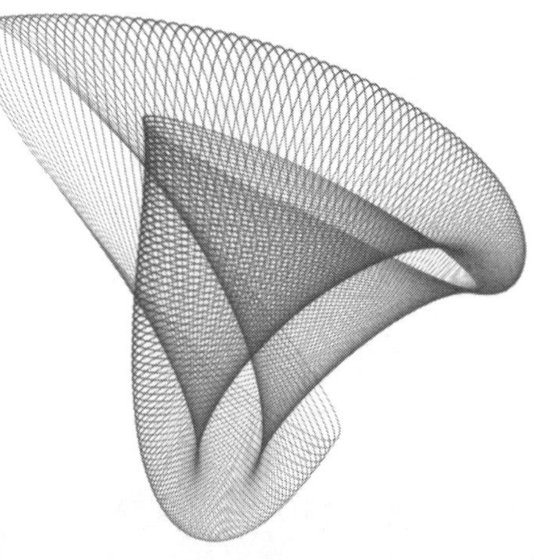

The J2EE platform provides a high level of service standardization. As such, the application developer can focus on core business functions, and the container tools generate most of the services-specific code pertaining to transaction management, security, remote connectivity, object-relational mapping, and so on. The application behavior for these services is configured at deployment time using deployment descriptors. These deployment descriptors were discussed in Chapters 4 through 7 for configuring platform services for various components. Figure 9-1 shows how a J2EE application is composed, and the various elements that make up the web, EJB, and application client modules. J2EE modules either can be deployed as stand-alone units, or they can be combined to create a J2EE application, as shown in the figure.

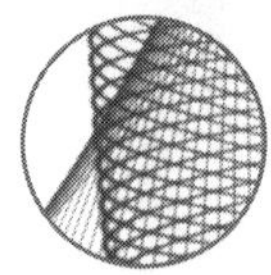

NOTE

The sample application GreaterCause was developed and tested on the WebLogic Server 7.0 (SP1). As such, all discussion in this chapter refers to configuration actions that pertain to WebLogic Server 7.0. WebLogic 7.0 uses J2SE 1.3.1 SDK.

A J2EE module is a collection of one or more J2EE components of the same component type (web, EJB, or application client). It is the basic unit of composition of a J2EE application. A web application contains the application's resources, such as servlets, JSPs, JSP tag libraries, third-party libraries, and any other static resources such as HTML pages and image files. The web applications deployed in a J2EE server use a standard deployment descriptor (web.xml file) and a vendor-specific deployment descriptor (weblogic.xml) to define their resources and operating parameters. These web resources and the deployment descriptors are bundled together for deployment in a Java archive file called the *web archive* with the .war extension. The EJB components viz. session, entity, and message-driven beans are bundled for deployment in a Java archive file called the EJB archive with the .jar extension. The EJBs are configured and deployed using the standard deployment descriptor (ejb-jar.xml file) and a vendor-specific deployment descriptor (weblogic-ejb-jar.xml). The ejb-jar.xml deployment descriptor describes the enterprise beans packaged in the EJB archive file. It defines the beans' type, names of their home and component interfaces, and implementation classes. It also defines the security roles and transactional behavior for the beans' methods. For beans with container-managed persistence, there will be a vendor-specific deployment descriptor (weblogic-cmp-rdbms-jar.xml). It is used for specifying the mapping between the container-managed fields (and also the container-managed relationships) to the underlying RDBMS table schema.

The web archive (.war) and EJB archive (.jar) can be bundled into an enterprise archive with the .ear extension. Each enterprise archive file is packaged with an XML-based application.xml deployment descriptor that contains the application's name and description, and a list of the J2EE modules that comprise the application. The .ear file represents all the entities required to deploy the application on the server side. Each application component (web archive and

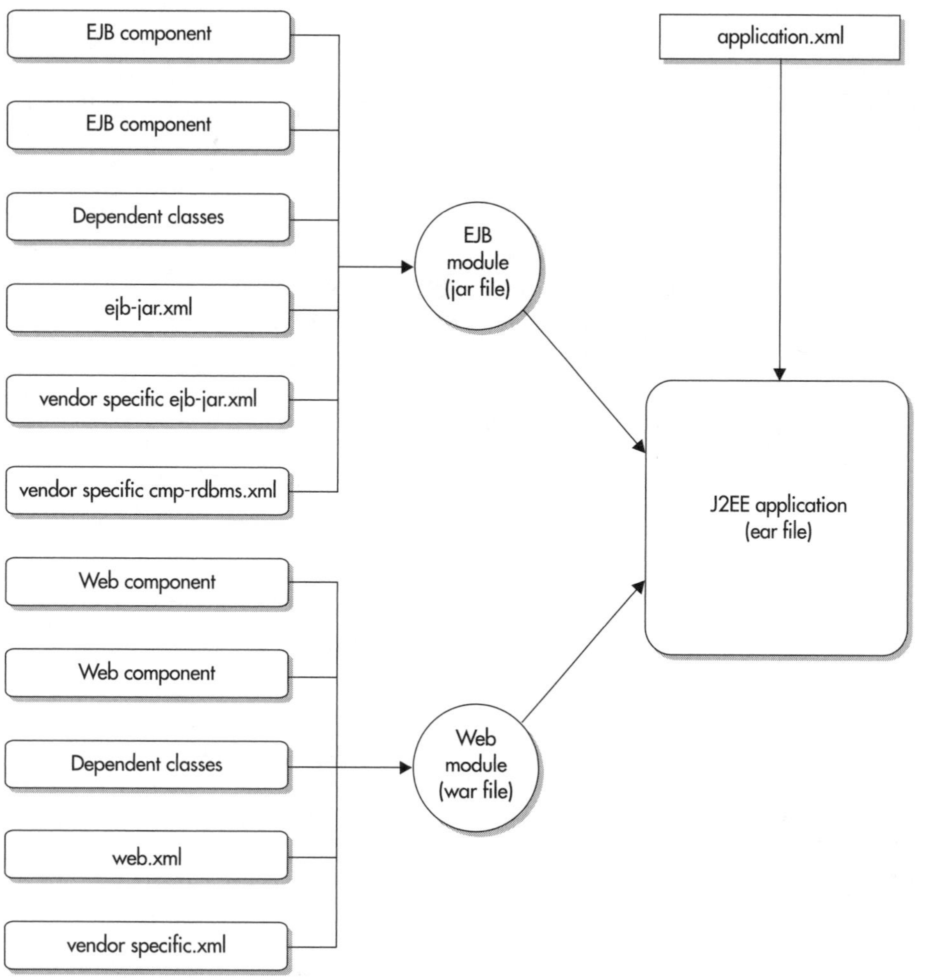

Figure 9-1 *Elements of a J2EE application*

EJB archive) is listed as a module in the application.xml deployment descriptor. Figure 9-2 depicts the steps involved in creating an application archive. We will apply these steps in the configuration and deployment of the sample GreaterCause application.

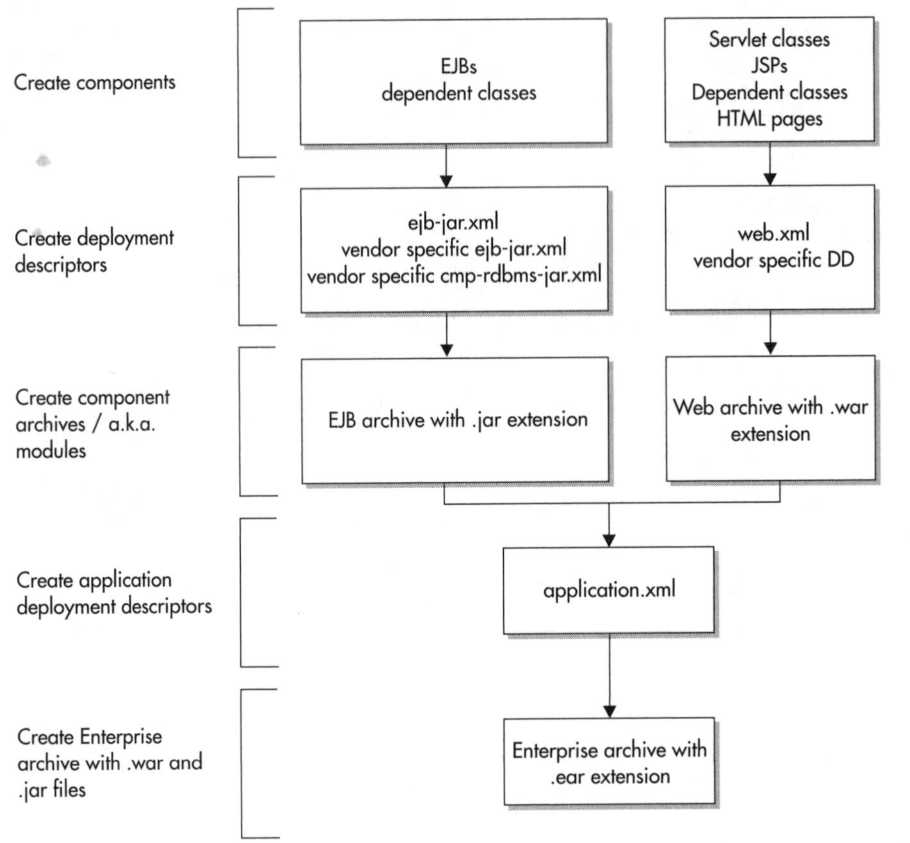

Figure 9-2 *Creating a J2EE application archive*

Installing and Configuring Struts

Although all Struts binaries required by the sample GreaterCause application are made available with the GreaterCause download, you can refer to http://jakarta.apache.org/struts/userGuide/installation.html to find out more about Struts installation and configuration. The binaries provided with the GreaterCause download pertain to Struts 1.1 beta release 2, which was used to test the application.

If you want to install the most current binaries, you will need the following from the Struts binary distribution for testing the sample GreaterCause application:

- **lib/commons-*.jar** These JAR files contain packages from the Jakarta Commons project that are used by the Struts framework. Copy these files into the WEB-INF/lib directory of the GreaterCause application.

- **lib/struts.jar** This JAR file contains all classes used by the framework. Copy these files into the WEB-INF/lib directory of the GreaterCause application.
- **lib/struts-*.tld** Copy these tag library descriptor files into the WEB-INF directory of your web application.

Chapters 4 and 5 explain the deployment descriptor (web.xml) configured for using the Struts controller servlet. The following Struts-related tag library declarations are included in the web.xml deployment descriptor:

```
<taglib>
  <taglib-uri>/WEB-INF/struts-bean.tld</taglib-uri>
  <taglib-location>/WEB-INF/struts-bean.tld</taglib-location>
</taglib>
<taglib>
  <taglib-uri>/WEB-INF/struts-html.tld</taglib-uri>
  <taglib-location>/WEB-INF/struts-html.tld</taglib-location>
</taglib>
<taglib>
  <taglib-uri>/WEB-INF/struts-logic.tld</taglib-uri>
  <taglib-location>/WEB-INF/struts-logic.tld</taglib-location>
</taglib>
```

These tag libraries are referenced in the GreaterCause JSPs using the following declarations:

```
<%@ taglib uri="/WEB-INF/struts-bean.tld" prefix="bean" %>
<%@ taglib uri="/WEB-INF/struts-html.tld" prefix="html" %>
<%@ taglib uri="/WEB-INF/struts-logic.tld" prefix="logic" %>
```

For modifying the characteristics of GreaterCause application, follow the instructions provided in Chapter 4 and 5 for creating/modifying entries in the WEB-INF/struts-config.xml file.

When compiling request handlers, form beans, or any other class that makes use of Struts components, include the struts.jar and commons-*.jar files in the CLASSPATH.

Configuring the Struts Validator

The sample application makes use of the Validator plug-in. The Validator services are injected into the Struts framework using the following declaration in the struts-config.xml file:

```
<plug-in className="org.apache.struts.validator.ValidatorPlugIn">
    <set-property property="pathnames"
        value="/WEB-INF/validator-rules.xml,/WEB-INF/validation.xml"/>
</plug-in>
```

The following two files are configured in the GreaterCause web application's WEB-INF directory:

- **Validator-rules.xml** This file contains the basic validators that are packaged with the framework.
- **Validation.xml** In this configuration file, we specify the validations associated with the form bean properties.

A detailed discussion of Validator is available at http://home.earthlink.net/~dwinterfeldt/overview.html.

Configuring the WebLogic Domain

Installing the WebLogic server is very simple and intuitive. You can download the WebLogic Platform 7.0 http://commerce.bea.com/index.jsp. Detailed instructions for installing the WebLogic Server 7.0 are available at http://edocs.bea.com/wls/docs70/install/index.html. For quick installation steps, please read on. For detailed information on configuring and using BEA WebLogic Platform 7.0, please refer to documentation available at http://edocs.bea.com/platform/docs70/index.html.

The following are fast-track instructions for creating a development environment:

1. During the product download, BEA Installer will be launched. After you accept the BEA license agreement, provide the BEA home directory.
2. For Install Type, choose Custom Installation.
3. When on the Choose Components screen, at the minimum, choose WebLogic Server. This will also install the WebLogic Workshop IDE that will be used for developing Web services. The installer is now configured to download the required archives to continue installation.
4. Specify the download directory and continue with the download.
5. After the download is completed, you will be prompted to provide a product installation directory. If your home directory was c:\bea, the default product directory will be c:\bea\weblogic700. Provide a suitable directory name and continue with the product install.
6. Completion of product install will launch a configuration wizard. Select Yes to run the Domain Configuration Wizard. The wizard is used to set up WebLogic domains. The WebLogic installation provides a preconfigured WLS Examples domain (for running the Examples Server). You may choose the Examples Server to deploy the GreaterCause application, or you can configure a separate domain.

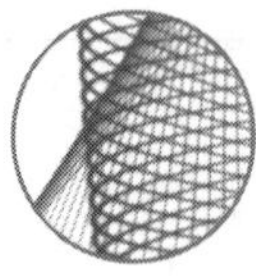

NOTE

A domain is an interrelated set of WebLogic Server resources that are managed as a unit. A domain includes one or more WebLogic servers and may also include WebLogic Server clusters. Detail information on domains is available at http://edocs.bea.com/wls/docs70/admin_ domain/index.html.

7. Select WLS Domain from the template list to create a WebLogic Server domain, or select WebLogic Workshop for creating a Workshop domain that is used in Chapter 8 for creating Web services. Creating a WebLogic Workshop domain is recommended because it can be used for developing and testing the GreaterCause application, as well as the Web service. Name the domain appropriately. The discussions to follow will refer to the domain name as *mydomain*.
8. When prompted to choose Server Type, select Single Server. This configuration is suitable and adequate for development and testing. In this case, the domain contains a single WebLogic Server instance that acts as both the Administration Server and application host server.
9. When prompted for domain location, you can leave the default (for example, c:\bea\user_projects\).
10. On the Configure Standalone / Administrative Server screen, provide the server name (default is *myserver*). Leaving the Server Listen Address blank will assume localhost. You may choose to leave the port setting as is. Review the section Listen Address Considerations in the document Creating and Configuring WebLogic Server Domains at http://edocs.bea.com/wls/docs70/admin_domain/index.html for further information on Server Listen Address.
11. On the Create Administrative User screen, provide the User Name and Password. This username and password will be required to start and manage the server. The default security realm myrealm will contain this user. Accidental removal of this user from the security realm will create an unusable domain.
12. When prompted to Create Start Menu Entry, provide a suitable selection.
13. Finally, review the Configuration Summary and create the new domain.
14. If a single domain is sufficient for your needs, select End Configuration Wizard. If at a later time you choose to create more domains, run the Domain Configuration Wizard from the Start menu.

The downloaded GreaterCause package has a GC.properties file that is referenced by the Ant build script. You must update the WL_DOMAIN property in the GC.properties file to reflect the location of the domain directory. For example, you may specify this property, along with the WL_HOME property (WebLogic home directory), as shown here:

```
WL_HOME=C:\bea\weblogic700
WL_DOMAIN=C:\bea\user_projects\mydomain
```

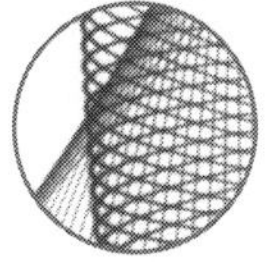

NOTE

After WebLogic server is installed, you can start the server either from the Windows Start menu or using the **startWeblogic.cmd** ***script provided in the ${WL_DOMAIN} directory. For testing the Web Service, ensure that the domain name refers to a Workshop domain.***

Configuring the JDBC Connection Pool

For development and testing, we used an Oracle database server. In this section, we discuss the procedure for setting up a JDBC connection pool for the Oracle database server. We must first start the WebLogic server according to the instructions provided in the preceding section. The rest of the instructions are as follows:

Start the console using http://localhost:7001/console.

1. Select mydomain | Services | JDBC | Connection Pools in the left-hand frame.
2. Select the Configure A New JDBC Connection Pool link in the right-hand frame.
3. Provide the following information and select <Create> to complete:

Form Field	**Value**
Name	GCPool
URL	jdbc:oracle:thin:@*myhostname*:1521:*mySID*, where *SID* is the service identifier
Driver Classname	oracle.jdbc.driver.OracleDriver
Properties	user=*username*
Password	*password*

5. We must now assign GCPool to a target server. Select the Targets tab on the same page that was used in the previous step. Select the Servers tab. Select myserver and move it to the Chosen window. Apply the changes before exiting.
6. Once the connection pool is created, we proceed to creating a JDBC Tx Data Source. Select mydomain | Services | JDBC | Tx Data Sources.
7. Select Configure A New JDBC Tx Data Source link in the right-hand frame.
8. Provide the following information and select <Create> to complete. The JNDI name provided here is the JNDI name referred to in the deployment descriptor of the entity beans. The two names should match for successfully deploying the application.

Form Field	**Value**
Name	GCTxDataSource
JNDI Name	jdbc/gcOracleTxPool
Pool Name	GCPool

9. We must now assign GCTxDataSource to a target server. Select the Targets tab on the same page that was used in the preceding step. Select the Servers tab. Select myserver and move it to the Chosen window. Apply the changes before exiting.

Configuring GreaterCause Users

At this point, we assume that you have installed the WebLogic server. If you have not done so, you may want to do it now. The "Implementing Application Security" section of Chapter 5 identifies three administrator roles supported by the application for performing administrative-related functions. The principals (users and groups) are defined in the default security realm myrealm in the WebLogic Server Domain mydomain.

The principal-to-role mapping is declared in the WebLogic-specific deployment descriptor *weblogic.xml*, as follows:

```
<security-role-assignment>
    <role-name>NPOAdministrator</role-name>
    <principal-name>NPOAdmin</principal-name>
</security-role-assignment>
<security-role-assignment>
    <role-name>PortalAdministrator</role-name>
    <principal-name>PortalAdmin</principal-name>
</security-role-assignment>
<security-role-assignment>
    <role-name>SiteAdministrator</role-name>
    <principal-name>SiteAdmin</principal-name>
</security-role-assignment>
```

The roles identified in the vendor-specific deployment descriptor are mapped to the roles used by the web components in the web.xml deployment descriptor using the *security-role-ref* elements, as follows:

```
<security-role-ref>
    <role-name>SiteAdminRole</role-name>
    <role-link>SiteAdministrator</role-link>
</security-role-ref>
<security-role-ref>
    <role-name>PortalAdminRole</role-name>
    <role-link>PortalAdministrator</role-link>
</security-role-ref>
<security-role-ref>
    <role-name>NPOAdminRole</role-name>
    <role-link>NPOAdministrator</role-link>
</security-role-ref>
```

The principals identified in the vendor-specific deployment descriptor are created in the default security realm *myrealm*, as follows:

1. Bring up the WebLogic console using the URL http://localhost:7001/console.
2. Select mydomain | Security | Realms | myrealm | Groups in the left-hand frame. Configure three new groups: SiteAdmin, PortalAdmin, and NPOAdmin. These groups are the principals mapped to their respective role names in the weblogic.xml deployment descriptors.
3. Select mydomain | Security | Realms | myrealm | Users in the left-hand frame. Configure users and associate them with a group created in Step 2. These usernames can be used for signing on to the GreaterCause application. Use the Groups tab for assigning a user to a group.

A Portal-Alliance administrator (Group PortalAdmin) can only be associated with one Portal-Alliance registration. Similarly, an NPO administrator (Group NPOAdmin) can only be associated with one NPO registration. Therefore, for each new PortalAlliance or NPO registration, create a user entry under the appropriate group. The preconfigured test data accompanying the download requires the existence of certain Portal-Alliance and NPO Administrators. The Portal-Alliance administrators that must be added to the group PortalAdmin can be located in the ADMIN table with a non-null value in the column Portal_ID. The NPO administrators that must be added to the group NPOAdmin can be located in the ADMIN table with a non-null value in the column EIN.

When signing in as SiteAdmin (using the username created for this purpose), any attempt to change Portal-Alliance or NPO information will be preceded with an Enter Portal ID or Enter EIN page to identify the Portal-Alliance or NPO being modified, respectively. However, signing in as PortalAdmin (using the username created for this purpose), the system will detect the associated Portal-Alliance profile based on the relationships stored in the system—this is true for NPOAdmin as well. This facility allows the SiteAdmin to be a super-user by being able to access and modify information for any other type of administrators.

Deploying the GreaterCause Application

In this section, we discuss the steps involved in installing the Greater Cause application. The accompanying download contains the source code and the installation scripts.

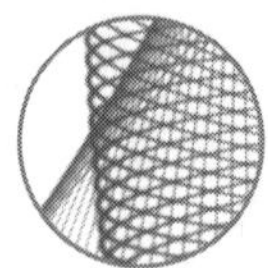

NOTE

The configurations explained in this section are geared toward a Windows-based installation.

The contents of the downloaded GreaterCause directory that will be used for installing the GreaterCause application are described briefly here:

Directory	Contents
GreaterCause	Ant build script and the corresponding properties file for building the application from source.
GreaterCause\bin	Command script that uses Ant build script for building the jar, war, and ear files.
GreaterCause\build\archives	Pre-built binaries for direct deployment of the GreaterCause application; also binaries built by the Ant script provided in this chapter.
GreaterCause\conf	See the following table for complete explanation.
GreaterCause\lib	Binaries used by Struts and Ant. (All binaries with the exception of ant.jar, xercesImpl.jar, and xmlParserAPIs.jar are required by Struts.)
GreaterCause\src\java	Complete source code of the application.
GreaterCause\src\sql	DDL script and script for loading sample data.
GreaterCause\src\web	GreaterCause JSPs.
GreaterCause\src\web\en_US	en_US locale-specific JSPs.
GreaterCause\src\web\images	Default image files referenced by default ApplicationResources.properties file (see the following table).

The following is a list of files in the configuration directory (GreaterCause\conf) together with their usage:

Name	Usage
web.xml	Deployment descriptor for the web application
weblogic.xml	Vendor-specific deployment descriptor for the web application
weblogic-cmp-rdbms-jar.xml	Vendor-specific deployment descriptor for cmp- and cmr-fields mapping to the database schema
ejb-jar.xml	Deployment descriptor for the enterprise beans
weblogic-ejb-jar.xml	Vendor-specific deployment descriptor for the enterprise beans
application.xml	Deployment descriptor for the J2EE application
struts-config.xml	Struts-specific configuration file
ApplicationResources.properties	Default resource bundle as specified by the *message-resources* element in the struts-config.xml file
validation.xml	File containing basic validators packaged with Struts
validation-rules.xml	Configuration file for specifying validations associated with form-bean properties
*.tld	Tag library descriptors files

Priming the Database

At this point, we assume that you have started an instance of the Oracle database server. This section will help you create the necessary tables required for the application (explained in Chapter 6), and load some test data. Before the tables can be created, update the GC.Properties file provided in the GreaterCause directory. The GC.properties must have values specified for the following properties:

- DBSERVER=
- DBPORT=
- SID=
- USER=
- PASSWORD=

For creating tables, provide the following at the command prompt:

```
GreaterCause\bin> build db_create_tables
```

For populating test data, provide the following at the command prompt:

```
GreaterCause\bin> build db_load_tables
```

Deploying GreaterCause.ear

The following steps are for deploying the GreaterCause application using the .ear file provided in the GreaterCause/build/archives directory:

1. Bring up the WebLogic console using the URL http://localhost:7001/console.
2. Select mydomain | Deployments | Applications in the left-hand frame.
3. Select the Configure A New Application link in the right-hand frame. This will show the Locate Application Or Component To Configure page.
4. Locate the GreaterCause.ear in the directory GreaterCause\build\archives and choose [select] to proceed to the next step.
5. Select myserver from Available Servers and move it to the Target Servers window. Select <Configure and Deploy>.

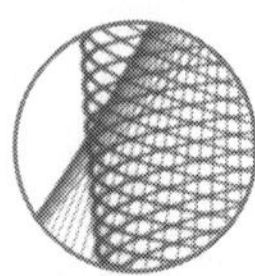

NOTE

You can access the home page of GreaterCause by using the URL http://localhost:7001/GreaterCause or http://localhost:7001/GreaterCause/1_HomePage.jsp.

Building the GreaterCause Application

The following steps are for building and deploying the GreaterCause application using the source files provided in the GreaterCause\src directory:

1. Set the WL_Domain in the GC.properties file provided in the GreaterCause directory.
2. For creating and deploying the .ear file, provide the following at the command prompt:

   ```
   GreaterCause\bin> build All
   ```

3. Bring up the WebLogic console using the URL http://localhost:7001/console.
4. Select mydomain | Deployments | Applications | _appsdir_GreaterCause in the left-hand frame.
5. Select the Deploy tab in the right-hand frame. Ensure that the Deployed status is true for GreaterCause.jar and GreaterCause.war.

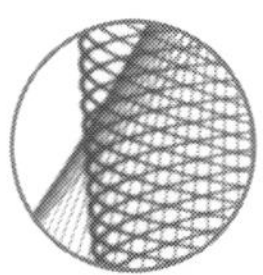

NOTE

The ejb-client-jar element in the ejb-jar.xml deployment descriptor specifies the name of a jar file that will contain the classes required for accessing the EJBs on the server. This jar file is automatically included by the build script in the WEB-INF/lib directory of the web application.

PART III

Appendixes

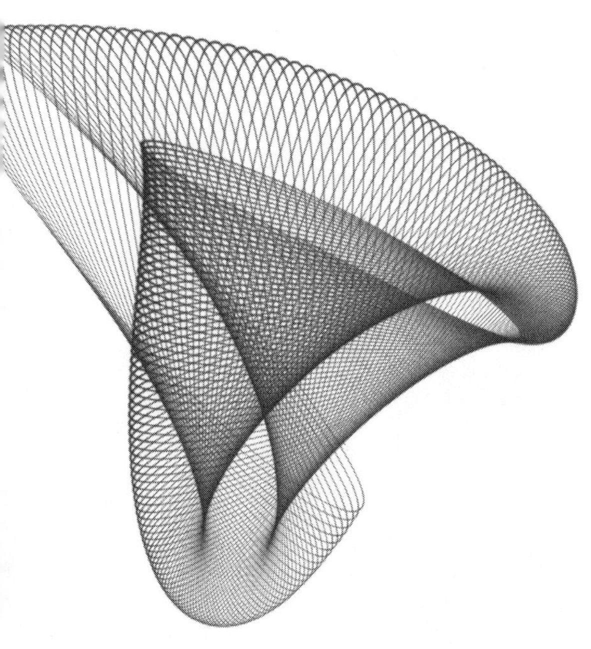

APPENDIX A

Detailed Use Case Description Template

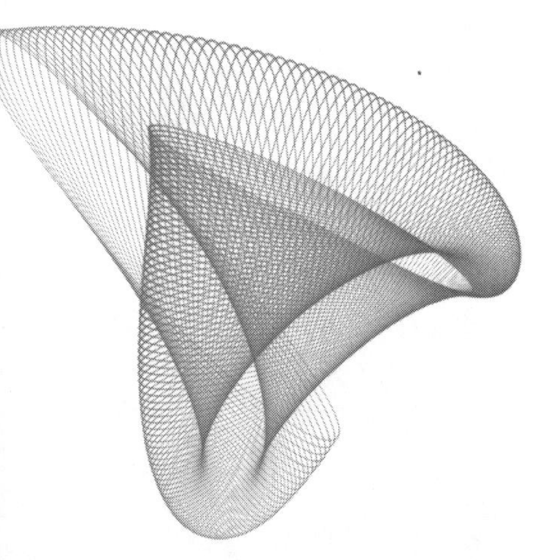

The following template is used for capturing detailed use case description as explained in Chapter 2. You may tailor this according to the dynamics of your team and project.

Use Case Name Provide a brief description and the purpose of the use case.

Actors Specify all the entities that interact with this use case, including other packages (or subsystems) of the application and other external systems.

Precondition(s) Preconditions are assertions that must be true at the beginning of the use case. The use case is responsible for keeping its part of the contract only if these preconditions are satisfied.

Postcondition(s) Assertions that must be true at the conclusion of a use case. The state of the system is stable and consistent only if these assertions are satisfied.

Include/Extend Use Cases Specify use cases that are subordinate to this use case. The subordinate use cases factor common behavior and provide a means for creating atomic units that become part of a whole.

User Interface Illustrate the user interface being serviced by this use case. These are typically wire frames that may be used to articulate the flow of events.

Main Flow of Events This flow of events is at a more granular level than the flow of events in use case summary. We take advantage of the fact that we can illustrate the flow of events in conjunction with user actions in the context of a user interface depicted by wire frames.

Exceptional Flow of Events This flow of events expresses exception or optional behavior of the system that deviates from normal flow of events. The availability of wire frames helps in identifying exceptional flows by examining the choices the users have in exercising various options provided by the navigational schemes.

Activity Diagram Use activity diagrams to explain complex scenarios.

Sequence Diagram For use cases, sequence diagrams provide lesser value when compared to activity diagrams. Use it only when there are several entities interacting with the use case.

APPENDIX B

GreaterCause Wire Frames

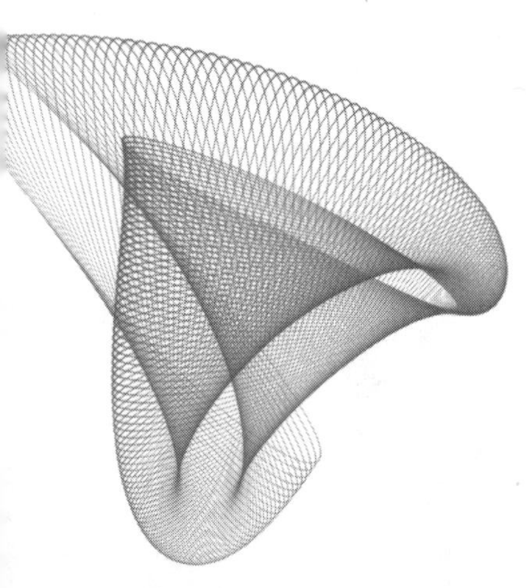

This appendix contains the wire frames for the sample application. The wire frames do not represent all the screens of the GreaterCause site but sufficient enough to get a general feel of the user interface, associated fields, workflow, and navigation semantics. It incorporates various aspects of the information architecture as explained in Chapter 2. The navigation semantics associated with the wire frames are explained using the site flow in Appendix C. For pages with complex navigation, a side bar can be helpful for mapping the navigation elements of a page to the page numbers used in wire frames; you may also add callouts to navigation elements for improved readability.

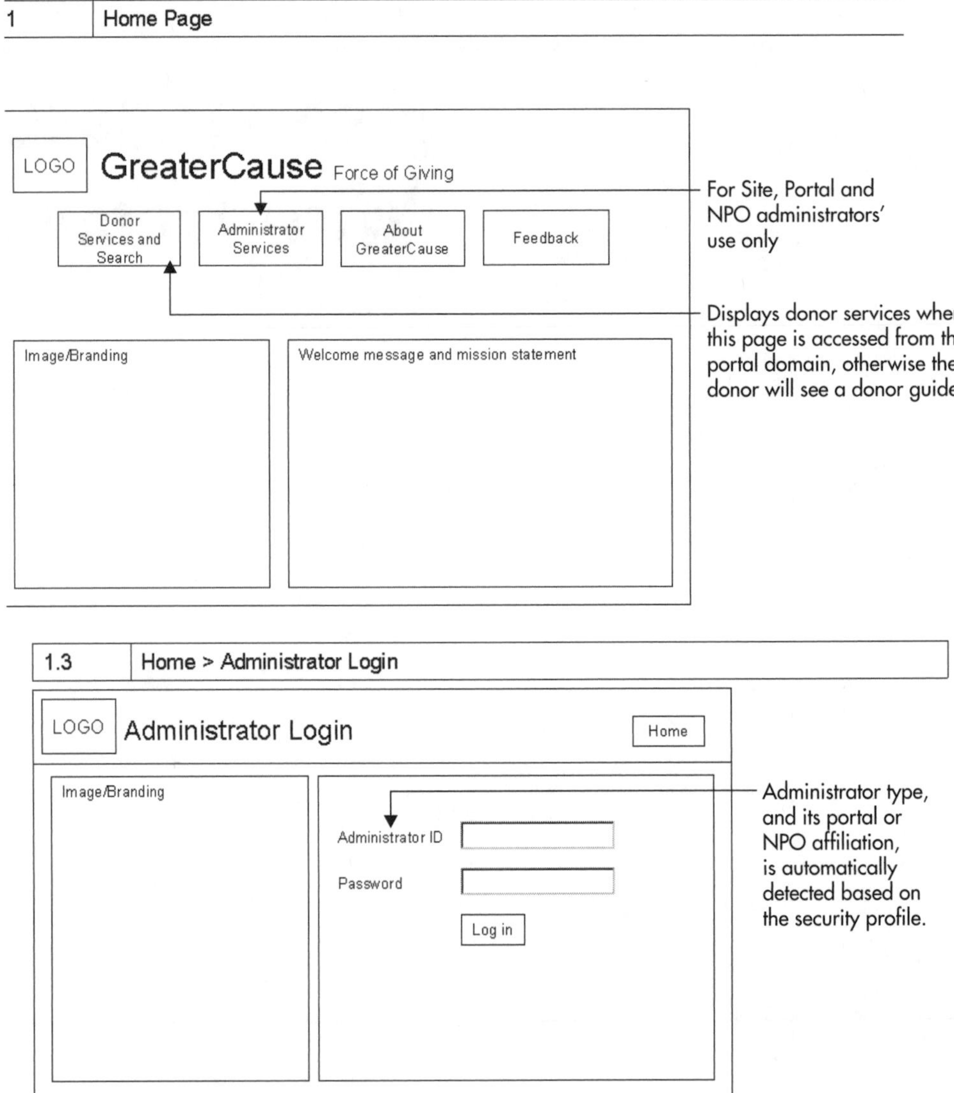

2	Home > Site Administrator Services

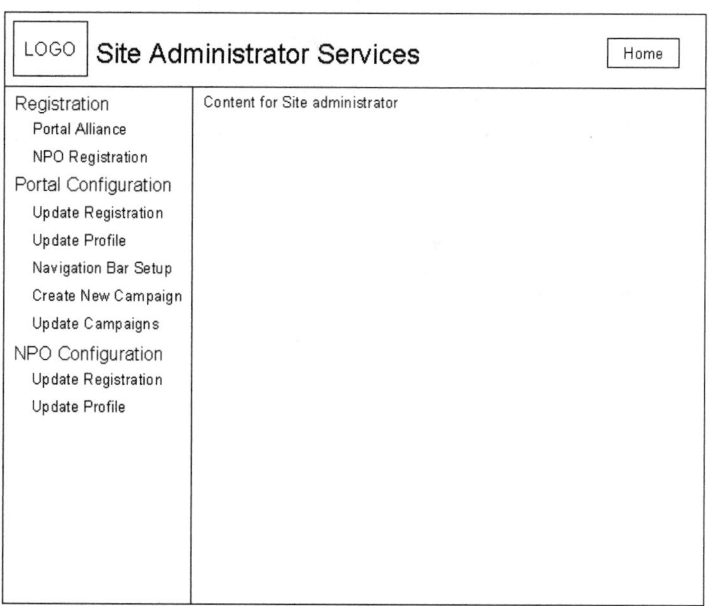

2	Home > Portal Administrator Services

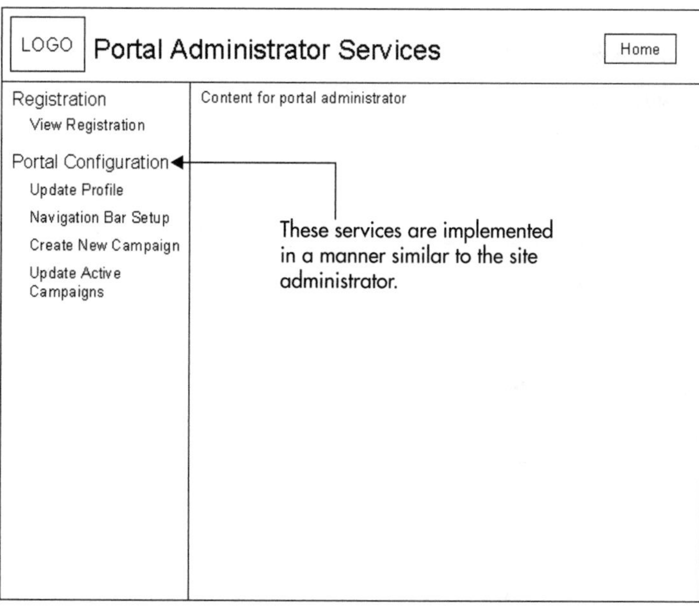

2	Home > Non-Profit Administrator Services

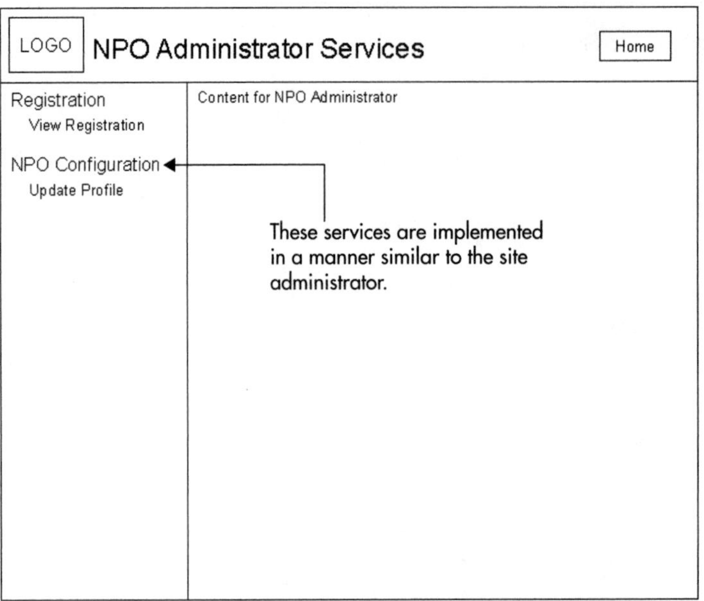

2.1	Home > Site Administrator Services > Registration > Portal Alliance Registration

LOGO Site Administrator Services Home

Registration
- **Portal Alliance**
- NPO Registration

Portal Configuration
- Update Registration
- Update Profile
- Navigation Bar Setup
- Create New Campaign
- Update Campaigns

NPO Configuration
- Update Registration
- Update Profile

Portal Alliance Registration

Portal ID

Administrator ID

Portal Name

Contact Email

Activation Date

Test Certification ○ In Progress ○ Completed

Register

2.2	Home > Site Administrator Services > Registration > NPO Registration

LOGO Site Administrator Services Home

Registration
- Portal Alliance
- **NPO Registration**

Portal Configuration
- Update Registration
- Update Profile
- Navigation Bar Setup
- Create New Campaign
- Update Campaigns

NPO Configuration
- Update Registration
- Update Profile

NPO Registration

EIN

NPO Administrator

NPO Name

Address

City

State

Zip

Country

Activation Status

Register

Identification Number provided by IRS

2.3	Home > Site Administrator Services > Portal Configuration > Enter Portal ID

LOGO Site Administrator Services Home

Registration
- Portal Alliance
- NPO Registration

Portal Configuration
- **Update Registration**
- Update Profile
- Navigation Bar Setup
- Create New Campaign
- Update Campaigns

NPO Configuration
- Update Registration
- Update Profile

Portal Configuration > Enter Portal ID

Enter Portal ID

Submit

Content for Site administrator

Site administrators must identify the portal ID that they want to administer. Portal ID is not required for portal administrators because this information is part of the portal administrators' profile.

2.1	Home > Site Administrator Services > Portal Configuration > Update Registration

LOGO Site Administrator Services Home

Registration
Portal Alliance
NPO Registration
Portal Configuration
Update Registration
Update Profile
Navigation Bar Setup
Create New Campaign
Update Campaigns
NPO Configuration
Update Registration
Update Profile

Portal Alliance Registration

Portal ID Acme
Administrator ID AcmeAdminID
Portal Name
Contact Email
Activation Date
Test Certification ○ In Progress ○ Completed

Update

2.3.2	Home > Site Administrator Services > Portal Configuration > Update Profile

LOGO Site Administrator Services Home

Registration
Portal Alliance
NPO Registration
Portal Configuration
Update Registration
Update Profile
Navigation Bar Setup
Create New Campaign
Update Campaigns
NPO Configuration
Update Registration
Update Profile

Portal Configuration > Update Profile

Portal ID ACME

Contact Info
First Name
Last Name
Email
Phone

Search Optimization
Limit my searches to [ ] non-profits.

Update

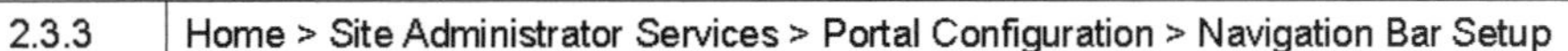

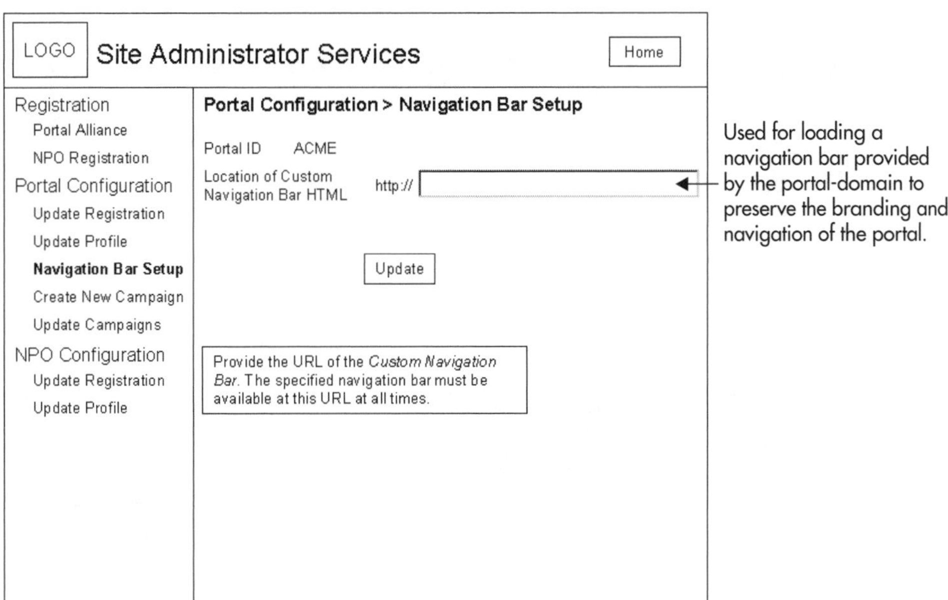

2.3.4 Home > Site Administrator Services > Portal Configuration > Create New Campaign

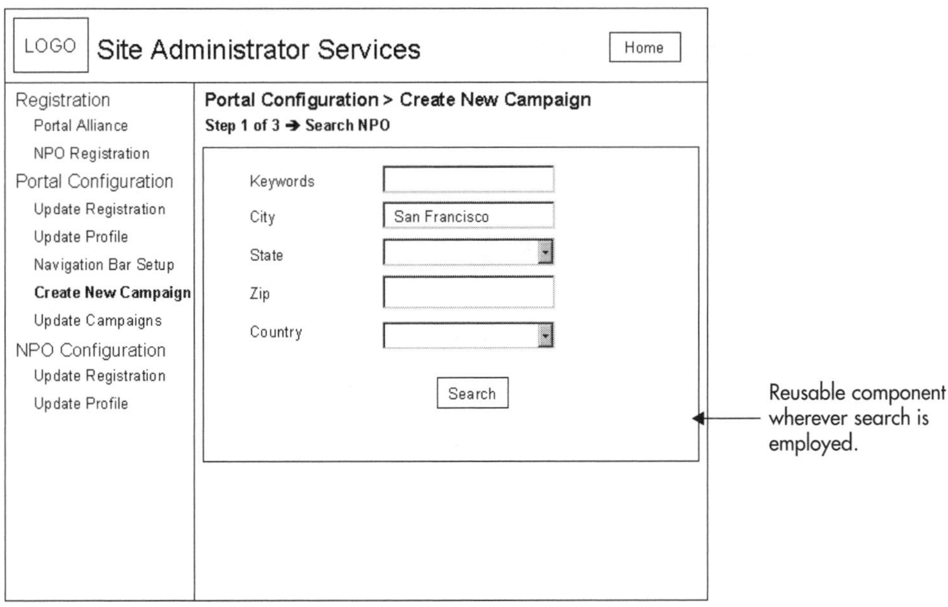

2.3.4.1	Home > Site Administrator Services > Portal Configuration > Create New Campaign

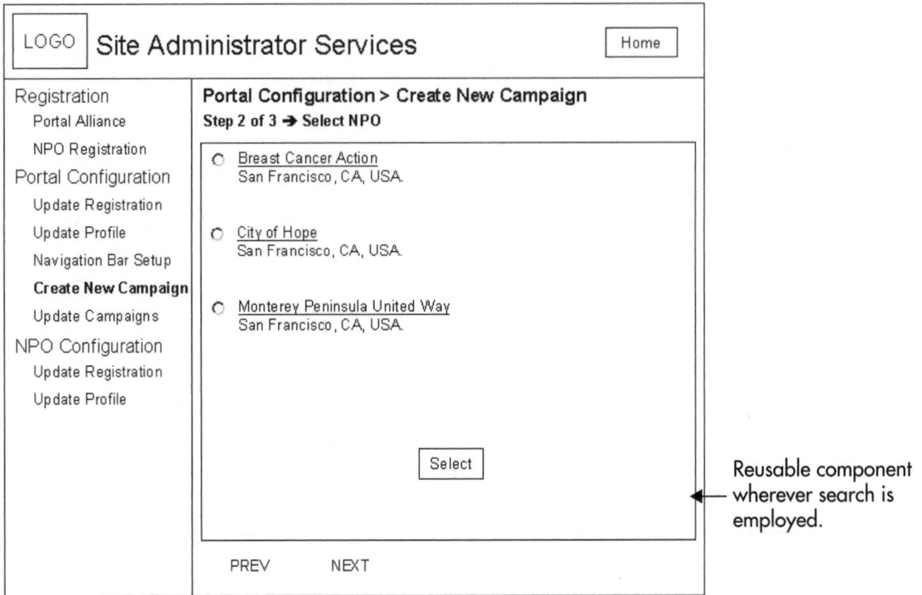

2.3.4.2	Home > Site Administrator Services > Portal Configuration > Create New Campaign

LOGO Site Administrator Services Home

Registration
Portal Alliance
NPO Registration
Portal Configuration
Update Registration
Update Profile
Navigation Bar Setup
Create New Campaign
Update Campaigns
NPO Configuration
Update Registration
Update Profile

Portal Configuration > Create New Campaign
Step 3 of 3 ➔ Enter Campaign Details

Portal ID ACME
EIN 123456789
NPO Name City of Hope
Start Date
End Date
Region Code Leave blank for National Campaigns

Create

2.3.5	Home > Site Administrator Services > Portal Configuration > Update Campaigns

LOGO Site Administrator Services Home

Registration
Portal Alliance
NPO Registration
Portal Configuration
Update Registration
Update Profile
Navigation Bar Setup
Create New Campaign
Update Campaigns
NPO Configuration
Update Registration
Update Profile

Portal Configuration > Update Campaigns
Step 1 of 2 ➔ Enter Region Code

Enter Portal ID [ ]

Enter Region Code [ ]

Next

2.3.5.1	Home > Site Administrator Services > Portal Configuration > Update Campaigns

LOGO Site Administrator Services Home

Registration
Portal Alliance
NPO Registration
Portal Configuration
Update Registration
Update Profile
Navigation Bar Setup
Create New Campaign
Update Campaigns
NPO Configuration
Update Registration
Update Profile

Portal Configuration > Update Campaigns
Step 2 of 2 ➔ Update Campaigns

Portal ID **ACME**
Region Code **PACIFIC**

123456789 City of Hope San Francisco, CA, USA	Start Date End Date	01/01/2004 12/31/2004
123456789 Monterey Peninsula United Way San Francisco, CA, USA	Start Date End Date	03/15/2004 04/07/2004

Update

2.4	Home > Site Administrator Services > NPO Configuration > Update Registration

Site administrators must identify the EIN that they want to administer. EIN is not required for NPO administrators because this information is part of the NPO administrators' profile.

2.2	Home > Site Administrator Services > NPO Configuration > Update Registration

2.4.2	Home > Site Administrator Services > NPO Configuration > Update Profile

LOGO Site Administrator Services Home

Registration
Portal Alliance
NPO Registration
Portal Configuration
Update Registration
Update Profile
Navigation Bar Setup
Create New Campaign
Update Campaigns
NPO Configuration
Update Registration
Update Profile

NPO Configuration > Update Profile

EIN 123456789

Administration ID 123456789AdminID

Contact Info

First Name

Last Name

Email

Phone

NPO Detail Page Info

URL

Mission Statement

Update

P.1	Portlet (Gateway to GreaterCause)

Portlet Sample

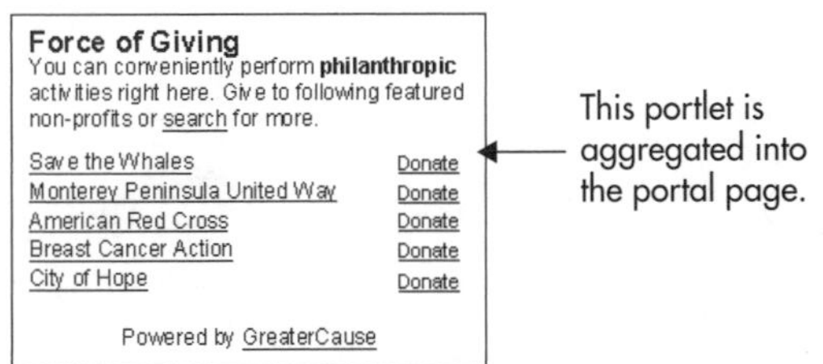

This portlet is aggregated into the portal page.

P.2	Registration

Custom or Default Navigation Bar to Preserve Portal Branding

Only the donors will see this portal-specific navigation bar.

LOGO Jane Doe, Making a Difference

Please take a moment to fill out the missing information. We are thrilled to have your support.

Registration ID Acme_Portal_User

First Name

Last Name

Email

Address

City

State

Zip

Country

Register

Most information is provided by the portal-domain.

P.2.1	Donor Preferences

Custom or Default Navigation Bar to Preserve Portal Branding

LOGO Jane Doe, Making a Difference

Search

Home	Donation Cart	Proceed to Checkout	Tax Record	Donor Preferences	Advanced Search

For best experience, customize following settings. All information is optional.

Default Donation Amount

Limit Search to non-profits

Primary Email*

Disclose Name and Address to Non-Profits Yes No

Submit Preferences

* Primary email will supersede registration email

Your Credit Card Information

Name on Card

Card Type

Card Number

Expiry Day Expiry Year

Following is your registration information. To change click here.

Jane Doe
555 Bay Drive
Fremont, CA 94555
USA
Email: jdoe@americaunited.com

P.3	Donor Services and Search

Custom or Default Navigation Bar to Preserve Portal Branding

LOGO Jane Doe, Making a Difference Search

Home	Donation Cart	Proceed to Checkout	Tax Record	Preferences	Advanced Search

Please enter search criteria to find non-profit of your choice

Keywords

Category

City San Francisco

State

Zip

Country

Search

Promotional Content for Donor.

For unregistered users, only Home and Advanced Search is available.

P.3.1	Advanced Search > Select Non-Profit

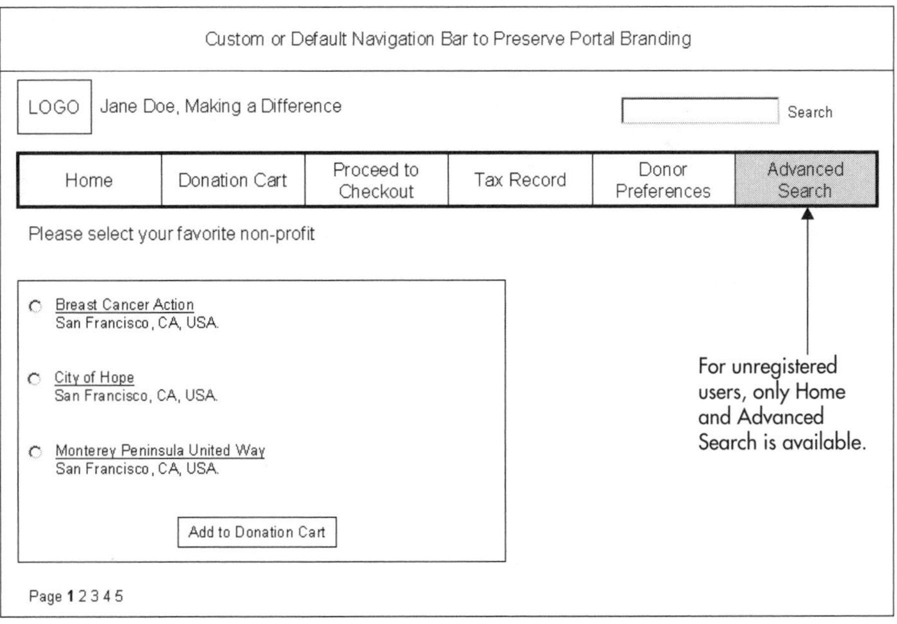

P.3.1.1	Donation Cart

Custom or Default Navigation Bar to Preserve Portal Branding

LOGO Jane Doe, Making a Difference Search

Home	Donation Cart	Proceed to Checkout	Tax Record	Donor Preferences	Advanced Search

Please enter donation amount and optionally the preferred cause

NPO Name	Amount	Preferred Cause e.g. Mississippi Flood	Remove
Breast Cancer Action San Francisco, CA, USA	$ 20.00		☐
Monterey Peninsula United Way San Francisco, CA, USA	$ 15.00	Oakland Fires	☐
City of Hope San Francisco, CA, USA	$ 25.00		☐
Total	$ 60.00		

Proceed to Checkout | Update Cart | Continue Donating

United Way will be accepting donations for several causes.

P.3.1.2	Checkout

Custom or Default Navigation Bar to Preserve Portal Branding

LOGO Jane Doe, Making a Difference Search

Home	Donation Cart	Proceed to Checkout	Tax Record	Donor Preferences	Advanced Search

You have chosen to support the following non-profits

Breast Cancer Action San Francisco, CA, USA	$ 20.00	
Monterey Peninsula United Way San Francisco, CA, USA	$ 15.00	Oakland Fires
City of Hope San Francisco, CA, USA	$ 25.00	
Total	$ 60.00	

Please verify your credit card information or select another

Name on Card

Card Type

Card Number

Expiry Day Expiry Year

Save changes for future use? ○ Yes ○ No

Confirm Your Donations

P.3.2	Tax Record

Custom or Default Navigation Bar to Preserve Portal Branding

LOGO Jane Doe, Making a Difference

Search

Home	Donation Cart	Proceed to Checkout	Tax Record	Donor Preferences	Advanced Search

Donation Summary for 2003. For 2002, click here.

Breast Cancer Action San Francisco, CA, USA	$ 20.00	12/25/2003	
Monterey Peninsula United Way San Francisco, CA, USA	$ 15.00	12/25/2003	Oakland Fires
City of Hope San Francisco, CA, USA	$ 25.00	12/25/2003	
Total	$ 60.00		

Printer Friendly Report

APPENDIX

C

GreaterCause Site Flow

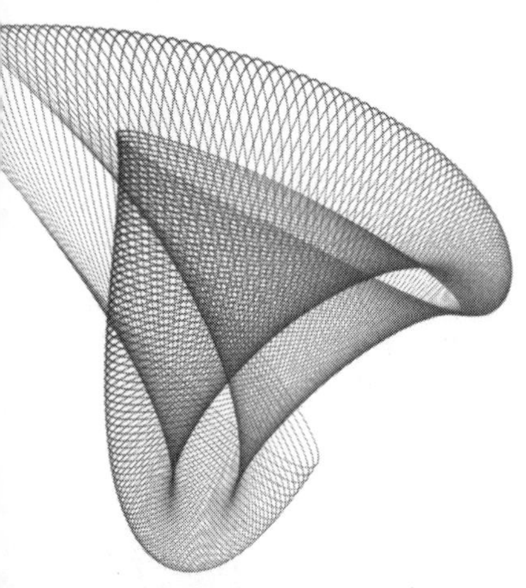

The navigation semantics of the UI illustrated in Appendix B is explained using a site flow that clearly articulates the page transitions associated with user actions. The site flow is an important artifact for articulating the navigation semantics and provides a bird's-eye view of the site. Site flow does not encompass each and every navigational aspect because doing so will make it less readable. To avoid the clutter, a common technique used for creating site flows is to draw it like a tree structure where every node has only one parent. The site flow will complete the story boarding effect by showing the transitions between various uniquely numbered wire frames according to the navigation semantics established for the functional web site.

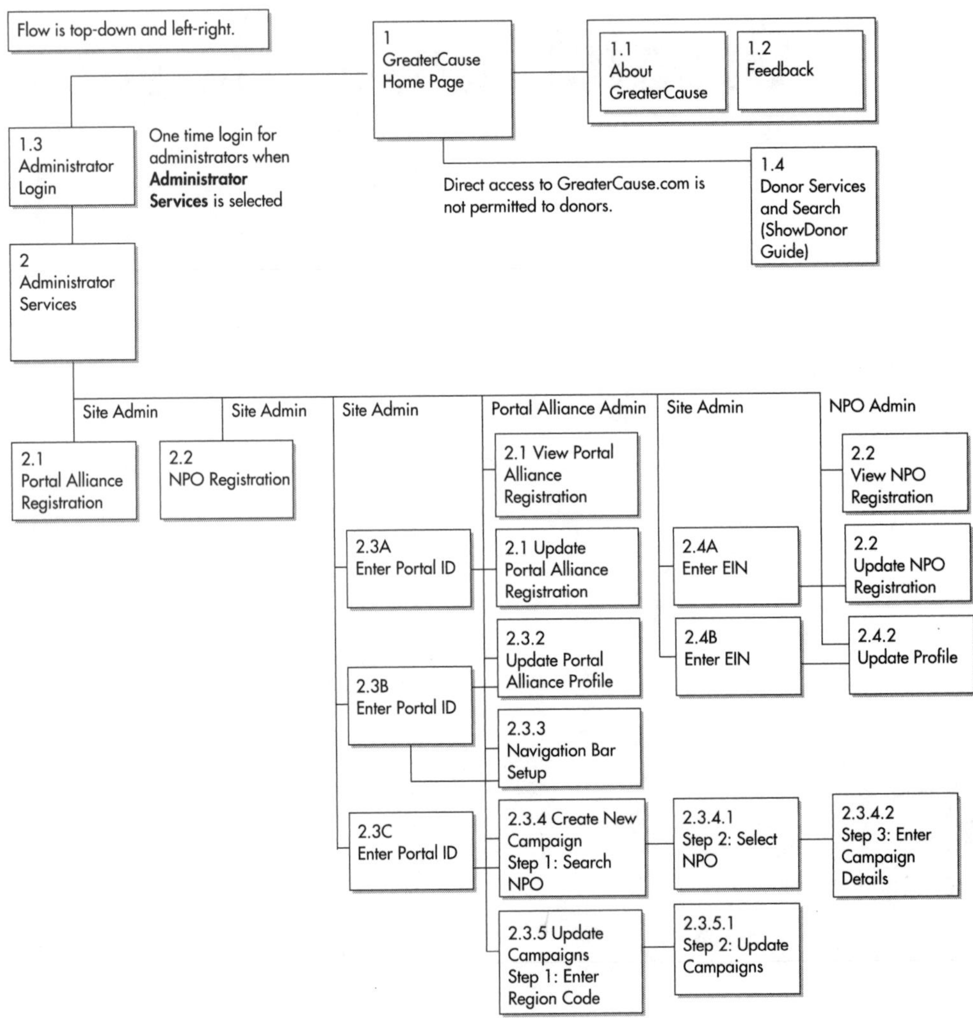

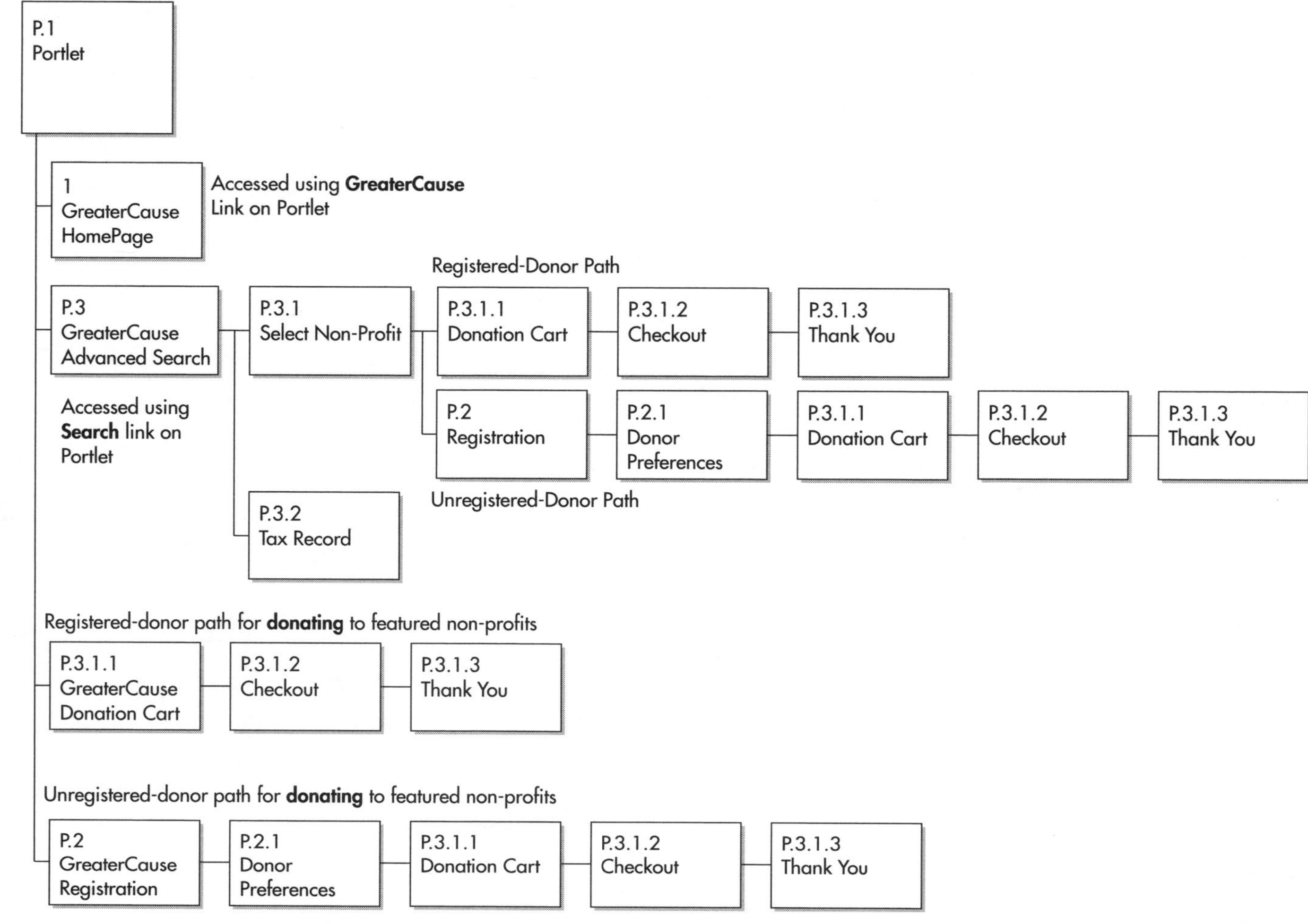
P.1
Portlet
1
GreaterCause
HomePage
Accessed using **GreaterCause**
Link on Portlet
P.3
GreaterCause
Advanced Search
Accessed using
Search link on
Portlet
P.3.1
Select Non-Profit
P.3.2
Tax Record
Registered-Donor Path
P.3.1.1
Donation Cart
P.3.1.2
Checkout
P.3.1.3
Thank You
P.2
Registration
P.2.1
Donor
Preferences
P.3.1.1
Donation Cart
P.3.1.2
Checkout
P.3.1.3
Thank You
Unregistered-Donor Path
Registered-donor path for **donating** to featured non-profits
P.3.1.1
GreaterCause
Donation Cart
P.3.1.2
Checkout
P.3.1.3
Thank You
Unregistered-donor path for **donating** to featured non-profits
P.2
GreaterCause
Registration
P.2.1
Donor
Preferences
P.3.1.1
Donation Cart
P.3.1.2
Checkout
P.3.1.3
Thank You

APPENDIX D

FeaturedNPOQueryService WSDL

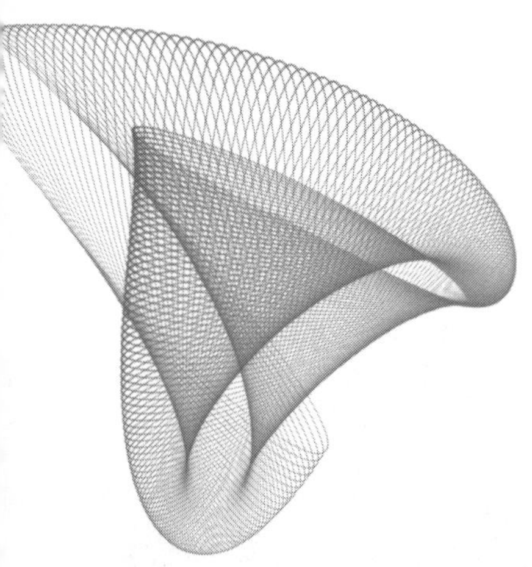

The following XML document was generated by the BEA WebLogic WorkShop tool for describing the FeaturedNPOQueryService Web service to the clients. Complete discussion on WSDL and the creation of FeaturedNPOQueryService is covered in Chapter 8.


```
<?xml version="1.0" encoding="utf-8"?>
<definitions xmlns:mime="http://schemas.xmlsoap.org/wsdl/mime/"
   xmlns:jms="http://www.openuri.org/2002/04/wsdl/jms/"
   xmlns:soapenc="http://schemas.xmlsoap.org/soap/encoding/"
   xmlns:cw="http://www.openuri.org/2002/04/wsdl/conversation/"
   xmlns:xm="http://www.bea.com/2002/04/xmlmap/"
   xmlns:soap="http://schemas.xmlsoap.org/wsdl/soap/"
   xmlns:http="http://schemas.xmlsoap.org/wsdl/http/"
   xmlns:conv="http://www.openuri.org/2002/04/soap/conversation/"
   xmlns:s0="http://www.GreaterCause.com/"
   xmlns="http://schemas.xmlsoap.org/wsdl/"
   xmlns:s="http://www.w3.org/2001/XMLSchema"
   targetNamespace="http://www.GreaterCause.com/">
   <types>
      <s:schema attributeFormDefault="qualified"
         elementFormDefault="qualified"
         targetNamespace="http://www.GreaterCause.com/">
         <s:element name="getCampaigns">
            <s:complexType>
               <s:sequence>
                  <s:element name="portalID"
                     maxOccurs="1" type="s:string" minOccurs="0"/>
                  <s:element name="regionCode"
                     maxOccurs="1" type="s:string" minOccurs="0"/>
               </s:sequence>
            </s:complexType>
         </s:element>
         <s:element name="getCampaignsResponse">
            <s:complexType>
               <s:sequence>
                  <s:element name="getCampaignsResult"
                     maxOccurs="1" type="s0:ArrayOfFeaturedNPODTO" minOccurs="0"/>
               </s:sequence>
            </s:complexType>
         </s:element>
         <s:complexType name="ArrayOfFeaturedNPODTO">
            <s:sequence>
               <s:element name="FeaturedNPODTO"
                  maxOccurs="unbounded" type="s0:FeaturedNPODTO"
                  minOccurs="0" nillable="true"/>
            </s:sequence>
         </s:complexType>
         <s:complexType name="FeaturedNPODTO">
            <s:sequence>
               <s:element name="startDate"
                  maxOccurs="1" type="s:string" minOccurs="0"/>
               <s:element name="regionCode"
                  maxOccurs="1" type="s:string" minOccurs="0"/>
```

```
          <s:element name="ein"
             maxOccurs="1" type="s:string" minOccurs="0"/>
          <s:element name="endDate"
             maxOccurs="1" type="s:string" minOccurs="0"/>
          <s:element name="npoName"
             maxOccurs="1" type="s:string" minOccurs="0"/>
        </s:sequence>
      </s:complexType>
      <s:element name="ArrayOfFeaturedNPODTO"
        type="s0:ArrayOfFeaturedNPODTO" nillable="true"/>
   </s:schema>
</types>
<message name="getCampaignsSoapIn">
   <part name="parameters" element="s0:getCampaigns"/>
</message>
<message name="getCampaignsSoapOut">
   <part name="parameters" element="s0:getCampaignsResponse"/>
</message>
<message name="getCampaignsHttpGetIn">
   <part name="portalID" type="s:string"/>
   <part name="regionCode" type="s:string"/>
</message>
<message name="getCampaignsHttpGetOut">
   <part name="Body" element="s0:ArrayOfFeaturedNPODTO"/>
</message>
<message name="getCampaignsHttpPostIn">
   <part name="portalID" type="s:string"/>
   <part name="regionCode" type="s:string"/>
</message>
<message name="getCampaignsHttpPostOut">
   <part name="Body" element="s0:ArrayOfFeaturedNPODTO"/>
</message>
<portType name="FeaturedNPOQueryServiceSoap">
   <operation name="getCampaigns">
      <input message="s0:getCampaignsSoapIn"/>
      <output message="s0:getCampaignsSoapOut"/>
   </operation>
</portType>
<portType name="FeaturedNPOQueryServiceHttpGet">
   <operation name="getCampaigns">
      <input message="s0:getCampaignsHttpGetIn"/>
      <output message="s0:getCampaignsHttpGetOut"/>
   </operation>
</portType>
<portType name="FeaturedNPOQueryServiceHttpPost">
   <operation name="getCampaigns">
      <input message="s0:getCampaignsHttpPostIn"/>
      <output message="s0:getCampaignsHttpPostOut"/>
   </operation>
</portType>
<binding name="FeaturedNPOQueryServiceSoap" type="s0:FeaturedNPOQueryServiceSoap">
   <soap:binding style="document" transport="http://schemas.xmlsoap.org/soap/http"/>
   <operation name="getCampaigns">
      <soap:operation style="document"
         soapAction="http://www.GreaterCause.com/getCampaigns"/>
      <input>
```

```
            <soap:body use="literal"/>
         </input>
         <output>
            <soap:body use="literal"/>
         </output>
      </operation>
   </binding>
   <binding name="FeaturedNPOQueryServiceHttpGet" type="s0:FeaturedNPOQueryServiceHttpGet">
      <http:binding verb="GET"/>
      <operation name="getCampaigns">
         <http:operation location="/getCampaigns"/>
         <input>
            <http:urlEncoded/>
         </input>
         <output>
            <mime:mimeXml part="Body"/>
         </output>
      </operation>
   </binding>
   <binding name="FeaturedNPOQueryServiceHttpPost" type="s0:FeaturedNPOQueryServiceHttpPost">
      <http:binding verb="POST"/>
      <operation name="getCampaigns">
         <http:operation location="/getCampaigns"/>
         <input>
            <mime:content type="application/x-www-form-urlencoded"/>
         </input>
         <output>
            <mime:mimeXml part="Body"/>
         </output>
      </operation>
   </binding>
   <service name="FeaturedNPOQueryService">
      <port name="FeaturedNPOQueryServiceSoap" binding="s0:FeaturedNPOQueryServiceSoap">
         <soap:address
            location="http://nadir1:7001/GreaterCauseWebService/FeaturedNPOQueryService.jws"/>
      </port>
      <port name="FeaturedNPOQueryServiceHttpGet" binding="s0:FeaturedNPOQueryServiceHttpGet">
         <http:address
            location="http://nadir1:7001/GreaterCauseWebService/FeaturedNPOQueryService.jws"/>
      </port>
      <port name="FeaturedNPOQueryServiceHttpPost" binding="s0:FeaturedNPOQueryServiceHttpPost">
         <http:address
            location="http://nadir1:7001/GreaterCauseWebService/FeaturedNPOQueryService.jws"/>
      </port>
   </service>
</definitions>
```

Index

Symbols and Numbers

A

B

C

D

E

F

G

H

I

J

K

L

M

N

Q

R

S

T

U

V

W

X

INTERNATIONAL CONTACT INFORMATION

AUSTRALIA
McGraw-Hill Book Company Australia Pty. Ltd.
TEL +61-2-9900-1800
FAX +61-2-9878-8881
http://www.mcgraw-hill.com.au
books-it_sydney@mcgraw-hill.com

CANADA
McGraw-Hill Ryerson Ltd.
TEL +905-430-5000
FAX +905-430-5020
http://www.mcgraw-hill.ca

GREECE, MIDDLE EAST, & AFRICA (Excluding South Africa)
McGraw-Hill Hellas
TEL +30-210-6560-990
TEL +30-210-6560-993
TEL +30-210-6560-994
FAX +30-210-6545-525

MEXICO (Also serving Latin America)
McGraw-Hill Interamericana Editores S.A. de C.V.
TEL +525-117-1583
FAX +525-117-1589
http://www.mcgraw-hill.com.mx
fernando_castellanos@mcgraw-hill.com

SINGAPORE (Serving Asia)
McGraw-Hill Book Company
TEL +65-6863-1580
FAX +65-6862-3354
http://www.mcgraw-hill.com.sg
mghasia@mcgraw-hill.com

SOUTH AFRICA
McGraw-Hill South Africa
TEL +27-11-622-7512
FAX +27-11-622-9045
robyn_swanepoel@mcgraw-hill.com

SPAIN
McGraw-Hill/Interamericana de España, S.A.U.
TEL +34-91-180-3000
FAX +34-91-372-8513
http://www.mcgraw-hill.es
professional@mcgraw-hill.es

UNITED KINGDOM, NORTHERN, EASTERN, & CENTRAL EUROPE
McGraw-Hill Education Europe
TEL +44-1-628-502500
FAX +44-1-628-770224
http://www.mcgraw-hill.co.uk
computing_europe@mcgraw-hill.com

ALL OTHER INQUIRIES Contact:
McGraw-Hill/Osborne
TEL +1-510-420-7700
FAX +1-510-420-7703
http://www.osborne.com
omg_international@mcgraw-hill.com